THE INDEPENDENT NUCLEAR STATE: THE UNITED STATES, BRITAIN AND THE MILITARY ATOM

The Independent Nuclear State: The United States, Britain and the Military Atom is a chronological account and overview of the 40-year history of British military research, development and production work in atomic energy. The United Kingdom's efforts in this field have always had close links with equivalent activities in the United States, and have often been conducted on a mutually co-operative basis. Through its description of these secret Anglo-American interactions, this study serves to highlight the degree to which the public debate in Britain over nuclear weapons has been conducted in a vacuum, as has American public policy-making over its nuclear links with the United Kingdom.

This book contains descriptions of the technical evolution of British nuclear weapon designs and production models, estimates of annual output figures for fissile material and weapon types, and indications of the nature of the weapon-testing programme. Decision-points are charted, such as the H-bomb development, and the factors that led to existing plans being changed are identified. The demonstrative nature of the programme until the late 1950s is illustrated, together with the rapidity with which stockpile targets were met at the turn of that decade. The impact of the agreements with the United States, both upon weapon development and production programmes and upon stockpiling, is analysed, as well as their effects upon the nuclear submarine programme. The consequences of the mid-1960s termination of weapon development are discussed, as is the later decision to restart it for the Chevaline programme. The impact of these events upon Anglo-American relations is identified, together with the recent British attempts to move to a closer political association with Europe.

The study concludes by evaluating the essential nature of four decades of United Kingdom military nuclear development, and identifying the practical limits imposed by past policies upon any attempt by a British government to implement a policy of unilateral nuclear disarmament.

John Simpson is Senior Lecturer in Politics at the University of Southampton. He acted as a specialist adviser to the Palme Commission, and is currently a member of the UN Secretary General's expert group preparing a report for the General Assembly on conventional disarmament.

THE INDEPENDENT NUCLEAR STATE

THE UNITED STATES, BRITAIN AND THE MILITARY ATOM

John Simpson

First published 1983 by
THE MACMILLAN PRESS LTD
London and Basingstoke
Companies and representatives
throughout the world

ISBN 0 333 23830 3

Filmsetting by Vantage Photosetting Co. Ltd,
Eastleigh and London
Printed in Hong Kong

Contents

Acknowledgements

It is not possible for me to offer public appreciation for all who have assisted in the preparation of this book, especially those who have been kind enough to read some of the draft chapters at various stages in their evolution. I am indebted to my former postgraduate students, Mark Imber and Tony McGrew, for initiating the line of investigation which stimulated the original research, for embarking upon the project with me and for commenting upon drafts and offering advice upon the areas of nuclear energy development they have specialised in. I am also grateful to Frank Barnaby, Professor Peter Nailor, Jim Schear and Ian Smart for comments made on draft chapters; to Richard Worcester for the opportunity to discuss with him some aspects of British nuclear weapon development, and to David Holloway for access to photocopies of American documents on early post-war military plans and assessments of Soviet nuclear progress. I have also received generous advice, assistance and encouragement from Duncan Campbell, Norman Dombey, Lawrence Freedman, Ross Hesketh, Bhupendra Jasani, David Page, Julian Perry-Robinson, William Walker and Lars Wallin. My colleagues and students in the Department of Politics at the University of Southampton have had the patience to bear with my ideas and inspirations throughout the lengthy gestation of this book, and in particular I wish to thank Peter Anderson, John Clements, Karen Dawisha, Frank Gregory and Phil Williams for culling relevant information from their own reading and research, and Peter Calvert for his active encouragement in the task of completing this study. I am also indebted to the University of Southampton for allowing me sabbatical leave in the summer term of 1980 to complete early drafts of some of the chapters.

Pam Powell and Mary McCray have endured the task of deciphering my handwriting, retyping drafts and producing the manuscript in its final form with unfailing good humour and fortitude whilst Margery Knight and Peter Lomas provided invaluable assistance in proof-reading the manuscript and preparing the index. I am profoundly grateful to all of them for their assistance. Last, but not least, I would like to thank my family for their forbearance while I struggled with a seemingly never-ending task: I hope that eventually my two sons will appreciate both its significance and my motives in undertaking it.

J. S.

Preface

This book was not planned: it was a product of curiosity and puzzlement. Its initial genesis was in a wide-ranging discussion with two research students, in which it emerged that certain of the published information about British nuclear energy activities in the 1950s appeared to contradict statements on the nature of nuclear weapons in a SIPRI study. This, plus a chance conversation some years previously in which it had been intimated that there had been considerable surprise in the United States in late 1957 at the progress Britain had made in nuclear weapon development, led me to investigate the hypothesis that the core of the Anglo-American nuclear relationship was that United Kingdom nuclear weapon designers had moved ahead of their colleagues in the United States by 1958, and the resultant Anglo-American agreements were thus negotiated from a position of British technological strength.

The manuscript that Macmillan commissioned my two research students and I to write in September 1977 was intended to examine the linkages between British civil and military nuclear energy facilities. It rapidly became apparent that it would not be possible to write about the military aspects without extensive research: fortunately the publishers were prepared to wait while this was undertaken and were prepared to accept this much amended version of the original commission. An interim report on the research formed part of a memorandum I prepared for the Defence and External Affairs Subcommittee of the House of Commons Expenditure Committee in February 1979, but a further three years' work proved necessary before the version which follows could be completed. In the course of this it became apparent that the original contradictions could be easily explained, but it was also clear that there existed in this area a hidden world of Anglo-American relationships.

The bulk of the text which follows offers a chronological account and overview of the 40-year history of British military research, development and production work in the area of atomic energy. Until 1952, it bases itself primarily upon the official histories of both American and British projects, with the American one being examined in some detail because it serves as a useful guide to understanding later British activities. After 1952, detailed information on both projects is sparse, as much of the technical data is still classified as part of both states' anti-proliferation policies. Fortunately a number of recent works, almost all of American origin, deal in some detail with the nature of nuclear weapon technology and its development, and by making use of them, the transcripts of hearings conducted by the United States Congressional Joint Committee on Atomic Energy, evidence presented to the House of Commons Defence Committee and a number of other key public statements, it has proved possible to construct a picture of what has occurred in the intervening years. At the same time, I felt that no book on this subject could avoid examining the practical implications of these past actions for the future of Anglo-American nuclear relations, and in particular any policy of attempting to create a nuclear disarmed Britain. The conclusions I reached were contrary to my own expectations, but in honesty I cannot but report them.

This study is open to criticism, as I would be the first to acknowledge, on the grounds that the areas I have examined are best understood in the context of broad political concerns and the aspirations, motivations and activities of individuals. I have not investigated either of these areas in depth, though I have included them in the account where information was readily available and they appeared appropriate. I accept that there is a great temptation to regard the walls of secrecy placed around nuclear technology as justification for ignoring connections with wider political issues. Yet up to 1964 I believe I have succeeded in identifying most of the broad linkages between politics and technology, for during that period nuclear technology was a prime driving force in strategic and tactical weapon development. Since 1964 development work has been aimed at more modest improvements in nuclear explosive efficiency than occurred over the previous 20 years, nuclear material shortages have ceased to be a pacing item in weapon production, and research work has focused on methods of hardening strategic nuclear warheads against the effects produced by anti-ballistic missile defence systems. The predominant focus of strategic debate has been delivery system capabilities rather than nuclear warhead development, with the consequence that the politics/technology linkages in the latter area have become more complex and problematic.

Readers may be surprised by some of the quantifications which are contained in the main text and the appendices. I have consistently attempted to indicate their basis, but am aware that they are, at best, crude approximations. I believe, however, that they provide a more accurate guide to events and processes than is available elsewhere, though it would be my hope that other scholars will be able to improve upon them.

The book is divided into eleven chapters. The first develops certain concepts or themes that are relevant to an understanding of the British nuclear weapon project. There then follow eight chapters which provide an account of the British project and its interaction with the American one. Next is the chapter which attempts to explore the practical problems of creating a non-nuclear Britain. The concluding chapter discusses the history of the United Kingdom's development of the military applications of nuclear energy in terms of the initial themes and then attempts to identify the 'essence' of these activities and the relationship with the United States.

Some will no doubt feel that this study should have taken a much more positive approach to issues such as the moral dimension of nuclear weapons possession or the planned purchase of Trident missiles and their parent submarines by Britain. I have consciously avoided these questions, as the principal task I set myself was to provide information which others could use. If both advocates and opponents of nuclear weapons and nuclear disarmament, and students of politics acquire greater understanding of what has happened in the past through reading this study, and use it to base their advocacy of future policies on more detailed and accurate foundations, or to gain insights into the politics of technological development procedures, then my modest aim will have been achieved.

Southampton J. S.

List of Abbreviations

ABM	Anti-ballistic Missile
AEA	See UKAEA
AEC	See USAEC
AGR	Advanced Gas-cooled Reactor
AWRE	Atomic Weapons Research Establishment (Aldermaston)
BEPO	British Experimental Pile O (Harwell)
CDT	Combined Development Trust
CFBR	Commercial Fast Breeder Reactor
CPC	Combined Policy Committee
CEGB	Central Electricity Generating Board
ERDA	Energy Research and Development Agency
EURATOM	European Atomic Energy Community
FBR	Fast Breeder or Fast Burner Reactor
GAC	General Advisory Committee (of USAEC)
IAEA	International Atomic Energy Agency
ICI	Imperial Chemical Industries Ltd
ICBM	Intercontinental Range Ballistic Missile
IRBM	Intermediate Range Ballistic Missile
JCAE	Joint Committee on Atomic Energy
JCS	Joint Chiefs of Staff (US)
LWR	Light Water Reactor
MAGNOX	British Gas-cooled, Natural Uranium Power Reactor
NATO	North Atlantic Treaty Organisation
NPT	Non-proliferation Treaty
NRX	Natural Uranium Reactor (experimental) – Chalk River, Canada
NRC	Nuclear Regulatory Commission
OECD	Organisation for Economic Cooperation and Development
PDRP	Power Demonstration Reactor Program
PWR-2	Second-generation Pressurised Water Submarine Reactor (UK)
RAE	Royal Aircraft Establishment
SAC	United States Strategic Air Command
SSEB	South of Scotland Electricity Board
TVA	Tennessee Valley Authority
UKAEA	United Kingdom Atomic Energy Authority
UNAEC	United Nations Atomic Energy Commission
USAEC	United States Atomic Energy Commission
ZEEP	Zero Energy Experimental Prototype Reactor

1 Prologue: Themes for Analysis in British Nuclear Energy Policy

Introduction

Nuclear energy can be distinguished from many other areas of modern technology by the intense emotional reactions and apocalyptic political and moral debate that it stimulates. The roots of these responses can be found in the events of August 1945, when two atomic bombs were dropped upon Japanese cities, with horrific consequences both for their inhabitants and their buildings. It also resides in the reaction of individuals to the intangible nature of the destructive radiation created by such explosions: phenomena which can kill or maim without being seen or felt. These emotive concerns have been reinforced, moreover, by the barriers of secrecy that have been erected around details of their associated technologies by the governments of Western states, initially with the intention of retarding the development of nuclear weapons by the Soviet Union, and later to make it as difficult as possible for other states to acquire the capabilities to make them. As a consequence, the public image of military nuclear activities that has been created is of state enterprises that are clearly very important, but also characterised by great secrecy, furtiveness and the suspicion that behind the screen of national security there may lurk a history of disreputable activities, dubious dealings and unethical decisions. The military aspects of nuclear energy thus present the democratic state with an acute dilemma: how to reconcile the demands of those citizens anxious to obtain proof that the powers of the state have not been abused, with the genuine and sincere concerns of those guarding its secrets that such information could assist other states to acquire nuclear weapons and detract from national security. There also exists an additional dilemma for the state: how to reconcile the pressures to exploit nuclear energy for non-military purposes, especially in the

1

context of an unregulated, free-market economy, with the
requirement to prevent both information and materials being
converted to military use either by non-state groups or non-
nuclear weapon countries. Inevitably, policy in both these issue
areas will involve judgements which are contestable, especially
by those outside of the state apparatus who only possess incom-
plete information.

A major aim of this book is to offer some historical insights
into the ways in which these dilemmas have been tackled by the
governments of the United Kingdom and United States, both
separately and in cooperation, over the last 40 years. Another
has been to assemble as much information on the military
aspects of the British nuclear energy project as possible. It is
inevitable that the resulting narrative suffers from being shaped
by the partial nature of much of the published data, which makes
the task of arriving at judgements on its accuracy perilously
difficult. To assist in this process, resort has been made to
reasoned estimates in such areas as annual rates of weapon
material production and related military stockpile figures. However, it cannot be too heavily emphasised that these *are* estimates, based upon overt, arbitrary assumptions and *not* a covert
method of publishing official figures. As a consequence, the
account which follows in later chapters is primarily an overview
of events, rather than a detailed description of the roles played
by individuals in generating them, and as such, it may differ
appreciably from the perspectives held by some participants.

Common sense suggests that in any study of the linkages
between the military development of nuclear energy and Anglo-
American relations a number of themes are likely to cut across
the historical narrative, and a preliminary discussion of some of
them may aid an understanding of certain of the controversies
described in it. These themes also serve the additional function
of providing a convenient starting-point for the concluding
analysis. Four such themes can be identified: the problems
created by the links between the civil and military uses of
nuclear energy; the forms of state decision-making processes
related to the military applications of nuclear energy; the time-
schedules and types of activity which determine the progress of
any attempt to translate a scientific idea into a production-line
article; and finally, ways of classifying the relationships that
arise out of a trade in military knowledge and materials between
allied states.

Distinguishing Nuclear Swords from Atomic Ploughshares

All technologies provide examples of the difficulty of distinguishing between military and civil activities: the development of nuclear energy has been no exception. Its problems arise from the nature of civil nuclear plants and processes, their genesis in defence programmes and their inherent military potential.

Logically, there are three methods available to distinguish between civil nuclear power activities and military programmes: by categorising plants; by classifying their mode of operation; and by demarcating the owners and end-uses of the material produced by them. All of these distinctions pose problems of implementation. Nuclear reactors in civil power stations and in experimental establishments can be operated in a manner which produces militarily useful materials:[1] indeed, some were built initially for this purpose and later converted to civil use. The plants to enrich uranium for use as civil power reactor fuel can also be altered to produce uranium which is suitable for weapons. Equally, factories designed to manufacture reactor fuel can make materials for both military and civil purposes, while facilities to separate out the constituents of this fuel, once it has been used, can similarly be operated to obtain weapon materials or additional civil reactor fuel.[2] The technology used to construct civil plants is thus inherently neutral between military and civil applications. Indeed, it was early recognition of this which impelled the United States government to advocate international ownership and control over all aspects of nuclear energy development in the immediate post-war years, and it also underlies much of the contemporary unease over the effectiveness of the international regime which is intended to limit the creation of additional nuclear weapon states.[3]

The manner in which reactors and uranium enrichment plants are operated offers a second method of dichotomising nuclear energy activities. Heavy chemical elements, such as uranium and plutonium, can exist in several physical forms, known as isotopes. These differ marginally from each other in weight, as a consequence of their atoms having a nucleus which has a slightly different number of neutrons. These differences are commonly signified by placing a number after the chemical symbol for the element, which represents the sum of the neutrons and another constituent of atoms, protons, found in the nucleus of each isotope. Certain of these isotopes, particularly plutonium 239

(Pu-239) and uranium 235 (U-235), are stable, yet will easily split or fission under specific physical circumstances and liberate large quantities of energy in several forms. Thus the use of almost pure Pu-239 or U-235 offers the easiest route to simple and reliable nuclear weapons and, in the case of plutonium, avoids certain handling difficulties caused by radiation. Such pure material is usually termed weapon grade,[4] and is generally regarded as only obtainable if power reactors and enrichment plants are operated in a manner other than that which leads to the most economic production of electricity.[5] This assertion has to be qualified, however, as weapon-grade plutonium may be produced in the start-up and de-commissioning phase of certain types of power reactor, while some civil experimental reactors use weapon-grade uranium as fuel.[6] Thus the civil/military divide tends to regress to considerations of who owns the material and its end-use, with the substances themselves remaining inherently neutral.

Ownership of fissile material may be of considerable importance in states such as the United States and the United Kingdom, whose systems of government are based upon legislation and administrative law, but it is unlikely to impress those who aggregate all elements of a nation's bureaucracy and state-funded activities into the single category of 'the state'. This leaves only the end-use of fissile material as a practical means of delineation. Such a distinction forms the basis of the Non-Proliferation Treaty (NPT) which was signed in 1968 and became operational in 1970.[7] The non-nuclear state parties to the treaty pledged themselves not to seek to develop or produce nuclear weapons, while the nuclear states promised not to assist in this. In return, it was implied that the non-nuclear states could have free access to all forms of nuclear technology and would be able to own nuclear weapon materials.[8] This emphasis upon the end-use of fissile materials, reinforced by the belief that the global safeguarding system operated by the International Atomic Energy Agency (IAEA) could give timely warning of the diversion of materials to military programmes, contrasts starkly with the early United States proposals for an international regime to control and own all nuclear materials and plants.[9]

The NPT's restrictions on the military use of fissile materials do not apply to nuclear weapon states, but they have been of significance to both United States and United Kingdom governments for external and internal reasons. Externally, both states have attempted to strengthen the international non-proliferation regime by agreeing to voluntary IAEA safeguards upon the material produced by their civil nuclear industries and certain of their plants.[10] This has forced these governments to attempt to draw a clear dividing line between the military and civil activities performed within their territory, either by excluding certain plants from such safeguards or distinguishing between civil and military material, and only performing safeguarding operations on the former. Internally, its significance rests upon the differences between the bureaucratic and commercial groups which own the civil and military nuclear capabilities and materials within the country, and the use made of these distinctions to legitimise the civil exploitation of nuclear energy.[11]

Nuclear technology thus possesses few inherent technical qualities which enable its civil applications to be distinguished from its military ones. Any attempt to do so inevitably leads to anomalies and exceptions. These problems are compounded if fissile materials are traded, for this may allow a state to use all its indigenously produced material in its military programmes, and fulfil its civil needs with material imported from other states. Do these trading activities constitute an act of assistance to a nuclear state's military capabilities, and if such activity has occurred in the past but has now ceased, should it be regarded as an important precedent? And what are the moral or instrumental reasons for regarding this type of substitution and transfer as either illegitimate or unwise? These are all difficult questions to answer in a positive and reasoned manner.

Two final problems inherent in the civil/military dichotomy are worthy of note. One, which is irrelevant to this study, is the concept of a 'peaceful' nuclear explosion, which could enable a state to justify the possession and use of nuclear devices for civil engineering purposes, despite the technology involved being similar to that utilised in weapons.[12] A second is the use of nuclear reactors to power submarines and warships. The NPT is only concerned with the proliferation of nuclear weapons and thus ignores this technology, despite the preferred fuel for such reactors being weapon-grade uranium. The IAEA statutes allow such material to be withdrawn from safeguards to fuel submarines, but the implications of these provisions remain unclear as no non-nuclear state has yet attempted to build and operate one.[13]

The preceding discussion has highlighted the difficulties of distinguishing between a civil and a military nuclear energy programme. It has suggested that sound arguments exist for regarding any attempt at dichotomising between the two in an absolute fashion on technical grounds as inherently misguided. Yet this distinction has been seen as fundamental to the internal and external policies of successive British and American governments. In such circumstances, it can be anticipated that the inherently contestable nature of all such distinctions will be identified as a cause of many political controversies in the nuclear energy area.

Who Makes What Type of State Decisions?

In any study of state technology policy, the degree to which the politicians, the administrators or the technicians and scientists can be regarded as both determining its nature and the outcome of specific projects will be of considerable interest. There now exists a sizeable literature on the nature of state policy-making and decision-taking which is applicable to the development of nuclear energy. Although some writers feel that certain of the ideas contained within it are too heavily conditioned by the experiences of the United States political system from which it is mainly derived, and thus not directly applicable to the British environment, there is little doubt that it offers useful guidelines for the current study.[14] This literature can be broken down into a number of components, including types of policy decisions, decision-making processes, participants, implementation and cross-national decision-making.

A useful categorisation of policy decisions in the United Kingdom context is that developed by Wallace to assist his study of British foreign policy. He argues that there are three distinct types of policy, which he labels high, sectoral and low.[15] High policy issues concern broad strategic choices, and they result from the interaction of politicians and higher civil servants, usually in the context of the Cabinet or Cabinet committees.[16] An example would be decisions on categories and numbers of weapons to be procured. One of the key elements in these decisions is the need to allocate national resources to implement them, thus necessitating the involvement of a wide range of groups and interests. By contrast, sectoral policy issues are 'those which are perceived as affecting only certain sections of society, only a limited number of interests and a limited range of concerns'.[17] Moreover 'it would often be more accurate to describe them in Whitehall terms as departmental rather than as governmental policies, for in sectoral policy issues, vertical divisions between different areas are evident'.[18] He appears to regard nuclear energy policy as falling largely into this latter category, both because of its insularity from other policy areas, and because of the somewhat tautological argument that if it has low political visibility and does not often generate acute domestic political problems, it cannot be categorised as high politics.[19] Thus the suggestion is that the broad, high-politics decisions will set the general goals, context and limits for sectoral policies, such as nuclear energy ones, and bureaucratic organisations charged with implementing them will have considerable freedom of action in undertaking these tasks. This is a product of the nature of the British political system, and a result of the inherent problems of developing and administering policy towards complex technological issues which politicians may find difficult to master. In the nuclear energy context, it is also a product of the security restrictions surrounding its military aspects.

The distinction made by Wallace between high and sectoral politics is similar to that made much earlier by Snow between open and closed politics.[20] Snow defines the latter as any kind of politics 'in which there is no appeal to a larger assembly – larger assembly in the sense of a group of opinion or an electorate, or on an even bigger scale what we call loosely "social forces"'.[21] He suggests that there are three characteristic forms of interaction within a situation of closed politics. The first is committee politics, where each member of a committee 'speaks with his individual voice, depends upon his personality alone for his influence, and in the long run votes with an equal vote'.[22] The second is the 'hierarchical politics' found in a chain of command of the services, of a bureaucracy or a large industry, where 'to get anything done . . . you have got to carry people at all sorts of levels. It is their decisions, their acquiescence or enthusiasm (above all, the absence of their passive resistance), which is going to decide whether a strategy goes through in time.'[23] In

short, policy-making is as much about the politics of implementation as it is about decision-taking. The third is court politics
where attempts are made to 'exert power through a man who
possesses a concentration of power'.[24] Snow has the wartime
relationship between Lord Cherwell and Churchill in his mind
when suggesting this third category.

Investigating these types of interaction in a situation of closed
politics, such as the British weapon procurement system, presents major problems because such activities are almost entirely
hidden from public view.[25] Published studies suggest that
decision-making and implementation are greatly influenced by
the actions of individuals in strategic positions throughout a
bureaucratic structure and remind the analyst of the need to
investigate both their ability to change the course of events and
the effect of the availability of resources and the neo-
determinist nature of technological development processes in
limiting their freedom of action.[26]

The pluralist American political system is one where there is a
much greater opportunity for public debate concerning technical issues, as well as considerably more published information
on them. This arises from the role of Congress in legislating on
the legal foundations, limitations and rules under which federal
agencies will operate, and the constant conflict with the President and government departments over its claims to play a
significant role in policy formation. This struggle for power
between the Executive, the Congress and the federal agencies
over policy formulation in the United States has led some
scholars investigating such interactions to draw a clear distinction between two types of decision processes. The first, variously described as rational actor or analytic, regards such activities
as ones in which 'decisions will be taken which maximise the
decision maker's values, given the constraints of the situation
[and] competing, directly pertinent objectives will be deliber-
ately balanced or "traded-off" by the decision maker as an
integral part of his reaching a decision'.[27] All decisions and
actions are seen as purposive, in the sense that to explain them it
is sufficient to offer an ends/means explanation, in the form of
'to achieve A, he did B', or 'he is doing B in order to achieve A'.
While this is a very attractive way of analysing state or group
behaviour in the absence of detailed information, it implies that
a collectivity is behaving as though it were an individual.

Moreover, for it to form the basis for explaining state behaviour, it requires that goals have to be publicly articulated, and that ends/means calculations be both observable and acceded to by all elements of the collectivity. Such explanations are difficult to verify in a situation of closed politics, and, in addition, there is considerable empirical evidence to suggest that this form of personification is misleading.[28] As a consequence, attention has been focused upon a diametrically opposed set of ideas, which suggest that the behaviour of bureaucratic organisations is not value-maximising but is largely routine, and that public policy is made via processes of political bargaining rather than rational calculation.[29]

In his study of the Cuban missile crisis, Allison suggests that bureaucratic behaviour can best be understood through an 'Organisational Process Model' based on the proposition that 'governmental behaviour relevant to any important problem reflects the independent output of several organisations partially coordinated by governmental leaders'.[30] He argues that organisational actions are heavily conditioned by 'standard operating procedures' designed to deal with situations encountered previously.[31] Steinbruner and Coulam, in studies of the Multi-lateral Force (MLF) and F-111 aircraft, have expanded on these ideas with the aid of what they call the 'cybernetic paradigm'.[32] This argues that to manage uncertainty and lack of data, decision-makers will simplify the environment in which they are operating by monitoring only a limited amount of information about it. They interpret that data in a manner which reinforces existing actions and act in a routine manner without making any attempt to investigate the consequences of their operations. This is a rather abstract way of describing the empirical observation that projects being administered by bureaucracies acquire an 'organisational momentum' which both allows them to continue beyond the point at which they fulfil any purposeful end, and makes them very difficult to cancel. In effect, what is being suggested is that the criteria used by people in bureaucracies to judge the success of their organisation may well be internal ones rather than the achievement of goals which are set by external groups, including political decision-makers. The survival of the organisation may be a more important goal to people within it than, for example, the state acquiring a military artefact which is fully capable of meeting the threat from potential enemies in the most efficient way. Thus reorganisation in order more effectively to achieve externally generated goals will be resisted if it threatens elements that are perceived to represent the essence of the organisation.[33] Sapolsky makes this point in a rather different manner in his study of the activities of the Special Projects Office set up to manage the United States Polaris missile programme. He argues that this had two separate roles; the technical, detailed management of the project and the political role of ensuring that it survived in the defence environment and obtained the necessary resources and priorities. He concludes that 'Absence of criticism ... can be taken as a mark of success'.[34]

These studies all point to the proposition that the policy-making activities of bureaucracies cannot be understood solely in terms of end/means relationships and the attainment of public goals or Cabinet directives. Rather a process of decision-making and policy implementation is involved which may be distinctively non-purposive, especially if the promotion and future survival of the responsible organisation are major objectives of the groups within it. This political aspect is emphasised in Allison's third model of organisational behaviour, the 'Government (or Bureaucratic) Politics Model'.[35] Here, the 'leaders' of bureaucratic organisations are viewed as a disunited group who act 'in terms of no consistent set of strategic objectives, but rather according to various conceptions of national, organisational and personal goals', with decisions being made 'not by a single rational choice but by the pulling and hauling that is politics'.[36] It remains to be seen to what degree these characteristics can be identified in the field of United States nuclear policy and in the 'closed' decision-making environment of the United Kingdom.

The idea that 'sectoral' nuclear policy-making centres around political activities between bureaucracies can be extended beyond the boundaries of the state to encompass international relationships between such organisations. This type of activity has been labelled 'multi-bureaucratic decision-making' by Kaiser, who distinguishes it from more normal government-to-government interactions through foreign offices and heads of state, and from interactions between non-governmental organisations.[37] He defines this activity as one where 'the decision making structures of different national governmental and international bureaucracies intermesh within specific issue areas for the allocation of values'.[38] He is concerned about its implications for the future of democratic forms of government, especially the characteristic features of secrecy: the performance of politically important activities by bureaucracies; the general lack of direct political control over their actions and the ceding by political leaders of the power to negotiate where they lack the detailed competence to discuss specific issues involving a considerable depth of technical detail. The work of Kaiser and Wallace suggests that two levels of interaction can be anticipated in transatlantic nuclear relations; the 'normal' political one and the multi-bureaucratic. The most interesting question arising from this for the operation of democratic political systems is the degree to which political leaderships are able to monitor and control the activities of their bureaucracies in implementing high-level policy decisions, or whether the latter's ability to offer expert information and advice results in policy being made from the 'bottom up', rather than from the 'top down'.

Why a Weapon Cannot be Developed Overnight

The evolution of a weapon project appears to be subject to unique uncertainties and difficulties. These enable it to be differentiated from other types of economic activity,[39] and can be categorised into those internal and those external to the project. Internal uncertainties reside in the 'possible incidence of unforeseen technical difficulties in the development of a specific weapon system'[40] and it is inevitable that they will be present in any programme involving significant technical advances. External uncertainties involve 'factors external to an individual project and yet affecting the course and outcome of the project. They originate in the pace of technological change in weaponry, changes in strategic requirements and shifts in governmental policy.'[41] Given the existence of these uncertainties there are a limited number of strategies available to policymakers to safeguard against their effects. One is the parallel development of radically different approaches to achieving a performance goal; another is the production of 'essentially similar items of test hardware' in order to 'prevent the interruption of testing by unforeseen accidents'.[42]

Investing heavily at an early stage in one line of development, and hoping that the predictions upon which it is based turn out to be correct, is one method of achieving rapid progress, especially if resources are limited. This strategy may save both time and resources, but if the gamble does not pay off, the results could be disastrous[43] unless the performance goals are rewritten around what is attainable.[44] The alternative technique is to 'avoid all but the broadest specification to start with and make no major commitment until a substantial jump in knowledge about the item being developed has been attained'.[45] Thus the most significant weapon development decisions are those involving the shift from a broad-based investigation of alternative weapon ideas to a concentration upon the development and elaboration of a single design, the freezing of that design and heavy investment in the facilities and materials to produce it.

This means that any weapon procurement project will almost certainly pass through a necessary number of sequential stages, each with differing expenditure implications. The latter have been illustrated by Peck and Sherer as shown in Figure 1.1.[46]

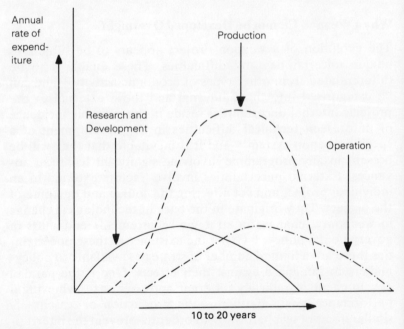

FIGURE 1.1   Incidence of expenditure on weapon projects.

The sequential phases that are involved in a weapon project can be listed as:[47]

(i) Broad-based component research and preliminary design work;

(ii) Initiation of the development processes and the acquisition of materials;

(iii) Reduction of design options and concentration upon a few alternatives for detailed elaboration;

(iv) Selection of one or several options, and construction and testing of basic prototypes;

(v) Freezing of a design for production, and the organisation of a production line;

(vi) Production of an initial (development) batch and testing under semi-operational conditions;

(vii) Full-scale production of weapons modified in the light of operational tests, and introduction into service.

Although the timescale of projects can be shortened by early commitment of resources to a successful design, the history of aircraft, naval and missile projects in the post-war period suggests that a six- to ten-year period normally elapsed between the start of work and entry into service with the armed forces. Within this period, the basic research and development activities and completion of an initial prototype took as long as the process of developing that prototype to the production stage.[48] There is no overt reason why such a series of sequential phases, and their associated timescales, were absent from the British nuclear weapon project. This assumption has important political and military implications, for the overt sign of nuclear weapon status, a first nuclear test explosion, can be equated with the basic prototype stage listed above. Thus it can be anticipated that a period of years will elapse between this politically important event and the militarily significant date when a number of production weapons ready for rapid use enter the national stockpile.

When is Independence not Independence?

In 1945, the world powers and their leaders regarded access to the technologies of nuclear energy as a vital element, if not the most vital element, determining the future of international relationships and the survival of their states. As a consequence, it became an issue area separated from other relationships between states, and some of this insulation has continued for five decades. The apparent necessity to possess a detailed knowledge of the technological and scientific issues involved in order to make informed policy decisions has given people connected with nuclear energy the appearance of guardians of religious secrets. Yet despite this exclusiveness, there is no overt reason why interstate interactions in this field should not be similar to those found in other, more open international forums. Indeed, the major element which differentiates these linkages from others is the dominance of the state and its subsidiary institutions in them, in contrast to better-known areas such as the trade in oil and petroleum products, where multinational corporations and other non-governmental institutions play a more central role.[49] One consequence of the significance attached to this kind of activity, however, has been that Britain's formal external relationships in the military applications of nuclear energy have been confined to bilateral links with the United States, rather than taking place in a multilateral context. It is thus unnecessary to go beyond an examination of bilateral relationships in seeking guidance for analysing these activities.

Many different types of relationship have been observed between two countries. These can be divided up in several ways, but one of the most common methods is to regard them as taking place along a spectrum ranging from self-reliance to dependence.[50] Self-reliance implies the ability to fulfil a state's needs by utilising its indigenous resources; dependence means that these needs can only be met through the use of resources controlled by other states.[51] This distinction can be used both to explore the degree to which any state is now self-reliant, and to attempt to draw a distinction between absolute and relative dependence, or, as it is more usually termed in the specialist international relations literature, vulnerability and sensitivity.[52] Absolute dependence or vulnerability implies that it is physically impossible to fulfil needs if a relationship is severed, because, for example, only a single source of a particular raw material exists and other substances cannot act as effective substitutes for it. Relative dependence or sensitivity implies that needs can be fulfilled in other ways or via other linkages. Indeed, this usage of the term may signify merely that an interaction exists.

These ideas of dependency and interdependency can be explored further if, for the purposes of analysis, they are seen to possess separable political and economic dimensions. The political usage of terms such as dependency, independency, self-sufficiency, mutual dependency and interdependency is illustrated by the spectrum of relationships displayed in Figure 1.2.

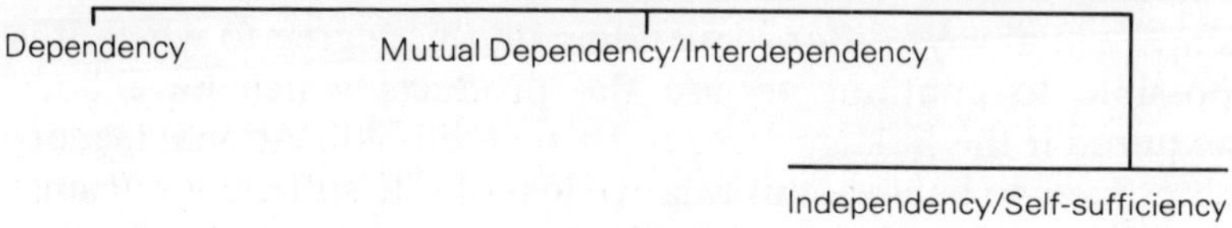

Dependency   Mutual Dependency/Interdependency

Independency/Self-sufficiency

FIGURE 1.2

Such a spectrum relies heavily upon traditional ideas of the state being a sovereign entity which, in a 'state of nature', recognises no superior authority and is in a position of independence and self-sufficiency. It has now been forced into a rather different situation, involving some element of dependency upon others, by the nature of the contemporary international environment.[53] Given this degradation from the ideal of self-sufficiency, the distinction between dependency and interdependency appears to involve the difference between a situation where one state, Alpha, can perform actions which adversely affect the members of another state, Beta, and Beta has no ability to make a reciprocal response, and one where such a countervailing capability exists, hence the synonymous use of the term mutual dependence.

The employment of this concept in political analysis leans heavily upon certain ideas found in economics, such as the relative amount of resources employed in performing a task in one way rather than another, or one task rather than another (opportunity costs); the economic benefits to be derived from concentrating upon producing a limited number of products, conducting extensive trade in them and thus having larger production runs which reduce unit costs (division of labour and returns to scale); and the existence of certain goods and services which are capable of being used by more than one person, group or state (collective goods). International relationships can be viewed as a form of trading relations, and thus the prime reason for engaging in them can be argued to be the economic one of maximising the attributes, or comparative advantages, of individual states, thereby increasing the total goods and services available to two or more states. This is a consequence of the greater efficiency that results from specialisation and the lower unit costs of longer production runs. In short, the disposable income of a state should in theory increase as it moves from a position of self-sufficiency to one of interdependence through external trade.[54] The nature of such interdependent relationships will always differ, depending on the degree to which it is possible to continue to use the products which have been acquired if the linkage were to be severed. All national leaderships have to balance this relative loss of self-sufficiency against the increased total of goods and services available to the state or, to put it another way, they have to assess the opportunity costs involved in returning to a state of greater self-sufficiency. Dependency upon another state is thus rarely absolute: more often what is involved is a greater or lesser degree of interdependence. Some countervailing pressures will usually exist and judgements on whether such a relationship is acceptable revolve around the opportunity costs or loss of economic product involved in returning to and sustaining self-sufficiency and whether or not a state is prepared or able to accept them.

The opportunity costs involved in a trading relationship are rarely static: they alter over time. A conscious initial decision to engage in it often occurs at a time when a practical option of continuing to be self-sufficient remains in existence. Unfortunately the logic of a trading relationship implies that maximum benefit can only be obtained from it if no resources are allocated to the task of sustaining any residual capacity for self-reliance. Thus what was originally only a position of relative sensitivity to the imposition of an embargo by a trading partner, as a result of the capacity to revert rapidly to self-sufficiency, tends, over time, to move towards a position of absolute vulnerability, as the plants and other facilities which comprised the capability to return to self-reliance deteriorate and are demolished. The choices confronting the state may then be to try to create a series of countervailing dependencies with its bilateral partner; to invest high levels of resources in the creation or refurbishment of new reserve capacity, to sustain the option of self-sufficiency; or to take the view that the specific needs which a particular type of trade meets can, in the last resort, remain unfulfilled.[55]

The maintenance of military security is perceived as the prime goal of most states, though whether any particular method of attempting to achieve it has an absolute quality attached to it is a much more difficult question to resolve. Yet bilateral and multilateral security alliances have qualities analogous to trading systems, for the same choices between self-reliance and mutual dependency are applicable to these linkages, while economic concepts have been used directly in the analysis of such military activities as collaborative weapon procurement.[56] Specialisation and division of labour, rather than the maintenance of balanced national forces, has been extensively canvassed as a solution to the perceived problem of shortages of certain NATO military capabilities, while joint weapon production has been advocated as a means of increasing the military resources available to the alliance. In this kind of security context, the types of possible trading relationships that may exist can be visualised as lying along a spectrum illustrated by Figure 1.3.

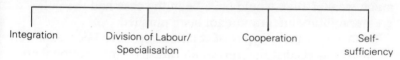

Integration   Division of Labour/   Cooperation   Self-
           Specialisation   sufficiency

FIGURE 1.3

A shift away from military self-sufficiency towards increased linkages with other states may be accompanied by a change in decision-making and management patterns, as a situation of division of labour progresses towards one of integration. Whereas the former implies maintenance of a capacity for self-sufficiency in some fields, integration, in which national organisations are absorbed into a larger transnational structure, may ultimately result in the loss of this attribute. A state's view of security integration is thus likely to be heavily dependent not only upon the perceived linkage between its sovereignty, its security position and the military advantages offered by these arrangements, but also upon its ability to retreat to a situation of self-sufficiency if forced to do so. Moreover, its judgements will be heavily influenced by the relative sizes and resource bases of the states involved in a military alliance. If all possess roughly equal capabilities, the losses and gains arising from the withdrawal of an individual state are likely to be spread randomly between the partners. If one state is much stronger than the others, then the actions of a lesser state in integrating its military capabilities with the greater one, such as engaging in specialisation, accepting unbalanced forces and sacrificing its latent power of self-sufficiency for the collective good, may be perceived by the dominant power merely as an act of cooperation. The dominant state would continue to retain an ability to revert to a policy of military independence and self-sufficiency, albeit at some opportunity cost to itself, whereas the lesser state might well regard this option as being increasingly unavailable to it. Thus an integrative relationship creates a position of vulnerability when viewed from the perspective of lesser powers, but to an alliance leader, it will merely be one of sensitivity. This presents the leadership of the lesser state with an acute dilemma, for whilst the integrative option, if sustained, appears to offer the opportunity to increase its security, any collapse of such an arrangement, especially after a considerable period of time has elapsed, could leave it in a position where its military stance was much weaker than would have been the case had the policy of greater military integration not been pursued.

In so far as these types of relationship have been explored within the specialist theoretical literature on international politics, the focus has been upon the problems that they present to the dominant state. The theory of collective goods has been applied to investigate the position of states which are military alliance leaders and which are seeking to convince lesser partners that they should contribute additional resources to the collective good of security.[57] All states can be argued to benefit from such military arrangements, but there is no simple method for deciding on the level of contribution each partner should make. Alternatives include fixing it in line with the opportunity cost of withdrawal to the individual state and the rest of the alliance, or attempting to calculate the positive benefits derived by each state from the arrangements. The most extreme case which arises when evaluating benefits is that of the 'free rider' in the system, the relationship between France and the North Atlantic Treaty Organisation often being alluded to in this context.[58] It can be argued that successive French governments have only been able to pursue their policy of nuclear self-sufficiency because of NATO's existence, yet they have not contributed directly to its peacetime military organisation.

This discussion suggests that states engaging in a military trading relationship, especially the junior partners in such a structure, will be constantly pushed towards the integration end of the spectrum by economic forces, but will be loath to move too far in that direction by the nature of state sovereignty and its links with national security and self-sufficiency. Thus, while a division of labour is attractive, so long as a retreat back to self-sufficiency is always feasible at an acceptable cost, military integration with a larger state will always lack appeal, both because it contradicts the whole idea of state sovereignty, and because it creates an unbalanced dependency relationship *vis-à-vis* that state, and places the lesser one in a position of great sensitivity, if not vulnerability. Any military trading relationship between the United States, as the greater power, and the United Kingdom, as the lesser one, can thus be expected to exhibit similar characteristics, especially one involving weapons, such as nuclear ones, which are regarded as the dominant military capability in safeguarding national security.

2 Conception: 1940–6

The Manhattan Transfer

The exploitation of nuclear energy always has been, and probably always will be, an international enterprise. Its birth is frequently dated from Chadwick's discovery of the neutron in Britain in 1932, but its subsequent progress during the 1930s took place in laboratories in several European countries and the United States. Many of the scientists involved formed a coherent transnational group which built upon each other's work, and the result was that by 1939 experiments basic to what is now termed nuclear physics were proceeding in Germany, Denmark, the USSR, Austria, France, the United Kingdom and the United States. This cosmopolitan enterprise was disrupted with the outbreak of war in Europe in 1939, and with the surrender of France in 1940 it became compartmentalised into four separate sets of activities, one in Germany, one in the USSR, one in Britain, incorporating refugee German and French scientific workers, and one in the United States.

It had been proved experimentally by 1939 that heavy atoms such as uranium could be split by bombarding them with neutrons,[1] and that this fission released enormous amounts of energy. It was apparent that such a process could be of practical use in two ways: to create a new form of explosive, and to act as a heat source for the generation of electricity. What remained unclear was whether these theoretical possibilities would ever become practical realities. Some of this uncertainty was removed in the spring of 1940 when Otto Frisch and Rudolf Peierls, two refugee scientists working at the University of Birmingham in Britain, produced a short theoretical explanation of how a bomb could be constructed using the uranium isotope U-235. Their paper discussed the amount required, techniques for manufacturing it, methods of detonation and the likely explosive effects.[2] Reports were also reaching Britain from France of German interest in both conducting atomic energy research and acquiring stocks of substances which could be used for fissile material production, thus suggesting that Germany was actively engaged in work on nuclear explosives.[3] An independent committee of leading scientists, sponsored by the Directorate of Scientific Research in the Ministry of Aircraft Production and known as the Maud Committee, was set up in Britain in April 1940 to evaluate this situation and develop policy proposals. This both co-ordinated a programme of research within British universities into the practical implications of the Frisch and Peierls paper and sponsored an intelligence-gathering operation into German activities.

The Maud Committee produced two reports in June and July 1941; the first on the use of uranium for a bomb and the second on its potential as a source of power.[4] The first report suggested that it would be possible to make a U-235 bomb by the end of 1943. It further stated that 'even if the war should end before the bombs are ready, the effort would not be wasted, except in the unlikely event of complete disarmament, since no nation would care to risk being caught without a weapon of such decisive possibilities'.[5]

The Maud reports reached the Scientific Advisory Committee of the British Cabinet at the end of August 1941. This committee concluded that the power project was unlikely to reach fruition in the near future, and should be pursued as an intergovernmental venture with the United States and Canada. A proposal that responsibility for its development should be transferred to Imperial Chemical Industries (ICI) was firmly rejected, but this firm was asked to second its Research Director, Mr W. Akers, to the Atomic Energy Project, now code-named Tube Alloys, as its Executive Director.[6] It was recognised that a bomb could probably be produced in two to five years, and a recommendation was made that high priorities should be given to developing fusing mechanisms for it; to conducting additional fundamental research into the nature of fission processes in U-235; and to laboratory and industrial work to aid the design of a plant to separate this material from the other isotopes of uranium. It was recommended that, if this research work proved successful, a full-size U-235 separation plant should be built in Canada, using components manufactured in the United States, as the necessary resources of men and materials were not available in wartime Britain.[7]

Nuclear energy research in the United States had proceeded in a rather fragmented fashion during 1939 and 1940, with the only work on its practical applications being focused upon its potential as a source of power. The United States Navy was displaying interest in the possibility of developing compact power plants fuelled by U-235 for submarine propulsion, and they were sponsoring work on a thermal diffusion process for separating out this material.[8] Despite the neutral status of the United States in the war with Germany, an Anglo-American exchange of general scientific information had begun in the autumn of 1940. This focused heavily upon radar technology but included some material on atomic energy. Copies of the Maud reports were sent to the United States under this arrangement and these enabled Vannevar Bush and James Conant, respectively chairman and deputy chairman of the US National Defense Research Council, to initiate a more structured American investigation into the production of nuclear explosives.[9] It also led to approaches being made to the United Kingdom at both the official and the highest political levels for the initiation of a jointly-controlled, integrated Anglo-American project to make atomic bombs, rather than just a programme to exchange information and coordinate research.[10] The British chose not to respond to these proposals because of the uncertain consequences of transferring a potentially dominant defence project to a neutral country.[11] The first American approach for more extensive cooperation in this field had thus been met with a *de facto* British rejection.

The United Kingdom and United States projects now proceeded independently, with the British concentrating upon the theoretical design of a U-235 bomb and the gaseous diffusion method of obtaining the material for it.[12] Work was also undertaken on the possibility of building an experimental nuclear reactor for development work on heat sources, using natural uranium as the fuel and heavy water as the moderator.[13] This project was led by refugee French scientists who had escaped from France in 1940 with their stocks of heavy water.[14] The United States was exploring three methods of producing U-235 in addition to gaseous diffusion: electromagnetic separation, enrichment in gas centrifuges and thermal diffusion.[15] Research had also started into both the use of the recently produced heavy

element, plutonium, as a fissile material, and methods of manufacturing substantial quantities of it in large nuclear reactors.[16]

Three of the leading scientists associated with the British
project visited the United States in the first three months of
1942, following the United States entry into the Second World
War, and discovered that considerably more scientific and
engineering resources and effort were being put into the American project than the British one. Indeed, it became clear to them
that 'the Americans who had been well behind the British in the
race for the bomb had drawn level and were indeed passing
them by'[17] and that the British had underestimated the potential
of plutonium in bomb manufacture. They reported that the
massive input of resources into the United States project would
soon enable it to outstrip the British one. A recommendation,
based on this report, that detailed proposals should be put to the
United States government for the merging of the two projects,
was made to the British political leadership in June 1942. The
British Prime Minister, Churchill, approved this suggestion
after considerable debate and an initial approach was made to
Bush in August,[18] but by then it was too late. It had been decided
to drive through the United States project with the utmost
speed, and to build full-scale production plants on the basis of
existing information without waiting for the completion of pilot
experimental facilities of the type that Britain planned to
construct.[19]

The change in the nature of the American project from a
scientific investigation to the engineering design and construction of production plants had led to the United States Army
being placed in charge of it in June 1942. Brigadier General
Groves was given the task of managing the work in September,
with headquarters in New York, hence its overall title of the
Manhattan Engineering District, usually shortened to the Manhattan Project.[20] This change of leadership and organisation led
to compartmentalisation for security reasons and induced a
rigorous single-mindedness of purpose, with all activities being
judged against the criterion of their ability to contribute to the
early production of a bomb. Britain's participation in a joint
project appeared unlikely to expedite this task, and its persis-
tence with this proposal started to breed mistrust among America's scientific administrators. The fact that the executive director of the United Kingdom project was seconded from ICI led

Bush, Conant and Groves to believe that Britain's motivation was to obtain information which would be of commercial value to Akers's parent firm, ICI, in developing a post-war nuclear power programme.[21] In addition, British insistence on access to all aspects of the Manhattan Project, if a joint project was to be initiated, was believed to stem from a desire to use American knowledge in a post-war national weapon project, rather than a belief that their existing expertise could be of value in expediting the production of a bomb for use in the existing conflict.[22] Their judgement was that British scientists could make no positive contribution to the American project and they regarded suggestions for cooperation as a method of allowing the United Kingdom to have access to any commercial and military discoveries made by the United States in the course of it. They stalled the British during the remainder of 1942 and gradually restricted transatlantic exchanges in this field. Finally, at the end of December, President Roosevelt approved a recommendation that these exchanges of information were to be restricted to those few items which could be used by the United Kingdom for immediate wartime purposes.[23]

This decision contrasted sharply with almost all other areas of defence research where a much freer Anglo-American interchange was the norm. It also foreshadowed the post-war discontinuity between cooperation on nuclear and non-nuclear defence projects. The British responded by reviewing once more the costs in money and resources of an independent wartime project: the conclusion was that a production project was possible but at a considerable opportunity cost in the diversion of resources from more pressing war work. The plans for the national project now envisaged the setting up of a government corporation to build a full-scale diffusion plant in Britain; the building of a nuclear reactor and an associated plutonium extraction plant in Canada; and the production by ICI of heavy water and uranium metal for the reactor in England. It was decided that before going ahead with such a plan one last attempt would be made to revive Anglo-American nuclear cooperation, which had become virtually non-existent by May 1943.[24] This proved very difficult, in part because it was unclear which person or group of people in the United States had effective decision-making powers in the area. Agreements were reached between Roosevelt and Churchill on the subject, but it did not prove easy for the British to persuade the United States representatives at lower levels to translate them into practical arrangements.[25] Eventually Churchill was able to discuss the matter with Bush and the United States Secretary for War in London in July, and an understanding was worked out between them. This formed the basis of the document signed by the President and the Prime Minister on 19 August 1943 at the Quebec Conference.[26]

This Quebec Agreement bound the two states never to use atomic weapons against each other, only to use them against another country with the other's consent, and never to transfer atomic information obtained as a consequence of the agreement to third parties without the other's acquiescence. To meet American suspicions of British commercial motivations, the President was to have the right to specify after the war the terms under which the United Kingdom government could make commercial or industrial use of nuclear information obtained from participation in the American project. Finally, a Combined Policy Committee (CPC) of three Americans, two Britons and one Canadian was to be set up in Washington to agree a joint programme of work and allocate materials for it. The members of the CPC and their technical advisers were to be informed of the general progress of all aspects of the American project, but at lower levels this interchange was to be restricted to data relevant to work in hand, and any exchange of detailed information on production plants was to be the subject of later *ad hoc* arrangements.[27] The Quebec Agreement was an executive one between the heads of government and was not an international treaty: the distinction meant that Roosevelt was not obliged to inform Congress about it, and that body was later to legislate in ignorance of it.

Cooperation did not resume immediately, despite the presence in Washington of a number of the leading British nuclear scientists. It seems to have taken two weeks for the United States members of the CPC to become seized of the agreement, and they then made it clear that it would not be implemented if Akers, with his ICI connections, acted as a technical adviser to the British members. Professor James Chadwick was therefore appointed Executive Director of Tube Alloys, the code-name for the British project, and head of its mission in Washington, with Akers returning to Britain to coordinate domestic activities.[28] This attitude of responsiveness to American wishes was reinforced when the resumption of a full exchange of information revealed the extent of United States progress towards producing the materials for a bomb.

Cooperation during the remainder of the war took three substantive forms. First, the Combined Development Trust (CDT) was formed in June 1944 to acquire raw materials, particularly uranium ore. Britain and the United States supplied equal funding for this venture, which was mainly concerned with ensuring the largest possible supply of uranium from the Belgian Congo. Existing ores from that source and others from Canada proved sufficient for the wartime project, and it was the postwar implications of this procurement activity that proved to be important, as the funding arrangement meant that these supplies of raw materials were jointly owned and controlled.[29] Second, a multinational British, Canadian and French research team was created in Montreal, headed by Professor Cockcroft, to design and build a heavy water moderated, natural uranium research reactor, using materials supplied mainly by the United States. This project resulted in the construction of both a zero-energy reactor, ZEEP, and the Chalk River NRX reactor, though neither was operational before the end of the war. It meant that the British, Canadians and French had considerable knowledge of how to build plutonium-producing reactors by 1945, and could look forward to acquiring supplies of this material to investigate its properties.[30] Third, British scientists were sent to the United States to become an integral part of certain elements of the Manhattan Project.

The two main activities in which the British scientists played a part were in the operation of the electromagnetic separation plant to produce U-235 and in the work of the Los Alamos laboratory, which had been given the job of designing and manufacturing nuclear bombs. Thirty-five British engineers, physicists and chemists went to Oak Ridge, Tennessee, and Berkeley, California, and became integrated into many sections of the electromagnetic separation project. They acquired sufficient technical knowledge through this participation to build such a plant in England, if it were to prove necessary.[31] At Los Alamos, British scientists were attached to almost all the divisions in the laboratory, though the majority were concerned with developing conventional explosive techniques to create a critical mass in a plutonium bomb through the implosion method.[32] This meant that at the end of the war the British members of the Los Alamos team possessed considerable detailed knowledge of how to design the type of plutonium bomb which was dropped upon the Japanese city of Nagasaki. In addition, British nuclear physicists had formed part of a group considering the possibility of an hydrogen bomb.[33] It was ironic that the British played only a very limited, consultative role in the construction of the gaseous diffusion plant at Oak Ridge, despite the fact that most of their early work had been concentrated in this area. Commercial considerations appeared to have played a major part in this situation.[34]

Participation in the North American projects thus left the British at the end of the Second World War with a theoretical veto on the United States use of atomic bombs, detailed knowledge of both how to make a plutonium bomb and how to produce U-235 using the very inefficient electromagnetic separation method, and an ability to design and build a plutonium production reactor using heavy water as a moderator. They had negligible knowledge of the design and operation of either the more efficient United States Oak Ridge gaseous diffusion plants for the production of U-235, or the graphite-moderated, water-cooled plutonium production reactors at Hanford, and their associated chemical separation plants to extract fissile material from reactor fuel. A small group of perhaps 50 to 60 British scientists and engineers was in collective possession of this information. The key questions in mid-1945 were whether it was to be used to further an independent British programme or a collaborative Anglo-American one, and how the United States government system would resolve its suspicions of the United Kingdom's commercial motives in pressing for any continuation of the wartime arrangements.

United States Policies towards Control over Atomic Energy

A number of elements combined to give United States policy towards control over atomic energy the appearance of being ill-coordinated and often contradictory from 1944 onwards. One was the limited attention which key decision-makers, such as the President, could devote to the subject, given the overwhelming problems of ending the war and attempting to con-

struct a new post-war international system. A second was the
need to bring Congress into the decision-making system at the
end of the war, both to allow the executive to account for their
wartime spending on the project, and to enable private industrial activities in the nuclear area to be firmly controlled. A third
was the lack of a clear boundary between the scientific knowledge underlying the wartime project and the industrial and
technical knowledge of how to build production plants and
make bombs. This generated strong pressures within the United
States scientific community for the creation of conditions which
would allow the normal transnational interchange of nuclear
physics information to be renewed, if necessary within the
context of international control mechanisms. A fourth was
demands for civilian, rather than military, control over nuclear
energy in the United States. A fifth element was the belief that
exceptional efforts had to be made to gain Soviet acquiescence
to international control mechanisms for nuclear energy. It was
accepted that this might necessitate the severing of existing
cooperative ties with Britain, though it was not to include any
premature termination of the United States monopoly over
nuclear weapons or any transfer of their 'secrets'. This stance
was compounded by a lack of understanding of the inherently
transient nature of the 'secret' of nuclear weapons, which was
reinforced by contemporary estimates, ranging from four to
twenty years, of the time it would take the Soviet Union to
explode a nuclear device. Finally, there was the contradiction
between the increasing emphasis placed upon nuclear weapons
in United States defence policy from 1946 onwards, and the fact
that any agreement on international control of nuclear energy
would have required its total reorientation. In short, different
elements in the United States political and governmental process had policies towards one or more aspects of nuclear energy
but no single coherent policy was dominant. This environment
made it very difficult for Britain to devolop a satisfactory
post-war nuclear relationship with the United States.[35]

The issue of post war planning had first been raised in the
United States in mid-1944 when the scientists designing the
Hanford plutonium-producing reactors had almost finished
their task, and it was clear that any further design work they
would undertake would have post-war, rather than wartime,
applications. The initial stance was to discourage such work, on

the grounds that the Manhattan Project was concerned only with those activities which would reach fruition in the course of the war.[36] This attitude was soon reversed and, by late 1944, two technical committees had been set up to make recommendations on the United States future nuclear research and development programme, as well as on domestic and international control systems. Their work had little immediate impact as the political leadership of the country was not yet seized of these issues.[37]

Bush and Conant at the National Defense Research Council had also been attempting to formulate a policy for the post-war control of nuclear energy. The core of their thinking was that 'While they looked with favour on joint Anglo-American efforts to acquire raw materials and contemplated extending interchange into the years of peace, they did not want the United States to commit itself so completely to Britain as to prejudice its relations with Russia.'[38] Professor Niels Bohr, who had been brought out of Denmark by the British in late 1943 in order to act as a consultant to the Manhattan Project, had also met both Churchill and Roosevelt and attempted to impress upon them the need for international control. He urged them to facilitate this by informing the Russians about the project at the earliest opportunity.[39] Bohr and Roosevelt had a cordial discussion but the encounter between Bohr and Churchill was a failure. Before Roosevelt had a chance to consult with his advisers in detail about international control, he met Churchill informally on 18 September 1944, at his Hyde Park residence in New York State. This meeting led to the Hyde Park *aide-mémoire* being initialled by the two leaders, which flatly rejected any public or secret disclosure to other states of information about the Manhattan Project. It was decided to initiate an investigation into whether Bohr had been leaking information to the Russians,[40] while the *aide-mémoire* asserted that 'Full collaboration between the United States and the British Government in developing Tube Alloys for military and commercial purposes should continue after the defeat of Japan unless and until terminated by joint agreement.'[41] This document bore all the hallmarks of having been drafted by Churchill and acquiesced to by Roosevelt, and the latter does not appear to have informed either Bush or his Secretary for War of its existence.

Bush was becoming convinced that the President contemplated signing an Anglo-American agreement to restrict nuclear information to the two states alone, and enable them jointly to 'control the peace of the world'.[42] He feared that this would lead to an arms race with the USSR and believed that international control was the only way to prevent it. The need for action on this issue became urgent in December 1944, when it became known that a number of French nuclear scientists, who had been working in Canada, wished to return to their newly-liberated homeland. This placed Britain in a dilemma, for although commitments had been made to them regarding their right to exploit wartime work, the original leader of the group, Joliot-Curie, was known to be a member of the French Communist Party. The British political leadership felt they could not prevent their return, but the leaders of the Manhattan Project argued that this would endanger its security, pose a risk of information leaks to the USSR, and lead to United States nuclear secrets passing into the possession of third parties in violation of the Quebec Agreement.[43] Eventually the scientists were allowed to return to France, but British support for their request both reinforced the existing distrust of the United Kingdom's motives in participating in the project, and demonstrated the difficulties the United States was likely to face in retaining a monopoly of nuclear weapons.

In the autumn of 1944 and spring of 1945 Bush made great efforts to convince the War Department, and especially Stimson, its Secretary, of the need to formulate a clear plan of action for both the end of the war and the possible use of the atomic bomb. This pressure was reinforced by renewed demands from the scientific community for a liberal post-war policy on atomic energy research, and the increased reluctance of certain congressmen to acquiesce in the budgeting of hundreds of millions of dollars for the Manhattan Project without any detailed explanation of its use. Stimson was able to see Roosevelt in mid-March and explain that there existed two schools of thought on future control of nuclear energy, one arguing for a continuation of the existing arrangements with Britain and the pursuit of a policy of minimum disclosure of information, the other arguing for international control to allow free interchange of scientific information and open access to nuclear laboratories. Roosevelt took no action following this meeting, and on 12 April he died.[44]

The new President, Truman, was rapidly acquainted with the details of the Manhattan Project and readily agreed to set up an 'interim committee' on atomic energy. This was to consider the issues of domestic and international control, and serve as a link with whatever permanent institutions Congress might eventually create for managing the development of nuclear energy in the United States. Its first task was to make recommendations on how the bomb might be used against Japan, and it was not until July that it was able to turn its attention to the question of post-war arrangements. It had been realised that to allow the wartime activities to be continued, an Atomic Energy Commission, with a full-time board of technical experts, would have to be established by congressional legislation after the war. One area of potential disagreement over such legislation was between the scientific community, who wished for full freedom of action in research, and those in the budget organisations and Congress who believed that all federal monies had to be spent only on the purposes for which they had been voted.[45] War Department lawyers were given the task of producing a draft bill, but this led to further divergencies of view on whether the regulatory and research function should be performed by a single organisation, and whether active or retired members of the armed forces should be eligible to become commissioners. The major area of disagreement was over the sweeping powers proposed for the Commission, which would give it a much greater ability to inspect and regulate the activities of private industry than any comparable United States organisation.

The War Department's draft bill was an attempt to carry the structure and organisation of the Manhattan Project over into peacetime, and it was ready for submission to Congress when it reconvened in September 1945. The necessity for the State Department to sponsor the bill provided an opportunity to inject into it sections on international control. The most important of these was that the Commission was to be subject to the guidance of the Secretary of State in international matters. There existed a more fundamental and paradoxical difference between the heads of the two organisations, however, in that Stimson in the War Department believed in the necessity of negotiating international control of atomic energy, whereas Byrnes in the State Department believed it was impossible to cooperate effectively with the USSR, and was concerned to use and retain the nuclear monopoly of the United States as a diplomatic tool in negotiations with that state.[46]

Throughout the early part of September the issue of international control versus United States monopoly grew in importance among Truman's advisers, fuelled by much misunderstanding over the existence of a 'secret' of the bomb which was seen as the 'property of the American people'.[47] A direct approach to Russia was suggested, with the US, USSR and Britain suspending work on the bomb, but it was clear by the end of September that the administration had little time left to formulate a policy on the issue, as the question of control of atomic energy had become a topic of major public controversy. This debate was fuelled from two sources. Scientists who had worked on the project found themselves still subjected to War Department restrictions, and started to campaign for greater freedom, arguing that this was necessary to allow the United States to move ahead with an extensive nuclear research programme. Some of them insisted that such a programme was vital because there no longer existed any secret about the atom bomb, and United States inactivity would allow other states to catch up with her. Others were campaigning for international control as a prerequisite for such a programme. A number of bills and resolutions were brought forward in Congress aimed at creating a domestic management system for nuclear energy, and the trend of congressional thought appeared to be moving in the direction of continuing the rigid wartime security system in order to retain the 'secret' of the bomb for the United States.[48] The administration finally chose to act through the medium of a Presidential Message to Congress on 3 October. This proposed the setting up of an Atomic Energy Commission with the minimum powers necessary to control all atomic energy activities. Discussions were also to be initiated with other states on the international control of atomic energy, starting with Canada and Great Britain.

The administration, in the shape of the War Department, then introduced legislation aimed at transferring control of atomic energy from the army to the full-time civilian commission. The hope was that it would rapidly be passed into law, but it became entangled in a conflict within Congress over how the bill should be handled, with certain senators advocating the creation of a joint committee to deal with it. The bill itself was attacked by certain of the nuclear scientists for giving them too little freedom, and then by congressmen because they would have no powers other than budgetary ones over the activities of the commissioners. Finally, the President became convinced that the bill would not allow the Executive effectively to control the activities of the commissioners, and by mid-November it was clear that it was unlikely to be adopted without drastic revision. The only positive move that had occurred was that the Senate had set up a committee on atomic energy with the rather junior senator, McMahon, as chairman.[49]

The Senate Committee believed its initial task should be to acquire a greater understanding of the detailed background to the legislation, but their educative aspirations soon brought them into conflict with General Groves, who still remained the head of the Manhattan Project. The committee requested details of wartime relations with Britain, stockpiles of bombs and other restricted data. Groves refused to supply them on the basis that they had no clear 'need to know', and a conflict then ensued between the War Department and the committee over the latter's rights with regard to all information on atomic energy issues. These questions were brought out into the open at a conference at the White House on 4th December attended by representatives of all the interested parties. At this meeting the President persuaded the committee members not to press for the information they had requested on the grounds that it would adversely affect the negotiations for an international control system, and he made it clear that he was seeking greater presidential controls over the commission than had been allowed for in the War Department's bill. It was in this situation of legislative deadlock and conflict over the rights of Congress that McMahon introduced his own bill into the Senate on 20 December. This had been drafted by some of his staff members after extensive consultations with interested scientists.[50]

The President had been pressured to take action on international control of nuclear energy by both the internal interest groups and Britain. Attlee, the new British Prime Minister, had written to the President on 25 September suggesting discussions on the future of Anglo-American nuclear relations, but Truman's reply set no date for a meeting. Attlee therefore wrote back on 16 October offering to visit Washington immediately for such a discussion, and it was agreed that the British, Cana-

dian and American leaders would meet there on 10 November
to discuss both the wider question of international control and
the narrower question of future trilateral cooperation.[51] This
meeting produced a three-power declaration containing a recommendation that the UN should set up a commission to make
specific proposals on three issues: the international control of
the peaceful uses of atomic energy; the elimination of atomic
bombs; and the safeguards necessary to deter evasion of international regulation. The question of the future basis of Anglo-
American collaboration was dealt with by two memoranda. The
first merely stated that the existing institutions of cooperation
should continue in a suitable form. The second contained
guidelines for a new document to supersede the Quebec Agreement. This was to be negotiated within the CPC, which had
continued to meet despite the termination of hostilities. The
guidelines said nothing about industrial and commercial rights;
they required only consultation, not consent, prior to decisions
to use the bomb against third parties, or to disclose information
to them, and they subjected all raw materials to joint allocation.
Full cooperation in basic scientific research was promised, but it
was stated that the CPC was to regulate by *ad hoc* arrangements
only any mutually advantageous interchange on the development, design, construction and operation of fissile material
production plants.[52] (45)
    The fact that the three-power declaration and the bilateral
memoranda might be seen as contradictory to each other,
especially if the tie with the United Kingdom was to jeopardise
the possibility of wider arrangements with Russia, is a good
indication of both the fragmented nature of United States
decision-making on these issues and the equivocal nature of
both states' commitment to the idea of international control.
Equally, failure to consult members of Congress throughout
these proceedings made it difficult to see how any successor to
the Quebec Agreement could be promulgated as a treaty and
given Senate approval. Britain had obtained, by default, a significant concession in the negotiations, as it was clear that the
American President was not going to take advantage of the
terms of the Quebec Agreement by placing limitations upon
Britain's ability to develop nuclear energy for civil purposes.
Whether this clause could have been enforced, however, is an
open question, as is the degree to which Britain could realistical-

ly insist upon being consulted before the use of nuclear weapons by the United States.

The next stage was to try to bring the Soviet Union into the discussions on international control, and the most convenient forum for this was the mid-December foreign ministers' conference in Moscow. This meeting was preceded by internal consultations between Byrnes, the United States Secretary of State, and members of the Senate atomic energy committee. They informed him that Congress would not agree to any exchange of information with the USSR unless prior agreement had been reached on a system of safeguards. The senators then expressed their concern over safeguards to the President, who distinguished clearly in his reponse between interchange of scientific information and interchange of production and ordnance data. However, the Soviets proved less suspicious of this initiative than the Senate and agreed to the setting up of the United Nations Commission in a joint communiqué of 27 December. This action alarmed certain of the senators who once again sought assurances from the President.[53] It was clear that henceforth no formal international agreement on atomic energy was going to be possible unless it could gain congressional approval.

The November meetings had remitted the drafting of a definitive post-war agreement for Anglo-American nuclear cooperation to the CPC. This met to start on the task early in December. It appointed a small subcommittee, which soon succeeded in producing a draft memorandum of agreement, containing wide-ranging provisions for a full exchange of information to meet the requirements of the respective national programmes. General Groves actively opposed these provisions, as he regarded them as tantamount to an overt military alliance with Britain, and believed they would have to be registered with the UN as a treaty under article 102 of the Charter. He was also aware that the British would soon ask for information on large-scale plants for manufacturing fissionable materials, and he believed that both of these developments would adversely affect the attempts to establish international control over atomic energy.

The result of this controversy was that the United States representatives on the CPC refused to agree to the draft memorandum, and also turned down suggestions that collaboration should continue under the terms of the Quebec Agreement. The British pointed out that this effectively nullified the November agreements, and by mid-April it was clear that this issue could only be settled by Attlee and Truman. The President responded by using the distinction between classes of information, which he had employed with the senators in December in connection with the negotiations with Russia, and asserted that the November statement only obligated the United States to a full interchange of basic scientific information and did not include production and ordnance data. He indicated that any other exchanges could be regulated by *ad hoc* arrangements, but was of the opinion that it was unwise to make arrangements while efforts were being made to establish international control.[54] The United States was thus only prepared to cooperate over raw material supplies and the exchange of basic scientific information, and any British programme for the production of fissionable materials would have to be based upon its own unaided efforts. The action by the President, while understandable in the context of the American objective of constructing an international control system for atomic energy, was regarded as a personal affront and grave injustice by many of the British atomic scientists and engineers, and it served as a significant motivation in their support of the subsequent independent British project.

The President's stance was in part an attempt to escape from some of the contradictions inherent in the *ad hoc* way United States policy had evolved, but it may also have been influenced by the first of the nuclear spy disclosures, that concerning Alan Nunn May.[55] This reinforced the school of thought in Congress which saw the atom bomb as an American 'secret', in the absence of positive information on the role played in its development by Britain, and which believed that any renewed interchange with the new socialist government of the United Kingdom would threaten the security of the American nuclear programme, and thus the United States. The choice between international control and Anglo-American cooperation, originally envisaged by Bush in September 1944, was finally made in April 1946 in favour of the former. A contributing factor was the pressure from Britain to make a decision, because it wished to proceed with its own national project. Although the United States President had chosen international control, the decision could also be interpreted by members of Congress as one which enabled the United States to retain a monopoly over the atomic bomb.

The presidential decision to refuse to transfer information on fissile material production technology to Britain was taken prior to the passing of any atomic energy legislation by Congress. The progress of the debate on this domestic legislation was very slow and haphazard. It centred upon the balance between civilian control over atomic energy and the need for military participation in an enterprise which had as its primary objective the production of weapons. This issue merged into that of maintaining effective security over the atomic 'secret' which, after the Nunn May revelations, was perceived by many to necessitate military control over the project. It was also affected by personal antagonisms within the Senate, and the problem of attempting to persuade the House of Representatives first to ignore the original army-sponsored bill, which they had accepted, and then to adopt an amended version of Senator McMahon's bill. This legislative process was one whose outcome and timing were very difficult to forecast, which proceeded in an almost autonomous manner, and over which the Executive either could not or would not exercise influence and control. The bill was viewed primarily as an instrument for domestic regulation, and little conscious attempt seems to have been made to inform Congress of the existence of the wartime agreements with Britain and the contradictions between their terms and the proposed legislation, which gave no powers to the Commission to exchange information with other states on the design of atomic weapons and the technology of fissile material production facilities. Exchanges of those special nuclear materials which could assist in a weapon programme were also outside its jurisdiction. The bill also created a unique, statutory congressional committee, the Joint Committee on Atomic Energy (JCAE). This comprised members of both Houses, and had the potential to be a policy-making body. Its members and staff were subjected to security checks to enable them to have access to all of America's nuclear secrets, and many of its hearings were conducted in secret Executive sessions, the transcripts of which were never published. Thus the relationship between the JCAE and the rest of Congress had similarities to that between members of a British Cabinet Defence committee and the other members of the Cabinet and the House of Commons. The final format of the bill was still in

doubt on 23 July when the conference committee of both
Houses met. The next day, it was agreed that exchanges of
information with other countries on industrial applications
should be made dependent upon Congress passing a joint
resolution confirming that an effective international control
regime for atomic energy had been created. This meant that
until this regime existed, it would be illegal for the new Atomic
Energy Commission (AEC), which was to be the owner of all
American nuclear information, to engage in any exchanges with
Britain on the industrial development of nuclear energy. On 27
July both Houses accepted the conference report, and the
President signed the Atomic Energy Act of 1946 on 1 August.[56]
Britain had been 'squeezed between the multilaterally-minded
internationalists and the nationalists',[57] although the possibility
existed that this restrictive legislation could be amended by
Congress if it, or the executive, were to decide that such changes
were advantageous to the United States.

In assessing these events it must be recognised that the United
States lacked a centralised system of government decision-
making similar to that of the United Kingdom, which meant that
there was no firm guarantee that agreements and promises
made by the President would be either passed into law or
legitimised as a treaty by the Senate. Congress was prepared in
wartime to accord considerable executive powers to the President, but when peace returned it was determined to exert its
rights over budgetary issues, in legislation and in treaty-making
once again. In addition, the familiar United States activity of
'bureaucratic politics' was being conducted between the numerous agencies of government,[58] and this was exacerbated in the
area of atomic energy by the fact that prior to the setting up of
the AEC by the 1946 Act there was no single agency responsible
for this area, or for coordination of domestic and external
activities in relation to it. The passing of detailed legislation was
the only effective way of giving this federal agency the powers to
control and develop American activities in the field. To these
elements were added the political uncertainties of the immediate post-war period, and the resultant division between
those sections of Congress and the Executive who believed that
first priority should be given to the setting up of an international
system of control, and those who saw the future in terms of
atomic isolationism. Few people at this time foresaw the evolution of United States security policy taking the form of the

construction of semi-permanent security alliances of the NATO type. In this environment, the idea of Congress ratifying a public agreement to set up an 'atomic alliance' with the United Kingdom was unrealistic.

The 1946 Act made the continuation of the wartime information and personnel interchanges impossible without congressional approval. It obligated the Executive to lay such arrangements before Congress in order that the President could be voted specific powers to implement them. The problem was that in the prevailing congressional atmosphere there was no guarantee that it would approve of such interchanges, and the President was unlikely to ask for amendments to the Act unless he was reasonably certain of success. In the absence of these restrictive clauses it might have been possible for the United States government to change its policy in 1948 when it became clear that the plans for international control of atomic energy would not succeed: their existence meant that changes would have to wait for a radically different international and congressional environment. The lesson for the future was that British governments would have to be clear about the type of agreement they wanted with the United States, and accept that there was an inverse relationship between the confidentiality of the agreement and its ability to bind the United States in perpetuity. They would also have to accept that a crucial element in dealing with the United States was to convince personnel at all levels of government and key members of Congress, rather than just the president, of the value of nuclear energy agreements with Britain.

Only three elements of the wartime arrangements remained operative after the April presidential decision and the passing of the 1946 Act. One was the agreement for securing joint control over supplies of uranium; the second, the United States material support for the heavy water moderated NRX reactor in Canada; and the third, the continued presence of certain British scientists and ordnance specialists at Los Alamos and in the team which carried out the post-war United States weapon effects trials at Bikini Atoll in July 1946. This latter arrangement allowed Dr Penney[59] to take part in discussions on the results of these trials, which had been conducted with the type of plutonium bomb dropped on Nagasaki.[60] His participation was made possible because the 1946 Act did not classify information on nuclear weapon effects as restricted atomic data. Both this type of information and that on certain Russian nuclear activities were classified as military restricted data, and could be exchanged with other states subject to the arrangements and limitations applicable to interchanges of non-nuclear defence information.[61]

One effect of the prolonged domestic conflict over the atomic energy legislation was that although fissionable material, especially U-235, continued to be produced in the United States during 1946, no new investment in plants or improved weapons was made, nor was there any attempt to train new teams to assemble standardised bomb components.[62] At the end of 1946, the United States had still not transferred its atomic project from an emergency wartime programme into a long-term peacetime one, and in many respects it was further from possessing an operational atomic bomb than it had been in early 1945. A random collection of bomb components existed, but few people had any information on what or where they were, and there were no personnel immediately available to assemble them into weapons. In addition, the output of plutonium from the Hanford reactors had been curtailed because of operational difficulties associated with the expansion of their graphite moderator. In a word, the American military nuclear project was in a shambles.

A British Independent Nuclear Programme

The amount of research into nuclear energy being undertaken in Britain declined sharply following the Quebec Agreement of August 1943. Many of the personnel who had been working in the field moved to North America during 1944, and this made it difficult to convene meetings of the Tube Alloys technical committee to discuss exclusively British concerns. Professor Chadwick,[63] the scientific adviser to the British members of the CPC, was reluctant to press for such meetings as he was anxious to avoid any impression that Britain was not putting all its effort into furthering the aims of the American project. As a result, Britain undertook little positive planning during this wartime period. It had been accepted that the Americans should be informed of all proposals for nuclear energy development in the United Kingdom, and in line with this policy the Prime Minister told President Roosevelt in February 1945 that Britain would

start its own atomic energy project after the war, while in April
the CPC was informed of the government's intention to start
work on plans for a national experimental establishment.[64]

The lack of any positive action to implement these aspirations
prior to the end of the war was partly a product of a desire to
avoid hostile American reactions, partly a result of the realisation that many scarce resources would have to be devoted to
such a project, and partly a consequence of the difficulty of
reaching a firm conclusion on the best method of producing
fissile material in significant quantities. Early in 1944 the advice
on the latter issue had been to build plutonium-producing heavy
water moderated reactors, but by mid-1944 this had changed to
the construction of a low enrichment U-235 plant to provide
fuel for a water-cooled and moderated reactor.[65] Design work
on a low separation plant started and cost estimates were
produced but, even in April 1945, the United States project was
still in such an uncertain state that Chadwick felt unable to offer
a firm view on the best option for Britain. His recommendation
was to delay any decision until the American project reached
fruition and firm evidence was available on the most effective
types of plant.[66] In the meantime, planning for the experimental
establishment went ahead. The Tube Alloys consultative council authorised its creation in April 1945, and in July, Professor
Cockcroft,[67] who was leading the Canadian heavy water reactor
project, was offered the post of its director. The decision to set
up this establishment was announced to Parliament in October
1945.

Such an establishment required a supply of fissile material
and thus the question of production plants was resurrected. The
technical committee set up to consider this issue based its work
on the assumption that the aims of the establishment would be
'development to the point of the construction of the smallest
working bomb and of a prototype "boiler" large enough to solve
the problems of the design of large scale power units'.[68] In order
to provide fissile material for it at the least cost, it was decided to
build a graphite-moderated reactor with design activity on it
starting as soon as the bulk of the work on the Canadian heavy
water reactors had been completed.[69]

The change of government in July 1945, when Attlee replaced Churchill as Prime Minister, did little to affect the
continuity of policy-making on atomic energy.[70] In September
the *ad hoc* Cabinet committee (Gen 75) dealing with atomic

energy approved the recommendation to set up the research
establishment, with the choice of Harwell as the site following
soon after. In the same month Chadwick indicated that he now
favoured building a production plant in Britain, while in October the Chiefs of Staff urged that a start should be made on
production plans, despite the concurrent negotiations for international control of atomic energy. The issue was then examined
by the Advisory Committee on Atomic Energy chaired by Sir
John Anderson, who had been the Conservative minister with
executive responsibility for atomic energy in Churchill's wartime Cabinet.[71] Although the technical committee had recommended in October that both plutonium and U-235 production
should be attempted, it was soon recognised that resources
could not be made available for this, and a choice would have to
be made. The advice of the British scientists who were still in the
United States was to produce plutonium, as this was a more
efficient fissile material for bombs on a weight-for-weight basis
than U-235,[72] and the British had extensive knowledge of how
to make such a bomb. It was also calculated that it would be
much cheaper to produce fissile material via a reactor than by
building a U-235 diffusion plant, because British electricity
costs were very high compared with the United States and such a
plant would consume a huge amount of power. Set against this
was the fact that Britain possessed little information on the
Hanford plutonium production reactors, but had participated
extensively in the operation of the Oak Ridge electromagnetic
separation plant and had had considerable experience in attempting to design gaseous diffusion plants. There also seems to
have been a recognition that the design and construction of
plutonium-producing reactors could in itself form part of a
research strategy for developing civil power reactors, whereas a
U-235 plant would merely produce potential fuel for such a
reactor. On these grounds the decision was taken to concentrate
on the production of plutonium for use in the development of
weapons. This led to a number of related issues being raised,
such as the size and number of reactors, their type and where
they would be built.

    The initial assumption was that any reactor built in Britain
would be a copy of the water-cooled, graphite-moderated reactors at Hanford, with design data being obtained from the
United States. The scant information on these reactors available

to Britain at the time led to an understandable error, as it was falsely assumed that they were of 300 megawatts thermal capacity, and produced about 100 kilograms of plutonium a year. This was believed to be sufficient material to make 15 bombs of the Nagasaki type.[73] In fact they were 250 megawatt (thermal) reactors, and were probably capable of producing only about half this annual plutonium output.[74] The initial choice seemed to be between building one or two reactors of this size. The decision was submitted to the Gen 75 Cabinet committee in December, which decided that work on one reactor should start immediately, but that the Chiefs of Staff should be asked for advice on the number of bombs they believed would be required before any decision was taken to build a second. The chiefs argued that it was necessary to have a stockpile of hundreds, rather than tens of bombs and therefore that two reactors should be constructed.[75] The Minister of Supply who, in theory, was now responsible for atomic energy,[76] suggested that a decision on the second reactor should be postponed, and the issue was not raised again.

A definite decision had thus been taken by January 1946 to produce fissile material in the United Kingdom for use in a weapon development programme before either the prospects for interchange of information had been quashed by the President, or the United States 1946 Atomic Energy Act had been passed. The Americans were informed of the decision at a CPC meeting in February 1946, and were asked for certain technical information concerning the Hanford reactors. It was this request which led to the United States administration adopting the position that it was only committed to exchanging basic scientific information with Britain.

The design, construction and operation of the British nuclear reactor and its associated uranium metal and chemical separation plants was to be handled by a new industrial organisation with headquarters at Risley in Lancashire, whose formation was announced in January 1946. The organisation was headed by Christopher Hinton, who had been a chemical engineer with ICI before the war and the deputy director general of the government's munition-filling factories during it. The first tasks tackled by this organisation were to build a plant at Springfields, near Blackpool, to produce uranium metal from ore, and to manufacture reactor fuel by machining it into rods and enclosing it in aluminium cans or cartridges. The decision to build this plant was announced publicly in March 1946. Its completion was critical for the overall progress of the nuclear programme, as construction of the first experimental air-cooled reactor, BEPO, at Harwell, had started in June 1946 and it was programmed for completion in mid-1948. Although some pure uranium oxide had been acquired from the United States before the passing of the 1946 Atomic Energy Act and ICI was able to cast it into uranium metal for the initial fuel charge of BEPO, later fuel would have to be manufactured at Springfields from British-owned uranium ore.[77]

The second task of the Risley organisation was to design and build a single Hanford-type reactor. This decision was to prove very difficult to implement. Since water absorbs more neutrons than air, any loss of coolant in a water-cooled reactor is likely to increase its nuclear reactivity. If the water loss was associated with a failure of the neutron absorbing control and safety rods, the reactor might go out of control, the temperature rise to levels at which the fuel melted and radioactive particles would be spread over a wide area. This danger had led to the Hanford reactors being sited in a very remote region, and the same geographic restrictions were judged to be necessary for a similar British reactor, which would also require a large supply of very pure water to prevent corrosion in its core. These two technical requirements led Hinton to conclude by mid-1946 that there was only one feasible site in Britain for the reactor, close to Arisaig in North-western Scotland on the route from Fort William to Mallaig. This location had many disadvantages, and it was estimated that it would take at least four years and considerable expense to build the reactor there. The Risley design team had originally looked at the possibility of an air-cooled design, which would both considerably ease the siting problem and make possible a smaller unit, as air cooling would enable a chain reaction to be sustained by a smaller mass of natural uranium, but in early 1946 such a design appeared to be technically impossible. In addition, neither a heavy water nor a helium-cooled reactor could be contemplated because of the lack of indigenous supplies of these materials. By the end of 1946, however, conceptual breakthroughs in the design of the air cooling system and the construction of the fuel cans had led to the recognition that an effective air-cooled design was feasible. Yet the Controller of Atomic Energy in the Ministry of Supply, Lord Portal, remained opposed to any change in the existing plan to build a copy of a Hanford reactor because it appeared to provide a cast-iron guarantee that an output of plutonium could be produced.[78] This viewpoint was somewhat undermined in the course of a visit to the United States project in May 1946, when General Groves advised Portal against building a Hanford-type reactor on safety grounds.[79] Thus, at the end of 1946 it was still not clear what type of reactor would be built, or where it would be sited.

The decision to concentrate on plutonium production and temporarily abandon the idea of producing U-235 was also being questioned by June 1946, mainly because it was realised that by enriching the depleted uranium from used reactor fuel rods, much greater use could be made of the finite amount of uranium then available. Either plutonium or U-235 could be employed to produce enrichment, but to use the former would drastically reduce the material available for the bomb development programme.[80] In addition, it was believed that the most promising area for future civil power development was the fast reactor, and enriched uranium would be needed for this research programme. These deliberations led to a Gen 75 committee decision in October 1946 to start preliminary design work on a plant to produce uranium with 14 per cent U-235, though it was accepted that existing commitments made it unrealistic to expect building work to start much before 1949. This was reinforced by ministers setting a low expenditure ceiling on this design work, which meant that a further Cabinet committee decision would be necessary if it was to proceed beyond the preliminary planning stages.[81]

In parallel with these decisions on plants to produce fissile materials, activities were proceeding to procure and design operational bombs. The RAF stated its requirement for an atomic bomb in August 1946, and for a high-speed, high-altitude bomber later in the same year. The Ministry of Supply specification for this aircraft (B35/46) was issued in January 1947 and stated that it had to be capable of carrying a 'special bomb' 1500 miles to a target.[82]

One of the key members of the Los Alamos weapon development team, Dr Penney, had returned to Britain during 1946 to take up the post of Chief Superintendent of Armament Research in the Ministry of Supply, and informal discussions had been taking place on the arrangements which would enable him to supervise the work of atomic bomb design. He proposed that a group of 18 people should be formed within the Armaments Research Department for this purpose, and that he should be responsible to Lord Portal for its work. It was the need to formalise this arrangement which seems to have led to the realisation that although it had always been assumed that the work of the experimental establishment and the production division was aimed at exploding a British atomic bomb with yields similar to the Nagasaki weapon, no formal decision to develop and stockpile it had ever been taken by the Cabinet. This was not entirely suprising, as it was only with the formation of Penney's group that concerted design work on such a weapon started, though it would have proved difficult to justify the resources already allocated to the project had the objective been pure scientific research, rather than the development and experimental production of a military weapon. The *ad hoc* Cabinet committee (Gen 163) which made the formal bomb decision in January 1947 also appears to have been affected by the evolution of the nuclear relationship with the United States, for the Foreign Secretary justified the decision by asserting that 'We could not afford to acquiesce in an American monopoly on this new development.'[83] Thus, not for the first–and certainly not the last–time, British nuclear weapon activities were justified not on the basis of the need to deter an enemy, but on the diplomatic need to have bargaining power in relation to a friend and potential ally.

In the 18 months after the end of the Second World War, Britain moved from a position of having personnel operating as an integral part of the United States atomic weapon project through one of attempting to create in Britain a dependent adjunct of the United States project to a posture of independence and insulation from that project. This independence was seen by some participants to be a positive virtue, in that it made Britain embark upon new lines of development, rather than just slavishly copy what the Americans had already done. In addition, the lack of suitable sites for water-cooled reactors reinforced doubts about the safety aspects of such designs and pushed Britain into the innovative development of air-cooled, graphite-moderated ones. The lack of readily available supplies of heavy water had a similar effect in making designs based on the Chalk River NRX reactor impracticable. The most striking contrast in this period, however, was between the unwavering British desire to acquire the ability to build a nuclear weapon, and the chaotic and fragmented nature of decision-making on nuclear energy within the United States political system, which must bear part of the responsibility both for the termination of the wartime nuclear information interchanges and the passing of the restrictive 1946 Act. Yet in the immediate aftermath of the war the British had little to offer the United States in the nuclear field, precisely because the Manhattan Project from 1944 onwards had been an integrated and not a cooperative one, and the United States had had access to all the work done by British personnel. Partially offsetting this was a need for an agreement on the future distribution of raw materials, and certain British scientists and technicians were seen to have potential value to the United States because of the expertise they had displayed in the wartime project. Yet a realistic basis for continued cooperation in a technology which was perceived to have great commercial potential no longer existed once the wartime exigencies were over, however much the British might desire it. Indeed it could be argued that they had been fortunate that no attempt was made to implement the clause in the Quebec Agreement related to the President's powers over British civil nuclear development. Between the uncertainties over the nature of the post-war international system, the internal conflicts within Congress, the disagreement between Congress and the Executive, and the legalism inherent in the American governmental system, the British had very little chance of making progress towards a new technical relationship with the United States. Little choice existed by mid-1946 but to plan to construct British production facilities for fissile materials on the basis of the knowledge which had been acquired in the course of the wartime collaboration. There might yet arrive a time when close technical cooperation with the United States could be reestablished on the basis of a mutually beneficial exchange of information, rather than a position which some American leaders sought to characterise as one of unilateral transfer of both militarily and commercially valuable data. Even then the central objective of British policy would still remain the development of a national nuclear weapon design and the construction of a small stockpile of operational bombs.

3 The American Nuclear Weapon Programme: Scarcity to Abundance

Second Generation Atomic Weapons

It was not until late in 1947 that a coherent policy started to emerge in the United States to guide its peacetime development and procurement of nuclear weapons. A number of factors accounted for this delay. First, the Manhattan Project had been rigidly aimed at producing 'laboratory weapons'[1] for use in the war. Peace led to emphasis being placed on new requirements for nuclear weapons, such as safety, ease of storage and long-term reliability. It also resulted in the break up of the wartime development and production organisation, with no immediate attempt being made to recreate it on a more permanent basis.[2] Second, the internal dispute between Congress, the armed forces and the administration over the structure and control of the government development and production organisation for atomic weapons meant that the AEC did not come into existence until 1 January 1947. During 1946 the project marked time, with some wartime production activities continuing but with little positive direction. This was coupled with a certain ambivalence at the highest levels towards active reinvigoration of the project, given the emphasis in external policy upon international control and the hopes of transforming the national project into an international one. President Truman displayed little interest in its status until April 1947, when he was first informed of the number of weapons in the existing stockpile (no more than 13, and none of them fully assembled): he expressed shock that it was only a fraction of what he, and the general public, imagined.[3]

A third element was that no clear technical targets existed for the peacetime programme, beyond the need for weapons that

48

could be more easily stored in a semi-assembled state. This resulted from the absence of permanent weapon development teams with an incentive for pressing ahead with new innovations; the focusing of the Bikini tests in 1946 upon investigations of the effects generated by the existing types of weapon rather than the development of new ones; and genuine technical uncertainty about what the next step in weapon development should be, and what types of device were possible. Both Britain and the USSR could direct their contemporary atomic programmes towards emulating the American achievement in creating a plutonium 'laboratory' weapon, secure in the knowledge that this was a technically feasible objective,[4] but the United States stood still until late 1947 because there was no clear view of where to go next.

Two organisations provided the impetus for the post-1947 United States nuclear weapon programme. One was the newly created AEC, which was attempting to organise fissile material and weapon production on a more directed basis. The second was the Joint Chiefs of Staff (JCS), who were developing plans for the operational use of nuclear weapons against the USSR and basing weapon stockpile targets upon them. Increases in the annual production rate of nuclear weapons could be attained either by expanding fissile material output or by making more effective use of it in the production of bombs. The main limitation upon the use of the existing stocks of fissile materials prior to late 1948 was that no work had been undertaken on the use of implosion techniques with U-235. As a result, stocks of this material were increasing, yet none of it was being incorporated into weapons.[5] Major operational difficulties existed with the plutonium plants, and the output from the three Hanford reactors had been reduced from their annual wartime production rate of approximately 165 kilograms to about 80 kilograms. This provided sufficient material for a maximum of about 13 bombs per year.[6] The oldest reactor had been shut down early in 1946 and the other two were being operated at reduced power and thus output, both to conserve their lives and to guarantee a continued supply of the polonium 210 initiator material. Moreover, the existing chemical separation plant did not allow recycling of uranium, and development of the replacement redox process, which permitted this, was urgent in the light of the United States dwindling uranium stocks.[7] Production of

U-235 had stabilised by early 1947 at a level significantly higher than the wartime one. Two new gaseous diffusion plants had been commissioned at Oak Ridge in March 1946 and from December they had been operated as an integrated high enrichment plant.[8] Uranium gun weapons were thus the only ones for which fissile material was readily available[9] but in early 1947 no nuclear components existed for them.[10]

The AEC gave highest priority to increasing plutonium output, and set itself a tentative target of five new production reactors at Hanford by 1950, two of these to be totally self-contained units, and three to be built in such a way as to replace the existing ones and use their ancillary equipment. This implied an annual weapon-grade plutonium output figure of 200 – 300 kilograms. Construction of both a new reactor and a replacement unit was authorised in October 1947, but in the meantime, it had become apparent that most of the difficulties with the existing ones could be resolved by repair and renovation work. This led to the third of the original reactors being recommissioned in mid-1948, and all three regaining their ability to operate at their wartime power outputs. In April 1947 it was also decided to embark upon the construction of the new redox reprocessing plant at Hanford. The management and construction on both the Oak Ridge and Hanford sites were in the hands of private chemical companies, rather than being the direct responsibility of the AEC.[11]

The only nuclear weapon components that had been manufactured since the end of 1945 were those for the Mark III Nagasaki-type 'laboratory weapons' which took two days to be assembled by a specialist team. It was not until December 1947 that the first such post-war team was mobilised and trained and the United States once more possessed a limited operational nuclear weapon capability.[12] Early in 1947 the AEC also started work on a positive bomb design programme with two major objectives. One was the creation of a lighter, smaller implosion warhead[13] that would both eliminate the need for specially modified aircraft and permit the nuclear core to be inserted into it by remote means immediately before operational use: the second the creation of core configurations incorporating both plutonium and uranium-235 to enable larger explosive yields to be obtained than was possible with plutonium warheads and make more efficient use of fissionable material. This would also allow the Oak Ridge output, known as Oralloy, to be in-corporated into weapons.[14] A bomb which allowed for remote insertion of the fissile core could be more easily stored, rapidly made ready for use, and then disassembled if it was not required, while the non-nuclear components would only be subject to harmful radiation or contamination during the limited number of occasions when the nuclear core was inserted.

These design objectives were met by the new Mark IV implo-sion assembly, which allowed for remote insertion, made possi-ble a more compact and lighter warhead design, used U-235 in the fissile core, and facilitated the production of non-nuclear components on a standardised 'assembly line' basis. Three experimental implosion cores were tested in the Sandstone series in the spring of 1948, and a design based upon them was integrated with the new assembly to create the Mark IV implo-sion bomb. It offered a 63 per cent increase in stockpile numbers compared to Mark III production and a 75 per cent increase in the yield of the total stockpile. By October 1948 the AEC was well advanced with plans to end Mark III production and switch output to the Mark IV in order to make fuller use of the fissile material stocks then in existence.[15] In addition, a large plutonium fabrication plant was under construction at Hanford, while final assembly of bombs on a production line basis started at Sandia Base in June 1949.[16] Thus both the ability to use U-235 in these weapons and their slightly increased explosive efficiency offered the United States the opportunity rapidly to expand its stockpile of weapons from mid-1949 onwards.

While the AEC was engaged in increasing United States nuclear bomb production, the JCS had been attempting to formulate military requirements for a stockpile of these weapons. The impact of the deteriorating world political situa-tion in 1946 had induced the JCS and the individual services to start planning in earnest for the next war. They examined the place of nuclear warfare in their strategic thinking, and the requirements for specific types and numbers of nuclear weapons and delivery systems. In February 1947 they informed the Secretaries for War and the Navy that their studies had led them to conclude that the existing supply of nuclear weapons was inadequate to meet national security needs, and they were attempting to draw up a set of target figures for the amount of fissile material and the numbers of weapons they believed had to be produced by the AEC over the next few years.[17] This statement of the military's long-term requirements for fissile material production was eventually completed in October 1947,[18] and it resulted in the Joint Chiefs informing the chairman of the AEC that they wished to have a stockpile of 400 20-kiloton yield atomic bombs by January 1953.[19]

In June 1947 there were only 13 nuclear weapon components in the United States stockpile together with 29 non-nuclear assemblies.[20] By July 1948 these figures had risen to 50 and 55 respectively, but the AEC had to inform the JCS that their 1948 target for bomb production could not be achieved. By October, however, the analysis of the Sandstone tests and the decision to move rapidly to production of the Mark IV bomb utilising U-235 led the AEC to inform the JCS that not only would this target be met but that a stockpile of 400 weapons would be available in January 1951, two years ahead of schedule.[21]

The military planners' ideas about a war with the USSR had meanwhile been evolving through a series of war plans with code-names such as Half Moon and Trojan. These exercises generated considerable disagreement over whether a strategic weapon offensive against the USSR would force that country to surrender, and would constitute a credible threat capable of deterring a Soviet attack upon Western Europe. This became politicised into a conflict between the US Air Force and the Navy, with the latter arguing that there was no evidence that nuclear attacks upon the major Soviet cities would lead to a termination of hostilities. Although this claim was publicly rejected by the air force, some reshaping of the war plans took place to make petroleum production installations priority targets, and planning was based on the assumption that an initial nuclear exchange would be followed by a long period of conventional warfare in Europe and elsewhere, interspersed with occasional use of nuclear weapons. This led the army to argue that high priority should be given to the direct use of nuclear weapons against the Soviet armed forces, including invasion fleets heading for the United Kingdom or other parts of Western Europe. The air force opposed this contention, as they believed that by assigning all fissile material and bomb production to the Strategic Air Command (SAC), the United States would have a decisive potential to destroy the USSR and that this would both deter any attack upon Western Europe and force a Soviet surrender if such an attack were to occur.[22]

This dispute was complicated by intelligence reports which indicated that the USSR would have the potential for threatening the United States with nuclear counterattack by 1955.[23] Some of the planners believed that once this capability existed, the United States nuclear resources would be more effectively deployed in a tactical role in Europe than in the alternative strategy of developing extensive air defence capabilities for the United States and giving priority in a nuclear war to counterforce strikes upon Russian bomber bases. In both cases, the United Kingdom was seen as an essential base, and considerable military concern was expressed that the British government might move towards a position of political neutrality.[24] These disagreements helped to precipitate a conflict over the way atomic bomb requirements were formulated, with the air force complaining that the Joint Chiefs were allowing the stockpile targets to be determined by anticipated fissile material output, rather than stating their optimum requirements and insisting that it was the AEC's responsibility to decide how and if it could meet them.[25] In parallel, the battle was joined over whether part of the limited United States supply of fissile material should be diverted from the Strategic Air Command to tactical forces in Europe.[26]

The AEC found it difficult to respond to these pressures as uranium was in short supply and the Truman administration had imposed severe fiscal limitations upon it in an attempt to balance the budget. The raw material problem was resolved in the short term by gaining British agreement to the use of uranium stocks in the United Kingdom, which were jointly owned by the two countries,[27] and it was hoped that an extensive programme of uranium prospecting and exploitation in the United States and Canada would eliminate any medium- and long-term supply difficulties.[28] Attempts were also made to expand fissile material production by building additions to the U-235 gaseous diffusion plant at Oak Ridge, with construction approved in March 1949 and commissioning scheduled for mid-1951.[29] The fourth reactor was completed at Hanford in 1949, and work was well advanced on completing the replacement for the first of the wartime ones. Thus by the end of 1949, Hanford was capable of an annual output of about 220 kilograms of plutonium,[30] while 300 bombs had been stockpiled.[31]

The Sandstone tests in the spring of 1948 stimulated production of the Mark IV bomb and demonstrated that weapons other than the standard 20-kiloton device were possible. The first of these was the Mark VI, a weapon of 20–100 kilotons yield intended for stockpiling in small numbers for use against the larger Soviet cities.[32] The second was a smaller, lighter assembly known as the Mark V, which, it was anticipated, would lead to weapons of 5–15 kilotons yield, suitable for tactical roles in ground, air or maritime warfare. Tests to examine this design concept, the Greenhouse series, were scheduled for Eniwetok Atoll in 1951.[33] A third was an earth penetrator weapon for use against hard military targets and dams which was based on a U-235 gun-type device.[34]

The existence of this weapon development programme plus the pressures to acquire more bombs for both strategic and tactical purposes, led the Joint Chiefs to demand an expansion of fissile material production from the AEC in May 1949. This received support from the statutory congressional Joint Committee on Atomic Energy (JCAE), which had itself started to press the AEC for an expansion of fissile material output early in 1949.[35] The commissioners were squeezed between these enlarged military requirements and the administration's desire to limit governmental expenditure, and, to try to resolve these conflicting demands, the President convened a special committee to review them and to make recommendations for future action.[36] This was still in the process of completing its report on the fissile material programme when the first Soviet nuclear explosion was detected in September 1949. The AEC responded with plans for a limited expansion of fissile material production. These included the conversion of the substitute reactor being built at Hanford to independent operation,[37] a further extension to the Oak Ridge plant, and the acceleration of work on the redox plutonium and uranium separation plant.[38] The Soviet test also caused the military planning staffs to alter their assessments of the likely rate of increase in the Soviet nuclear stockpile.[39]

The United States Decision to Develop a Hydrogen Bomb

Further expansion of the AEC's fissile material production programme now became inextricably linked with the question of whether the United States was to attempt to develop a thermonuclear bomb. The resulting debate focused on whether such a weapon was technically feasible, politically desirable and had any conceivable military functions, or whether it would be preferable to concentrate the AEC's resources on the development of smaller-yield nuclear weapons with war-fighting possibilities. The AEC's General Advisory Committee (GAC),[40] in its report of 30 October 1949, recommended against an immediate development and production programme for thermonuclear weapons, at least until there had been an opportunity to explore the possibility of a 'no-development' agreement with the USSR, and proposed as an alternative the acceleration of work on fission weapons.[41] Technically this recommendation was fully compatible with the anticipated development programme for a hydrogen weapon, as a smaller-yield device possessing high nuclear efficiency, the 'primary' or trigger, was known to be necessary to initiate a fusion reaction.[42] It also reflected a professional judgement that it was premature to commit the country to the production of hydrogen weapons before any design existed, and in the absence of convincing evidence that they could be made to work. Of even greater importance, however, was the belief that analysis of the airborne debris from the testing of such a weapon would give the USSR and any other interested states sufficient information to enable them rapidly to build it for themselves, thus making it likely that any United States lead in this new technology would be short lived.[43] These technical arguments, together with moral opposition to such weapons of mass destruction, were to be of no avail against the perceived political need for a visible commitment to the maintenance of military superiority over the Soviet Union following the Berlin blockade, the collapse of the Nationalist government in China, and the Soviet nuclear explosion. The possession of 'bigger and better' weapons was believed to be imperative if Soviet aggressive actions were to be deterred from the mid-1950s onwards, when it was estimated that their stockpile of nuclear weapons would run into three figures.[44]

The political arguments for a public commitment to a hydrogen bomb programme were vigorously advocated by a coalition of politicians, military officers and nuclear scientists, including Senator McMahon, Secretary of Defense Johnson, the scientists Teller, Lawrence and Alvarez, and the members of the AEC's Military Liaison Committee, which largely directed JCS policy on the issue as they alone had access to all the relevant technical information.[45] The special committee that Truman had set up to advise him on the request for expanded fissile material production was given the additional task of making recommendations on a thermonuclear weapon programme and it concluded that it should be pursued. Truman accepted this advice and on 31 January 1950[46] he announced that the United States was to start development of a thermonuclear weapon. At no point in this decision-making process was serious consideration given to the functions of weapons with potentially unlimited yields, though existing JCS studies had concluded that a military need existed for only a very small number of 100-kiloton bombs: it was the political and psychological impact of their existence which dominated the debate. The assumption was that the Soviet Union would inevitably advance in this direction, and the United States had to get there first.

Urgency was injected into the thermonuclear weapon programme in February 1950, when Klaus Fuchs was arrested in the United Kingdom on charges of passing nuclear weapon information to the USSR. This event, rather than the Soviet explosion in 1949, led the intelligence services significantly to change their evaluations of the existing state of the Soviet Union's nuclear weapon programme. It was assumed that Fuchs had given the Soviet Union all the knowledge about nuclear weapons possessed by the United Kingdom and this led to estimates of the size of the Soviet stockpile being moved forward by one year, and serious attention being paid to the possibility that the USSR's thermonuclear development programme had overtaken that of the United States, especially as undetected nuclear tests could not be discounted, and Fuchs himself had worked on theoretical calculations linked to possible designs for a hydrogen bomb. These assessments were reinforced by intelligence reports that both heavy water reactors and uranium enrichment plants were under construction in the USSR.[47] The AEC was galvanised into action by the fear that the USSR might be building hydrogen bomb production plants and plans were therefore made both for a development programme and to manufacture materials in quantity for production thermonuclear weapons.

The immediate problem facing the AEC was how to provide both plutonium for its weapon production programme and a supply of tritium for future experimental work on thermonuclear devices. Tritium is produced by exposing the light metal lithium to neutron bombardment, and the most practical way of doing this in 1950 was to make use of the Hanford reactors. Tritium production would absorb neutrons that would otherwise produce plutonium and this would lead to a significant decrease in the AEC's plutonium output.[48] Hanford could produce test quantities of the material but reactors with a greater supply of neutrons would be required if the thermonuclear bomb was to be perfected and placed into large-scale production.[49] At the end of May the AEC recommended to the President that the chemical firm Du Pont should build and manage two very large, efficient reactors, cooled and moderated by heavy water, each capable of producing 800 kilograms of plutonium and one and a half kilograms of tritium per year.[50] Truman approved this new programme early in June, and the Savannah River site in South Carolina was selected for the reactors.[51] It was not expected that they would be operational until 1956, and in the meantime, tritium was to be manufactured by fuelling the Hanford reactors with enriched uranium in order to obtain the required neutron intensities.[52] President Truman remained reluctant to commit substantial funds to achieve an expansion of fissile material production prior to 1956, despite the increased emphasis being placed in National Security Council and JCS studies on the need for additional nuclear weapons to supplement United States' conventional war-fighting capabilities in Western Europe. These studies culminated in the completion of NSC 68 in April 1950.[53] The air force continued to insist on priority being given to bomb production for the strategic role, and the other two services emphasised the need for nuclear weapons as an integral component of their war-fighting capabilities. It was accepted without question that the United States would use nuclear bombs, if militarily appropriate, at the outset of any act of Soviet aggression.

The interservice dispute over the allocation of fissile materials soon became irrelevant, however, as a result of the radical change in the political and fiscal climate in Washington which followed the outbreak of the Korean War on 25 June 1950. Financial resources were made available for a massive expansion of United States military capabilities, and the AEC decided it should plan to double the scheduled capacity of its fissile material production plants by 1956 in order to implement the JCS judgement that the tactical uses of nuclear weapons placed no limit on the military need for such material.[54] It proposed to accomplish this by building three additional heavy water reactors at Savannah River, a new gaseous diffusion plant at Paducah, Kentucky,[55] and a sixth reactor at Hanford.[56] Meanwhile, construction of the new redox plant at Hanford was scheduled for completion in August 1951.[57] This expansion would increase annual plutonium and tritium equivalent production from about 220 kilograms in 1950 to over 4300 kilograms after 1956.[58]

This massive expansion plan was still not sufficient to satisfy the AEC's critics on the JCAE. Senator McMahon requested that the commission should produce a detailed cost study on the feasibility of doubling and trebling planned levels of fissile material output, and this was completed in September 1951.[59] After prolonged negotiations between the AEC, JCAE, the Defense Department and the President, the latter signed a directive authorising a further expansion of production capacity on 25 February 1952.[60] This involved the building of two very large water-cooled graphite-moderated reactors at Hanford, additions to the gaseous diffusion plants at Oak Ridge and Paducah, and a third, completely new gaseous diffusion plant at Portsmouth, Ohio.[61] None of these additional plants would be operational before 1956, and this expansion programme continued to be criticised as inadequate by certain members of the JCAE.[62] In a nutshell, these decisions meant that over a two-year period, plans were drawn up and implemented to increase the United States' annual military plutonium production capacity from about 220 to 5000 kilograms: a 23 fold increase.[63]

When the decision to start development and production of a thermonuclear weapon was taken none of the United States weapon designers had a clear idea of how to obtain the necessary pressures and temperatures to trigger a thermonuclear reaction. Design work on thermonuclear weapons was difficult, because there was no obvious means of carrying out essential experimental work, while theoretical calculations were crucially dependent on the availability of improved computational facilities. A significant conceptual breakthrough was eventually made by Teller, Ulam and de Hoffman in March and April 1951, and this transformed the prospects of the United States producing a thermonuclear bomb. The central design problem had been finding a means of applying tremendous pressure to the thermonuclear fuel before thermal energy from the primary fission device reached it. Details of the nature of the break-through were published in the United States in 1979.[64] The Teller, Ulam and de Hoffman ideas were implemented in the design of a single experimental device, exploded at Eniwetok Atoll in November 1952. This device, code-named Mike, had a yield of 10.4 megatons, but used liquid deuterium as a fuel, needed extensive refrigeration facilities and was in no sense an operational weapon. It demonstrated that a thermonuclear explosion was possible, however, and as a result efforts were directed towards perfecting a design which was suitable for carriage by aircraft.[65]

The achievement of a thermonuclear explosion was helped by the work on fission weapons which started at Los Alamos in 1948. Explosive tests intended to assist in the development programme for the lightweight Mark V low-yield warhead took place in Nevada from January 1951 onwards.[66] Work on the Mark VI high-yield fission bomb also proceeded rapidly, and involved the design and development of a segmented fissile core. A U-235 test device based on this concept and yielding 500 kilotons was exploded at Eniwetok in November 1952.[67] A further design concept which used a fission device with a seg-mented core to ignite a small amount of tritium contained within it, which in turn 'boosted' the fission yield, was tested at Eniwetok on 24 May 1951, and it led to a family of nuclear bombs and warheads based on this principle being tested during the next three years.[68] This concept later formed the basis for the fission primaries in thermonuclear weapons.[69]

The extensive programme of experimental work on both fission and fusion weapons was reflected in a parallel expansion of work on production models, budgetary allocations having been requested from Congress in August 1951 for the develop-ment of approximately 20 new atomic bombs, shells and missile warheads.[70] The increase in the design load at Los Alamos as a result of this expansion was partially responsible for the creation of the separate Lawrence Livermore thermonuclear laboratory in California during the summer of 1952.[71]

The AEC's research and development programme from 1947 to 1953 had been primarily concerned with nuclear explosives, but some attention and resources were allocated to the development of military power reactors. These were intended for use as power plants for intercontinental bombers, as power sources for naval vessels and submarines, and to provide an electricity supply for remote radar stations. The air force's bomber project made very slow progress and after great expense had been incurred it was eventually abandoned in the early 1960s. The naval group under Captain H. G. Rickover had started an extensive study of the possibilities of a ship propulsion reactor in April 1946, and in December had encouraged the General Electric Company to produce proposals for a sodium-cooled, enriched uranium power plant for both surface vessel and submarine use.[72] This was not pursued, in part because the AEC wished to retain control over all reactor development and promote a broad-based programme of research into reactor types, materials and components. The detonation of the Soviet test device in August 1949 gave fresh impetus to this work. Westinghouse and a team from the Argonne laboratory near Chicago were given a contract to build a land-based model of a light water submarine reactor, while the General Electric research team at Schenectady, in New York State, was to work on a sodium-cooled reactor for both land and naval application. To assist this programme a large area of land near Arco in Idaho was acquired for the construction of experimental reactors and the Argonne/Westinghouse prototype was commissioned here in March 1953.[73]

The United States nuclear programme had been transformed out of all recognition by 1952, following the hiatus of the immediate post-war period. The combined effects of developing bombs with greater nuclear efficiency, increasing the output of fissile materials and adopting high-volume assembly techniques meant that there existed a stockpile of 400 nuclear weapons by the end of 1950 and it appears probable that in January 1953 the inventory exceeded 600.[74] This expansion had been stimulated by detailed military contingency planning for an attack upon the USSR and by the impact of the Fuchs spy case, and had been made possible by the changed economic climate following the outbreak of the Korean War.

Nuclear reactor development had been sluggish and disorganised, though Rickover's dynamic leadership, the stimuli of the Soviet explosion and the Korean War led to work being pushed ahead rapidly on submarine reactors. No attempt had been made to add turbines to production reactors to enable them to generate their own electricity, as the inexpensive power available from the hydroelectric stations of the TVA and other American utilities meant that such projects lacked financial appeal. At the end of 1952, the prospect was that the military planners and the JCAE would continue to press for an almost indefinite expansion in the number of United States nuclear weapons. Demand for fissile materials to manufacture those weapons and fuel military reactors appeared to have no limits, with annual output expanding throughout the 1950s as the plants ordered in the 1950–2 period became fully operational.

4 Gestation: The Programme to Explode a British Atomic Device, 1947–52

British Military Requirements and Civil Possibilities

The formal political decision of the Gen 163 Cabinet committee in January 1947, that design work should start on a British nuclear bomb, left most of the technical issues involved in its construction to be resolved by those managing the project. Their immediate aim was to build and test a fission device which would demonstrate both mastery of the nuclear physics principles applicable to atomic explosions, and an ability successfully to design, develop and manufacture the non-nuclear components necessary to trigger it off. This involved ordnance experiments which 'could be begun and completed without the need to use fissile material at any stage'.[1] In parallel, work was to be initiated on a production design for the bomb's nuclear explosive warhead, which would offer the same advantages of allowing the fissile core to be stored separately from the fully assembled non-nuclear components that had been incorporated into the United States Mark IV weapon. This activity had to be integrated with the design, testing and production of the fuses, ballistic case and other components of the complete nuclear weapon system. The bomb had many similarities to a ballistic missile, as it was intended to be dropped from several miles above the earth, though it had no direct means of propulsion.[2]

The most important pacing item in both the testing work and the programme to produce operational weapons was the availability of fissile material. It was inevitable that stocks of production weapons would only accumulate slowly, given the quantities of fissile material needed for their manufacture and the contemporary shortage of uranium, and that in the early years a choice had to be made between allocating material to the testing programme and to increasing the stockpile. The expectation that stockpile numbers would only grow slowly during the 1950s had been one of the main reasons behind Blackett's attempt in November 1945 to persuade the government not to embark on a bomb programme.[3] The key issue was whether 'Britain was going to spend a disproportionate effort in building up a stock of bombs too small to be of military value'.[4] Such considerations were tacitly ignored by those members of the Cabinet committee who made the political decision to press ahead with the programme, and the result was that for the first nine years of its existence it was unrelated 'to strategic and tactical needs and probabilities'.[5] A political goal had been set, and was to be pursued within the confines of judgements on the maximum amount of material and manpower resources that Britain could afford to divert to the project, given other demands upon national capabilities.

These political limitations resulted in the size of the facilities for the production of fissile material being based upon the minimalist technical criteria of the construction of a single reactor of Hanford size, which was assumed to generate 300 megawatts of thermal power. Calculations on the nature and plutonium production capabilities of this plant were based on limited information, for the first reactor to which the British had full access, the Canadian NRX, had only just started operations, and was of a different type to the Hanford ones. It was therefore not surprising that the calculations were eventually found in 1950 to be grossly in error.[6] Yet they had led to the setting of an annual production target of 100 kilograms of plutonium from 1951 onwards, which then persisted, despite the abandonment of the original planning assumptions. Final agreement on the type of production reactor to be built had still not been reached by early 1947, but design work was focusing upon a gas-cooled reactor of roughly half the physical size and anticipated plutonium output of the Hanford type of plant. Building a number of reactors to this new design had obvious risk-spreading attractions, for fissile material output would cease to be dependent primarily on the efficient operation of a single unit.

A decision to proceed with construction of two of these reactors at a site near Sellafield in Cumbria, subsequently known as Windscale,[7] was taken in May 1947, after considerable debate over the merits of two alternative gas-cooled designs.

One involved enclosing the reactor in a pressure vessel, circulating a coolant gas around it in a closed system, and using the heat generated to drive an electricity-producing turbine. This scheme had considerable attractions, for it would provide electricity to power the fans, pumps and other ancillary equipment of the reactor and also serve as a prototype for a first-generation nuclear power station. A simpler alternative was to blow air through the reactor core and exhaust it through a tall chimney. These possibilities, allied to the fact that two reactors were now envisaged, led Hinton to suggest that the first reactor should be built as a simple plutonium production unit to provide a minimum supply of fissile material for military purposes, and the second as a dual purpose plutonium/power reactor. Although this second reactor would take longer to design and construct, and embodied greater risks of failure, he believed that it would be a more efficient unit with considerable development possibilities. Lord Portal refused to go along with these proposals as they meant accepting an increased risk that the plutonium production targets would not be met. He believed, not unreasonably, that they had already been hazarded by the decision to substitute an untried air-cooled design for the proven Hanford-type reactor. Thus the result of this first interaction between military requirements and commercial possibilities was that the development and construction of a dual-purpose plutonium/power reactor was delayed for several years.[8]

Although little empirical information was available on reactor characteristics and operation, detailed design work proceeded rapidly once the decision to switch to a simple air-cooled reactor had been taken. The uncertainties were believed to be similar to those which had been encountered with the Hanford reactors, namely, the tendency of graphite to expand under conditions of radiation and heat, and the possibility that this would prevent fuel elements being pushed through the reactor. Some information on this phenomenon, known as Wigner expansion, was obtained from a group of visiting United States scientists in the summer of 1948, and formed the basis for the design of the reactor's graphite structure. In the autumn of 1948 a further discussion took place on plant location hazards with a second American delegation, in which the possibility of a reactor fire resulting from the storage of Wigner energy in graphite was raised. This was then considered by the British to be a minor risk as it was believed that adequate operating procedures could be devised to allow this energy to be released safely from time to time. However, it was inadequacies in the control and monitoring system intended to deal with this phenomenon which subsequently led to the Windscale fire in 1957 and the permanent closure of the two reactors.[9] A subsidiary design problem concerned the need for filters in the reactor chimneys to prevent radioactive particles from burst fuel cans escaping into the atmosphere. Information obtained by Cockcroft on a visit to Oak Ridge at the end of 1948 suggested that they were necessary, but by the time this data had been fully analysed, the chimneys were partially built and the filters had to be placed on top. Hence the construction of those menacing structures that continue to dominate the Sellafield skyline.[10]

The Springfields uranium fuel factory in Lancashire produced the first charge for the Windscale reactors by the early summer of 1950; the first reactor became operational in April 1951 and the second followed in October of that year.[11] In mid-1950 it was discovered that the early calculations on the reactivity of the Windscale reactors were incorrect, and, as had been the case with the early Hanford reactors, much more uranium fuel would be needed to achieve criticality than had been anticipated.[12] It was possible to increase the reactivity and thermal power of the reactors by altering the fuel cans, but the first one had to be operated initially at 76 Mw(th) and the second at 104 Mw(th), compared with the design rating of 115 Mw(th).[13] Outputs of about 120 Mw(th) were obtained after 1953 when very slightly enriched uranium was used to fuel the reactors, but plutonium production remained significantly below the 1946 target rate of 100 kilograms per year.[14] Prior to 1954 the combined plutonium output from the reactors was probably about 45 kilograms per year, rising after 1954 to about 60 kilograms.[15] A reduction in the amount of plutonium needed for each of the initial test devices and for early production weapons from about 6.7 kilograms to 5.67 kilograms served to offset this shortfall, and give a potential to produce about ten bombs or test devices per year from 1954 onwards.[16]

Work on the plutonium separation plant at Windscale proceeded in phase with the construction of the production reactors. It involved considerable innovation, as the plant was intended to recover both plutonium and uranium from the reactor fuel rods, in contrast to the existing Hanford plant which only recovered the plutonium and stored the uranium along with the other waste products.[17] This uranium could be recycled into the reactors after reenriching it to natural levels in the planned Capenhurst uranium enrichment plant, the amount of enrichment needed being very small. This made the British production cycle more efficient in its use of source material than the original American one. Research into the design of the plutonium separation plant, which included a French contribution, had started in Canada during the war, and by September 1947 the initial work was complete. A pilot plant was built at Chalk River and fed with irradiated material from the NRX pile to prove the process, achieving reassuring results. Early in 1948 three of the chemists involved in the work visited the United States and held discussions with American colleagues who were attempting to design a similar plant for Hanford. This visit provided insufficient data to increase British confidence in the effectiveness of their own design but a decision was taken to proceed to construction despite the lack of confirmatory information. However, the original analytical work proved very accurate, and the plant functioned successfully when fissile material was fed into it in February 1952. It went into operation before the American redox one and offered several advantages over it, resulting in British expertise in fuel-processing rapidly equalling that of United States.[18]

The production target for the United Kingdom's fissile material programme had been dominated by economic and technical factors but, like their transatlantic counterparts, the British military services in 1946 started to evolve plans for the post-war world. They were working within a political directive for all military development plans that assumed there would be no major war before 1957, and both the bomber and nuclear bomb development programmes were geared to this date. Although the assumption that the USSR was the most likely future enemy was resisted by leading members of the Cabinet until early 1948,[19] this did not prevent preliminary military planning work commencing on requirements for new weapons, including both atomic and biological ones. This work envisaged such weapons being used primarily against population centres, and a list was prepared of the 59 Soviet cities selected for attack, each of which was within 1500 miles of bases in Britain, Cyprus and Pakistan.[20] In 1948, freed from the political constraints of not assuming that the USSR was the prime enemy, an interservices subcommittee deliberated in detail on British stockpile goals. It concluded that in 1957 600 atomic bombs would be required effectively to deter the USSR; 400 of them to be procured by the United States and 200 by the United Kingdom. It was assumed that there was no need to build up a British capability for independently deterring the USSR.[21] These deliberations show that some liaison may already have taken place with the United States over planning figures for nuclear weapons stockpiles, as in December 1947 the US Joint Chiefs had decided to adopt a production goal of 400 Mark III bombs by 1 January 1953.[22] However, the Americans do not themselves appear to have given any thought to the contribution that a future British nuclear force might make to an allied stockpile until late 1949.[23] Thus the British production goal appears to have been determined by a desire to possess a politically significant capability compared to that of the United States, by the expected size of the British bomber force in 1957 and by the need to destroy specific targets in the USSR.

Unfortunately, the requirement for 200 bombs by 1957 could not be met with the production facilities under construction in early 1948. Several methods for increasing the output of fissile material to meet this target were available: one was to build an additional reactor at Windscale feeding into the existing chemical separation facilities; a second was to construct a high enrichment gaseous diffusion plant for operation from 1955 onwards, and use its U-235 to make mixed bombs of the United States Mark IV type. Another alternative was to do both, but even this would only enable the target figure to be attained by 1958.[24] These calculations were made before information became available on the shortfalls in plutonium output from Windscale, and were based on the assumption that 50 kilograms per year would be available from a single reactor. They suggested that bomb production would proceed at the rates shown in Table 4.1.[25]

The financial cost of these options varied considerably; the cost of an additional reactor was about 27 per cent of a high enrichment plant producing sufficient material to construct an additional 20–21 bombs per year. At the same time potential shortages of uranium made it imperative to build a low enrich-

TABLE 4.1　*Estimated projections of British Atomic bomb production made in 1948*

End of year	1952	1953	1954	1955	1956	1957	1958	1959	1960	1961
Existing programme (2 reactors) 15 bombs/year	15	30	45	60	75	90	105	120	135	150
3 reactors 23 bombs/year	15	38	61	84	107	130	153	176	199	222
2 reactors plus high enrichment plant 36 bombs/yr	15	30	45	66	102	138	174	210	246	282
3 reactors plus high enrichment plant 43 bombs/yr	15	38	61	90	133	176	219	262	305	348

ment plant if fuel was to be guaranteed for a three-reactor programme. No immediate action was taken to implement any of these alternatives, but in February 1949, with the Berlin blockade still in force, the Cabinet finally agreed to expand the fissile material production programme. One additional reactor was to be constructed at Windscale; development and construction was to start on a low enrichment plant at Capenhurst in Cheshire; and a research and development programme was to be initiated on a high separation plant. In December of that year work was discontinued on the third reactor, despite the fact that its foundations had already been laid, primarily because negotiations with the United States had reached a stage where it was hoped that U-235 and possibly production weapons would soon be available from that source. In addition, there was believed to be insufficient uranium to meet both British and American needs.[26] Work on the low enrichment plant continued, as this was intended to maximise the use that could be made of the limited national stock of uranium by reenriching it after it had become slightly depleted in U-235 as a consequence of passing through the production reactors. The plant was built to give twofold enrichment, and although it became fully operational in April 1953, four years after construction had been authorised, its output was initially restricted by difficulties over the supply of its feed gas, uranium hexafluoride.[27]

Design and development work on the high enrichment plant, which was to be capable of producing bomb-making material, was substantially complete by the summer of 1951, and so a

decision was taken to start its construction. The power requirements of the plant necessitated the construction of a new,
oil-fired power station at Ince, near Capenhurst, with an output
of over 200 Mw(e). The original idea was to build a second low
enrichment plant and use both low enrichment facilities to feed
the high enrichment one. Early in 1952 a decision was taken to
separate the low and high enrichment plants and build the latter
as a new self-contained unit with both low and high enrichment
stages, completion being scheduled for 1956.[28]

Some atomic engineers considered the Windscale reactors to
have a guaranteed operational life of only five years, so by 1952
there was an urgent need to consider ways of insuring against
their possible closure after 1956. In addition, plutonium output
remained significantly below the original target figures, while
closure would create difficulties over the supply of the short-
lived neutron initiator material, polonium 210, without which a
British stockpile of bombs would quickly become inoperative.
The stimulus for building additional production reactors arose
from a conference to review global strategy held at the Royal
Naval College in Greenwich in 1952 by the British Chiefs of
Staff. The defence of Western Europe was expected to be based
increasingly upon the deterrent threat posed by United States
nuclear weapons, and it was argued that Britain should possess
more nuclear weapons for two purposes: to be able to attack
strategic targets of no direct national interest to the United
States; and to enable smaller-yield weapons to be used in a
tactical role during any ground engagement in Western Europe
or at sea.[29] In the light of this reassessment of priorities and
expansion of roles, plus the fact that the 1948 production
schedule had suffered considerable slippage by August 1952
due to shortfalls in fissile material output, the Chiefs of Staff
recommended that the Cabinet order the building of additional
reactors in order to double plutonium production.[30] The issues
which then arose were how best to achieve this and whether any
of the options could be linked to the development of civil
nuclear power stations.

Serious studies of power plants were started in the United
Kingdom in 1950, when two types of reactor were investigated;
one, using enriched fuel, for submarine propulsion, and the
other, a fast breeder reactor, again using enriched fuel, for
land-based power generation.[31] The options open to Britain

were constrained because plutonium was reserved for the bomb programme, while enriched uranium was unlikely to be available in quantity much before 1958, and even then most of it would probably be reserved for military use. Britain had no indigenous source of heavy water, making reactors moderated with this material unattractive, and it was believed that the United States would refuse to supply helium, the most attractive coolant gas, because of restrictions in the 1946 United States Atomic Energy Act. Thus in the short term natural uranium reactors were the only feasible line of development, which automatically meant that they would have to be moderated by graphite rather than by light water because the former absorbed fewer neutrons. This type of power reactor would also be a natural extension of the technology of the Windscale plutonium production reactors.

The Harwell scientists who were responsible for the development of civil reactor technology believed that power generation from natural uranium reactors could only be justified as a by-product of plutonium production, and they regarded reactors using enriched uranium fuel as having greater commercial attractions. Initially their hope was that research into land-based power reactors using enriched fuel could be integrated with research into submarine propulsion systems. However, it became clear that a reactor fuelled by 3–5 per cent enriched uranium would be too heavy for use in submarines, and in October 1952 the development programme for these reactors was suspended until national highly-enriched uranium production had started.[32]

A nuclear power conference held at Harwell in September 1950 accepted that the expenditure on an initial nuclear power programme might be justified if the chosen design was intended to produce both power and plutonium. This type of reactor could be termed a near breeder because, it was argued, its plutonium output could be used in weapons and then as fuel by a later generation of fast breeder reactors. The aims of such a design would be to raise the temperature of the coolant gas to the point where the steam generated in the heat exchangers could drive electricity-generating turbines efficiently. This in turn meant increasing the temperature in the core of the reactor and therefore the intensity of the chain reaction. Such temperatures were not possible with the aluminium containers used for the Windscale reactor fuel, but the Harwell metallurgists evolved a magnesium alloy, known as magnox, which could resist corrosion both at temperatures up to 400°C and in the presence of the only available coolant gas, carbon dioxide. A proposal was therefore drafted early in 1952 to undertake a full-scale design study of such a reactor, but received far from unanimous support as the design used, or burned up, only a small proportion of the fissile material in its fuel charge, and heavy water reactors were technically a preferred line of development because their more efficient moderator gave better fuel utilisation. Eventually the design work was allowed to proceed, mainly on the grounds that it would bring industrial firms and the British Electricity Authority into the field of nuclear power generation.[33] By June 1952 the design study involved a reactor rated at 150 Mw(th) and producing about 40 kilograms of plutonium per year.[34] The estimated cost of building a prototype of this reactor was prohibitive, and had not the Chiefs of Staff decided that there was an urgent need to increase plutonium production to levels which would enable the original 1946 cumulative output goals to be achieved, it seem probable it would never have been constructed.[35]

The initial reaction of Harwell and Risley to the request for proposals to double plutonium production was to suggest that this could be done by building a third Windscale-type reactor, supplemented by the output from two planned research and development ones. However, the idea of building a further Windscale installation was opposed by Hinton and others as a technically retrograde step, an unsurprising attitude in view of the design's disappointing performance, while relying on experimental reactors for plutonium production would create major conflicts over their operating priorities. Although another Windscale reactor could be built within three years, limitation on the supply of graphite meant that it would be impossible to complete a second during this period. A proposal was then advanced for building two reactors designed to produce both power and plutonium which could benefit from information gained from operating the Windscale plants. These could only be built on a four-year timescale, and the Chiefs of Staff were asked whether it was absolutely necessary to achieve the three-year target figure. Their subsequent acquiescence to a four-year schedule allowed the requirement to be met with two combined power/plutonium reactors which would, together, have an annual target output of about 80 kilograms of plutonium.[36]

The central argument for building these reactors was that they produced cheaper plutonium than air-cooled ones. They would also use less graphite, and could produce enough electricity to power themselves and other plants on the Windscale site, plus a surplus for export to the national grid. No detailed considera-tion was given to their economy or efficiency in producing power: the crucial factor was that the coolant outlet tempera-tures made electricity generation technically feasible. One im-portant issue that remained unresolved for some time was whether the higher burn-up and temperatures of these designs compared with the Windscale reactors would lead to the pro-duction of a significant quantity of plutonium 240, the isotope which creates difficulties for weapon designers.[37] Studies later demonstrated that this would not occur and that the reactors could be run in such a way as to maximise either military plutonium output or power production.[38] Permission to proceed with the construction of the two reactors was given by the Cabinet in March 1953, after the failure of Churchill's first attempts to negotiate a new atomic energy agreement with the United States.[39]

The expectation was that these reactors would increase the annual rate of plutonium production for military purposes from about 45 kilograms in 1953 to about 140 kilograms by 1958: this output, plus that of the high enrichment plant, offered the potential for annual production rates of about 45 US Mark IV type atomic weapons. Thus it might still be possible to achieve the 1948 stockpile target of 200 bombs by the end of 1960.[40]

Constructing the First British Atomic Device

The detailed planning for Britain's first nuclear weapon and the scheduling of an explosive testing programme began in June 1947, following the formal decision to give Dr Penney responsi-bility for this work. The first task was to design and build an experimental nuclear device (that is, a bomb without its ballistic case and fusing mechanisms) along similar lines to the US Mark III 'laboratory' weapon. The British team was able to set out the principles of this device and list its components from the knowledge accumulated at Los Alamos. The theoretical problems of bomb design were well understood, and Britain had considerable experience in the design of explosive lenses, detonators and fuses, though knowledge was lacking on methods of manufacturing and testing these components. Despite cooperative work in New York during the war on the chemistry of polonium 210, the radioactive material with a half life of 138 days which, together with beryllium, initiated the chain reaction in nuclear explosives, there was little information on its compatibility with other bomb components. Material for experimental work on these issues only became available from the Windscale reactors in mid-1951, and in addition, considerable problems had to be overcome in the manufacture of explosive lenses.[41]

The United Kingdom's first experimental assembly, code-named Hurricane, was successfully exploded in the Monte Bello islands off the coast of Australia on 1 October 1952.[42] It was very similar in its construction to the United States Trinity assembly exploded at Alamogordo in July 1945.[43] This test demonstrated mastery of the purity requirements for fissile materials; the techniques for gold-plating the two solid plutonium hemispheres forming the fissile core to prevent oxidisation; the fabrication of the polonium 210/beryllium initiator; the design of the explosive lenses and their associated firing circuits, and the physics principles underlying the device. Work proceeded in parallel on the engineering design of an operational nuclear weapon code-named Blue Danube. It involved close coordination, especially over weight distribution, between the nuclear warhead team and those members of the Royal Aircraft Establishment (RAE) at Farnborough who were responsible for the fusing systems, the aerodynamics of the bomb casing, and the positioning of equipment within the 24-foot projectile. At least one aircraft company was closely involved in the RAE work, while responsibility for the environmental testing of the nuclear device, to ensure it would function under all conditions, rested with the warhead group.[44]

The production warhead design differed significantly from that of the first experimental device as it had a series of interlinked safety mechanisms to prevent it being detonated by accident or without authorisation. These included an internal structure which allowed the fissile core to be stored separately from the rest of the warhead, both on the ground and in the air, and a method for inserting the core into the weapon by remote control to arm it in flight. In addition, many of the materials had to be manufactured to rigorous standards to ensure reliability, and some had to be plated with protective coatings to prevent corrosion and avoid contamination.

In concept, the warhead design was similar to that used in the United States Mark IV assembly which had been in production from late 1948 onwards, and it generated about 20 per cent more yield from its fissile material than the initial American Mark III weapon of 19 kilotons.[45] At the end of 1952, work on the ballistic case and internal structures and systems of Blue Danube had reached a point where dropping trials of prototype projectiles and explosive tests of the operation warhead, complete with its remote arming mechanisms, were planned for the following year.[46]

The inherent dangers in experimenting with radioactive materials and manufacturing prototype and production weapon components from fissile materials meant that a new site and facilities had to be provided for these activities. The issue was also raised as to whether it was desirable to centralise all nuclear weapon research and production, something which was attractive from a security perspective. Penney initially opposed any move to create a separate nuclear establishment on the grounds that the most significant areas for nuclear weapon design improvement were to be found in refinements of conventional ordnance techniques, rather than in new nuclear physics concepts, but in early 1950 the decision was taken to build the new facilities at Aldermaston in Berkshire, and concentrate all development work on nuclear weapons there. Penney was placed in charge of the new establishment and relieved of his responsibilities for conventional ordnance development.[47] Thus, during 1951 and 1952, the work on manufacturing the first device, and designing a production warhead, proceeded in parallel with the construction of this new establishment, with the attendant disruptive consequences of moving personnel from their previous locations and creating a new organisation at a time when its precise future responsibilities were not clear. This latter issue was finally clarified in 1952, when Aldermaston was made responsible for nuclear weapon design, development and prototype testing, the manufacture of the fissile cores of production

weapons and their final assembly. Many components not directly connected with the nuclear assembly itself would be manufactured elsewhere, and delivered to Aldermaston for incorporation into production weapons.[48] The limited output of plutonium
from Windscale made this bomb production activity a very
low-volume operation for a number of years, although it was
organised on a production-line basis using remotely controlled
machines.

Late in 1951, with design work on the Hurricane assembly
and the Blue Danube warhead well advanced and most of the
new organisation *in situ* at Aldermaston, attention turned to the
future direction of British nuclear weapon development and the
new tasks to be allocated to Penney's establishment. It was clear
from the United States precedents that the options were either
to concentrate on the design, development and production of
new versions of fission weapons, or to attempt to develop a
thermonuclear bomb. The theoretical possibilities of producing
yields up to 1000 kilotons (a megaton) and higher yield to
weight of fissile material ratios from cores containing both
plutonium and U-235 had been recognised in 1948, while the
production shortfalls from Windscale gave added impetus to
any improvements which could add substantially to the future
stockpile of weapons. Such advances would also enable
weapons of reduced weight and size to be developed.[49]

The option of moving directly to a hydrogen weapon appeared unattractive at this time. The United States had yet to
demonstrate publicly that such a device was feasible, and it was
clear that resources were not going to be easily obtained for both
a fission and fusion weapon programme. The design team at
Aldermaston was still in the process of consolidation, and it
needed time to absorb additional personnel and tasks.
Moreover, the United States programme had demonstrated that
significant quantities of tritium were likely to be required, and
this material could only be obtained by duplicating the Hanford
method of bombarding reactor fuel rods containing lithium with
neutrons.[50] The Windscale reactors would have to be used for
this purpose, resulting in a reduction of their already limited
plutonium output, and a diminution in the potential British
nuclear weapon stockpile for several years ahead. In these
circumstances, it was hardly surprising that the decision was
taken to concentrate upon development work related to the

Blue Danube warhead with the aim of producing a refined design offering reductions in both warhead weight and yield.

At the end of 1952 the British nuclear programme was still divorced from a military planning base, despite the many attempts by the leaders of the services in 1948, 1949 and 1952, to link its production capacity to future operational requirements. The programme had been sustained by the political belief that, as long as Britain possessed the proven ability to make nuclear weapons, it was not necessary to be too concerned about the absence of a substantial stockpile or the means to deliver them upon the USSR. This was reinforced by the significance attached to the target date of 1957 for possessing a substantial inventory of bombs, and an effective force of V bombers, these aircraft being the only ones which could credibly deliver the large, heavy Blue Danube weapon. In 1952 this year still seemed distant but it was obvious that the existing and planned fissile material production facilities were inadequate in comparison to the size of British bomber force envisaged for the end of the decade. The haphazard process of decision-making in the production area, in contrast to the United States situation, was encapsulated by General Morgan, the successor to Lord Portal as Controller of Atomic Energy in the Ministry of Supply, when he wrote:

> the output figure for weapons ... was arrived at originally by some sort of process akin to that known as a Dutch Auction. It seems to me that the requirement has never been keyed in any definite way to any plan of strategy or tactics. This is in a way understandable since we know that the atomic bomb ... has been regarded as a political far more than as a military weapon.[51]

Atomic Energy Negotiations with the United States

Substantive Anglo-American exchanges on nuclear weapon designs and fissile material production had ceased following the presidential directive of April 1946, and had been made legally impossible without the agreement of Congress with the passing of the US Atomic Energy Act in August. The only exception to this freeze was information on weapon effects and on phenomena associated with Soviet tests. Also, the machinery for collaboration was still extant in the shape of the CPC, together with the Combined Development Trust, which was responsible for the procurement and allocation of uranium ore.

The break with the United States generated resentment among those associated with the British project, because of its suddenness and its completeness. Memories of the earlier break in 1943 were recalled, and there was a determination that the United Kingdom should never again be placed in such an exposed position. Any offers of renewed collaboration would only be acceptable if they contributed to the fulfilment of the objectives of the national project, and enabled Britain to retain the option of 'going it alone'. Mr Attlee and his Cabinet colleagues were deeply committed to the concept of an independent project, and their political relations with the Truman administration in nuclear matters hinged on the absolute need for Britain to possess the technology to manufacture weapons. This contrasted sharply with the underlying attitude of Churchill, who continued to see the independent British project not as an end in itself, but as a means to the reintegration of the nuclear projects of both countries, if necessary through the sacrifice of many of the independent elements in the British project. He was prepared to forego a capability for the national manufacture of nuclear weapons if this furthered Anglo-American security interests: Attlee was not.[52]

The severance of the Anglo-American nuclear energy linkage was unique as other examples of wartime integration of defence research, especially the fields of biological and chemical weapons, remained intact into the post-war period.[53] At the time these were regarded as having a similar military potential to nuclear weapons, and suspicions grew in Britain that the real motive behind the breach was a commercial one. This attitude was reinforced by the knowledge that Akers, from ICI, had been rejected by the United States as the resident director of the British contribution to the Manhattan Project. On a more personal level, considerable pique was felt among some of the British scientists and engineers that their expertise in the nuclear area had been spurned, and a feeling grew up that an independent programme would enable British abilities over the whole field to be demonstrated to the Americans. Although close personal relationships were sustained between colleagues on both sides of the Atlantic, the restrictions of the 1946 Act

prevented any useful information being transmitted on an informal basis, while such information as was obtained often proved
to be inaccurate or misleading.

The break with the United States occurred at a time when
great international diplomatic activity, partly stimulated by
Attlee, was taking place to reach agreement on the international
control of atomic energy. Until this issue had been resolved
there was little hope of any further progress in negotiating a
more positive basis for Anglo-American nuclear relations, as
the United States government believed that international control would be very difficult to achieve if it became known that
America was making secret agreements to assist the United
Kingdom to become a nuclear power. The United Nations
Atomic Energy Commission (UNAEC) began its work in June
1946, but after 14 months of exhaustive and detailed negotiations the talks became deadlocked. The United States was only
prepared to destroy its atomic weapons and hand its facilities
over to international control once an international system
guaranteeing its security had been established: the USSR
wanted to see all atomic weapons destroyed first, and only then
negotiate on a security system.[54] This impasse was not openly
admitted until the third report of the UNAEC in May 1948, but
the new United States Secretary of State, General Marshall, and
his advisers, had reached a consensus by September 1947 that
little further progress was possible, and that the time had come
to reestablish a dialogue with the British and the Canadians.[55]

The Truman administration had two additional reasons for
reopening bilateral atomic energy discussions with Britain. The
members of the JCAE had been informed in mid-May 1948 of
the nature of the Combined Development Trust; of the full
extent of United Kingdom participation in the Manhattan Project, and of the nature of the Quebec Agreement under which
the United States President had bound himself not to use the
atomic bomb without British consent. Many members of the
committee had been shocked by the limits to United States
freedom of action implied by the arrangements, and were
demanding rapid action both to assure a greater supply of
uranium ore for the United States, and to negate what was seen
to be the totally unacceptable and unconstitutional limitations
upon their country's ability to use nuclear weapons. Some
members even suggested that the negotiations over the Marshall

Plan might be used as a lever to obtain British agreement on these matters, but this proposal was rejected by the President. The implicit threat that this might still happen nevertheless formed the backdrop for the bilateral atomic energy discussions.[56]

The second pressing reason for negotiating with Britain was that unless the United States could obtain access to both the entire 1948 and 1949 production of uranium ore from the Belgian Congo and to stocks of ore held in Britain under the Combined Development Trust arrangements, the American production plants would be unable to operate at full capacity. It was anticipated that the United Kingdom would use this issue to demand the establishment of a new information exchange arrangement, despite the fact that Section 10 of the 1946 Atomic Energy Act made any exchange of data on industrial uses illegal unless effective international safeguards existed. It was suggested, however, that the Act permitted some information on weapons and fissionable materials to be passed on to Britain, so long as the Department of Defense determined that this was in the interests of 'the common defense and security'. This interpretation was accepted by all parties, including the members of the JCAE, prior to a full meeting of the CPC in December 1947.[57] Nine areas for potential Anglo-American information exchange were identified at this meeting. In return the British agreed to the United States taking all the 1948 and 1949 Congo ore production, plus two-thirds of the unallocated stocks held in the United Kingdom, and recognised that the Quebec Agreement was no longer operative. These elements were written into the record of the CPC (becoming known as the *modus vivendi*), and national representatives stated that they intended to proceed on this basis, thus eliminating any need to refer the agreement to Congress or register it at the UN.[58]

The *modus vivendi* guaranteed positive and substantial benefits to the United States but few to the United Kingdom, as the CPC record was silent on how the information exchange was to be handled and what its objectives were to be. This asymmetry created increasing friction as 1948 progressed, despite the worsening international political climate produced by East–West tensions over Berlin, yet initially the positive and friendly atmosphere in which the arrangements had been negotiated offered hope for a new and fruitful relationship. In

February 1948 it was agreed that information would be exchanged on certain types of reactors and on plutonium extraction chemistry, and a number of British scientists made visits to
the United States for this purpose, while three Americans
visited Harwell in June and were given information on the
design of the Windscale reactors.[59] They reported to the AEC
that these were to be plutonium production reactors, thus
corroborating the warning delivered in March that Britain was
about to announce publicly its intention to develop atomic
weapons.

One of the AEC commissioners, Strauss, claimed ignorance
of Britain's aims, though most other participants in the American programme had always assumed that this was the British
objective. When the AEC was asked to approve an exchange of
information on the fundamental properties of reactor materials,
he argued that Britain's military pretensions altered fundamen-
tally the basis for the technical exchange agreement and that the
JCAE should be informed of the situation. In July, the British
requested that consultations should take place on the basic
metallurgy of plutonium, but Hickenlooper, the Republican
JCAE chairman, having been told of the 'discovery' that Britain
intended to make atomic weapons, insisted that the request
should be rejected.[60] It was clear that the existence of this,
mainly Republican, isolationist element within the AEC and
JCAE was going to make it very difficult for the information
exchanges to be continued, let alone expanded. In August and
September the British attempted to press the case for an exchange of information on weapon designs, but were advised to
wait until after the presidential election in November.[61] In the
meantime, a limited exchange of information continued on the
chemistry of plutonium extraction, and Cockcroft acquired
information on a number of topics during an autumn visit to the
United States.[62]

No further progress could be expected until the State and
Defense Departments, the JCS, the AEC, the JCAE and the
President could agree on a common position. The process of
interagency consultation produced a consensus by March 1949
that what was required was a completely new agreement under
which nuclear weapon production would be undertaken in the
United States, with some bombs stockpiled in Britain in accor-
dance with common war plans. This proposal was in part

motivated by fears that an independent British programme would ultimately assist the USSR, either by leaks of technical information caused by lax security measures or by the USSR invading the United Kingdom and capturing her uranium ore stockpile, production plants and weapons.[63] Such a radical shift in United States policy would need congressional approval, and there was little optimism that this could be obtained rapidly or easily. In addition, the North Atlantic Treaty had been sent to the Senate in April for ratification, and it was felt that discussion of Anglo-American nuclear cooperation should not be allowed to become entangled with this process. The attitude of the JCAE was also uncertain as Hickenlooper, who had been displaced as chairman of the JCAE by McMahon after the Democrats' election victories in 1948, had accused the commission of 'incredible mismanagement', and long and acrimonious JCAE hearings had resulted. McMahon felt that he could not guarantee JCAE approval for the plan, and that the committee would probably split on the substantive issue of the desirability of the proposals and on the constitutional question of whether the President had been given the authority to make such an agreement by the 1946 Atomic Energy Act. This judgement was confirmed at a meeting the President held in July with representatives of the State and Defense Departments and the AEC, plus certain members of the JCAE, when some isolationist Republicans expressed the view that they could see no justification for the United States 'bailing out' the British by making bombs for them. The resulting compromise was that negotiations with Britain should commence, but any agreement that resulted would have to be ratified by the JCAE.[64]

Negotiations started in the CPC on 20 September, the day after traces of the USSR's first nuclear explosion had been detected. The American objectives in the discussions were to facilitate the planned expansion of their nuclear production programme by preventing any shortage of uranium ore, and to apply the idea of a division of labour in defence activities to nuclear weaponry. Both aims involved concentrating the output of nuclear materials and weapons in the United States, and minimising nuclear production activity in the United Kingdom through arrangements acceptable to both the British government and the JCAE. The intentions of the United Kingdom delegates were to acquire information to assist their existing programme, and to reject any proposal which abrogated their state's rights either to possess nuclear weapons under national control or to develop the industrial and commercial aspects of nuclear energy.

The initial American stance was to propose that fissionable material production should be concentrated in the United States or Canada, because of the vulnerability of the British plants to attack and capture; that no additional plants should be built in Britain and that nuclear components of atomic weapons should only be stored in Britain if they formed part of common war plans. The United States would be allocated 90 per cent of all uranium ore, and would lead an integrated research, development and production programme.[65] It appeared that the only way in which sufficient uranium ore could be obtained for the expanded United States plutonium production programme of five Hanford reactors was to terminate construction work on the third British reactor at Windscale. This was the cornerstone of a potential package deal, covering the years up to 1955, that emerged from the discussions. Britain would restrict her production facilities to the two Windscale reactors and the low enrichment plant then under construction, and in return would participate in a full exchange of technical information, receive complete cooperation in the design, production, and storage of her own atomic weapons, and would be provided by the United States with the U-235 and other materials to make improved weapons. Certain of the American negotiators felt that Congress was unlikely to approve such a package and it was decided to consult the members of the JCAE on this issue. The impression gained by the British was that the main problem remained 'an ill-defined and almost unconscious feeling that atomic energy is and should remain an American monopoly, both for military and industrial purposes'.[66]

The adjournment enabled the British military and political leaders to review their position on these issues. They agreed to accept any proposal under which the United States would supply Britain with U-235 for weapon production and agree to fabricate the nuclear cores and initiators for the bulk of the British weapons, but at least some of these had to be stored in the United Kingdom under national control. To safeguard their independence, however, the United Kingdom intended to build prototype plants for U-235 and initiator production and for the casting and machining of fissile materials. It was anticipated that most of the British atomic bombs resulting from these arrangements would be stored in Canada and that there would also be common Anglo-American testing ranges. The British leaders felt sufficiently encouraged by the progress of the negotiations to terminate work on the third Windscale reactor, as it was accepted that any agreement would make its completion unnecessary.[67]

The talks reopened in Washington at the end of November, but the American delegation indicated that they now envisaged an integrated Anglo-American programme along lines similar to those in 1943–5. They argued that a small British production programme would not make the most efficient use of the available materials, and that the proposals for cooperation in research and production would prevent them incorporating British scientists, especially Dr Penney, into the weapon design teams at Los Alamos.[68] The proposals for integration were discussed at length in London, and a revised British position emerged. A small number of the best United Kingdom staff were to be offered to the United States, but work was to continue on the creation of a national atomic weapons establishment and facilities to provide fissile material for it. A comprehensive interchange of technical information was envisaged, but Britain had to remain free to pursue any line of nuclear development she judged to be in her interests. Some of the plutonium from the Windscale reactors would be fabricated into British atomic weapons in the United States, and some would be traded for U-235 to increase their efficiency. There would also be cooperation in weapon-testing. Two further elements were essential for any agreement. One was acceptance that 'about 20 bombs' would be stockpiled in the United Kingdom: the second was that the national stockpile had to be sacrosanct against any later attempt by either Congress or a new United States President to renegotiate the arrangements.[69]

These proposals were presented to the United States negotiators at the end of December, and in the meantime, the British government had decided to create a separate weapons laboratory at Aldermaston to enable the United Kingdom's independent project to continue should Dr Penny leave for Los Alamos.[70] The AEC's response to the proposals was unenthusiastic, although the State Department took a more optimistic view of the situation. On 2 February 1950, before the proposals could be put to the JCAE, negotiations were effectively terminated by the public disclosure of the arrest of Klaus Fuchs, the German-born Harwell physicist. Given the JCAE's obsession with atomic security and the growing belief in the AEC's military liaison committee that Fuchs's espionage might have enabled the USSR to move ahead of the United States in the development of thermonuclear weapons, any resumption of the negotiations was dependent on the outcome of his interrogation and trial. It must be doubted, however, whether the JCAE would have accepted the December proposals.[71]

The net outcome of the 1949 negotiations was that the United States gained access to uranium supplies for their expanded production programme while Britain reduced its potential plutonium output by one-third. The termination of negotiations left the British military and political leadership in the unsatisfactory position of having accepted United States arguments in favour of a division of labour to avoid waste, especially in view of the more efficient nature of American fabrication processes and weapon designs, but realising also that there was now no alternative to the continuation of the existing programme for an independent development and production capability.

The American desire to increase fissile material production following the outbreak of the Korean War soon led to informal discussions on the renewal of negotiations. It was now acknowledged that Britain's two Windscale reactors and associated low enrichment plant would be more efficient converters of uranium into fissile material than the existing Hanford processes. Rumours reached Britain of Pentagon proposals to acquire plutonium from the United Kingdom in exchange for modern nuclear weapons. Such an arrangement remained dependent upon the administration's ability to persuade Congress to amend the 1946 Atomic Energy Act, and the informal contacts yielded no result.[72] Congress did agree to one minor amendment to the 1946 Act late in 1951, but its main purpose was to allow the United States to make greater use of the Canadian Chalk River NRX reactor. During 1949, Britain and Canada discussed using this reactor to provide the British weapon programme with additional plutonium, but no agreement was reached, although standby arrangements were negotiated in respect of polonium 210 production.[73] The large surplus of neutrons produced by the NRX reactor made the AEC increasingly anxious to have access to it in order to develop fuel elements for both their new Savannah River plants and their submarine reactors, and to produce plutonium and isotopes such as tritium for weapon development purposes. To make fuller use of this reactor and also to improve uranium production techniques in their mines, it was necessary to pass restricted data to Canada, and the Act was amended to permit this. However, Senator Hickenlooper continued to express concern during the JCAE hearings on the amendment that information passed to the Canadians would reach socialist Britain, and that Canada did not have an adequate security system for the retention of nuclear secrets.[74]

The amendment did facilitate an expanded interchange of information with Britain in atomic energy intelligence, and uranium processing and purification, with the result that a joint investigation took place into apparent uranium losses at the British Springfields works. It also made possible the export of fissile material to and from the United States, if the President judged that 'the common defense and security' were not going to be adversely affected,[75] though this appears to have been applied only to material irradiated in the Chalk River reactor. It was made clear to the AEC by the JCAE that any exchange of information or materials with Britain would have to be decided on a case-by-case basis, and that the amendment could not be used as authorisation for any general Anglo-American agreement. The sensitivity of the JCAE to the apparent laxity of British security procedures stimulated the holding of a security conference with the United States in June 1951, in which the British delegation accepted that they should amend their security procedures to include 'positive vetting' of some personnel, although wholesale changes were not actually implemented until the mid-1950s.[76]

During 1950 and 1951 information continued to be exchanged on some of the topics agreed in 1949, but knowledge of the behaviour of graphite in reactors was sparse, and there was no interchange on power reactors. Britain passed information to the AEC on its butex chemical process for separating the plutonium and uranium in reactor fuel rods, in exchange for similar data on American processes, and also requested the use of United States nuclear testing facilities. However, the fear that the United States might take political advantage of Britain's dependence upon their facilities, led to the decision to test in Australia.[77]

Although the United States became less dependent on Britain for access to raw material supplies as sources of uranium ore diversified during the early 1950s, its need to have access to United Kingdom strategic bomber bases increased. Arguments about the strategic vulnerability of Britain's independent weapons programme were somewhat paradoxical, as the characteristics of the existing United States bombers made it imperative to have equally vulnerable bases and stockpiles of weapons for them in Britain or other Western European states if they were to mount nuclear attacks upon the USSR. Anglo-American military staff talks had been held regularly since 1948, and American war plans assumed that the RAF would make a major contribution to the allied bomber fleets, although all British requests for discussions on the operational aspects of the strategic use of atomic weapons had been refused. This led to mutual consent on the use of nuclear weapons, which the United Kingdom had abandoned in the *modus vivendi*, becoming a political issue again. The United States ambassador to Britain was believed to have given an oral assurance in 1948 that Britain would be consulted before atomic bombs were dropped by aircraft operating from British bases, but nothing was ever committed to paper. The issue achieved prominence at the end of 1950 when Attlee flew to Washington to investigate rumours that the United States was contemplating the use of the atomic bomb in the Korean War. He believed that in the course of this visit he obtained a promise of consultation over its use in circumstances other than in the aftermath of a surprise attack upon the United States, despite the fact that the Secretary of State appears to have been at pains to impress upon the British delegation that no American President could constitutionally make such a promise, as it would limit both his freedom, and that of Congress, to make war.[78]

Britain was dissatisfied with the continued lack of clarity over the conditions under which United States nuclear forces stationed in England might be used against the USSR. Eventually, in September 1951, a high-level meeting was held in Washington at which it was formally recognised that there would have to be consultation before the United States could use atomic weapons from bases in England, and that Britain had the theoretical right to veto such an action. A document was drafted stating that the use of air bases and other facilities in Britain would be a matter of joint decision in the light of circumstances at the time, and its contents were reported to the House of Commons in December.[79]

This disclosure occurred just after Churchill's Conservative government had been formed, following the October 1951 general election, and it was expected that he would make an immediate attempt to negotiate a new atomic energy exchange agreement with the United States, and seek to achieve a resumption of the 1943–5 situation of merged nuclear projects. Churchill and Lord Cherwell visited Washington in January 1952 and indicated that their initial objective was to try to maximise cooperation within the terms of the amended 1946 Act. It soon became clear that little progress was possible, due to the AEC and the Department of Defense holding different views on the scope provided by the Act. The Defense Department's representatives argued that information on the production of nuclear weapons was specifically excluded from discussion by the 1951 amendment, thus eliminating most areas of potential cooperation.[80] The only hope for progress was on a case-by-case basis, and although Cockcroft visited Washington later in the year to explore this possibility, he found that the process for gaining agreement to a specific information exchange within the United States governmental system was so complex and tortuous that it was unlikely to be attempted unless America desperately wanted access to specific British data.[81]

Areas in which it did prove possible to expand cooperation included nuclear intelligence matters and access to information on the United States strategic air plan. Churchill was given a personal briefing on this, and the United States Secretary of Defense allowed informal discussions to start on its strategic and tactical consequences.[82] However, it was accepted that as 1952 was a presidential election year, there was little immediate possibility of introducing amendments to the 1946 Act or changing congressional and Defense Department attitudes towards it. Churchill's policy throughout 1952 was to mark time, explode the first British atomic device, and hope for a more liberal attitude from the new American President. The election of Eisenhower led to renewed hopes for a change in United

States attitudes and the Prime Minister refused to sanction the building of the Calder Hall plutonium/power reactors until he had explored the possibility of implementing the earlier proposals for Britain to be supplied with a small stockpile of bombs in return for an integration of British research, development and production work with American efforts.[83] This meeting took place in January 1953, but failed to achieve the desired result, and, as a consequence, the construction of the reactors commenced. Eisenhower's·election appeared to offer the prospect of a President who was anxious to improve Anglo-American technical cooperation in atomic matters, but personnel changes in the AEC made this cooperation more difficult to envisage. Strauss, who had been hostile to earlier British attempts to extend cooperation, became its chairman, and its general manager, Nichols, was also viewed with little enthusiasm by his British counterparts.[84]

The period 1946–52 thus saw Britain involved in a number of attempts to expand the exchange of nuclear information with the United States, but emerging with little to show for them. The conflicting attitudes of the AEC and the Department of Defense; the fear by both that they would be accused by the JCAE of exceeding their powers under the 1946 Act; the legalism which permeated the administration of atomic energy policy; and the unwillingness and political inability of the President to give a positive lead in this area, gave Britain no clear idea where the decision-making centre in nuclear matters rested in Washington, and thus where to apply the most effective pressure. Superficially, the faltering Anglo-American negotiations had led to Britain making substantial sacrifices in order to further joint interests. The United States had been provided with much needed uranium ore and with nuclear bomber bases, and had been relieved of a duty to consult the United Kingdom before using nuclear weapons, while Britain had cancelled the construction of a third Windscale reactor yet had acquired very little information through formal channels to assist her independent nuclear programme. However, the two states were members of the NATO security system, which could be argued to have made such considerations of sectional interests irrelevant, and the United States had no obligation to extend its nuclear umbrella over the Western European states, as some of the old fashioned isolationists in Congress were quick to point out. The

American nuclear guarantee convinced Britain that it should make cuts in its national programme to assist the common defence effort, but the unyielding commitment to sustain nuclear independence – in the shape of production facilities, fissile materials and bombs under national control – remained.

5 Translating the Art into the Article:[1] Initial British Nuclear Weapon Testing and Production

Producing Blue Danube

In early 1953 the British nuclear weapon programme was in much the same position as that of the United States in 1948. The proof tests of a production physics package suitable for long-term storage, safe military handling and rapid deployment and arming were scheduled to take place in Australia later that year, and design and initial development work on the Blue Danube weapon system was almost complete. The original political directive had only specified the development of this bomb with its maximum yield of 20 kilotons and steps had been taken to increase plutonium production after 1956 in order to achieve, by the end of the decade, the stockpile target set eight years earlier of about 200 weapons. Production of the high-flying V bombers, which were to carry Blue Danube, had been initiated and the implications for future procurement policy of the American work on thermonuclear experimental devices were slowly being absorbed. Yet there was still no great demand for the immediate acquisition of large numbers of Blue Danube bombs, as was demonstrated by the decision to divert 15 kilograms of plutonium to civil fast breeder reactor experiments.[2] The lack of any modern bomber capable of carrying Blue Danube was partly responsible for this, as was a continued belief among the political leadership that agreement might still be reached with the United States on a package deal, under which nuclear bombs could be acquired from America in return for access to British materials and manpower.

In October 1953, two tests of experimental devices similar to the warhead planned for incorporation in production Blue Danube weapons took place at Emu Field, near Woomera in

90

South Australia.[3] Assembly of the first Blue Danube production bomb was by then virtually complete and, following these tests, it was delivered to the RAF in November.[4] During 1954 an intensive ground instruction programme was conducted at RAF Wittering to train technical personnel in the handling and servicing of the weapon.[5] Release and bombing trials with suitably weighted Blue Danube bomb casings had started in April 1953, and these continued during 1954 using the first production Vickers Valiant bombers. The initial Blue Danube bombs were built on a 'cottage industry' basis in very small numbers, being more a development batch rather than the start of a major production run. They were used to uncover operational deficiencies and sources of unreliability in the bomb and the design of succeeding weapons was modified to correct these shortcomings. Blue Danube evolved through a series of changes to its casing, internal systems and nuclear warhead, and was more a family of weapons than a single design. Due to the restricted availability of plutonium and U-235, annual output remained in single figures until its termination in early 1958. Cumulative plutonium output was significantly below the 1948 projections throughout the period, and the impact of this shortfall on bomb production rates was exacerbated by high initial scrap rates for fissile materials and the difficulty of quickly recovering such scrap when it was contaminated with other substances. In addition, it had become apparent that the ongoing research and development programme would involve the consumption of more fissile material than had originally been anticipated. As a consequence, projections in late 1954 of plutonium output and the growth of the United Kingdom's stockpile of Blue Danube bombs probably approximated to the figures in Table 5.1.

The initial work on British nuclear weapons had all been linked directly to variable yield Blue Danube 20 kiloton strategic bombs but pressures were growing by 1953 within the operational requirements branches of the services to develop nuclear explosives which were capable of being used in other military roles.[6] These ideas were resisted by a political leadership which regarded nuclear bombs as diplomatic instruments, rather than war fighting weapons, although it was accepted that nuclear weapon development would not now end with Blue Danube. In the course of 1954 the staff at Aldermaston there-

TABLE 5.1 *Estimate of British stockpile figures and projections in late 1954*

Year ending	1952	1953	1954	1955	1956	1957	1958
Gross annual plutonium production in reactors[a]	69[b]	45	63	55	55	95	135
Net annual usable plutonium output (kg)[c]	12	29	35	57	50	50	83
Cumulative net plutonium output (kg)	12	41	76	133	183	233	316
Cumulative U-235 output (kg)[d]	—	—	—	—	20	170	470
Plutonium for civil use (kg)	—	15	15	15	15	—	—
Cumulative total of plutonium consumed in tests (kg)[e]	6	18	18	18	54	54+	54+
Maximum size of weapon stockpile[f]	1	1	7	16	20	40	74
Estimate of actual size of weapon stockpile[g]	0	1	4	10	14	22	40
1948 projections (2 reactors only)[h]	15	30	45	60	75	90	105

(a) The basis for this calculation is explained in detail in Appendix 3 and 4b. It was assumed in 1954 that the power rating of a Calder Hall reactor would be 150 Mw (th), not 200 as subsequently proved to be the case.
(b) This figure includes production in both 1951 and 1952.

(c) The assumptions underlying these figures are explained fully in Appendix 4b. They exclude scrap material undergoing purification, though the 1955 figure assumes that the process to reclaim it was operative by that date.

(d) In the absence of any detailed data, it has been assumed that the estimated increase in bomb production by 20 units, as a consequence of the operation of the high enrichment plant, was based upon the need for a critical mass of 15 kilograms of U-235. Thus, at full power, the Capenhurst plant as originally designed would produce about 300 kilograms per year. The figures for 1956 and 1957 are arbitrary guesses based on the assumption that the plant was brought into operation in stages and by gradual increases in power levels and thus throughout of materials.

(e) It has been assumed that an average of 6 kilograms of plutonium was contained in each device either tested or planned for testing at the end of 1954. Although this figure is higher than the amount used for the Hurricane assembly, explosive safety tests which were not publicly reported are likely to have led to the destruction of some additional fissile material, thus justifying the higher figure.

(f) These are based on 6 kilograms of plutonium or 15 of highly enriched uranium or a 6:15 mixture of these materials per weapon.

(g) See Table A.4c.

(h) These figures are based on the magnitudes given in Table 4.1, supra p. 68.

fore turned their attention to two further design projects. The first was a logical extension of the Blue Danube warhead line, namely, the development of a nuclear warhead in the 20–200 kiloton range, for fitment to a ballistic missile, code-named Blue Streak, and an air-launched cruise missile, code-named Blue Steel, both of which had commenced development during 1953.[7] The requirement for increased yield arose from the relative inaccuracy of these delivery systems compared with strategic bombing aircraft. For technical reasons it was anticipated that fissile cores utilising U-235 would have to be designed to enable these high yields to be obtained.[8] The second project, code-named Red Beard, was to construct a second-generation version of the Blue Danube warhead and its associated weapon components, whose much reduced dimensions and weights would enable it to be carried not only by the RAF's new strategic bombers but also by the Canberra aircraft which were already in RAF service in considerable numbers, and by advanced naval strike fighters then in the early stages of development. Its physics package was similar in concept to the US Mark V warhead, its development programme ran three to four years behind that of Blue Danube, and its design yield appears to have been variable within the range of 5–20 kilotons.

Both these projects involved significant increases in the ratio of yield to weapon weight compared with the initial Blue Danube warhead design, and they, and further Blue Danube development work, were linked to a common experimental programme. This had the goal of investigating methods of reducing weapon weight and increasing yield. Unlike the equivalent United States efforts in this direction, no use was made initially of nuclear explosive testing, in part because prospects for improvement appeared to be greatest in areas other than the configuration of the fissile core, but also because the United Kingdom lacked a nuclear testing range close to its laboratory, similar to Los Alamos's Nevada site. Full-scale explosive testing was difficult and expensive to organise, and it also entailed depletion of the small stock of plutonium available for the manufacture of production weapons. As a consequence no such tests occurred in 1954 or 1955, and the staff members at Aldermaston came to view them in a significantly different perspective to that held by those at Los Alamos. Whereas the latter used nuclear explosive tests to assess rapidly a range of possible weapon configurations, the British laboratory performed this process by more laborious methods, and came to regard such tests as the culmination of the development process, and a means of 'fine tuning' designs. The most visible effect of these differing policies was that whereas between five and ten explosive tests were used to develop British warhead designs, 20 to 30 tests might occur before an American bomb or missile warhead was judged to be fully optimised.

Expansion and Acceleration

Work on the three atomic weapon development programmes progressed steadily during 1954, but it was accompanied by increasing pressures for a radical change of direction in British nuclear weapons policy. Eisenhower had asked Congress to amend the 1946 Atomic Energy Act to facilitate expanded nuclear cooperation with the United Kingdom and other NATO states, but the resulting legislative process, dominated by members of the JCAE, produced a bill which offered little overt possibility of any arrangement under which stocks of British-owned atomic bombs could be acquired from the United States.[9] The placing of additional V bomber production contracts[10] meant that unless moves were made rapidly to increase the output of fissile material, it would be the early 1960s before sufficient Blue Danube bombs were available to arm all of the RAF's new strategic bombers.

Interlocking with this weapon production problem was a realisation that the tests of American and Russian thermonuclear devices had demonstrated both a quantum jump in explosive power and the impossibility of mounting any effective defence against operational weapons developed from them.[11] The only conceivable method of dissuading a thermonuclear-armed Soviet Union from aggressive action was seen to be the possession of a similar countervailing military capability, and this strengthened the belief among the British political leadership that only states armed with megaton weapons would, in the future, be able to deter the USSR. As a consequence, in late 1954, development of a megaton thermonuclear weapon was made the overriding political and technical objective of the British weapon research and development programme.[12] This change in policy was reinforced by judgements that future technical cooperation with the United States in nuclear weapon development would only be achieved if the United Kingdom could demonstrate it had the will and the technical ability to produce these new weapons.

It was obvious from its initiation that a thermonuclear programme was going to be subject to much greater political pressures, imperatives and constraints than the Blue Danube one. One major area of concern was the rapidly evolving nature of the nuclear arms race. Instead of the acquisition of atomic weapons becoming a finite development plateau, as had been widely anticipated, the United Kingdom had barely acquired the capability to make production atomic bombs when this technology was supplanted by the infinite possibilities inherent in thermonuclear explosives. Thus the Cabinet recognised that Britain had a clear security interest in halting further Soviet thermonuclear development work once it also possessed this technology. Yet international pressures for an immediate halt to the thermonuclear arms race already existed.

The unintended consequences of the United States Bravo thermonuclear test at Bikini, in which a number of Japanese fishermen were affected by nuclear fall-out, had made the biological and genetic consequences of explosive testing a major international political issue, and demands had been voiced for a ban on all further tests.[13] At the end of March 1954, a number of

British Labour MPs tabled a motion in the House of Commons calling for an end to such nuclear trials, and it was soon clear that this concern would generate very strong domestic pressures for an international testing moratorium.[14] This placed the British Cabinet in a dilemma for it was felt to be imperative that the United Kingdom should develop a thermonuclear weapon, but it was also realised that it might soon be faced with a US – USSR agreement to halt thermonuclear testing and irresistible domestic and international pressures upon them to accept it. Thus it became politically vital both to develop a thermonuclear weapon design concept in the shortest possible time, and to have available for deployment the 'insurance' high-yield fission design, capable of carriage by the Blue Steel and Blue Streak missiles, if a test ban had to be signed before thermonuclear weapon development was completed. To add to Britain's difficulties, the United States government was pursuing an active policy of attempting to persuade the USSR to divert fissionable material to peaceful uses, and the United Kingdom government could not ignore possible consequences of this upon its nuclear weapon production programme.[15] Three political imperatives had thus come to dominate the British nuclear weapon policy by the end of 1954: the need to develop a thermonuclear warhead as rapidly as possible; the necessity of pursuing work on fission warheads with greater nuclear efficiency, both as triggers for thermonuclear devices and as insurance against the thermonuclear programme being stopped before its completion; and the demand for a rapid increase in fissile material output in order both to safeguard against an international ban on further production and to provide material for large-yield atomic weapons. Yet the British leadership remained fully committed to support the existing attempts to negotiate effective disarmament and arms control measures, so long as they would not freeze the United Kingdom in a position of qualitative nuclear inferiority compared with the superpowers.

The administrative structure for the atomic energy project was also changed during this period. Lord Cherwell, who became the Cabinet minister responsible for the project in 1952, believed that the existing arrangements, whereby detailed administrative control was vested in the Ministry of Supply, were unsatisfactory. He favoured the creation of an organisation similar to the USAEC, funded by the Treasury and responsible to the Ministry of Defence. This idea produced considerable opposition, but in April 1953 the Cabinet was persuaded to accept the idea and a committee under Lord Waverley was set up to plan the changeover and recommend a structure for the new organisation.[16]

The Waverley Report,[17] and the resultant British Atomic Energy Act of 1954, led to the creation of the United Kingdom Atomic Energy Authority (UKAEA) on 19 July of that year, which was financed by its own parliamentary vote, but was responsible to the Lord President of the Council rather than to the Minister of Defence.[18]

It was divided into three groups; research, weapons research and production, the latter known as the industrial group. In practice the weapons research group became semi-autonomous, as a deliberate policy decision had been taken in 1953 to concentrate all military work at Aldermaston and leave Harwell to focus on civil technology. These two national nuclear laboratories increasingly came to operate in isolation from each other, with no interchange of classified information, though Aldermaston maintained close links involving restricted data with military research establishments such as RAE. One consequence of both this enhanced security policy of isolating military research from other nuclear energy activities and limiting nuclear explosive testing was that the United States government remained totally ignorant of the progress being made at Aldermaston in nuclear weapon design and development between 1952 and 1958.[19] The inability of their agencies to monitor the detailed nature of those British tests which did occur, due to their detection and evaluation system being focused upon events in the northern hemisphere, sustained this situation.[20]

The impact of political imperatives upon the military nuclear programme was discernible during 1955–8 in three main activities: experimental testing; the construction of new fissile material production plants; and the manufacture and assembly of bombs for the RAF's nuclear weapon stockpile. The value of a permanent and well-equipped site for experimental testing of nuclear devices had always been recognised, and its importance was underlined during visits made early in 1955 by British observers to the American site in Nevada.[21] A main stumbling block to an extensive testing programme had previously been its cost, but the political decision in late 1954 to allocate more resources to the nuclear programme and accelerate its progress removed this restraint. In the spring of 1955 negotiations commenced with the government of Australia to acquire a permanent testing site there, and agreement was rapidly reached on the use of an area near Maralinga in the state of South Australia.[22] William Cook, the energetic Deputy Director at Aldermaston, was given overall responsibility for organising an accelerated development and experimental programme, and plans were made to use explosive nuclear testing in a much more positive manner as part of the weapon design process.

The first series of experimental explosions stimulated by these relaxed financial restraints, code-named Buffalo, was planned for Maralinga in the late summer of 1956. The intention was to combine a number of tests of experimental devices with investigations into the effect of the detonations upon military and civilian artefacts and animals.[23] The timing of these tests was linked to the completion of airfield and base facilities at Maralinga, but in June 1955 it became clear that the programme of modifications to the Blue Danube warhead would benefit from two additional experimental detonations at an earlier date. A decision was taken to conduct these proof tests, the Mosaic series, in the Monte Bello Islands, the site of the initial 1952 detonation, in May/June 1956.[24] Detailed arrangements and schedules for these two test series had only just been agreed when, in early August, it was decided that preliminary work should start on selecting a site under United Kingdom control for a third series of tests of megaton-yield weapons, code-named Grapple, which were to start in early 1957. It was accepted that the radioactive fall-out from such a weapon made it impossible to contemplate holding these tests in Australia, and the Line group of islands in the central Pacific, about 1000 miles south of Hawaii, was tentatively selected as the site for them. After an air reconnaissance of the area, a decision was taken in November to use one of them, Christmas Island, to support a continuing series of trials on a regular basis, if its legal status could be clarified. This was necessary because there was a remote possibility of a United States claim to sovereignty over the island. In 1856, Congress passed what come to be known as the Guano Act, under which any American citizen who found phosphate from guano (that is, bird-droppings) on uninhabited Pacific islands gave the President the discretion to annex that territory for the United States. Research indicated that there were no grounds for such a claim in the case of Christmas Island, although the United States had constructed an airstrip there during the Second World War.[25] The need to resolve this issue was partly responsible for the lack of any immediate public announcement of the date and place of the tests, as was the desire not to provoke political protests. But international law demanded that adequate warning of the closure of safety areas in the surrounding international waters had to be given, and as a consequence details were publicly announced on 7 July 1956, well before final design choices had been made and it could be guaranteed that successful demonstration devices were capable of being constructed.[26]

These decisions, taken between May and November 1955, to build facilities at two testing grounds on the other side of the globe, give some indication of the additional resources the political leaders in Britain were prepared to mobilise in support of the objectives that they had set the Aldermaston team. The acceleration of experimental work also led to a limited sacrifice of stockpile numbers in favour of development devices until additional plants to produce fissile material could be built. Such a construction programme was under consideration in early 1955, in parallel with the accelerated schedule for explosive testing. When the decision had been taken in early 1953 to build the two additional plutonium production reactors at Calder Hall, there was an expectation that they would be joined eventually by a further pair which would replace the Windscale installations. A major limiting factor in deciding on the timing of further reactor orders was the supplies of uranium available to Britain, as the planned expansion of American plutonium and U-235 production after 1952 meant that the United Kingdom was inhibited from claiming anything other than a small proportion of the output of Belgian Congo and South African ores, which were being jointly procured under the CDT arrangements with the United States.[27] Britain had no sources of uranium ore other than these arrangements and it was mainly to make the maximum use of the material in its possession that the Capenhurst low enrichment plant had been built. This was commissioned in April 1953, and enabled the slightly depleted uranium recovered from the Windscale reactor fuel cans to be enriched for re-use. By the end of 1952 a total of 3000 tons of uranium had been allocated to Britain by the CDT, compared with a throughput of material in the Windscale reactors of about 600 tons per year.[28] Available stocks were thus sufficient only for about five years operation of these two reactors without recycling, which illustrates both the relevance of the Capenhurst plant and one of the major reasons why no decision was taken to build additional reactors in 1950, when it was first realised that the output from Windscale would be below expectations.

By 1955, the uranium supply position had eased considerably. The United States had started to recycle uranium from spent fuel that had been accumulating since 1945,[29], and was obtaining increasing supplies of ore from Canadian mines and domestic production. The CDT had signed an agreement to acquire the output from four South African mines which were capable of producing 1500 tons annually, while similar agreements had been concluded with Australia.[30] Of greater significance, however, were the 'Mary Kathleen' deposits, discovered in Queensland, Australia in 1954, and destined to become a major source of supply for the UKAEA.[31] Thus by early 1955 the British government could start to plan for an expansion of fissile material production, secure in the knowledge that uranium supply problems were no longer constraints on the future United Kingdom military programme.

The fissile material production position early in 1955 is illustrated by Table 4.1, and Appendix 4b. Annual output of plutonium from the reactors could be expected to rise to about 135 kilograms by 1958, sufficient for about 22 warheads. The high enrichment plant at Capenhurst, when fully operational, could be expected to add a further 20 to that figure, giving an anticipated annual output in 1958 and subsequent years of about 42 physics packages. Yet the military requirements for free-fall bombs, warheads for missiles, smaller, lighter and larger-yield weapons, not to mention thermonuclear devices, suggested that this annual rate of output would be insufficient to meet the demands for fissile material in the 1960s. It would also deprive the V bomber force of adequate stocks of Blue Danube bombs when it became fully operational in the late 1950s,[32] and the maximum working life of the Windscale reactors was also a matter for speculation. All of these factors indicated a need to build additional military production reactors.

Political fears of the need to accede to any international

agreement on a cut-off of fissionable material production for military purposes reinforced these arguments for a rapid and substantial increase in the output of fissile material by the end of the decade. The Cabinet therefore decided to allocate additional resources for the attainment of this objective and in June 1955, the UKAEA was directed to start construction of the two additional reactors at Calder Hall, and a further four at Chapel Cross in Dumfriesshire, Scotland. All were to be of a similar size and design to the two untested plutonium/power reactors under construction at Calder Hall, and all would feed their irradiated fuel into the Windscale works for reprocessing.[33] The effect of this expansion was that annual military output of plutonium could be expected to grow from 50 to 60 kilograms to about 375.[34] This was still only a very small proportion of American output, but it alone could theoretically sustain an annual production of more than 60 Blue Danube warheads per year.[35]

Further extensions to the Capenhurst high enrichment plant were sanctioned at the same time, and the entire fissile material expansion programme was scheduled for completion by 1960. The planned size of the Capenhurst plant was small in comparison to the United States ones, due largely to the belief that a strictly limited proportion of the nation's electrical supply capacity could be preempted for this purpose.[36] A number of ancillary plants were also built, such as those required to convert uranium hexafluoride feed gas from the Capenhurst plants back into uranium metal.[37] Finally, to enable bomb manufacture to move from a 'cottage industry' to an 'assembly line' basis, a purpose-built production and check-out facility was constructed at Burghfield Common Royal Ordnance Factory, close to Aldermaston.[38] This was intended speedily and efficiently to convert the increased supply of fissile material into operational bombs. The entire new construction programme appears to have been aimed at manufacturing sufficient fissile material to enable at least 90 atomic warheads of 20 kiloton yield to be produced each year from 1960 onwards.[39] Yet no significant increase in the weapon stockpile could be expected before 1959 and until then the number of operational weapons would be very limited and their mode of manufacture made their reliability somewhat suspect. The link between these decisions and British official strategic thinking and equipment procurement policy was first spelled out by Macmillan in the 1955 Statement on Defence, although it was not until Duncan Sandys's 1957 version that its full implications began to be grasped by the general public.[40]

Developing New Types of Nuclear Warhead: the Thermonuclear Demonstration Programme

The government made the public announcement that it intended to develop a thermonuclear bomb in the course of Macmillan's February 1955 Statement on Defence.[41] It is still not clear when the relevant Cabinet decision was taken, but it was probably in late 1954.[42] Little research work had been undertaken in support of such an enterprise prior to the run up to the Cabinet's decision, although some British scientists, in particular Fuchs, had participated in the early theoretical work at Los Alamos, and Penney had favoured a concentration on thermonuclear weapon research from the start of the British project.[43] Studies of such a project in 1951 and 1952 had resulted in a decision to concentrate on the development of fission weapons.[44] The United States still had to demonstrate that such a device could be made to work, and there was no guarantee that it could be produced in a weaponised form. Aldermaston had only just been set up as an independent laboratory, and was still in the process of creating an effective research, development and production organisation to meet the RAF requirement for a strategic atomic bomb. To have started a thermonuclear weapon project in 1953 would have prejudiced these efforts, and left the RAF with only a handful of 'laboratory weapons'. In addition, the need to use the Windscale reactors to produce tritium for a thermonuclear weapon development programme would have reduced still further their already limited plutonium output.[45] Cherwell had therefore advised Churchill and his Cabinet in the second half of 1952 that such a programme was 'quite beyond' the nation's means and they had accepted his judgement.[46] Yet two years later, the technical situation had changed considerably. The United States had demonstrated that thermonuclear weapons were feasible. British development work on atomic bombs offered the possibility of constructing effective trigger mechanisms for them and the debris from American and Russian tests offered clues to methods of producing effective weapons.[47] These changes, plus the international pressures for a testing ban, led to Cherwell's earlier assessment being reversed. It was now believed that with an exceptional mobilisation of national resources in support of the project, the United Kingdom could achieve a successful megaton nuclear test before the earliest possible date for a test ban. As a consequence, the political decision was taken to proceed with the enterprise.

The first half of 1955 thus produced a series of decisions on the military exploitations of nuclear energy which led to a transformation of the nature of the project as it had evolved over the previous ten years, and injected a pervading sense of urgency into it. It no longer had a single, finite and limited aim but was concerned now both to develop new types of weapons and achieve a substantial stockpile of operational ones.

Nuclear weapon testing recommenced in May and June 1956 at Monte Bello, with the two proof tests of modifications to the initial Blue Danube warhead design. These involved the minimum of range instrumentation, unlike the next four experiments conducted in late September and October at Maralinga, when many investigations were conducted into the nature of nuclear weapon effects.[48] All these Maralinga tests involved experimental devices whose characteristics were capable of being incorporated into the Blue Danube weapon. Two of the experimental devices were mounted on towers and had a yield greater than 20 kilotons. Two further devices were of a lesser yield, one a ground burst and the other an air burst, and appear to have been intended to prove the system for varying the power of the Blue Danube warhead and to examine the effects of using a small-yield weapon in a tactical context. The air burst involved the first full test of the Blue Danube weapon system, which was released from a Valiant aircraft at 35 000 feet. It was seen to have considerable political significance, as it demonstrated conclusively that Britain possessed an operational nuclear weapon capability.[49]

Maralinga was also the site for three further tests in September and October 1957, code-named the Antler series. Two of them involved devices exploded on towers and the other an air burst of a device suspended below a balloon. These experiments served the dual purpose of furthering the research work into improvements in the yield to weight ratio of nuclear explosives, and of acting as proof tests for the second-generation warhead which was to be fitted to the Red Beard bomb capable of being delivered by tactical aircraft.[50]

The public announcement of the decision to demonstrate a United Kingdom megaton weapon capability was followed by exceptionally rapid progress towards that goal. This is illustrated by the comparative timescales contained in Table 5.2.[51]

TABLE 5.2 *Timescales of US, USSR and UK nuclear programmes*

	US	USSR	UK
Number of thermonuclear devices exploded within 42 months of the political decision to proceed with a programme	1	1	7
Time from political decision to proceed to demonstration of an experimental device dropped from an aircraft (in months)	76	60	28

This exceptionally rapid progress was the result of the improved level of knowledge about atomic and thermonuclear reactions available to the British weapon designers in 1955 compared with that available to their United States counterparts in 1950; the resources deployed into the project from other government research establishments; and dynamic management and leadership. The country's rapidly expanding atomic weapon design knowledge formed an essential basis for the thermonuclear programme. The construction of a primary nuclear device, which triggers off a thermonuclear reaction, demands a mastery of advanced techniques for constructing atomic warheads of low weight and yield, and a significant understanding of nuclear explosive effects. Both the Blue Danube and Red Beard research and development programmes enabled this knowledge to be obtained, and the primaries used in the thermonuclear testing programme were based on their design concepts.[52]

The supply of materials for thermonuclear test devices was resolved initially by using plutonium in the primary devices, and producing tritium in the Windscale reactors from 1955 onwards.[53] When they were shut down in October 1957, following the fire in one of them, production of tritium was transferred to the Calder Hall reactors.[54] In addition, an enrichment plant to produce the lithium 6 isotope used in the production of lithium 6 hydride, one possible thermonuclear fuel, was commissioned at Capenhurst during the mid-1950s.[55]

The creation of a viable design concept for a thermonuclear device, within the short timescale dictated by political impera- tives, meant that the development strategy had to involve short cuts and high risks, with the exploration of a number of alterna- tive lines of development in parallel to insure against failure of some of them. Designs of the initial experimental devices were frozen at an earlier stage than was normally desirable in order to meet the political timetable, and this, plus the general impetus behind the project in comparison with the American situation after 1953, accounted for its rapid progress.

The thermonuclear experimental devices were tested by ex- ploding them at 15 000 feet following an airdrop from a Valiant bomber flying at 39 000 feet at a range of 30 to 40 miles from Malden Island, which was itself 400 miles south of Christmas Island. The presumption must be that these experimental warheads were fitted into a Blue Danube bomb casing, as this would have predictable ballistic properties. The tests were organised in this manner to prevent contamination of the base areas and to minimise local and global fall-out, both of a physical and political nature.[56] Although the mode of delivery gave the impression that a production weapon was in the final stages of testing, the devices were actually 'laboratory weapons', and the purpose of the programme was to examine a number of different design concepts along lines similar to the United States Castle series of experimental detonations in 1954.[57]

The first test explosion occurred on schedule on 15 May 1957, and two further experimental configurations were tested in the course of the next month, followed by another in November. An indication of the difference between the potentials of the early atomic and thermonuclear devices can be obtained by compar- ing the approximately 20-kiloton yield of the Hurricane assem- bly, and the 10 000 lb weight of Blue Danube, with the megaton yields generated by the thermonuclear assemblies from similar or reduced total weights. The experimental devices also seem likely to have been much lighter than the equivalent United States ones exploded in the Castle series. Two sources suggest that the yields of the first three devices were much less than predicted and may have only been in the high kiloton range.

Hasty redesign, however, produced a megaton yield in November.[58]

Once the political objective of appearing to explode a megaton device had been achieved, the central objectives of the explosive testing programme became the design of an efficient production weapon which would be resistant to Soviet countermeasures, including nuclear weapons exploded in anti-aircraft roles; which could be carried by the Blue Streak missile; and which offered greater yields in relation to the fissile and fusion materials incorporated in them than in the initial devices.[59] Five further tests, involving almost 6000 personnel, took place near Christmas Island in April, August and September 1958; three air drops of possible production designs resulting in individual yields of approximately ten megatons,[60] and two tests from tethered balloons involving explosions in the kiloton range. These latter tests appear to have been experiments with primary devices, probably involving boosting, but were also linked to the design for a small third-generation atomic weapon capable of tactical use. Macmillan, who was both British Prime Minister and Minister for Atomic Energy at the time, noted on 29 May 1958, prior to the second of these tests, that 'if all goes well, we shall need only two explosions; but if (as is very possible) we have failure in the new and very special system which we want to test, we shall need two more ... if we give up now we shall *not* have a reliable weapon or one which the enemy cannot neutralise'.[61]

Similar technical concerns are also reported to have permeated discussions with the United States during 1958 and on 20 August Macmillan sought assurances from Eisenhower that amendments to the 1954 Atomic Energy Act, which had just been agreed by Congress, would 'permit the exchange of "full information" on "vulnerability" of the bomb ... [This] is essential for we believe that otherwise the bomb can be "minimised".'[62]

A test on 23 September 1958 proved to be the last British atmospheric explosion, as a US–USSR–UK moratorium on all nuclear testing, and negotiations on a testing ban, started on 31 October and lasted through to 1961.[63]

Although the United Kingdom had tested seven thermonuclear devices since May 1957, the weapon designers still had several tests they wished to perform to perfect production warheads, particularly ones intended to be fitted to strategic missiles, and the testing programme was terminated solely for political reasons.

The effects of the international and domestic political pressures for a testing ban had thus been accurately assessed by the British political leadership in late 1954, and this had enabled the Aldermaston weapon design and development teams to be provided with sufficient resources to acquire the experimental information needed to produce a number of thermonuclear devices in the four years between the anticipation of a ban or moratorium on nuclear testing and its implementation. By October 1958, the United Kingdom was in possession of proven thermonuclear design concepts capable of generating megaton yields, but considerable further effort was necessary to translate this knowledge into a manufacturing programme to meet the RAF's need for optimised physics packages for gravity bombs and warheads for the Blue Streak and Blue Steel missiles.[64] In addition, it had also acquired knowledge to enable a third-generation advanced tactical weapon to be constructed.

A testing ban had first appeared imminent in June 1957, when both Eisenhower and Dulles, his Secretary of State, had publicly stated that the United States was willing to accept such a ban, providing it was coupled to a parallel agreement on the termination of weapon manufacture. In July the United States delegate to the UN Disarmament Subcommittee, meeting in London, formally proposed that there should be a ten-month test suspension, during which it was hoped that agreement could be reached on a test monitoring and inspection system, and a halt made to the production of nuclear weapons. The Soviet Union responded by proposing an extended test ban, but no curb on weapons manufacture.[65]

The British government, under intense domestic pressure to cease testing, had no choice but publicly to support the United States proposal, yet ministers were probably relieved that Soviet opposition prevented the plan being agreed, as if the weapon cut-off proposal had been immediately implemented it would have left the United Kingdom in possession of some 20 completed Blue Danube weapons and two thermonuclear test devices. Macmillan described this situation as 'the terrible dilemma in which we find ourselves, between the Scylla of test suspension and the Charybdis of "cutoff" of fissile material'.[66]

The Soviet objective was to achieve a test suspension without any limitations on weapon production, as their leadership, in common with that of Britain, viewed nuclear warheads as primarily political in their effects, rather than war-fighting weapons that had to be perfected and shaped for specific military tasks and roles. As a consequence, they rejected a succession of United States proposals during 1957 which attempted to link a test suspension with wider disarmament measures, and then, on 31 March 1958, announced that they were unilaterally suspending nuclear weapon testing and called upon the United States and United Kingdom to do the same.[67] In the meantime, a congressional subcommittee on disarmament chaired by Senator Humphrey had been holding hearings at which the idea of accepting a separate test ban, backed up by an international inspection and control system, had been strongly advocated. In April Eisenhower proposed that technical discussions be initiated on the inspection system for a future test ban regime, and accepted explicitly that future negotiations on this issue would be separated from those on a cut-off in weapons production.[68] This led eventually to the agreement that there should be a testing moratorium from the end of October, when negotiations were to start on a comprehensive treaty banning all nuclear tests. As a consequence, the attention of the superpowers became focused upon efforts to achieve agreement on this treaty,[69] and the objective of terminating weapon production receded into the background, though the existence of such proposals reinforced the determination of the British government to acquire a substantial stockpile of operational nuclear bombs as soon as possible.

The means to achieve this objective were being constructed during 1957 and 1958 at Calder Hall and Chapel Cross. The first two reactors at Calder Hall went critical during 1956 and their plutonium started to emerge from the Windscale reprocessing plant by the second half of 1957. The second pair were completed during 1958, while the first Chapel Cross reactor achieved criticality in December 1958 and all four were operating by the end of 1959.[70] For a short period of time following the Windscale fire in October 1957 the first pair of Calder Hall reactors were the only plutonium production ones operative in Britain: the Windscale reactors were never restarted, as the Calder Hall type proved to be very efficient military plutonium producers, and the necessary modifications to the Windscale ones made their further operation uneconomic.

The public announcement, in June 1955, of the increase in the number of military production reactors occurred some four months after a government White Paper had been published, laying out a programme for the construction of civil power reactors by commercial companies, using Calder Hall technology. This plan proposed the building of four stations with twin reactors of the Calder Hall type, followed a little later by four with larger, modified designs of reactor, and finally by four with liquid-cooled reactors giving a total capacity of 1500–2000 Mw(e) by 1965.[71] In March 1957, following the Suez crisis and an acute oil shortage, this target figure was increased to 5000–6000 Mw(e). By 1958 three civil magnox stations (Berkeley, Bradwell and Hunterston) were under construction with reactors of 530–555 Mw(th). The next five stations with larger reactors ranging from 840–970 Mw(th) (Dungeness, Sizewell, Trawsfyndd, Oldbury and Hinkley Point) were at the stage of detailed design. There is no evidence to suggest that the initiation of this civil programme was motivated by anything other than a belief that these stations would assist in overcoming the contemporary energy shortage in a manner which would also place Britain in the forefront of an important area of industrial development, and there was no initial expectation that they would have any direct military role. On 1 August 1957, however, the Paymaster General, Mr Maudling, stated in a written parliamentary answer that three of the new civil power stations were being modified to enable them to operate on a military fuel cycle, in order to provide an insurance against future defence requirements.[72] Five weeks earlier, the *Economist* journal had reported that four stations were to be modified in order to provide additional plutonium for the production of considerable numbers of tactical atomic weapons, including missile warheads. It had also forecast that the eight Calder Hall type military production reactors would collectively produce about 300 kilograms of plutonium a year.[73] Each of the three stations under consideration for operation on a military cycle were in the second batch of reactors rated at about 900 Mw(th), and collectively they would be capable of producing about 1200–1400 kilograms of weapon grade material annually after commissioning in 1963–4.[74] Thus, if the British government decided to follow the United States lead and manufacture nuclear weapons for a number of tactical roles, the use of thé three civil power stations as weapon-grade plutonium producers would enable military material output to be expanded from approximately 300–400 to 1500–1800 kilograms per year, permitting annual nuclear warhead production to be trebled, if not quadrupled.[75]

It was clear that if this plan was to be implemented, the existing reprocessing plant at Windscale would have insufficient capacity to deal with the 8–12-fold increase in the quantity of irradiated fuel that could be expected to be produced by the operation of these reactors on a military fuel cycle. As a consequence, work started in 1957 on the design of a new plant of greatly increased capacity. This plant, known as B205, was completed in 1964, and was equipped to process 2400 tonnes of used fuel per year.[76]

The British military nuclear programme was thus poised to make a rapid transition from the art to the article at the end of 1958. The programme for increasing fissile material production was about to come to fruition, and steps had been taken to enable it to be expanded even further from 1964 onwards. Yet the existing nuclear stockpile was miniscule compared with the contemporary United States inventory, probably numbering no more than 50 bombs, despite increasing numbers of RAF strategic bombers.[77] Steps had been taken to increase bomb production, but the thermonuclear and tactical weapon explosive testing programmes had been suspended before their planned completion, due to the long-anticipated agreement on a nuclear testing ban. The possibility also existed that agreement would be reached on a cut-off of weapon production, and this made the rapid achievement of the stockpile target of about 200 bombs a matter of the utmost urgency if the country was not to be left in a disadvantageous diplomatic (and military) position. Fortunately, assistance in this task, and the completion of thermonuclear weapon designs suitable for production, was to be forthcoming from the United States.

6 The Making of an Atomic Alliance

Hopes, Disappointments and United States Domestic Political Intrigues: Anglo-American Nuclear Negotiations, 1953–6

Early in 1953, the casual observer might have been forgiven for believing that excellent prospects existed for renewing the wartime Anglo-American nuclear relationship. Churchill was Prime Minister of Britain, and he judged that a diminution in the independence of the national nuclear project was an acceptable price to pay for new cooperative linkages. The only non-negotiable items were the independent research and development base and a small stockpile of bombs stored in Britain under national control: the art was more important than the article.[1] The new Republican President, Eisenhower, was known to believe that Britain had been unfairly treated in 1946, and he had had close links with several British Cabinet Ministers, notably Macmillan, during the war. He was supported by a Republican majority in Congress: the omens appeared to be propitious. Moreover a covert exchange of intelligence data on the Soviet atomic programme had already been organised through meetings of a group of British and American nuclear scientists, code-named the Nomination Committee.[2]

But it was not to be. Although attempts were made by British political leaders to negotiate on nuclear issues with the new administration, it was clear by late 1954 that the amended United States atomic energy legislation would permit little change in the existing situation. Also, Eisenhower had antagonised members of the JCAE by appointing Strauss to the dual positions of chairman of the AEC and presidential adviser on atomic energy, thus undermining the independent position created for that organisation in the 1946 legislation, and challenging the role of Congress in the making of atomic energy policy. The tensions created by this appointment were compounded by the existence of a deep-rooted political conflict

111

within Congress over the strategy to be adopted by the AEC for the development of civil nuclear power plants. From 1950 onwards, the AEC had been conducting studies into alternative designs for civil power reactors, but the new Republican administration proposed leaving all industrial-scale development of this power source to private industry, in line with its general policy of encouraging greater 'privatisation' of the energy supply network. In contrast, many Democrats favoured the maintenance of federal control over nuclear energy development and the use of federal funds to support the building of prototype power reactors. This division was further exacerbated by the Dixon–Yates controversy, which was sparked off by a contract to permit the AEC to build a conventional power station for the supply of electricity to domestic users, in return for certain of the Tennessee Valley Authority (TVA) hydroelectric installations being used to power the AEC's new uranium enrichment plant at Paducah. Democrats were hostile to this idea because it reduced the role of the 'New Deal' TVA, while some Republicans argued that it would constitute a further act of federal 'socialism'. As a consequence of these activities, Congress appeared unlikely to accept any proposals for a radically different nuclear relationship with Britain and, whatever his personal aspirations, this constrained the President from instituting initiatives to change the situation. Moreover, the Democrats regained control of Congress and obtained a majority on the JCAE in the elections in late 1954, leaving a Republican administration facing a Democratic Congress, whose initial acts included the cancellation of the contentious Dixon–Yates contract.[3]

The 1946 United States Atomic Energy Act contained no provision for private ownership of nuclear plants. It had to be amended before civil nuclear power plant design and development for domestic utilities and overseas customers could commence, although the AEC was to remain the owner of all nuclear fuel used by private operators. In parallel, the administration had engaged in two external nuclear energy initiatives, which necessitated legislative changes. In December 1953 Eisenhower proposed in his 'Atoms for Peace' speech to the UN General Assembly that an international agency should be created to promote and regulate the development of the peaceful uses of nuclear energy.[4] He also informed Churchill, at their

Bermuda conference in the same month, that he believed it was in America's interests to pass sufficient information on its nuclear weapons to the NATO allies to allow them to train their forces effectively for nuclear warfare. Legislation to achieve these objectives was included in his 'state of the union' message to Congress, recommending that 15 amendments should be made to the 1946 Act.[5] This led Churchill to publish the full text of the 1943 Quebec Agreement, in the belief that it would assist the administration in its negotiations with the JCAE.[6]

The administration had grouped its amendments to the 1946 Act into two draft bills, one dealing with international and security issues, the other with domestic concerns. The JCAE chairman and vice chairman, Cole and Hickenlooper respectively, decided to amalgamate these two measures to facilitate their passage through Congress, so JCAE staff were instructed to draft a completely new bill to replace the 1946 Act. A revised, committee-sponsored version of this resulted from political 'horse trading' between Democrat members wishing to prevent private industry from acquiring technical information owned by the AEC free of charge, and Republican members advocating both isolationism in external affairs and the preservation of the 'secrets' of the atomic and thermonuclear bombs.[7] The JCAE then lost control of the legislation in the full Congress as a result of its links with a parallel dispute over federal policies on public energy supply systems. After considerable amendment, the bill was passed by the Senate on 16 August, and the Atomic Energy Act of 1954 become law two weeks later.[8]

The Act's international provisions enabled the President, with JCAE concurrence, to share data with allies on the external characteristics of nuclear weapons and their yields: he could also set up procedures for them to receive the benefits of the peaceful applications of atomic energy.[9] These transfers were to be initiated through bilateral 'Agreements for Cooperation', which would only become operative after being laid before the JCAE for 30 days, during which time hearings could be held upon them and objections registered.[10] The AEC would then draw up its own federal legal rules to govern the transaction. The 1954 Act did not permit any interchange of nuclear design information with allies, but positive advantages accrued from the ability to conclude 'Agreements for Cooperation'. These were executive agreements rather than treaties, and thus any future Anglo-American arrangements for nuclear cooperation need not be ratified by either two-thirds of the Senate or a majority in both Houses of Congress: they would merely need presidential and JCAE approval.

The next move was to open negotiations for the signing of such agreements with America's wartime nuclear allies, Canada and the United Kingdom. Meanwhile, Secretary of State Dulles had been actively lobbying the NATO states to incorporate American nuclear weapons into their war plans. This resulted in the adoption of a declaratory policy of being prepared to use nuclear weapons to defeat any Soviet conventional attack upon Western Europe at the December 1954 NATO Council of Ministers.[11] In parallel, the British Cabinet had concluded that the imminence of nuclear testing and weapon production restrictions made it imperative to accelerate its nuclear weapon development and production programmes, rather than continue to wait for a major breakthrough in Anglo-American relations which might make these actions unnecessary.

Negotiations with the United States to maximise the limited opportunities offered to Britain by the new legislation reached fruition on 15 June 1955, when parallel civil and military 'Agreements for Cooperation in the Use of Atomic Energy' were signed in Washington. The civil agreement[12] was comprehensive, but specifically prohibited any interchange of data which was judged to be of military significance,[13] or was not 'relevant to current or planned programmes'.[14] This excluded military power reactors and isotope separation plants, although heavy water and U-235 could be supplied under the agreement, provided it was for civil research purposes.[15] Information on reactors was to be exchanged on the basis of reciprocity.[16] The military agreement[17] was considerably more restrictive and less detailed than the civil one, and held out the prospect of an expanded dialogue only in the areas of atomic intelligence and coordination of planning for nuclear attack and defence.[18] Its initiation enabled Her Majesty's Government to obtain some assurance that American targeting plans included the destruction of those Soviet military capabilities which were regarded as most threatening to Britain.[19]

The implementation of these civil and military agreements soon ran into difficulties, due largely to the chaotic and non-purposive nature of the American legislative processes surrounding the 1954 Act. This appeared to have assigned ultimate political and legal authority over military nuclear exchanges to the President, but it was silent on which agency was to recommend action in this area. The civil situation was even more confused, as the State Department had no clear role in the process of negotiating such agreements for cooperation, the AEC had to function as both a promotional and regulatory agency in relation to them, while the JCAE believed it had a positive policy-making function in this area, because the AEC could not spend any money from its budget unless the JCAE approved. In practice, atomic energy had become a no-man's-land, with both the President and the JCAE asserting a right to make policy, while the AEC was sandwiched between them.

The signing of the military agreement led to a meeting between British and American representatives at Quantico, near Washington, in mid-1955, at which it was agreed that the United Kingdom should be given details of the size, weights and attachment systems of American nuclear bombs, thus ensuring that the V bombers could be adapted to carry them if future circumstances permitted.[20] Such information had been made the legal property of the AEC by both the 1946 and 1954 Acts and, in December 1955, the Department of Defense requested that it be transferred to the UKAEA in order to implement the agreement.[21] The commissioners refused on the grounds that the 1954 Act gave them no legal authority to do so,[22] thus initiating a prolonged dispute over which organisation was authorised to determine areas for military interchange with other states. Two substantive issues were involved. The first was whether the AEC could legitimately overrule a Department of Defense judgement that the exchange would strengthen United States security. The second arose because the two parts of Section 144b of the 1954 Act were contradictory, and if the more restrictive part was regarded as dominant, little interchange was possible.[23] The AEC took the view that only weapons essentially similar to those which the United Kingdom had itself developed could be discussed with the United States,[24] and even then, no weapon design information could be exchanged. The President chose not to intervene in this conflict, or exercise his legal authority over military issues, thus creating a decision-making vacuum. This situation remained unresolved until 1959 when Eisenhower made an Executive Order which delegated his powers to the Department of Defense and the AEC acting jointly, and specified that he should only be involved if they disagreed. It also made the Secretary of State responsible for the negotiation of Agreements for Cooperation.[25] Whether this order was a consequence of the departure of Strauss from the atomic energy scene in mid-1958 is unclear. Thus the limited scope for dialogue offered by the 1954 Act rapidly diminished once the AEC chose to place restrictive interpretations upon its language.

The desire of the American military services to discuss with their British counterparts operational aspects of collaboration in the nuclear field was also the cause of disputes concerning the civil agreement within the United States' governmental system. The USN's first nuclear submarine *Nautilus* had been handed over on 22 April 1955, its development having been pushed through by the then Captain Rickover, USN, with strong support from the JCAE.[26] The Subcommittee on Agreements for Co-operation of the JCAE chose to regard nuclear submarine propulsion reactors as a new 'secret' of the atom, and during the hearings on the two Anglo-American agreements, members insisted that this technological lead should be preserved for purely national exploitation,[27] and wrote a provision into the civil agreement which specifically prohibited any discussions involving this technology.[28] In parallel, the Defense Department had asked the Attorney General for a confidential opinion on whether it was legal for the AEC to transfer information on submarine technology to other states. He concluded that data on military power reactors could be exchanged, as the new military agreement with Canada made provisions for such transfers linked to the continental early-warning radar system, but he declined to offer an opinion on the specific case of submarine reactors. The JCAE was informed of this opinion in January 1956, but made no response.[29]

Soon afterwards the Attorney General sent a further letter to the Secretary of Defense and the AEC chairman stating that, in his opinion, the 1954 Act gave legal authority for information to be exchanged on submarine reactors, but suggesting that no action should be taken without the informal approval of members of the JCAE.[30] Events had by then moved on, as initial discussions on such a transfer had occurred at the highest level between the Royal Navy and the USN in November 1955 when

Admiral Lord Mountbatten, the First Sea Lord, visited Admiral Burke, the Chief of Naval Operations in the United States. Mountbatten told Burke that the Royal Navy was actively planning to acquire a fleet of nuclear submarines as enriched uranium for fuel would be available from Capenhurst after 1956, and he offered to support the USN's aspirations in this field in return for technical assistance.[31] He may also have invoked an informal interservice agreement on the exchange of different types of submarine technology which was allegedly concluded in 1953.[32] The visible result of his visit was that a British naval liaison officer joined the United States Polaris project team: the hidden consequences were that the USN chose to drive through submarine technology exchanges with Britain despite known opposition from the JCAE. Negotiations between the Department of Defense, the AEC and Britain were therefore opened with the objective of drafting an amendment to the 1955 civil agreement specifically to authorise exchanges of information on nuclear propulsion technology.[33] The JCAE was kept in ignorance of this move, and to exacerbate the situation, the civil agreement, unlike the military one, specified that all exchanges were to be on the basis of reciprocity; yet Britain had no information to exchange, as it had undertaken little research and no development work on this type of reactor.[34]

The situation was complicated both by Strauss's dual role and Captain Rickover's linked position within the USN and AEC. Rickover was the manager of both the navy's and the AEC's submarine reactor development branch and the AEC's Shippingport civil power reactor project,[35] and was also the centre of a battle between the JCAE and the navy over his promotion to Admiral, with the latter wishing to retire him.[36] He and the JCAE tended to view all these activities as interrelated, and thus any transfer of submarine reactor information to Britain was also regarded by the JCAE as a transfer of civil power reactor data.

There was considerable controversy within the Democrat-controlled committee concerning nuclear power development work, and the AEC was the somewhat reluctant sponsor of a Power Demonstration Reactor Program. The JCAE was not convinced of the effectiveness of this initiative, and the Gore–Holifield bill was introduced into Congress by the Democrats in the middle of 1956 to legislate for an expanded programme of federally funded power demonstration reactors, one of which was to be a gas-cooled graphite-moderated design similar to that at Calder Hall. This bill was passed by the Senate, but defeated in the House.[37] Thus any transfer of civil power reactor data to Britain without reciprocity was certain to generate hostility within the JCAE. No legal duty existed for Britain to pass information on Calder Hall to the AEC under the 1955 military agreement, as its status as a military production facility excluded it from these exchanges. Such information could not be requested under the civil agreement, however, because this arrangement was based on reciprocity, and the United States had no civil magnox-type reactors under construction. In addition, detailed information on the design of specific civil power reactors being built for the CEGB and SSEB was the property of the consortia of companies constructing them, and not the UKAEA, unlike the American position, where the AEC owned all nuclear information. Thus the British government would have to gain access to this information before it could exchange it. The subtleties of this 'Catch 22' situation escaped most JCAE members, and their disquiet at the apparent British ability to obtain something for nothing was reinforced by the widespread publicity given to the claim that Calder Hall was the world's first nuclear power station.[38] American opinion in general, and the Republican members of the JCAE in particular, were convinced that the United Kingdom had forged ahead and gained a dominant position in the potentially lucrative world nuclear power plant market by unfair 'socialist' methods of state subsidy. In this fertile soil, the idea took root that Britain was obliged to reciprocate the unilateral transfer of nuclear submarine technology by providing information on her civil power technology. At the same time, the Democrats on the JCAE continued to press for the construction of a large plutonium/power reactor at Hanford, which was eventually built in two stages from 1958 onwards as the 'N' reactor.[39]

It was against this background that negotiations on a draft agreement to transfer United States submarine technology to the United Kingdom were concluded in June 1956, and Strauss submitted its text, written in the form of an amendment to the 1955 civil agreement, direct to the President for his signature. JCAE members first heard about it at a special Excutive Hearing of the Subcommittee on Agreements for Cooperation on 8 June, just prior to the President signing it on 13 June.[40] It was then officially laid before the committee for the statutory 30 days on 15 June.

Not surprisingly, several members of the JCAE were outraged by these events, for the amendment had arrived towards the end of the session in a presidential election year, and bore all the hallmarks of political sharp practice. At least one member claimed that the amendment was illegal under the 1954 Act, and, on 25 June, AEC Commissioner Murray notified the committee that he disapproved of it because of inadequacies in British security procedures. Excutive session hearings were held on 9 July, to receive material on both the security and legal objections to the amendment, and on 17 July the issue was raised on the Senate floor. On 23 July a report on British security procedures was submitted to the JCAE,[41] and three days later the full committee decided to request the President not to implement the agreement until investigations were completed. However, Congress adjourned the next day and did not reconvene until 3 January 1957; meanwhile the Middle East War, the Suez intervention and the presidential elections had occurred. In January 1957 there was also a change in the British political leadership, with Macmillan, the architect of Britain's nuclear defence policy in 1954 and 1955, replacing Eden as Prime Minister. Eisenhower made no move to implement the submarine agreement during this period, but on 5 February 1957 he informed the chairman of the JCAE that the Secretary of State, the Secretary of Defense and the chairman of the AEC had been instructed to initiate the exchanges.[42]

The conflict over the 1956 amendment to the Anglo-American civil agreement was, in retrospect, a very significant turning point in the relationship between the JCAE, AEC, Defense Department, State Department and the administration. For the first time since 1946, the four latter organisations had banded together in a determined attempt to open up an exchange of nuclear information with Britain in the face of active opposition within Congress. The tactics used were rather crude, not to say opportunist, but they underlined a new-found determination to evade the congressional stranglehold on those international actions on nuclear energy which the administration judged essential for national security.

The JCAE's hostile reaction to these tactics revolved around two procedural points. First, the provisions of Section 202 of the 1954 Act, which stated that the Commission was to 'keep the joint committee fully and currently informed with respect to its activities', had been ignored;[43] second, the JCAE's 30-day monitoring powers under the 1954 Act had been demonstrated to be ineffective as the President had implemented the amendment despite several members' vocal opposition to it. The immediate consequence of this action was to create hostility to further Anglo-American collaboration and to make even worse the relationship between the members of the JCAE and Strauss. The JCAE were determined to reassert their legal powers over such agreements for cooperation, and this was to have a potent influence upon future Anglo-American negotiations.[44]

Submarines and Sputniks

The Suez intervention of November 1956 had a traumatic effect upon Anglo-American relations, as it demonstrated not only that there were situations in which British and American external policies and interests might differ, but also that Britain's capability for independent military action was very limited in the face of superpower hostility. In addition, the widespread domestic opposition to the action, led by Labour MPs, broke the post-war consensus on external security policy and proved as inhibiting as the superpower pressures and hostility.

The reaction of leading members of the Conservative Party was to argue that Britain either had to restore its ability to act independently of the United States, or to take steps to prevent a Suez-type schism recurring, to heal the political breach as rapidly as possible, and to recognise that no British government could now take effective independent military action without tacit American support. The policy of the new Prime Minister, Macmillan, was to satisfy the first school of thought by continuing to support the 1954–5 plans to accelerate the national development of the military applications of nuclear energy, while attempting to negotiate a closer security relationship with the United States, inspired by the Churchillian vision of an integrated defence community. Macmillan was assisted in this process by his close personal ties with Eisenhower, having been the latter's political adviser for part of the Second World War, and he was soon able to reestablish an effective Anglo-American dialogue at the highest level. The result was an incremental process in which collaborative ties with the United States in several defence-related fields were slowly expanded. This trend concealed a number of reverses and difficulties, and culminated in a dramatic change in American nuclear policy towards Britain following the politically significant Soviet technological achievement of launching the world's first artificial earth satellite. It was also characterised by fragmentation of American policy-making in the atomic energy area, and difficulties in turning high-level Anglo-American decisions into working-level arrangements.

The incremental process was preceded by a positive decision to continue seeking collaboration with the United States, rather than adopt an alternative policy of assistance to France. In 1955 France requested British help in building a gaseous diffusion plant for separating out U-235. This appears to have found a favourable response amongst some of the older British scientists and engineers, who recalled the contribution made by the few outstanding French scientists to the wartime Canadian reactor project. The request was ultimately rejected, probably on the political grounds that the United Kingdom government would not assist in the likely proliferation of nuclear weapons, but the episode made both America and Britain very sensitive to the danger of the French regarding Anglo-American cooperation as a form of unjust discrimination directed against them.[45]

Five separate sets of Anglo-American discussions connected with nuclear energy were taking place by late 1957, involving a wide range of personnel. They were dominated by the attempts of the two sets of military services to work out mutually acceptable methods of improving their capabilities *vis-à-vis* the common adversary, the USSR, this objective now being seen by the United States Department of Defense to outweigh any considerations of maintaining a monopoly over nuclear secrets. The first of the areas of discussion concerned the implementation of the amendment to the civil agreement, giving Britain access to United States nuclear submarine technology. Commissioner Murray's assertions about the inadequacy of British security procedures meant that this issue had to be tackled first when moves were made to implement the agreement in February

1957 but then, in Admiral Rickover's words, 'we gradually gave them the information'.[46] 'A group of 25 leading engineers and scientists from British industry and from their Admiralty ... spent two weeks in the United States.'[47] The idea was that Britain would use the information obtained to assist its submarine reactor design programme which had restarted in 1956.[48] Unfortunately, the visit produced considerable friction caused by accusations that some of the representatives of the British firms involved were using the opportunity to obtain commercially valuable information from Westinghouse, the major American submarine reactor building company, for use in civil reactor development.[49] The link between the American submarine reactors and their land-based power reactor programme made such suspicions almost inevitable. In addition, Admiral Rickover, while committed to the idea of the United Kingdom acquiring United States submarine reactor technology, was understandably concerned that attempts by British firms to obtain detailed technical information through his project management organisation were going to divert it from the priority task of progressing the USN's nuclear reactor programme. He argued that 'if we acceded to any extent to requests of that kind, we would be tying up our people and we would not be able to do our work'.[50]

Neither side appears to have felt that the procedures for this initial interchange were satisfactory. The Royal Navy pressed for the stationing of numerous permanent liaison officers in the AEC and Navy Department: Rickover complained that British attempts to obtain information threatened to delay work on USN projects. By December 1957 relations had deteriorated to the extent that, according to Rickover, 'the British naval attache delivered an unsigned, undated letter to the Navy Department, stating that they were not getting adequate information from us. We finally resolved that issue.... Lo and behold, as soon as they agreed to that with the Navy Department, it was taken up with the Atomic Energy Commission, the same thing.'[51]

Despite these problems, the United States Navy leadership was still strongly committed to assisting the Royal Navy to create a nuclear submarine force, and exporting this technology to other interested allied states. Such an offer was made to the NATO allies in the course of the December 1957 NATO summit meeting in Paris.[52] In the same month Admiral Rickover held discussions in London with representatives of the Royal Navy at which he argued that friction would be reduced if Britain dealt directly with the commercial firms developing and building American submarine reactors. He reported that he had 'suggested to them, and they have bought, the idea that they would make a commercial arrangement ... to buy a complete submarine propulsion plant from an American company on a purely commercial relationship, and install it themselves in the submarine they were building in England'. He further observed that the Royal Navy was 'currently spending about $7 million a year on their nuclear submarine development, and at that rate, it will take many, many years before they are ready'.[53]

This proposal was discussed and accepted by the British Nuclear Submarine Advisory Committee in March 1958, with Admiral Rickover in attendance.[54] The potential savings in time and money were substantial, and from the United States perspective it meant that the exchange could proceed with a minimum of interference to their own programme, while still achieving the objective of creating a submarine reactor building capability in Britain in the minimum possible time.[55] Accordingly, it was decided formally to request that the British government should be allowed to purchase a submarine reactor from a United States commercial company. As the existing atomic energy legislation gave no legal authority for such a transaction, Congress would have to make appropriate amendments to the 1954 Atomic Energy Act before it could proceed. Its willingness to do so was no doubt influenced by public statements made by Rickover, who argued that the primary role of such reactors was to power submarines designed to destroy those Russian boats which carried offensive missiles.[56] Since Soviet cruise or ballistic missile firing submarines travelling to firing stations off America's eastern seaboard would have to pass through waters which Britain was anxious to dominate for reasons of her own security, any enhancement of the Royal Navy's ability to destroy Russian submarines in the Eastern Atlantic and Norwegian Sea would automatically reduce the nuclear threat to the Continental United States, and thus be a direct contribution to the strengthening of America's own territorial security.

The RAF was engaged in two areas of collaboration with the United States Air Force in the mid-1950s related to nuclear weaponry. The first was the procurement of ballistic missiles. Britain had under development the Blue Streak intermediate range ballistic missile (IRBM), powered by a licence built version of the rocket motor developed for the USAF's Atlas intercontinental range ballistic missile (ICBM). Its inertial guidance system was also of American origin.[57] Blue Streak was not expected to be available for deployment until the early 1960s, yet there had already been a Soviet threat to fire rockets with atomic warheads at Britain during the November 1956 Suez Crisis. This, and the British government's 1955 decision to embrace fully the idea of preventing attacks upon the United Kingdom by a policy of strategic nuclear deterrence, made the Macmillan Cabinet anxious to deploy IRBMs in Britain as rapidly as possible. At the same time, the USAF was engaged in the competitive development of the Thor IRBM with the United States Army, using components already developed for the Atlas ICBM,[58] but its restricted range necessitated it being sited in Europe, if it was to have an operational role. A suggestion that Thors should be based in Britain emerged from these diverse sources and pressures.

Preliminary discussions between the RAF and USAF took place in December 1956, and an agreement in principal to proceed with the deployment was reached between the two Defence Ministers in early February 1957. This agreement was then ratified by the US President and British Prime Minister at their Bermuda conference in March.[59] The precise terms of the agreement took some time to negotiate as the AEC's interpretation of the information exchange provisions of the 1954 Act made it difficult at first to hold detailed discussions on storage and safety of the warhead and methods of joint control over the complete system.[60] The initial proposal was that the Thor squadrons would be manned by the USAF until RAF personnel were fully trained, but this merely heightened British determination to obtain some form of direct control over them. The arrangements finally agreed in February 1958 were that the United States would supply the missiles free of charge, and the RAF would provide the infrastructure services, and would man and maintain them. The warheads would be supplied by the United States, and remain totally in United States custody on the bases until orders were received that the missiles were to be readied for firing, thus complying with the legal requirements of the 1954 Atomic Energy Act.

British and American officers had separate firing keys for each missile, and both had to be inserted before its engines would start. This was termed the 'double key' system and it ensured that the governments of both states had to be in agreement before the missiles could be fired.[61] British ministers were at pains to stress, however, that their government was free to mount indigenously designed and manufactured warheads on these missiles at some future date, should it choose to do so, in which case the control system would be modified by discontinuing the United States firing key.[62] This agreement acted as the prototype for later arrangements under which the United States supplied strategic nuclear delivery systems to the United Kingdom on favourable terms. It also meant that the deployment of the Thors in Britain in 1959 would require modifications to the 1954 Act if the operational arrangements were to be effective.

The second area of USAF collaboration with the RAF concerned both the targeting plans which the two forces intended to implement in the event of war with the Soviet Union, and the ability of the V bombers to carry American nuclear bombs. In November 1954, 'no arrangements had yet been made to specify which enemy targets, especially those most important to the United Kingdom, would be dealt with immediately by American bombers'.[63] Progress was limited because the USAF was forbidden by the AEC from disclosing details of United States weapon yields and numbers. The first British nuclear bomber squadrons became operational in 1956, but it was apparent that it would be some years before an adequate inventory of nuclear weapons would be available to arm all aircraft in the new force. This made access to American weapons imperative if its military potential was to be exploited fully in the event of global nuclear war. At the Bermuda conference in March 1957, however, agreement was reached on both an expansion of joint intelligence activities and the formal initiation of military planning, though no mention of this appeared in the communiqué.[64] Subsequently, Eisenhower appears to have directed the AEC to allow information on nuclear weapon dimensions and weights to be transferred to Britain to ensure that the RAF could carry American hydrogen bombs in its modern strategic bombers, and the United Kingdom reciprocated with similar information on its designs.[65] During 1957, interchanges between RAF Bomber Command and SAC expanded, direct communications links were created and, in

November, an initial exchange of ideas on operational planning and targeting occurred.[66]

The collaborative activities of the United States Navy and Air Force, plus the expansion of nuclear intelligence activities stimulated by the 1955 military agreement and the 1957 Bermuda meeting, reinforced the pressures from within the Department of Defense for a much wider interchange of nuclear information with Britain. To enhance this process, American observers were invited to attend the three nuclear test explosions linked to the Red Beard development programme scheduled to take place at Maralinga in September and October 1957.[67] Yet the USAEC, the legal owner of nuclear information, continued to insist that their very restrictive interpretation of the 1954 Act and thus the 1955 agreements was correct. They were also engaged in a struggle with the Department of Defense to reconcile their duty, embodied in the atomic energy legislation, to sustain civilian control and custody of nuclear weapons with the emerging military realities of a deterrence system geared to preventing surprise attack by being in a state of instant readiness for retaliation, which implied always keeping a proportion of the nuclear bomber force fully armed. In addition, one of the USAEC commissioners, Thomas Murray, was openly hostile to Britain's acquisition of thermonuclear bombs, as he believed it should concentrate its efforts and resources in developing and producing small-yield atomic weapons for tactical use.[68]

The dialogues between the two sets of armed forces on nuclear issues were paralleled in the period 1957–8 by two further interdependent interchanges between American and British political and atomic energy leaders. Declassification conferences provided convenient initial vehicles for meetings of the leading atomic scientists and engineers. They enabled Cockcroft to visit Washington in May 1956, and discuss the British and American programmes to develop civil power plants fuelled by thermonuclear reactions,[69] a series of six conferences being held on this topic between October 1956 and March 1958.[70] In June 1957, a further civil agreement was signed to facilitate the exchange of information on power reactors. This covered 'the Calder Hall and various American experimental reactors in addition to other areas of cooperation between the two countries'.[71] In practice, if not in theory, this agreement was viewed as being linked to the submarine reactor agreement, and it encountered considerable criticism in Britain as it was argued that 'immediately valuable commercial information is being exchanged for information about a reactor system that is only suitable for military usage'.[72] However, the United Kingdom still refused to transfer data on Calder Hall's magnox fuel cans under this agreement, and continued to argue that information on the reactors being built for the CEGB and SSEB by the commercial consortia was outside its terms as this data was not owned by the government but by the companies concerned.[73]

Discussions at the highest political levels continued to be underlain by suspicions that each side was attempting to take advantage of the other. Although the Bermuda conference in March 1957 had been followed by a widened dialogue on nuclear energy matters, hopes of an early initiative by the administration to produce a more positive allied division of labour in this area, by pushing permissive amendments to the 1954 Act through Congress following the first British H-bomb tests in May, soon faded. Fears that the Bermuda agreement would prove to be yet another false dawn were heightened when Mr Stassen, the United States representative at the UN Five Power Disarmament Subcommittee, submitted a proposal to this international forum in June for an early end to the production of fissile material for military purposes, without consulting the British government. It then transpired that the State Department had not been consulted either! Throughout the period since 1955 Stassen, the presidential adviser on disarmament, and Dulles, the Secretary of State, had been feuding over who was responsible for United States policy-making on disarmament, and this fissile material cut-off proposal appears to have been an independent initiative by the former.[74] Macmillan's reaction to the proposal was not surprising, given the background to the acceleration in the British military programme. He wondered whether it was 'America's reply to our becoming a nuclear power – to sell us down *before* we have a stockpile sufficient for our needs? Some of my colleagues suspect this.'[75]

This event brought to the fore the underlying distrust of United States intentions which had been a constant feature of the wartime and post-war nuclear relationship and had been reinforced by the Suez episode. However, Eisenhower rapidly disowned Stassen's actions, and Plowden, the head of the UKAEA, who had been having talks in Washington on a new civil agreement, was able to confirm that the initiative had not originated within the AEC. Macmillan saw Stassen on 18 June and made it plain to him that, while Britain was in favour of an ultimate ban on testing and a cut-off of fissile material production, these would be 'fatal things for us if they came too soon'.[76] The situation was further complicated by a Russian proposal for a two- or three-year internationally supervised moratorium on testing. This was only acceptable to Britain if it could be postponed until such time as the testing of new design concepts for hydrogen bombs and tactical weapons could be completed. Fortunately for Macmillan, the USSR's rapid rejection of Western counterproposals swiftly removed this difficulty.

Nuclear testing was to be debated at the autumn session of the UN General Assembly, and Strauss, the AEC chairman, visited London on 9 October to formulate a common Anglo-American position in anticipation of the UN debate. On 4 October the USSR launched its first Sputnik, which was seen by many Americans as visible evidence that the United States was being overtaken by the USSR in technological capability. Macmillan used this event to urge the President, both directly and via Strauss, that 'countries of the free world should try to pool their resources to meet the increasing threat'.[77] Eisenhower's response was to ask Macmillan to visit Washington immediately, and Dulles, in conveying the invitation, hinted that some amendment to the 1954 Act was being contemplated. Macmillan and his Foreign Secretary arrived on 23 October, and the next day the President held a meeting of the National Security Council to approve proposals for a full interchange of information on military applications of nuclear energy with Britain. Two joint Anglo-American committees were instituted, one concerning weapons systems and the other nuclear collaboration, while a pledge to amend the 1954 Act was included in the Declaration of Common Purpose which served as the communiqué for the meetings.[78] An immediate result of these developments was that Britain invited two United States' observers to attend its fourth thermonuclear test on the 8 November.[79] Thus a Russian 'peaceful' satellite, the close personal relationship between Eisenhower and Macmillan, a decade of patient negotiations, and six months of increasingly detailed technical interchanges resulted in a decision that was to have considerable consequences for future British nuclear weapon development and production. The issue now confronting the United States administration, however, was how to obtain congressional approval for the legislation which would give legal authority for the negotiation of the new nuclear alliance.

A month later, a final item was added to the list of amendments that Congress would be required to make to the 1954 Act. The leaders of the NATO states, meeting in Paris, agreed not only to sanction formally the deployment of American tactical nuclear weapons in Western Europe, but also to support the idea that an earmarked NATO stockpile of United States nuclear weapons should be created. This stockpile would be held in American custody in peacetime, as required by the 1954 Act, but could be transferred to individual West European states, for use with their own delivery systems, once an attack had occurred.[80] The move was intended to discourage allied states from spending scarce military resources on nuclear programmes that merely duplicated US capabilities by offering many of the deterrent benefits that possession of independently developed nuclear weapons were alleged to offer. Its implementation necessitated the transfer of additional information to NATO states on weights, dimensions, fusing systems and attachment points for American nuclear weapons, hence the need for revision of the existing atomic energy legislation.

The Ideas behind the Nuclear Alliance

The high priority accorded by Eisenhower to revising the American atomic energy legislation was underlined by the attention devoted to it in his State of the Union message on 9 January 1958, in which he stressed that it was '... wasteful ... for friendly allies to consume talent and money in solving problems that their friends have already solved'. On 27 January, bills incorporating the proposed amendments were introduced in both the House and Senate, and referred to the JCAE Subcommittee on Agreements for Cooperation, which started hearings on them two days later.[81] The JCAE was also holding hearings on two further issues: the proposed EURATOM Agreement for Cooperation and the AEC's Power Demonstration

Reactor Program, and issues arising from one set of hearings had a tendency to spill over into the others.

The amending bills were intended to give the President discretion and authority to sanction four types of activity which were illegal under the 1954 Act: passing additional information to allies to enable them to deploy American nuclear weapons on their own delivery systems in the event of war; physically transferring to allies military nuclear power plants, their fuel and certain non-warhead components of nuclear weapon systems, such as bomb attachment mechanisms;[82] physically transferring to allies who were nuclear weapon states 'special nuclear materials' for all types of military and non-military uses, and non-nuclear components of nuclear weapons;[83] and exchanging detailed information with an allied nuclear weapon state in order to improve its weapon design, development and production capability. The legislation permitted the implementation of four sets of Anglo-American nuclear arrangements whose nature had already been discussed informally at official level. Their overriding purpose was to make the most effective use of the resources which both states were devoting to the military applications of nuclear energy.

The first set of arrangements concerned the supply of fissile materials and fusion fuel, and were based upon the complementary needs and outputs of both states for three nuclear weapon materials: uranium 235, tritium and plutonium. It was recognised that the relatively limited throughput of the Capenhurst high enrichment plant, plus the high cost of coal-fired electricity production in the United Kingdom compared to hydroelectricity in the United States, would result in British unit costs for U-235 being at least three times their American counterpart.[84]

The Royal Navy's aspiration to construct a nuclear submarine fleet and the need for fissile material to construct substantial numbers of thermonuclear warheads also meant that military demand for U-235 from Capenhurst was likely to exceed planned output levels throughout most of the 1960s. Tritium production plants had been built in Britain, linked to the operations of the Windscale and Calder Hall reactors, but the unit costs of producing nationally the gram quantities of this material required for nuclear weapons were much greater than equivalent figures for American output, which was being produced at annual levels of several kilograms in the much larger American plants at Savannah River. It thus made economic sense to import these products from the United States if a reciprocal flow of materials could be arranged to pay for them. Fortuitously, the potential for this existed within the British civil nuclear programme. The CEGB and SSEB magnox power reactors, which would be commissioned from 1962 onwards, were based on the Calder Hall design, and were thus producers of substantial quantities of plutonium, even when optimised for electricity production. Plans were being discussed to modify certain of them to operate on a military fuel cycle, but in any event the operating cycles of these civil reactors would result in substantial quantities of plutonium containing high percentages of Pu-239 being produced in the initial years of their operations. [85] By mid-1958, civil power stations of some 5000 Mw of thermal capacity were under construction, with capacity for another 11 000 Mw at the planning stage.[86] Although the United States had plutonium production reactor capacity of approximately 25 000 Mw in operation, there was no federal programme to build operational civil reactors other than demonstration models, and thus almost all the plutonium being produced and separated there was earmarked for its weapon programme.[87] While the AEC was producing sufficient U-235 to meet all America's military and civil needs, doubts were being voiced about the adequacy of its plutonium production capacity, especially in view of the commitments to build up the NATO stockpile and to supply quantities of this material to West European states under a EURATOM agreement for non-military research.[88] Thus the motivation and potential existed for a mutually beneficial trade in fissile materials, with the USAEC supplying the UKAEA with both highly enriched uranium, for military weapon and submarine propulsion purposes, and tritium, for tactical and megaton warheads, in exchange for supplies of British plutonium.[89] A more extensive trade in fissile materials with America's allies had originally been envisaged, under which 11 000 kilograms of plutonium, including some obtained from the civil power and experimental reactors exported to European states and Japan under the 'Atoms for Peace' programme, would be available for unrestricted civil or military use under the 'buy-back' provisions of enriched uranium fuel supply contracts. However, this plan was strongly opposed by the State Department, on the grounds that it negated the aims of the 'Atoms for Peace' initiative, while Japan had refused to participate and had requested substitute fuel supplies from the IAEA.[90] The diplomatic advantage of an arrangement with the United Kingdom was that its reactors were not part of either the 'Atoms for Peace' programme or the EURATOM agreement.

These trading proposals also facilitated the formulation of a common Anglo-American policy on the cut-off of fissionable material production for military purposes, which the United States was strongly advocating. Both states could now vigorously press for a complete cut-off, secure in the knowledge that neither of their military nuclear programmes was likely to be seriously disadvantaged in the unlikely event that the USSR was to agree to the proposal. The Capenhurst, Oak Ridge, Paducah and Portsmouth (Ohio) enrichment plants could be converted to the production of civil reactor fuel with little effect upon either state's military position, as the United States had a stockpile sufficient for all foreseeable military purposes, and adequate reserve stocks could be imported into the United Kingdom before any international agreement came into effect.[91] The Windscale, Hanford and Savannah River reactors would cease to operate, but the British CEGB and SSEB reactors were civil power reactors and could be expected to continue to function under international supervision, as could Calder Hall and Chapel Cross. They would provide the Western allies with an ability rapidly to restart fissile material production for military purposes, should a cut-off agreement break down, while both polonium 210 and tritium production remained outside the scope of these negotiations.

One curious aspect of these proposals is that part of the justification for the trade, and the pricing policy inherent in it which was presented to the JCAE, was that Britain had intended to use its plutonium to enrich the fuel for its new generation of advanced gas-cooled (AGR) civil power reactors. Although this proposition was useful in convincing the JCAE that the plutonium had considerable value to the United Kingdom, as in its civil role it was claimed it would have to be replaced by low enriched uranium, it played no part in the detailed intergovernmental negotiations.[92]

The second set of collaborative arrangements resulted from Britain's recognition that her resources in the nuclear weapon field were limited, and there was no point in reinventing warhead designs which were already in production in the United States. For some types of nuclear weapon, reliance would have to be placed upon the new NATO stockpile arrangements. Britain agreed that it would not attempt to develop nuclear artillery shells or nuclear warheads for US-supplied short-range artillery rockets, nor produce nationally all of its requirements for nuclear bombs and depth charges, but would rely on these armaments being made available by the United States in the event of hostilities under the standard NATO arrangements.[93] To assist in this process, information to enable British delivery systems to carry these weapons would also be exchanged. This military division of labour had the effect of reducing the quantity of fissile material required for British national nuclear weapon production, and also served as an additional justification for exporting this material to the United States, as directly or indirectly it would be assisting America to provide NATO with its nuclear stockpile in Europe.

A third area of collaboration concerned the interchange of both nuclear warhead (that is, physics package) design information and non-nuclear components for similar types of nuclear weapons which had been developed independently by both states. The interchange was restricted initially to those types of fission and fusion bombs which were specified by the United States, but the United Kingdom could expect in the future to acquire nuclear information relevant to any new type of weapon which it had under active development. It was anticipated that Britain would also wish to purchase non-nuclear weapon components from America, either because they were cheaper due to the longer production runs there or because they were more immediately available. The United States would also have the opportunity to use British-designed components in its own weapons.[94] In addition, it was envisaged that, to save money, Britain might be supplied with complete sets of non-nuclear components for certain standard fission weapons, but would have to manufacture the fissile cores for these weapons itself, as the guiding principle of all American atomic energy legislation was, and is, that no complete nuclear weapon could ever be transferred to another state in peacetime.[95] However, these 'do-it-yourself' kits were to be restricted to atomic weapons.[96] In addition, both states would monitor the development of each other's strategic delivery systems, and would have the option of purchasing or licence-producing either complete systems or some of their components.[97]

The fourth set of understandings related to the transfer of the submarine reactor and its fuel to Britain in return for the transfer of information on the design of the Calder Hall fuel cans.

The overall package comprised a balanced set of Anglo-American arrangements, under which both states could increase their national nuclear capabilities, and those made available to NATO, at a reduced cost in money, resources and scientific manpower. Britain could embark on a revised and considerably less expensive nuclear and thermonuclear weapon production programme, and would also attain its stockpile targets much more rapidly than previously envisaged, as well as expediting its nuclear submarine programme. The United States would, after about 1963, gain access either directly or indirectly to additional supplies of plutonium for its small weapons programme, without investing in additional reactors and reprocessing facilities, and could obtain full information on the prototype of Britain's civil nuclear power plants. There were no proposals for exchanges of information on existing production facilities for U-235 or plutonium, other than the Calder Hall reactors, as neither side had a pressing need for them and both were aware of the commercial possibilities inherent in these technologies.[98]

There appears to have been no expectation among the American weapon designers that Britain's nuclear warhead technology would assist the United States own programme, as American information on British progress was misleading. They anticipated that these technological exchanges would have a similar asymmetrical quality to those on nuclear submarine reactors, and, given this context, the United States motivations in embarking upon these arrangements appear to have been remarkably generous. It was understood that once the agreement had been implemented, the United Kingdom would continue to develop nuclear weapons and carry out research independently of the United States, but both countries would maintain close liaison on similar projects on a 'need to know' basis and there would be a continuing technological exchange in certain component areas. There was to be limited British dependence upon America in a number of areas of fissile material and non-nuclear component supply, and in the acquisition of strategic and tactical missile delivery systems.

Amending the 1954 United States Atomic Energy Act

It would have been surprising if the amendment bills and their associated collaboration arrangements had been accepted by Congress without question, and the AEC-sponsored draft rapidly ran into difficulties within the JCAE Subcommittee examining it. The attempt to change Section 55 of the Act to allow the AEC to purchase British plutonium on the basis of a long-term contract encountered the greatest difficulties. It was planned that the AEC would create a $200 million 'revolving fund' to finance the Anglo-American trade in fissile materials, though the precise mechanism envisaged remains somewhat obscure. There is a strong suggestion that the money was initially to be lent to Britain, which would then use it to pay for some or all of the enriched uranium and tritium purchased from the AEC prior to 1964. Receipts from this transaction would then be used to purchase plutonium produced in Britain. This procedure would have the effect of making the transaction a virtually cost-free exercise for the United Kingdom government.

Hostility to this proposal arose from a number of sources. Some committee members asserted that the United States should be self-reliant in the production of fissile materials, while others opposed it on the grounds that it was a political device to enable the AEC to evade the JCAE veto over its expenditures which had been inserted into the 1954 Act.[99] It was also alleged that such a contract would give the British state-sponsored nuclear industry commercial advantages over United States enterprises. The proposal then became entangled in the acute conflict that already existed between the JCAE and AEC over the latter's civil Power Demonstration Reactor Program (PDRP). Parallel committee hearings were taking place on this issue, focusing upon whether the AEC should build and own power plants, and the degree to which domestic and foreign sales of them by private firms should be subsidised through the price of American enriched fuel and the buy-back price for the plutonium in used fuel rods.[100] Claims that UKAEA only valued plutonium at $10–$11 a gram, but were negotiating the sale to the AEC on a $30 per gram price basis, led to allegations that Britain would obtain huge windfall profits from the arrangement and that it would subsidise the economics of the United Kingdom's gas-cooled graphite-moderated magnox reactor designs. This contradicted the AEC's own policy on domestic nuclear power development, based upon the same section of the 1954 Act, where the 'plutonium credit' was calculated at $12 a gram with the AEC persistently refusing to quote any 'military' plutonium price.[101] The proposed price of $30 a gram was therefore alleged to be a direct subsidy to foreign commercial competition.[102] The State Department also publicly opposed the arrangements, because both civil and military receipts from enriched uranium sales would be paid into the same revolving fund, thus discrediting the concept of 'Atoms for Peace'.[103] After threats to block the passage of the bill and attempts at compromise, those parts of the proposed legislation relating to the AEC's long-term contracting power and the revolving fund were withdrawn,[104] though the right to trade in fissile material remained, so long as the JCAE concurred with any contractual and financial arrangements that resulted.

The Democrat-dominated JCAE extracted a domestic price from the AEC for agreeing to permit these transactions, as the latter had to accept that the United States had a need for additional supplies of plutonium. The JCAE was thus able to force upon it the construction of the 'N' reactor at Hanford, which was to be designed so as to accept an 'add on' power-generating plant at a later date. In this way, the JCAE succeeded in initiating the building of a power reactor based on similar plutonium/power concepts to Calder Hall, though its thermal capacity was 4000 Mw as compared to the 200–268 Mw generated by the British military reactors and the 950 Mw produced by the second generation of magnox civil reactors which started construction in 1959–61.[105]

Additional controversy arose from allegations that the wording of the proposed bills could be used by the Executive branch to transfer components for nuclear weapons to a non-nuclear state: a 'do-it-yourself' kit for creating additional nuclear powers.[106] Although this was strenuously rejected by the AEC witnesses, certain members of the JCAE, still embittered by the dispute over the 1956 nuclear submarine information agreement, were determined to deny the Executive any possible freedom to adopt such an interpretation. The bill was, therefore, amended by the JCAE to make it clear that any nation which was the subject of such transfers had to have made 'substantial progress' in the development of atomic weapons, this being defined as possessing the plant to produce materials for a number of types of bomb, and having successfully tested such weapons.[107] Only Britain met these requirements, though some concern was voiced as to how the Executive would judge whether and when France had done so.[108] The revised wording meant that transfers of equipment to non-nuclear states were restricted to missiles and guns, minus their warheads or shells, and attachment equipment for bombs.

The belief, held by some members of the JCAE, that the prospective Anglo-American arrangements would give disproportionate benefits to the United Kingdom, and would amount to little more than a unilateral transfer of technology and materials from the United States to Britain also created difficulties. Attempts were made to investigate this assertion by seeking to obtain judgements on the value of the weapon design information likely to be obtained from Britain, but it was pointed out that such an evaluation could only occur after a full exchange of information had taken place. The lack of reciprocity in the submarine reactor agreement was also criticised,[109] though this was diffused by hinting at an implicit link between this exchange and the willingness of the United Kingdom to use the civil agreement to transfer details of the Calder Hall's magnox fuel cans.[110] None of these objections and criticisms ever extended to direct opposition to military cooperation with Britain, however, and their motivation was a suspicion that military assistance would be converted into disproportionate commercial benefits by the United Kingdom's state-owned nuclear industry.

A further area of diplomatic delicacy was provided by the intention of the legislation to discriminate against France and in favour of Britain. Only Admiral Rickover was prepared to state publicly that he favoured nuclear cooperation with Britain and no other European ally,[111] and it was clear that the members of the JCAE Subcommittee were very concerned at the possibility of France acquiring nuclear weapons, not least because of the perceived instability of its political system during the period when the Fourth Republic was being replaced by the Fifth.[112] The problem was thus how to word the legislation to avoid giving a French government grounds for either arguing that their state was being unfairly treated, or for claiming immediate nuclear assistance from the United States.

The final area of criticism arose out of the submarine reactor saga, and concerned the procedures under which the JCAE could review Agreements for Coorperation. The original bill was amended by the Subcommittee to allow such agreements to lie before Congress for 60 working days, rather than the 30 specified in the 1954 Act, and to prevent their implementation if Congress passed a concurrent resolution of disapproval.[113] Thus all future agreements would have to have at least the negative acquiescence of Congress before they could be implemented.

These controversies over parts of the amending bill delayed its passage from the JCAE to the full Congress until June. Meanwhile, the USSR had announced a unilateral suspension of nuclear weapon-testing, and called upon the other nuclear states to do the same, thereby placing the United Kingdom government in a difficult diplomatic situation. Strong domestic political forces in Britain continued to press for a suspension, and despite opposition from Strauss and the Department of Defense, the President had decided to support a separate test ban in early June.[114] Yet the scientific advice received by Macmillan was that the earliest date for testing a British thermonuclear design concept which was both reliable and resistant to technical countermeasures was September.[115] It was believed that the United States had such a design, and if the amendments to the 1954 Act were passed by Congress, a new military agreement was ratified and the relevant information transferred to Britain, Macmillan would be in a position to support the test ban.[116] Until this happened, the British leadership felt it had no option but to stall the Moscow initiative and attempt to continue with its testing programme. Macmillan visited Washington in early June, conscious that, unless the amendments to the 1954 Act were passed into law by Congress in the first week of July, the adjournment of Congress in early August would prevent the new Anglo-American military agreement from being laid before Congress for the full period prescribed by the legislation, and it would thus not be implemented until Congress reconvened in February 1959.[117] The progress of the amending bill was discussed by the Prime Minister and the President in a series of meetings between 7 and 8 June, and a provisional military agreement was negotiated which would be laid before Congress as soon as the bill was passed. In addition, the two leaders 'initialled an agreement about the use of bombs or warheads under *joint* control. So far as the bases are concerned, which the Americans have in England, this regular agreement replaces the loose arrangement made by Attlee and confirmed by Churchill.'[118]

The bill was passed to the full Congress in June, where it was amended further by both the House of Representatives and the conference of both Houses. The purpose of these amendments was to prevent any possibility of the President sanctioning the transfer of non-nuclear parts of atomic weapons to allies other than Britain.[119] It was also emphasised that 'non-nuclear parts of thermonuclear weapons are not to be transferred in the forseeable future'.[120] The bill was eventually passed by both Houses at the end of June and was signed by the President on 2 July. The next day a new Anglo-American Bilateral Agreement for Military Cooperation was formally concluded in Washington.[121] It was approved by the JCAE after brief Executive hearings and came into force after the 30-day period which applied only to the 85th Congress: for the 86th and subsequent Congresses it was to be 60 days.

In mid-1958, 12 years after President Truman had decreed that nuclear cooperation with Britain should be suspended, the changed international environment, and Britain's progress over the whole field of nuclear energy, had made it possible both to reverse the bureaucratic and political inertia within the United States which had assisted the retention of the 1946 *status quo* on nuclear relations with other states, and to forge a new cooperative relationship. However, the old problems of the conflicting demands created by the need to cooperate in military matters, and the competitive position of both countries in the civil nuclear field, remained, being highlighted by the requirement for reciprocity in exchanges in the latter field, and the commitment to the use of information obtained from military exchanges for defence purposes only. The existence of a complete range of capabilities for manufacturing fissile materials in Britain meant that there was no longer any pressing need for interchanges on enrichment, plutonium production reactors and reprocessing technologies, as equipment to perform these roles was already in operation. In addition, the civil potential of these plants, the technology underlying them and the exploitation of nuclear energy by private companies in both states meant that commercial and industrial property rights, rather than military secrecy, would henceforth be the major barrier to information exchanges on a government-to-government basis. Although the United States had been forced by its 'Atoms for Peace' policy, and the rigorous commercial logic underpinning the AEC's approach to civil reactor development, to refrain from contemplating the active use of its civil reactor types for producing military materials, Britain was in a somewhat different position. Her civil power plants, plus Calder Hall and Chapel Cross, could be operated on a military fuel cycle if a political decision was taken to do so. The ambitious programme of nuclear power station building announced in 1955 was not started overtly with military production in mind, but there seems little doubt that it later proved to be very important in furthering Anglo-American military cooperation. Obtaining access to key aspects of the Calder Hall technology made full military collaboration appear particularly attractive to all parties in the United States, and was of great assistance in convincing members of the JCAE, who had been advocating the AEC's development of a similar reactor, that the new arrangements constituted an equitable bargain. Thus the ambitious civil production programme directly assisted in the transformation of Britain's military nuclear position. Yet ultimately, the decision to reverse the well-established atomic energy policy of the United States was a product of a logic of events which was already moving the President and his advisers in this direction before the catalyst provided by the launching of Sputnik. Amendments to the 1954 Act would have been necessary in 1958 to legitimise the Thor arrangements, the submarine reactor sale, the implementation of the new NATO doctrines on the planned use of nuclear weapons, targeting collaboration between the RAF and USAF, and to deflect British objections to the American decision to alter its policy on negotiating a separate testing ban. The Sputnik episode added urgency to this movement of events, and made it rather easier to convince Congress that it was necessary to take steps to make maximum use of the NATO alliance's nuclear resources. As Macmillan recorded in his diary: 'While this sense of unity and understanding exists between us, we should try to create something definite to leave to our successors.'[122] There is little doubt that between 23–25 October 1957, spurred on by the 'peaceful' Russian Sputnik, Macmillan and President Eisenhower forged the basis for the creation of a substantial stockpile of operational nuclear weapons in Britain at a reduced cost and faster rate than would otherwise have been possible.

7 The Nuclear Alliance in Operation, 1959–63

Initial Exchanges and Arms Control Negotiations

The Anglo-American Military Agreement for Cooperation of 1958 had two substantive articles. Article II concerned the exchange of classified information, which was now to extend beyond the limits specified in the 1955 Agreement and was to include the data required to allow existing and future British delivery systems to be fitted with American nuclear weapons. Exchanges of information on military reactors were now incorporated into the military agreement, while paragraph 13 specified that all types of classified information on atomic weapons could be exchanged if the communicating state believed that this was necessary to improve the recipient's atomic weapon design, development and fabrication capability. Article III specified the terms under which the submarine reactor and a ten-year supply of replacement fuel were to be transferred to Britain. The United States was also to supply information on methods of reprocessing nuclear submarine fuel elements, including information on the design, construction and operation of appropriate facilities. The only other substantive elements in the agreement were that there could be no transfer of fully-assembled atomic weapons between the two states, and that any information received under it was to be used exclusively for defence purposes and was not to be communicated to third parties without mutual consent. This latter prohibition was of indefinite duration. Nowhere in the agreement was reciprocity stated to be the basis of the exchange, unlike the situation in the civil agreement, though mutual advantage had to be involved. This meant that the United States would not transfer information to the United Kingdom unless this was judged to contribute to its own security.

The agreement allowed the two states to commence detailed negotiations on the type of data that was to be exchanged,[1] and a

142

conference of technical experts was convened on 27 August 1958, followed by a second two weeks later.[2] Prior to this meeting, Macmillan had traded British agreement to an American initiative to suspend nuclear testing for a personal promise from Eisenhower that the United States would transfer to the British participants 'full information on "vulnerability" of the bomb and on making small bombs, but with megaton power'.[3] The latter information was imperative if Britain was to design operational rocket warheads without embarking upon a further test series. He regarded this promise as more important and effective than the official understandings but, as in 1943, the existence of high-level agreement on an interchange did not immediately produce the intended results at the working level.

Neither side was eager to be the first to reveal its nuclear secrets when the meeting of experts commenced, and the United States representatives still had little idea of the full extent of British progress. At the end of the first meeting, after three hours of unproductive talks, the British delegation seriously considered returning home. The only alternative appeared to be for the United Kingdom to risk all and reveal details of at least one of its weapon designs. At the start of the next day's meeting, the British representatives described the physics of the device they believed best illustrated the current state of their knowledge. The American representatives then recessed for a ten-minute discussion and returned in a much more optimistic mood. It was indicated that a full and free exchange would henceforth be possible, so long as it could be directly related to problems and weapons the United Kingdom was working on. At the end of this initial round of meetings, Teller, one of the United States weapon designers involved in the discussions, is reported to have said that the remarkable result of the 12-year total separation was that both countries had achieved broadly the same physics understanding, although the greater resources allocated to the United States programmes had given them more sophisticated engineering designs. Two weeks later a more detailed exchange of information occurred, as a result of which it became clear that the United Kingdom had developed certain techniques that the United States did not possess.[4] Thus the result of the interchange was that Britain was able to 'give information on advances in which the American scientists were anxious to share'.[5]

The second area for immediate negotiations concerned the

sale of the submarine reactor and the fuel to power it. The former involved a company-to-company agreement between Westinghouse and Rolls-Royce, who were chosen partly because of their existing links in the aeroengine field. The latter resulted in an unpublished agreement whose details were revealed to the JCAE. This committed the United States government to supply 300 kilograms of highly enriched U-235 over a ten-year period on a 'need to use' basis. Article III of the agreement implied that this uranium would be supplied in the form of manufactured fuel elements, which would only be transferred when it became necessary to refuel the submarine reactor. It was anticipated that the latter could theoretically operate for six months at full power on a single fuel charge, but it was recognised that the 300 kilogram figure was a permissive one, and that in operational use the reactor would not be run in such a manner as to consume its fuel at this rate. It was assumed that Britain would reprocess the used fuel to reclaim the remaining U-235, which would then be manufactured into new fuel elements. The 'need to use' procedure, which was similar to that employed in the civil agreements, involved United States officials having regular access to the reactor in order to ascertain the state of the fuel charge.[6] Unlike the weapon design and production relationship, the purpose of this agreement was solely to create a British nuclear submarine development and production capability, and there was no expectation that the transfer of technology would necessarily continue after the initial ten-year period.

The third area of potential negotiations, the exchange of fissile materials and non-nuclear components, was one in which the initial understandings had been undermined by the JCAE's refusal to allow the AEC to sign long-term contracts. As a consequence, a fresh basis had to be found for these exchanges, and no bilateral agreement covering them could be concluded during 1958, while agreements on the transfer of non-nuclear parts of weapons were premature until both states had explored the detailed nature of each other's designs and made decisions on future production plans.

By late 1958 the objectives that the Churchill Cabinet had set for Britain's military nuclear development programme in 1954–5 had been substantially achieved. A thermonuclear weapon design capability had been created in Britain, and this, plus access to United States information on similar types of weapons developed by both states, meant that it would be possible to start an expanded production programme rapidly. The major pacing item in this expansion was the increased fissile material output expected by 1960. Britain had thus succeeded in passing through the thermonuclear barrier to a position of being able to accept the superpower testing moratorium with equanimity, leaving France and China on the other side. Macmillan and his Cabinet then concentrated on a three-pronged strategy to consolidate Britain's international security position. This comprised the achievement of the national atomic and thermonuclear weapon stockpile goals as rapidly as possible; the signing of a comprehensive test ban agreement and possibly a fissile material cut-off, to achieve the internationalist aims of both a halt in the arms race and the exclusion of further states from the nuclear club; and the pursuit of all measures which would limit the ability of the two superpowers to develop methods of neutralising atomic and thermonuclear weapons, and thus once more relegate Britain to an inferior military position. There were thus positive national security objectives inherent in the vigorous pursuit by Britain of internationalist disarmament and arms control measures after 1958, for these measures were seen as the most effective way of sustaining the military credibility of the British inventory of strategic nuclear weapons. Britain had at last caught up in the qualitative arms race in nuclear technology and did not wish to be rapidly left behind again, as had happened between 1952 and 1954.

The nuclear policies of Britain in the military sphere after 1958 were thus focused upon sustaining the test ban moratorium and attempting to negotiate a comprehensive test ban treaty on the one hand, and on the other, organising the rapid manufacture of a limited inventory of nuclear weapons. The Cabinet specified yields and numbers to be procured and it was the responsibility of the UKAEA and the Ministry of Supply to determine the production arrangements. The UKAEA was involved in activities in three main areas: weapon development, weapon production and fissile material production. The pre-1956 nuclear weapon production plans to meet service requirements had envisaged that as the high enrichment plant at Capenhurst was progressively commissioned after 1956, increased production of Blue Danube bombs with modified warheads, using both plutonium and U-235 as the fissile material, would commence. This weapon would then be replaced on the production line at Burghfield Common by the Red Beard bomb, development of which was substantially complete by 1958. This had a warhead which used the same design concepts as Blue Danube, but offered a significantly better weapon weight to yield ratio. As a consequence a smaller, lighter warhead could be built using less fissile material, and offering the same variation in yields as the Blue Danube one. When married to the bomb casing and fuses developed by RAE, the result was a weapon which almost certainly weighed less than 2300 kilograms and was of sufficiently small dimensions to fit into the bomb-bay of a Canberra light bomber, several hundred of which were in service with the RAF. This meant that these aircraft, with a radius of action at high altitude close to that of the V bombers, could threaten attacks upon Soviet territory if operated from British bases on the periphery of that country, as well as destroy fixed military targets, such as airfields, to the rear of any European battle zone.[7] One major technical change between the Red Beard and the Blue Danube designs was that the fissile core had to be fitted into the newer weapon before flight, rather than in flight.[8] Red Beard bombs carried by the Canberras and V bombers were located internally in the aircraft bomb-bay and the casing had to be substantially altered to make them suitable for external carriage in the Scimitar naval strike aircraft, when the latter entered service on the Royal Navy's carriers in 1959 and 1960.[9] It was originally envisaged that these Red Beard variants would be followed into production by a large-yield fission warhead for the Blue Streak and Blue Steel missiles, but by late 1958 it was accepted that the substitution of a thermonuclear design for the large fission one would both save money and make it unnecessary to manufacture additional quantities of weapon-grade plutonium in the CEGB magnox reactors. Production plans for the services were thus in a state of flux in early 1959 because of both the possibilities for cost-savings offered by the new bilateral agreement, and the options created by the thermonuclear experimental programme for producing nuclear weapons with a wide range of yields, yet utilising reduced amounts of fissile plutonium and uranium.

The initial Anglo-American conferences on the exchange of weapon information were the first steps in a process in which the

British slowly revealed details of all aspects of their existing and projected designs, and the United States representatives discussed those American models which they believed were of interest to the United Kingdom and would 'fulfill a mutual defense need'.[10] Delegations visited each others' research, development and production plants, and the British representatives evaluated a range of United States' non-nuclear components that could be used in existing bombs, as well as a number of American nuclear weapon types which were either under development or in production.[11] As a result, a revised manufacturing schedule for British nuclear weapons was drawn up to cover the period until 1969. This involved a detailed plan to produce specific types and quantities of warheads in the early part of the period, to be carried by delivery systems either under development or in production, and a rather more general schedule covering the latter part. A major feature of this revised plan was its emphasis upon the rapid achievement of the 1948 stockpile figure of 200 strategic bombs. No final decision had been reached by May 1959 on the future weapon programme, particularly on the degree to which American non-nuclear components, either individually or in totality, would be used in future British weapons, but the approximate target figures for the inventory of weapons by yield and type did enable an assessment to be made of the total amount of fissionable material which Britain would require through to 1969.[12]

The 1958 amendments to the 1954 Atomic Energy Act gave authority to the AEC for an exchange of British plutonium for American enriched uranium, even though the original financing arrangements had been vetoed by the JCAE. This resulted in detailed negotiations taking place on both the mechanisms and nature of possible Anglo-American exchanges of materials over the next ten years and British plans to use enriched uranium in weapons and as fuel in submarine reactors. There was an immediate, once and for all requirement for material to be incorporated into weapons, but by the end of the decade it seemed likely that there would also be a small continuing demand for the material as a consequence of the increased numbers of submarine reactors within the fleet and their steady consumption of uranium fuel. In addition, there was a need to possess a reserve stockpile for both of these military applications.

It was envisaged that Britain would obtain American assistance in acquiring supplies of fissile materials at reduced cost in two ways. Plutonium produced in United Kingdom reactors could be bartered for American materials on agreed exchange rates, or they could be obtained by straight purchase for dollars. A major attraction of the barter arrangement over simple cash purchase was that it clearly fulfilled the requirement in the American atomic energy legislation that the transaction would be mutually advantageous. Two technical issues heightened the importance of this exchange: the revised British production programme involved a greater role for U-235 in weapons production and submarine propulsion than had been envisaged in 1955, and consequently the output of the Capenhurst plant would need to be expanded if production targets were to be met on a purely national basis.[13] Secondly, the nature of the new weapon designs was such that by substituting a combination of plutonium and U-235 in fissile cores for plutonium alone, bombs with greater nuclear efficiency could be produced. This meant that if plutonium could be exchanged for U-235 on satisfactory terms, British bombs could be produced at a considerably reduced overall cost.

Agreement was reached by mid-1959 on an exchange of a proportion of the annual output of plutonium from the British reactors for highly enriched U-235 at the rate of one unit by weight of plutonium for 1.76 units of U-235, the total quantities not to exceed a ceiling figure. No foreign exchange costs other than transport charges would be incurred under this arrangement. The AEC's schedule of prices for both plutonium and highly enriched uranium up to the end of June 1963, makes it difficult to ascertain whether the plutonium involved was to be material obtained from a military fuel cycle or a civil one.[14] The United Kingdom also had the option of acquiring additional U-235 for cash rather than by barter after 1964, while the United States could directly purchase British plutonium. The rationale behind this cash purchase option was that the dollar/sterling exchange rate might have moved in Britain's favour by the mid-1960s. Tritium was also to be traded directly for plutonium, or purchased.

One aspect of these arrangements was that the United States appears to have been prepared to accept plutonium produced by the civil reactors when they entered service after 1962, either as a result of having the technical knowledge to use this material in weapons or because it was intended for non-weapon purposes. As a consequence, the plan to alter the CEGB reactors to enable them to operate on a military fuel cycle was reassessed, and it was decided that these insurance modifications would now only be made to the two reactors being designed for Hinkley Point.[15] The 1958 Electricity Act had to be amended to permit the CEGB to operate a military cycle and to produce other isotopes, and this was accomplished in late 1960.[16]

Several options were discussed with the United States representatives as a basis for the trade in nuclear materials, but not proceeded with. Evidence presented to the JCAE in 1959 indicated that initial talks had aimed at 'permitting the exchange of U-235 at 20 per cent enrichment for Pu for unrestricted use on a gram for gram basis'.[17] One explanation for this proposal is that Britain intended to acquire feed material from the United States for further enrichment in the Capenhurst plant. This procedure could in theory have increased the plant's annual production of weapon-grade uranium at least sixfold, thus allowing the output anticipated from 18 years of operations to be produced in three.[18] As American atomic energy regulations drew the line between weapon and non-weapon-grade uranium at 20 per cent enrichment, such an arrangement could have involved an exchange of 'civil' materials only.[19] However, there is no evidence in the public domain to suggest that this type of exchange was ever implemented.

Anglo-American exchanges and purchases of fissile and thermonuclear materials had been made possible by the 1958 amendments to the 1964 United States Atomic Energy Act, but to implement such activities it was necessary to amend the 1958 Military Agreement for Cooperation between the two states. This was an enabling measure, however, and the substance of the relationship was contained in detailed and secret protocols between the two states. These specified the isotopic composition of the materials to be exchanged, the quantities involved and the schedule of deliveries.[20] These documents appear to have covered limited periods of time, and were negotiated, and possibly renegotiated, in the light of revisions in the plans for the procurement of British nuclear weapon types and American tactical nuclear weapons.

The necessity to amend the 1958 bilateral agreement to

provide authority for these exchanges created an opportunity to consolidate in one text two additional Anglo-American agreements, thus completing the formal changes in their nuclear relationship. The first of these additions covered the transfer of non-nuclear components involving weapon design information. The text also provided for the transfer of complete non-nuclear assemblies for atomic weapons, though this possibility was never exploited.[21] The second addition was similar to that negotiated with a number of other NATO allies, including Canada, Holland, Turkey, Greece and West Germany. Its purpose was to transmit sufficient information and non-nuclear equipment to the United Kingdom to enable it to purchase and operate delivery systems which could, in the event of hostilities, be equipped with American nuclear warheads. It was envisaged that use would be made of the equipment transfer provisions to enable Britain rapidly to acquire a thermonuclear weapon delivery capability for strategic purposes. In the longer term, they would allow the acquisition of a wide range of nuclear delivery systems, without Britain having to incur all of their associated development and production costs.[22] The consolidated text covering these amendments was signed on 7 May 1959, and entered into force on 20 July 1959.[23] The amended military agreement had rather complex provisions for terminating the five types of transfer it encompassed, namely weapon information; submarine reactor technology; submarine fuel; fissile and thermonuclear weapon materials; and non-nuclear weapon materials. The transfer of weapon information under Article II could be terminated at any time by mutual agreement, or unilaterally by giving one year's notice to the other party on 31 December 1968, or at the end of each succeeding period of five years. The transfer of submarine technology and fuel under Article III was originally to terminate on 8 August 1968, ten years after the entry into force of the 1958 agreement, but this date was extended to 31 December 1969 by the May 1959 amendment. Finally, the provisions covering the transfer of both nuclear and non-nuclear weapon materials under Article IIIb would cease to be operative on 31 December 1969, unless agreement was reached to extent them. There were no specific provisions for the supply of weapon-grade uranium to fuel British-built submarine reactors. However, since these were all enabling provisions, and the crucial documents were the detailed, secret protocols which specified information to be transferred, and types and quantities of materials and equipment to be traded, the exchange agreements could, in practice, be made inoperative by unilateral action. The obligation on both parties to maintain the security of each other's information was timeless, however, and only capable of termination by mutual consent.

Two further changes were incorporated into the 1959 agreement to modify important sections of the 1958 one. One concerned the patent clauses in Article IX. This extended to the non-nuclear components of nuclear weapons the obligation placed upon each state to give the other free access, for governmental, military purposes only, to any new technology produced as a consequence of an exchange. The second involved Article VII, which regulated the dissemination to third parties of information transferred under the agreement. This specified in greater detail the processes to be followed in the event of dissemination, and extended its scope to include materials as well as information. This latter change masked another element of the Anglo-American nuclear relationship that had its origins in the wartime uranium acquisition arrangements organised through the CDT; in attempts to prevent supplies of uranium reaching the socialist bloc and in the efforts of the United States State Department to formulate a coherent strategy against nuclear proliferation following the 'Atoms for Peace' initiative in late 1953. These activities had coalesced in the creation of a secret international club of uranium suppliers and consumers, where members regularly exchanged information on sales and shipments and attempted to agree a standard policy on the safeguarding rules to be applied to materials and facilities supplied by them to non-nuclear states. A series of technical meetings on this question had been held during 1957 and 1958, mainly in Ottawa, and agreement between the United Kingdom, the United States, Canada, South Africa and Australia on a common policy was reached in London at the end of February 1959.[24] This also formed the basis for the IAEA's first safeguards agreement with Japan, INFCIRC/3 of 29 March 1959 and the more general 'safeguards system (1961)' or INFCIRC/26, agreed on 31 January 1961.[25] In late 1959, France, Belgium and Portugal joined this secret club, which used as the basis for its activities the COCOM list of prohibited nuclear exports to communist countries.[26] The club remained in existence until February 1967, when two of the uranium-supplying states, Australia and South Africa, dropped out and were replaced by technology exporters such as Germany, Sweden and Switzerland.[27] During its period of existence, the raw material suppliers club appears to have held frequent meetings to coordinate policy and exchange intelligence.[28]

The Revised British Nuclear Weapon Development and Production Programme

The 1959 amendments effectively moved control over the details of Anglo-American nuclear exchanges out of the hands of Congress and the Executive into those of lower-level officials in the Defense Department and the AEC, who became responsible for determining which information to release and what material to transfer. As a consequence, future congressional interest in these activities only arose either when parts of the agreement were due for renewal, or when information was received which reinforced suspicions that Britain might be deriving undue commercial benefits from them. The ability to sustain the relationship thus devolved to a level where the mutual respect of two groups of technical experts came to play an important part in its sustenance, together with a certain element of professional solidarity. In particular, the ability of the United States weapon designers to discuss professional matters with their British counterparts was something which, while intangible, appears to have been highly valued in an environment where it was impossible to conduct an open dialogue with groups outside of the government service.

This relationship of professional solidarity was born in the heady months after mid-1958 when both British and American weapon laboratories evaluated each other's designs, and discussed how they could be improved by adopting ideas the other had developed independently. Britain acquired many options for building up its inventory of nuclear weapons as a consequence of this process. These included continuing to use only British-made components and designs; to adapt British design concepts to incorporate American components and materials; to buy complete non-nuclear assemblies for atomic weapons from the

United States and fit British-manufactured fissile cores into them; to anglicise American design concepts using the best components available; to procure and deploy British-controlled delivery systems which could be fitted in wartime with American nuclear warheads or bombs; and to purchase United States nuclear delivery systems and fit them with British-produced warheads. Some of the weapons that resulted from the decisions on these options are still in service. Published data on them from official sources are sparse, but it is possible to construct a picture of what may have transpired from these and other public sources. The existence of functioning national production plants for non-nuclear weapon assemblies and fissile cores led to a decision to continue to produce the earlier all-British designs for a further two to three years. The ability of both the V bombers and the widely deployed Canberra aircraft to carry the Red Beard bomb, together with its more modern design, led to it replacing Blue Danube on the Burghfield Common production line in 1958. The stockpiling of significant numbers of this weapon from 1959 onwards appears to have been responsible for a widely-held assumption that they were production thermonuclear weapons.[29] This was reinforced by positive statements about the production of such weapons in the Defence White Papers of the period.[30]

The variant of Red Beard intended for use from the Navy's large aircraft carriers, when they were operating as part of NATO's strike fleet, took slightly longer to place into production than the RAF version, as it was designed to meet a very demanding operational requirement. The limited storage capabilities of these vessels meant that a single bomb design had to be capable of exploding under water, after earth penetration, on the surface or in the air, and produce low or high yields in the 5–20 kiloton range. This meant that it could be used against submarines or surface ships in a tactical role and against hardened harbour installations, military targets or cities in a strategic one. Production of this bomb for naval use started in 1959.

Until 1965 attempts to arrive at a firm national production programme for future nuclear warheads were complicated by frequent uncertainties and changes in the development programmes for dedicated strategic nuclear delivery systems. Between 1946 and 1955 delivery-system specifications had been dominated by the weights and dimensions of the early physics packages, but by 1960 the position had been reversed, and the bulk of nuclear warhead work was focused upon optimising design concepts to enable them to meet the requirements of delivery systems as cheaply as possible.

Several programmes of this type were in progress at Aldermaston by mid-1959. They included the design of thermonuclear warheads for both the British strategic ground-launched ballistic missile, Blue Streak and the V bomber's air-launched cruise missile, Blue Steel and an anglicised warhead for the short-range battlefield and air-launched strategic versions of the Blue Water ballistic missile, whose yield requirements ranged from a megaton to kilotons.[31] In addition, once design information from the United States had been assimilated, two linked third-generation free-fall bomb designs were being readied for production. The first was a thermonuclear bomb with a fixed yield of about 1 megaton, and the second, a lighter, variable-yield weapon, for use against tactical targets beyond the battle zone.[32] The RAF requirements specified that both these bombs were to be capable of detonation at altitude, following the use of either orthodox or lofted bombing procedures, or at ground level after the use of a 'lay down' technique.[33] These development programmes constituted a formidable workload for Aldermaston, and the situation was further complicated by the existence of the US, USSR and UK voluntary nuclear testing moratorium from November 1958 to August 1961.

Several of these projects were the subject of dramatic cancellations. In April 1960, Britain decided to abandon Blue Streak, its independently designed and developed strategic missile, because of the vulnerability of surface launch sites in the densely populated United Kingdom. Strategic missiles based in underground silos and submarine-launched missiles required access to large solid propellant motor technology not available at that time in Britain. This led to a decision to avoid duplicating United States work in this field, and rely in the medium term on American-manufactured strategic delivery systems.[34] It was formally agreed that Britain would purchase 100 Skybolt air-launched missiles from the United States, and tacitly understood that the Polaris submarine-launched system would be made available at a later date.[35] Development work on a warhead for Blue Streak was reorientated to meet the requirements of Skybolt, and this led to intensive consultations with the United States team developing this weapon, in order to modify a British design concept for the role.

It seems probable that the strategic warheads for Skybolt and Blue Water used similar design concepts, and their parallel development meant that the intention of the British government was to continue to pose a dual strategic nuclear threat from medium and light bomber delivery platforms into the 1970s, with the TSR-2/Blue Water combination taking over the role initially performed by the Canberra/Red Beard one.

Two development programmes that proceeded without interruption were those aimed at freezing the production designs for the advanced tactical weapon, intended primarily for use against military targets, and the linked megaton thermonuclear bomb. The latter's design concept had also been used in the Blue Steel warhead. These bombs weighed 600 and 950 lb (275 and 430 kg) respectively, and the latter was about nine feet long, far removed from the weights and sizes in the original specification for Blue Danube.[36] Although it was not possible to carry out extensive proof tests of production versions of the weapons due to the testing moratorium, data from previous British and American experiments gave sufficient confidence in their design to engage in detailed production planning during 1959. Initial versions of the megaton physics package entered the British stockpile in 1961,[37] with production rapidly accelerating by early 1963, first to provide Blue Steel warheads and then gravity bombs for the V force.[38] As these thermonuclear weapons entered the inventory, the large Blue Danube bombs were scrapped, their fissile materials recycled into the new bombs, and some of their specially built operational storage facilities decommissioned.[39] The same 'boosted' design concept involving tritium was probably used for both the primary fission devices in the megaton weapons and the advanced tactical bomb.[40] The latter was intended to replace the much larger and heavier Red Beard design in both RAF and RN service, and initial production probably started about 1964. As a consequence a single anglicised physics package served as the basis for all the 'third-generation' British nuclear weapons.

Access to United States nuclear weapons under 'key of the cupboard' rules, where the weapons were held in American custody in peacetime, was negotiated after 1959 for certain British-owned tactical and battlefield delivery systems and this had significant political overtones. In 1960–61, three of the RAF's Valiant medium bomber squadrons were assigned to NATO for the tactical bombing role, being equipped to drop either conventional bombs or American-owned nuclear weapons.[41] Britain had ordered the Corporal battlefield missile from the United States in 1955,[42] and this was eventually deployed with the British Army of the Rhine at the turn of the decade, the warheads being stored in United States custody. Honest John missiles were also acquired under similar arrangements. In addition, a conscious decision was taken not to develop nuclear artillery shells or demolition mines, and to rely upon access to the United States NATO stockpile for these weapons. It was also decided to equip British land-based maritime patrol aircraft with United States nuclear depth charges.[43] The political significance of these arrangements was that they enhanced the United States President's ability to control the course of any hostilities that broke out in Europe by giving him a near monopoly over the initiation of the tactical use of nuclear weapons in Europe, as no other NATO state had short-range battlefield nuclear weapons stockpiled on the Continent. However, in practice the position was ambiguous, as Britain remained capable of delivering nationally-owned nuclear weapons on European battlefield targets if its political leadership chose to order this.

Some broad idea of the effects of these production activities on the United Kingdom's stockpile of nuclear weapons is given in Appendix Table A.4c. The maximum output of completed bombs from Burghfield Common, and of fissile cores and non-nuclear components from Aldermaston and Cardiff, occurred between 1959 and 1964 and it led to a rapid increase in the size of the stockpile. Although the figures contained in Table A.4c are totally speculative, they do offer insights into the limited nature of British production activities; their peak concentration within a very short period of time in the early 1960s and the way the different elements in the nuclear production programme dovetailed into each other. They suggest that the size of the British stockpile of strategic devices has remained constant at 100–200 bombs or warheads since the early 1960s, and that the total number of items in the inventory has been considerably less than previously published reports have suggested.[44] One irony arising from these statistics is that it appears that, had the multilateral or unilateral disarmament campaigns of the late 1950s succeeded in achieving their aim rapidly, there would have been few nuclear arms for Britain to relinquish. Indeed, the process of arming Britain with a substantial stockpile of nuclear weapons took place while the CND campaign was displaying its greatest vigour and at a time of intensive international negotiations to halt the nuclear arms race.[45]

Firm and finite production targets had thus been evolved by 1961 to meet Britain's needs. They retained the old idea of a stockpile of about 200 strategic weapons, but added about 50 for maritime use and 200–300 for tactical roles in Europe and elsewhere, supplemented by 100–200 American weapons, available under 'key of the cupboard' rules, for battlefield use in Europe. The substitution of thermonuclear weapon designs for large-yield atomic ones and the dismantling of the Blue Danube weapons was expected to make available considerable quantities of plutonium and U-235 for inclusion in later warhead designs. This, plus the potential effects of material exchange agreements with the United States, invalidated most of the assumptions made in 1955 about the nature and length of Britain's weapon programmes, which had led to the expansion of fissile material production plants. The problem that faced Ministry of Defence and UKAEA officials after 1960 was thus no longer how to expand weapon development and production facilities rapidly, but how to contract them as painlessly as possible to meet the reduced demands, both of the steady state inventory of the 500–700 nationally-owned nuclear warheads planned for the 1970s, and those of the emergent civil nuclear power programme. A 12-year plan was prepared which envisaged a gradual rundown of Aldermaston's development and production activities and a reduction in staffing levels of 36 per cent by 1973.[46] The effect upon the fissile material production plants was even more dramatic and rapid, the complete closure of the military high-enrichment facilities for manufacturing U-235 at Capenhurst being envisaged in 1963, with a rundown period starting in 1962[47] and a switch in 1964 from a military to a civil fuel cycle at Calder Hall and Chapel Cross to optimise electricity production at the lowest possible cost.[48]

Atmospheric Testing and the Search for a Comprehensive Test Ban

Design and production activity related to nuclear weapons was accompanied by vigorous British efforts to halt the superpower nuclear arms race and prevent further nuclear proliferation in the period 1960–4. Although Anglo-American relationships at the working level remained good, especially in the weapon design area, higher-level relations became less harmonious because of differences in perspective over Soviet nuclear activities, the Common Market issue, the reciprocal nature of nuclear linkages and the spillover from American attempts to contain what they saw as the disruptive international effects of France's nuclear programme.

The Democratic administration of President Kennedy replaced Eisenhower's Republican one in January 1961, and this resulted in significant changes in the personnel dealing with atomic energy, including a new chairman of the AEC, Glen Seaborg. There appears to have been a feeling by 1961 that all that the British had to offer in the nuclear weapon area had already been secured, and that henceforth little reciprocity was likely. This led to differing recommendations for action, as some policy-makers regarded the fact that the United Kingdom now possessed no nuclear secrets not known to the United States as a cause for satisfaction, while others felt that the time had come to try to persuade both France and Britain to relinquish their nuclear independence. As a consequence, the new President approved a National Security Council Policy towards NATO on 21 April 1961, which stated that 'it would be desirable for the British, in the long run, to phase out of the nuclear deterrent business, since their activity in this field is a standing goad to the French'.[49] This thrust of policy was reinforced by the decision of Macmillan's government to seek entry to the EEC and EURATOM in early March 1962, and the vigorous negotiations undertaken by Edward Heath to attain these objectives. Macmillan had discussed nuclear cooperation with De Gaulle during the former's visit to France in June 1962, and attempted to convey to the French leader that 'while we might cooperate in some of the details which were within our own control, we could not part with these secrets which we only received from America as heirs of the original founders of nuclear science in the war'.[50] Thus Macmillan attempted to separate the British position *vis-à-vis* the United States from the French one by reference to the period of wartime integration, while at the same time indicating that the comingling of weapon design information had not yet proceeded to the point at which separate cooperative arrangements with France were impossible.

Something of the content of these discussions appears to have reached the United States, and led to fears that Macmillan and Heath would be prepared to pay any price, including the transfer of nuclear weapon design data to France, to persuade De Gaulle to allow Britain to enter the Common Market. These fears were reinforced by Macmillan's attempts during 1962 and the early part of 1963 to convince the President that he should release nuclear weapon information to France in return for De Gaulle's signature on a test ban agreement.[51] Moreover, it has been asserted that the French veto on British entry into the EEC in January 1963 served to increase these American fears of dissemination by a desperate British political leadership rather than reduce them.

The situation over nuclear weapons was complicated both by American attempts to persuade the NATO allies to buy the Sergeant short-range ballistic missile, and by a speech made by Robert McNamara, the United States Defense Secretary, to the NATO council in May in which he condemned national nuclear forces as 'dangerous' and 'lacking in credibility'.[52] The missiles the United States wished to sell to Europe were to be equipped with an American warhead under 'key of the cupboard' rules, and the favourable terms being offered were regarded by Macmillan as the major reason for Britain's inability to sell the Blue Water missile to its continental allies, and the cause of the cancellation of both its land- and air-launched variants in August 1962. This also destroyed the aspiration to develop the TSR-2/Blue Water combination as a supplementary strategic delivery system. The Prime Minister noted that 'to British eyes, the concept of interdependence with the United States seemed to be becoming a somewhat one-sided traffic'.[53]

This worsening in British relations with part of the Kennedy administration was counterbalanced by the particularly close links between David Ormsby Gore, the then British ambassador to the United States, and the President. This is illustrated by Macmillan's own account of the frequent consultations between the two leaders and the ambassador during the Cuban missile crisis.[54] As a consequence of these and other factors, the British government was remarkably successful in constructing a position where it acquired a near-permanent input into the American policy processes over arms control and nuclear affairs. Perhaps the best description of this role is provided by Henry Kissinger. He states that it

involved a pattern of consultation so matter-of-factly intimate that it became psychologically impossible to ignore British views. They evolved a habit of meetings so regular that autonomous American action somehow came to seem to violate club rules ... It was an extraordinary relationship because it rested on no legal claim; it was formalised by no document; it was carried forward by succeeding British governments as if no alternative were conceivable. British influence was great precisely because it never insisted on it; the 'special relationship' demonstrated the value of intangibles.[55]

A major element in Anglo-American nuclear relations during the Kennedy era was the attempt to negotiate a nuclear test ban with the USSR. The initial hopes that this could be accomplished soon after the start of the testing moratorium had been dashed by the failure of the May 1960 Paris summit due to the U-2 affair. Negotiations then became stalemated, and the Soviet Union resumed atmospheric testing at the end of August 1961, while the United States commenced underground testing on 15 September. The question that then arose was whether the United States should also resume atmospheric testing, and if so where? The problem was that the State Department believed that further testing at Eniwetok Atoll would be diplomatically damaging, as it was part of the Marshall Islands Trust Territory which the United States administered on behalf of the United Nations. Their other Pacific testing site was Johnston Island, 500 miles south-west of Hawaii, but this was too small to act as the base for a large series of tests. The obvious alternative was Christmas Island, but this was British and the United Kingdom was publicly opposed to further atmospheric testing. Seaborg, the AEC chairman, discussed its use with Sir Roger Makins, the UKAEA chairman, in London in September, and in the course of the discussions the latter raised the possibility of detonating a British test device underground at Nevada. As a consequence, a link between British access to Nevada and American use of Christmas Island became tacitly established.[56]

Atmospheric testing soon became the subject of direct negotiations between the Prime Minister and the President. Following a speech by Khrushchev to the 22nd Soviet Communist Party Congress on 17 October announcing a 50 megaton test on 31 October and the existence of a Russian 100-megaton weapon, Macmillan attempted to persuade the President to agree to a six-month moratorium on atmospheric testing in the hope that this would lead to negotiation of a test ban agreement.[57] The President rejected this suggestion, and Macmillan then made a formal request to conduct a proof test for the British Skybolt missile warhead at Nevada. There then ensued what was seen by the Americans as an exercise in reciprocal bargaining in that Macmillan was seen to be attempting to dissuade the United States from conducting atmospheric tests by insisting that Britain should have full details of the devices to be tested from Christmas Island and the purpose they would serve. This implied that the United States was being coerced by the United Kingdom to expand the areas within which data on the design of nuclear weapons was being exchanged.[58] The Geneva Test Ban Conference had meanwhile reconvened, though no progress resulted, and on the 29 January 1962 it adjourned indefinitely. An Anglo-American summit meeting had been scheduled for 21 December 1961 in Bermuda, and it was in this forum that the President and the Prime Minister attempted to reconcile their differences over atmospheric tests.

One major question discussed during the Bermuda talks was the military implications of the Soviet multimegaton warheads. On the one hand, Penney, who was attending the meeting as Macmillan's scientific adviser, 'estimated that eight of the existing multimegaton weapons would be enough to "make a terrible mess" of England'.[59] On the other hand, as Macmillan noted 'the last Russian tests are rather alarming. We know that they are working very hard on an "anti-missile" missile.'[60] Macmillan's approach to the problem was succinctly summarised by Seaborg when he noted that:

> [Sir William Penney] felt that both sides might now be forced to attempt setting up an anti-missile defense. This would be a fantastically difficult and costly effort. The Prime Minister was concerned about the piling up of bigger and bigger bombs if the arms race proceeded unchecked. He felt that the UK

on and on piling up sophisticated weapons. Meanwhile, 'everyone else' would have simple Hiroshima-type bombs within twenty-five years. This was an intolerable prospect. Mankind could not go on this way. We had to make another effort to reach an agreement.[61]

Eventually, a compromise was reached under which the President agreed to make a further effort to achieve a testing ban in return for American use of Christmas Island for an atmospheric test series starting in April and continuing to November. Formal agreement was reached on 8 February 1962, but Britain insisted that any testing at Christmas Island had to be a joint venture with United Kingdom participation in measuring weapon effects.[62] Macmillan was clearly very concerned about British domestic opposition to the resumption of tests, and particularly to the British Nevada one, and this, together with his profound belief that the arms race had to be halted, accounted for his strong pressure upon the President to reach agreement with the Russians on a test ban treaty.[63] One consequence of this 'leverage' was that the United States government decided not to request the use of the site when the AEC started to plan for a further atmospheric test series to start in June 1964.[64]

Two Anglo-American tests of British devices related to the development programme on the Skybolt warhead were held in Nevada in March and December 1962, while the United Kingdom had access to data on the 25 test explosions conducted from the Christmas Island base.[65] An ironic side-effect of one of the high-altitude tests conducted by the United States during this period was that an early British scientific satellite (ARIEL) had its communications facilities destroyed by it.[66]

Throughout the second half of 1962 and early 1963, negotiations proceeded with the Russians on a test ban treaty. The British appear to have taken a softer line in these negotiations than the United States, and in particular argued that there was no need for seismological stations in the USSR to detect clandestine tests, and that in any event such tests would not be able to change the strategic balance.[67] The negotiations eventually resulted in the signing of the Partial Test Ban Treaty in July 1963, which imposed no limitations on underground testing.

The next stage in Macmillan's 'Grand Design' was to deal

with the issue of nuclear dissemination and proliferation. This became entangled rapidly in American attempts, starting in December 1962, to persuade the European NATO states to forego national nuclear weapons and participate in a multilateral force, which was to be an internationally-owned and mixed-manned fleet of naval vessels carrying Polaris missiles with American-owned warheads.[68] Although part of the motivation behind this idea was to offer these states a collective strategic deterrent to reinforce their security, it was also aimed at the French, for 'their nuclear weapons program was a net liability to [US] efforts in arms control. It was an embarrassment to the West in negotiations with the Soviet Union and a hindrance in achieving our objective of preventing further proliferation of nuclear weapons capability.'[69] This policy had important consequences for the United Kingdom when, in December 1962, it became necessary for the President and the Prime Minister to negotiate at Nassau over the supply of Polaris missiles to Britain, following the cancellation of the Skybolt development programme by the United States. The numbers of Skybolt missiles to be acquired by the United Kingdom and the stockpile of warheads to be manufactured for them had not been agreed until July, and, as Macmillan noted, 'it was difficult to suppress the suspicion that the failure of Skybolt might be welcomed in some American quarters as a means of forcing Britain out of the nuclear club.'[70] The outcome of these negotiations was that Macmillan agreed that British Polaris missiles and the submarines to carry them, together with some of the RAF's bombers, were to be assigned to a new NATO nuclear force.[71]

The net outcome of this confused period of alliance and arms control negotiations was that a test ban treaty to prevent the development of anti-missile missile systems using high-yield, high-altitude thermonuclear explosions had been achieved, and thus some assurance had been obtained that existing British thermonuclear weapon technology would remain militarily viable for many years ahead. The principle of access to the United States Nevada testing grounds was also conceded, and the United Kingdom appears to have successfully extended the areas of nuclear weapon collaboration by its insistence on participating in the Christmas Island tests. However, the price paid for switching Britain's strategic delivery system from Skybolt to Polaris was not only considerable nugatory expenditure on the warhead for the former, but also acceptance that the Polaris force would be assigned to NATO, though it might be withdrawn if 'supreme national interests' were at stake. In addition, two linked elements of uncertainty continued to cloud the nuclear relationship. One was the American fear that Britain might attempt to buy its way into the EEC by offering nuclear weapon and submarine reactor design data to France. The second was the difficulty experienced by the Americans in distinguishing between the French and British when constructing a policy against nuclear proliferation, and the accompanying belief that France would only be restrained in its nuclear activities if similar measures were applied to the United Kingdom. This conflicted sharply with the British view that they had an historic right to be a nuclear power as a co-participant in the Manhattan Project.

8 The Mature Technology: From Polaris to Chevaline

Polaris and the Termination of Active Nuclear Weapon Development

Two arms limitation measures had been associated with the formation of the Anglo-American nuclear alliance: a testing ban and a halt to fissile material production. Macmillan, pursuing his policy of security through superpower arms restrictions, had seen the first of these partially achieved in 1963, but it fell to his successor, Douglas-Home, to preside over the limited attainment of the second. By 1964, a treaty to terminate all fissile material production for military purposes had been overtaken by events. The original American motive in making the proposal, the attempt to prevent the Soviet Union acquiring the capability for a knockout blow, was no longer relevant, but at the same time the needs of the US, USSR and UK for fissile materials had been significantly reduced as a consequence of the evolution of nuclear weapon technology from fission alone to fission plus thermonuclear reaction for both strategic and tactical purposes. All three states intended to reduce their output of weapon material in the near future, but the Soviet rejection of any system of intrusive inspection prevented these national decisions being consolidated into a treaty to limit or terminate the production of fissile material for military purposes. However, they all had a common interest in encouraging other states not to acquire nuclear weapons, and agreement was reached between them that simultaneous announcements of reductions in their national programmes for fissile material production should be made on 21 April 1964.[1] Sir Alec Douglas-Home made the British announcement which included statements that:

The civil reactors which have been, and are being, brought

165

into service in this country ... produce plutonium. Part of this will be used for civil purposes in the United Kingdom and part sent to the United States under an agreement ... whereby U-235 is supplied in exchange by the United States Government.

and

our plans do not envisage the use of any of the plutonium produced by our civil reactors in the United Kingdom weapons programme and I am informed by the United States that they have no intention of using the plutonium received from us for weapon purposes.[2]

This announcement was followed by a Defence White Paper in June which stated that:

We have now reached a point where supplies of fissile material already available or assured will be sufficient to maintain our independent nuclear deterrent and to meet all our defence requirements for the foreseeable future. This takes account of the fact that material already embodied in weapons can be returned and used again. Consequently, production of U-235 for military purposes at Capenhurst ceased in 1963 ... Military plutonium production is gradually being brought to an end. If at any time further supplies of fissile material are required for defence purposes, it will be possible to resume or increase production.[3]

These decisions had a significant, if somewhat unexpected, consequence for the defence budget. The eight Calder Hall type reactors; the new, large reprocessing plant at Windscale known as B205;[4] the Capenhurst low and high enrichment plants; part of the capacity of the Springfields nuclear fuel plant, and a substantial uranium ore stockpile had all been funded by the UKAEA on the assumption that their capital costs and interest charges would be recovered from the sales of fissile material for military use over the minimum ten-year production period of the 1955 programme. The uranium purchased by the UKAEA for defence purposes could still be used indirectly in this role, for in Britain, as in the United States, only the state nuclear agency was allowed to own fissile material. Thus plutonium produced in the magnox fuel rods used in the civil reactors was owned by the UKAEA, not the CEGB or SSEB. Thus no distinction could be made between British civil and military fissile material in terms of ownership: the UKAEA was the owner of both, and was thus free to exchange either type with the USAEC for U-235 and tritium.

The UKAEA attempted to recover their expenditure on fissile material production facilities from the Ministry of Defence via the Treasury and, after a struggle, succeeded in doing so. £302.5 m at 1964 prices was subsequently paid to the UKAEA by the Ministry of Defence in eight instalments between 1964 and 1972.[5] The result of this transaction was that when British Nuclear Fuels Limited (BNFL) was formed in 1971 to take over these plants and operate them on a commercial basis, they were shown in the accounts at a low book value, and the firm thus obtained what amounted to a subsidy from the defence budget in its early years. It also meant that during the 1970s the Ministry of Defence was reluctant to simplify the application of IAEA and EURATOM safeguards by building separate, unsafeguarded military plants as it had paid for the existing civil ones, some of which continued to be used for both civil and military purposes.[6]

The main development project undertaken at Aldermaston between 1963 and 1968 was to enable warheads to be provided for the British Polaris missiles. This represented a formidable challenge as a very restricted timescale was involved. In addition, after two experimental devices had been tested underground at Nevada in July 1964 and September 1965, the British Labour government, headed by Mr Wilson, decided to terminate further explosive testing. This policy appears to have been influenced by accusations that it had reneged on promises made while in opposition to renegotiate the Nassau Agreement on the supply of Polaris missiles to Britain,[7] but the Prime Minister also appeared to be unconvinced of the utility of such tests, particularly as he claimed that the one in 1964, intended to achieve reduced yield to weight ratios for future nuclear warheads, had been a costly failure and had had to be repeated in 1965.[8] He may also have been aware of the possible adverse impact of these tests upon the negotiations for a non-dissemination and non-proliferation agreement which culminated in the 1968 Non-Proliferation Treaty (NPT).

The weapon designers at Aldermaston do not appear to have started work on designing a new strategic missile warhead for Polaris until a decision was taken on 10 June 1963 to equip the submarines with the new A3 version of the missile. In the period between the Nassau Agreement and the A3 decision, at least one Cabinet Minister was pressing for the rejection of the Nassau arrangements on the grounds that they undermined the concept of an independent deterrent capability. The alternative he was offering was to fit a lightweight thermonuclear warhead to the successful Black Knight rocket used for testing reentry systems, thus creating a combination much smaller than the cancelled Blue Streak, and therefore more easily deployed in hardened silos or in a mobile mode.[9] A major consequence of this move would have been that British expertise in reentry vehicle design and manufacture could have been sustained: the effect of the Polaris A3 purchase was that the teams initially created to build the Blue Streak vehicle were dispersed, and a hiatus of a decade then ensued when little experimental work took place in the United Kingdom in this area.[10] The Black Knight idea gained little political support, however, and Aldermaston was left with the task of designing, developing and producing a Polaris warhead within five years. The procedure used was similar to that employed for the Skybolt warhead, with an initial design being developed based on British requirements, materials and production methods, and employing experimental data, materials and non-nuclear components from the United States if appropriate. It is possible that Britain also possessed some specific information on the American design as a consequence of the Frigate Bird test of a Polaris missile warhead off Christmas Island in May 1962.[11] The British design concept was then shown to the American laboratories, who commented on it and suggested ways of modifying it to create a production warhead similar to the equivalent American one. This procedure avoided the direct transfer of information on thermonuclear weapon designs, and its success was heavily dependent upon the professional concern of the American weapon designers in ensuring that their British counterparts should succeed in producing an effective product.

The Polaris warhead requirements differed significantly from earlier British nuclear designs in several areas. One was that the three nuclear warheads in each missile had to remain assembled for a prolonged period of time, and thus had to be engineered to an extremely high standard of reliability and require minimal maintenance.[12] A second was that they had to be integrated with the missile reentry system, and be capable of withstanding submarine storage and launch, space and reentry environments. These requirements led to the formation of an Anglo-American Joint Reentry Working Group to ensure that the British warhead would always be compatible with the rest of the system.[13] The work of this group benefited from considerable American assistance.

One issue permeating the Polaris warhead design process was the concern that it could eventually become vulnerable to disablement by Soviet anti-ballistic missile (ABM) systems, either through the effects of radiation or neutrons generated by defensive high-altitude explosions, or from direct physical destruction. Aldermaston's work was widened to include the study of countermeasures to ABMs and the development of designs which were hardened against ABM effects, but which still attained the space, weight and reliability requirements of submarine-launched missile warheads. In addition, Britain joined with the United States and Australia in a programme of reentry vehicle and anti-ballistic missile research, using the relatively large numbers of Black Knight rockets that had been ordered to test the reentry vehicle designed for Blue Streak and had become surplus to requirements after the latter's cancellation in 1960.

One significant effect of these Australian tests was that the United Kingdom was able to provide the United States with useful data on upper atmospheric conditions in the southern hemisphere in return for American data relevant to the operation of the Polaris system.[14] Some British personnel had also been involved in the American tests on the effects of high-altitude nuclear explosions conducted from Christmas Island in 1962,[15] and thus the Aldermaston team, in close association with the RAE at Farnborough, acquired some familiarity with the problems of warhead and missile hardening, reentry, missile interception, and deception of highly complex ABM radar systems. Considerable interchange took place with the United States on these topics during the 1960s, stimulated by events such as the towing of an ABM through Red Square in Moscow in 1964.

The original planning schedule probably envisaged that assembly of Polaris warheads would start in 1966, in order to provide an adequate stockpile for the initial patrol of the first of the 'R' class missile submarines in June 1968. In fact, it appears that the initial production models were not completed until 1967 (see App. Table A.4c), with the result that the first submarine went on patrol without its full complement of warheads. The necessity to produce large numbers of warheads for the missile submarine fleet by late 1969 meant that although the full inventory of thermonuclear warheads for Blue Steel and the megaton gravity bombs carried by the V bombers could be manufactured before Burghfield Common started assembling Polaris physics packages, volume production of the advanced tactical warhead did not begin until the early 1970s. Thus Red Beard bombs continued to be deployed with Canberra and Buccaneer aircraft throughout the decade, though no attempt was made to modify the Navy and Air Force's Phantoms to carry this British nuclear bomb when they entered service. Rather the squadrons of these aircraft allocated to a tactical nuclear role in Germany in the early 1970s were equipped with American nuclear bombs, for use in the event of hostilities, under 'key of the cupboard' rules.[16] However, during the 1970s substantial numbers of these new advanced warheads for tactical weapons were manufactured to reequip the Fleet Air Arm, both in the anti-submarine and strike role, and to enable British bombs to be fitted to the RAF's Jaguar and Buccaneer aircraft stationed in Germany and the United Kingdom. This allowed the Phantoms to revert to a conventional role and Britain's reliance upon access to American nuclear bombs for tactical purposes was appreciably reduced.

The period between 1965 and 1974 is notable for the lack of any British underground nuclear weapon tests at Nevada or elsewhere. A major reason for this was the unwillingness of both Wilson's Labour government and its Conservative successor to commit the country to active development of new physics concepts or warhead designs. The tactical warhead which was in production and the associated megaton weapon had service lives estimated at 20–25 years,[17] and there seemed little point in developing versions with marginally improved yield to weight ratios. Neither government was anxious to spend money immediately on improvements to the Polaris force, which in any event did not enter service until 1968, as one of its main attractions was its cheapness.[18] As a consequence, little weapon-orientated work was undertaken on missile warhead designs after Polaris, and the Labour government decided to run down the workforce at Aldermaston, and diversify its role to include responsibility for civil research and development projects, in particular the fast breeder reactor.[19] Denis Healey, the Minister of Defence, informed Parliament in June 1967 that the government had rejected the option of purchasing the Polaris successor, the Poseidon, from the United States, and thus had not attempted to obtain access to the technology of multiple independently targeted reentry vehicles (MIRVs).[20] Of perhaps greater significance, however, was a statement by Mr Wilson, the Prime Minister, a week later, in which he gave a categorical asssurance that he was not interested in the development of new generations of nuclear weapons. This committed the Labour government publicly to a policy of terminating British nuclear warhead and reentry vehicle development.[21] This move was then presented to De Gaulle as a positive example of Britain's intention to reduce its nuclear ties with the United States, at a time when a renewed attempt was being made to enter the EEC.[22] Thus the long-standing fears in the United States that the British government was prepared to buy its way into Europe with nuclear information were again reinforced.

These events led to the nuclear weapon development and production facilities taking on the appearance of organisations in decline, an impression reinforced by reductions of expenditure on special nuclear materials and nuclear weapon research.[23] This made it increasingly difficult for the British weapon designers to justify the continuation of the close working relationship with the American weapon laboratories at Los Alamos, Livermore and Sandia, organised through a range of joint working groups, as the areas where British experimental information could be offered in exchange for American data were somewhat limited.[24] An exception was in the nuclear intelligence field, where Britain's possession of Hong Kong enabled it to offer useful evaluations of the Chinese nuclear testing programme which had started in 1964.[25]

Rebirth through Chevaline

Given the political veto on any significant testing and exploratory development work, and the Wilson Cabinet's decision not to acquire Poseidon, Aldermaston had little choice but to concentrate its reduced research and development budget after 1967 upon paper studies of possible improvements to the Polaris warheads and their reentry system, to counter the emerging threat from Soviet ABM systems.[26] The extent of this threat became public knowledge in 1966 when the United States revealed that the Soviet Union was constructing an ABM defence of Moscow based on the Galosh missile.[27] Because of the absence of knowledge of the shelf-life of the original Polaris warheads, the Royal Navy's forward plans included provision to rebuild them as required towards the end of the 1970s. These plans were probably linked to the discovery by the United States that the slow build-up of helium in the tritium used to boost thermonuclear primaries and tactical weapons had a much greater adverse effect upon yield than had previously been calculated. This problem was identified at some point after 1962, and prior to this the expectation appears to have been that the tritium used in weapons would sustain their predicted yields for at least ten years. The only method of determining the effect of this tritium ageing process upon individual weapon designs appeared to be to test each type of boosted warhead when it reached the end of the shelf-life that had been attributed to its tritium, and then alter the design or the maintenance procedure to compensate for any unanticipated reduction in yield.[28]

The plans for a possible rebuilding of the Polaris warheads in the late 1970s became entangled with the idea of designing modified warheads when discussions with the United States on the ABM threat suggested that it would be prudent to have new designs matched to improved reentry systems available for rapid production by that date. The objective was to acquire the capability of manufacturing a reentry system, which would be able to penetrate the Moscow defences, irrespective of their capabilities, and thus maintain the credibility of the British strategic deterrent into the 1980s. The bulk of the associated studies, which continued through to 1974, concentrated on elaborating an approach partially developed in America some years earlier for the Polaris missile, but then discontinued when the United States decided to buy the Poseidon missile which was both equipped with MIRV and had a greater range.[29] This American design concept, known as Antelope, involved hardening the missile warheads against the effects of nuclear explosions and modifying the firing and reentry system to present radar defences with a confusingly large number of credible threats at the same time, and thus saturate them.[30]

These technical possibilities could not be realised without a political directive from the Cabinet to allocate resources to a development programme, including underground tests, and thus the evolution of this Polaris improvement concept was dominated by domestic political considerations, and the uncertainties arising from the changes of government from Labour to Conservative in 1970; to Labour in 1974 and back again to Conservative in 1979. Although Wilson had publicly rejected the idea of acquiring Poseidon in 1967, the option of improving Polaris as a British programme remained open. Preliminary studies had commenced in 1967 and the Labour government was close to making a decision to initiate a formal feasibility study when it was replaced by Mr Heath's Conservative one.[31] A feasibility study was authorised in 1970, followed by a project definition phase in 1972. This suggested that work should start on a five-year development programme but a variety of political factors relating to the change of government, such as the move to a closer economic and political relationship with other European countries as a result of Britain's acceptance into the EEC,[32] and the progress of the US–USSR strategic arms negotiations, plus reassessments of the best way for Britain to counter Soviet ABM development, led to a decision to proceed being deferred throughout 1973. Meanwhile, some work continued on the basis of funding extensions of three or six months duration.

This project definition study was largely a paper one. It cost £7.5m to complete and contained an estimate that total costs would be £175m.[33] Following the signing of SALT I in May 1972, ministers had conducted an extensive review of the future options for the Polaris fleet, stimulated both by the possibility that the imminent negotiations on a SALT II treaty to limit MIRVed missiles might contain technology transfer prohibitions similar to those in the ABM Treaty and the realisation that if an improved system was to be placed in service to meet the ABM threat with a reasonable expectation of future system life, a decision to embark upon a full development programme would have to be taken rapidly.[34] The subsidiary possibility of building an additional submarine was rejected on grounds of timescale and cost,[35] and the choice was narrowed down to one of either proceeding with the full development and production of an improved Polaris system, or purchasing Poseidon missiles from the United States and developing a British warhead and reentry vehicle for it. Heath's government had restarted studies of the Poseidon option in 1971, and although early exploratory talks suggested that the Nixon administration would be prepared to accede to a request for Poseidon, the progress towards the SALT I Treaty and the possible nature of SALT II made some agencies of the American government appear somewhat reluctant to provide Britain with the MIRVed reentry vehicle for it. The impression gained strength in the Ministry of Defence and among political leaders that even if an agreement to purchase MIRVed Poseidon was reached with the United States government, irresistible pressures might arise within both political systems and in international fora to abandon the contract in the following years. This would certainly occur if an agreement was reached between the United States and USSR to abandon both MIRV and ABM deployments. Since purchasing the Poseidon booster would mean that the submarines would require additional refitting work to accommodate and fire them, and many of the logistics, storage and training facilities would have to be modified, this option appeared likely to be much more difficult and expensive than simply altering the warheads of the existing Polaris missiles, and might not yield the same degree of resistance to ABM defences that appeared likely to be obtained if resources were focused upon reentry vehicle improvements alone.[36]

The political and technical uncertainties confronting any move to restart active nuclear warhead development and to renew work on missile reentry vehicle design made it unusually difficult for the Heath Cabinet to reach a decision on allocating money for the proposed five-year development programme. In particular, the necessity radically to change the existing system was heavily dependent upon technical judgements on both the likely advances in Soviet ABM defences over a 20-year period and the future of nuclear arms control negotiations, which by mid-1973 had advanced to the point where both superpowers had limited their ABM deployments to defending either a single city or missile complex. If no ABMs were to be deployed in the USSR through to 1990, then a programme to combat them became an insurance measure rather than an absolute necessity. Despite these difficulties of evaluation, which favoured delay and procrastination, the Heath Cabinet decided to proceed with the programme in January 1974, with the aim of deploying the system at the end of the decade.[37] The Ministry of Defence requested the provision of funds for completion, but due to the domestic political difficulties of the time[38] was only authorised to spend £15m on the next six months planned work.[39] Thus no effective actions to implement the decision to deploy the system had been taken when the future of the project was thrown back into a state of acute uncertainty by the result of the general election in February 1974, which returned a Labour government, led by Wilson, to power, though it lacked a secure majority in the House of Commons.

The advent of a Labour government made the Heath Cabinet's decision to adopt a national solution to the Soviet ABM threat appear politically astute, for any purchase of Poseidon would have had to be announced publicly. It would have been virtually impossible for the new government to sustain it, even if it had wished to do so, given its earlier public rejection of it while in office and its later commitment while in opposition not to replace Polaris. By contrast, the development of a modified reentry system, dependent for its effectiveness upon new nuclear warheads and based upon work initiated by the previous Wilson government, was a much more defensible political decision. Yet such was the political climate within the Labour Party that those few members of the Cabinet fully conversant with the programme chose to allow a wall of secrecy to be created around it. The impression was allowed to grow that a modest maintenance programme, including modifications to keep the Polaris system operative for a further decade, was all that was contemplated, rather than the drastic reversal of previous policies that was actually being implemented.[40]

The precarious parliamentary position of Wilson's first Labour government of 1974 persisted until a further election in October produced an enhanced majority. Meanwhile ministers did not reverse the previous administration's decision to develop and deploy the system, but in April chose instead to provide £46.5m to continue the work for a further year and keep the project teams together, while its future was subject to a detailed examination in the context of an overall defence review.[41] One result of this more detailed project definition study, which included some hardware development, was that a new estimate of programme cost was made raising the 1972 figure of £175 m to £235 m.[42] Given the two-year period of political indecision on whether or not to sanction completion of the project, it was not surprising that the formal action of the new Labour Cabinet in December to approve a further period of expenditure on it was regarded by those involved in the work as falling short of a convincing commitment to deployment.[43] This attitude was reinforced by the far-reaching defence review of late 1974 and 1975 during which the future of the project was reexamined. Although in retrospect it appears that a Poseidon purchase might well have been cheaper at this stage, the international and domestic political circumstances were judged to make this an unrealistic option.[44]

The review of the warhead improvement project in the context of the total defence programme was concluded in September 1975, and a definitive Cabinet decision was taken to complete development and plan for deployment.[45] In parallel, the management structure was altered and a new project management team formed. It was only at this stage that those involved appear to have become convinced that after three years of weak political commitment the project was at last going to be pushed through to completion, and there was an incentive to move ahead rapidly, though it was now unlikely to enter service much before the end of 1982. The new management team then recosted the project, included additional items which had arisen since 1972, such as the overhead costs at Aldermaston, the Navy's insistence on a statistically significant series of full-scale missile firing tests, changes in specification and underestimates of specific development costs, and in March 1976 arrived at a new figure for completion of £598 m at 1976 prices, £388 m at 1972 ones.[46] Little of this increase in cost originated in the warhead area: most was a result of embarking upon a development programme in a field (reentry vehicle design) where British knowledge was very limited and mainly theoretical.[47]

Despite public references to actions to maintain the effectiveness of the Polaris force, no overt indication of the extent of the programme emerged into the public domain until early 1980, when the incoming Conservative government led by Mrs Thatcher revealed some details of what had been taking place over the previous five years, together with the official code name for the project, Chevaline.[48] By then, costs had risen to £1000 m at 1980 prices, £530 m at 1972 ones, a trebling of the 1972 estimate, while deployment was expected to occur from 1983 onwards.[49]

One effect of this new programme was to regenerate the nuclear weapon data exchange relationship with the United States and inject a greater element of reciprocity into it than had been possible during the eight-year suspension of nuclear testing, thus alleviating the fears of some officials that the numbers and significance of the joint working groups would slowly decline if Britain was not working on more advanced ideas than those developed at the turn of the 1960s. The Chevaline concept differed significantly from America's MIRV systems, and it could be argued that the United Kingdom was developing, at minimal cost to the United States taxpayer, a strategic vehicle with features that America might find useful at some future date. This gave the United States authorities an incentive both to support the programme, on the basis that it represented a cooperative division of labour, and to extend the information exchange relationship to cover advanced technologies as the United Kingdom was again making a positive contribution to it. However, the degree to which it was genuinely expected that the United States would want to utilise technology from this United Kingdom programme must remain an open question. What could not be denied was that the existence of a development programme to counter ABMs, independent of that undertaken by the United States, did restore an element of reciprocity to the relationship. One of the more visible results of embarking upon the new programme was that the Labour government sanctioned a linked series of underground tests in Nevada. Seven explosions of British test devices occurred there between August 1976 and October 1980.[50] In addition, a test previously authorised by the Conservative government was allowed to proceed by the Labour government and occurred in May 1974.[51]

The main purpose of the seven-test series was to improve the weight to yield ratio offered by existing concepts, and to shape the nuclear warhead design to enable it to fit into the space available in the revised reentry vehicles. By reducing the weight of the nuclear warhead, either more of them or additional anti-ABM equipment could be carried in the Polaris payload package.[52] The procedures used to design the warheads seem likely to have been well-established ones of starting from an original British concept, and then modifying it in the light of advice and comments from the American weapon laboratories. This meant that extensive interchanges occurred with the United States Navy, their civilian contractors and the US Energy Department, which took over responsibility for weapon development when first the AEC and then the Energy Research, and Development Agency (ERDA) were abolished in the mid-1970s. As a result, the new physics package incorporated the latest American advances in weight reduction and yield enhancement and Britain probably succeeded in jumping a generation of warhead development. This may account for the apparent contradiction between the Labour government's commitment to not making preparations to acquire a successor strategic system and statements made to the Defence Committee of the House of Commons that any comprehensive test ban resulting from the tripartite negotiations started in Geneva in 1977 would not inhibit a Trident warhead development programme.[53] The fully proven Chevaline warhead appears to have commenced production during 1979, with deliveries planned to continue until the mid-1980s.

Supplies of fissile material had ceased to be a limiting factor on British nuclear warhead production by 1964, though the country had chosen to obtain supplies of certain materials necessary for nuclear weapon manufacture from the United States on grounds of reduced cost and immediate availability. One of these materials, tritium, is a substance subject to radioactive decay, and thus it had to be renewed at some time during the operational life of both the strategic thermonuclear weapons and tactical 'boosted' ones. It appears to have been this material that Wilson alluded to during a defence debate in 1965, in support of his argument that the British deterrent was not independent.[54] The nature of the United Kingdom's weapon production programme was such that supplies of tritium had been acquired from the United States for new weapons from 1961 onwards, and it was anticipated originally that its neutron generating qualities would degrade slowly and evenly. Thus, despite the use of this material in all the advanced nuclear weapons already in the British stockpile and planned for the future, it was believed that any refusal by the United States to provide further supplies to Britain would still allow time for manufacturing to restart in the United Kingdom before the potential yields of the existing weapons became unduly degraded. The discovery during the post-1962 period of a more rapid fall-off in the potency of tritium in United States weapons, and the possibility that the explosive test at Nevada in 1974 was of a British weapon which had attained the end of its calculated shelf-life, may indicate that by the mid-1970s there had been a change in technical policy concerning tritium.[55] If the 1974 test was for this purpose, and it involved one of the earliest production weapons using this material, then one may deduce that the original calculations indicated that the material could be retained in weapons for its full half-life of $12\frac{1}{2}$ years. The indications are that the consequences of this tritium 'ageing' problem led to the period for newly manufactured material to be retained in weapons being reduced to less than ten years, and possibly as low as five.[56] Leaving the tritium in nuclear weapons until the original shelf-life figure was reached would, so it has been claimed, introduce 'real uncertainties into the estimated yields of older weapons by some two orders of magnitude'.[57]

The effect of these discoveries was to increase the annual British demand for tritium to be used in weapons, to remove the cushion against a United States refusal to supply the material, and to make the United Kingdom dependent upon each and every future American President for the sustenance of the technical credibility of its nuclear forces. Its significance was further enhanced by the replacement of the Red Beard tactical weapons with the advanced tactical ones employing the 'boosting' principle, production of which was then at its height. In addition, two aspects of the United States scene were offering grounds for concern by 1976. Production of tritium from the AEC's Savannah River reactors had been progressively run down after the mid-1960s, leaving only three of the installations in operation at reduced power levels. Serious consideration was being given in the United States to developing and producing the 'neutron' warhead for tactical purposes, and this would require additional quantities of tritium. It is thus conceivable that some anxiety was felt about the impact of such an expanded demand upon the ability and willingness of the United States to transfer regular shipments of tritium to the United Kingdom. A second aspect was that a presidential election campaign was taking place in the United States, and the Democrat challenger, Mr Carter, had committed himself to push ahead vigorously with nuclear arms control policies, particularly in the non-proliferation area.[58] It was unclear what impact these commitments might have upon the ability of the United Kingdom to buy weapon materials from the United States, though the worst was feared. These uncertainties, plus the changed technical position and composition of the weapon inventory, resulted in the Labour Cabinet deciding to strengthen Britain's independent position *vis-à-vis* the United States by sanctioning the adaptation of one of the plutonium/power reactors at Chapel Cross for use as the basis for a national tritium production plant. This would have sufficient capacity to maintain the credibility of the nuclear weapons stockpile in the event of a sudden American decision to suspend deliveries of tritium to the United Kingdom.[59]

9 Reactors, the Trade in Military Nuclear Materials and Trident

Submarine Reactors

The essence of the Anglo-American nuclear submarine transfer arrangements, which were incorporated into the 1958 bilateral agreement, was that the contract to supply the Royal Navy with a submarine reactor was to be between two commercial companies, rather than their parent governments. They permitted a single example of a submarine reactor to be purchased by the United Kingdom company and installed in a British boat. Any further reactors would have to be built in Britain under licence from the American company and with the minimum of assistance from the United States. In this way, there would be no interruption to the United States Navy's large nuclear submarine building programme. In practice the arrangements meant that Britain acquired a single example of a submarine nuclear propulsion system and a set of blueprints and was left to get on with the job. Rolls-Royce at Derby was nominated as the British commercial concern and a company-to-company contract was rapidly concluded with the American reactor manufacturer, Westinghouse. This enabled HMS *Dreadnought*, the first British nuclear submarine, to be completed in 1963 with a Westinghouse reactor, followed by the first submarine with a British-built reactor system, HMS *Valiant*, in 1966. A land-based British submarine reactor prototype, HMS *Vulcan*, had also been installed at the Admiralty test station at Dounreay in 1965 to act as a training facility and limited test bed.[1] The agreement had provided for information on fuel fabrication and reprocessing to be supplied to the United Kingdom, with the intention that Britain should become self-sufficient in all the technologies of submarine reactor development as rapidly as possible. A fuel fabrication plant was built by Rolls-Royce using this data, and a storage pond for used submarine reactor fuel was completed at BNFL Windscale in 1964.[2] No reprocessing of submarine fuel has been undertaken in Britain, as the amount of material involved is insufficient to justify this activity.

The nature of the submarine exchange arrangements meant that they evolved after 1959 in a radically different way from the ones on nuclear weapon design. Admiral Rickover had made clear at the JCAE hearings on the bilateral agreement that his main purpose in supporting the sale of a reactor was to prevent the British having continuous and direct access to the American project, because he believed that responding to their queries would disrupt American progress and deflect him from his singleminded determination to develop nuclear plants for the USN. Thus, once the information exchange had been successfully completed, there was no incentive to change the terms of a relationship which would involve little reciprocal flow of information to the United States. Back-up services for HMS *Dreadnought*'s reactor and its associated propulsion machinery continued to be provided by both Westinghouse and the Electric Boat Company, but there was no continuing exchange of information on submarine reactors and their fuel. The UKAEA and Rolls-Royce Associates anglicised the original Westinghouse S5W reactor to provide a power plant for HMS *Valiant*, and continued this process through two further modifications to the core of the original design, commissioned in 1973 and 1981 respectively. Subsequently, work commenced on a new, advanced design, PWR-2, and this is expected to be installed in HMS *Vulcan*, the land-based trials installation at Dounreay, in the mid-1980s and in any new missile submarines commissioned in the 1990s.[3]

Admiral Rickover played an intermittent but important role in the initial years of the British nuclear submarine programme, as he was in a unique position to assist the British project when it encountered difficulties. In his relations with the United Kingdom over nuclear submarine technology, he had unique freedom of manoeuvre, as the American atomic energy legislation left him with a substantial measure of personal discretion over the provision of certain types of information and materials to the United Kingdom. In practice, he did not appear to be responsible to any superior body in the exercise of these powers. As a consequence, sustained efforts were made by British officials and naval leaders to cultivate and maintain good relations with him, and the value of his assistance was recognised by a number of gestures intended to convey appreciation for his efforts, including honorary awards. Lord Zuckerman, the Chief Defence Scientist at the Ministry of Defence, played a central role in this activity, as his excellent personal relationship with Admiral Rickover led to requests of a particularly urgent nature being channelled through him on an informal, rather than official, basis. The result was that assistance was occasionally forthcoming to resolve difficult problems affecting the British project, but this was offset by unpredictable episodes in which information which could have aided the United Kingdom programme was not made available. Thus whilst any information affecting reactor safety was passed to Britain without delay, and at one particularly difficult stage in the building of the 'R' class missile submarines, stainless steel tubing was transferred to the United Kingdom from limited American stocks, Britain was not forewarned of certain areas in which the United States had experienced technical difficulties, such as the welding of submarine reactor pressure vessels. While there was no legal or other obligation upon Admiral Rickover to supply this information, its non-availability often resulted in increased costs and slippages in the building schedules for the early British nuclear submarines.

The government-to-government agreement covering HMS *Dreadnought*'s reactor system had included a ten-year supply of fuel, but it contained no specific provisions for any additional regular transfer of highly enriched uranium from the United States to fuel British-built reactors. This resulted in the nine reactors constructed in Britain during the 1960s[4] being fuelled either with nationally produced U-235 withdrawn from reserve stocks or from material obtained from the United States by general purchase or barter.

Since it was necessary to replace the material consumed in these reactors, it was clear that when the bilateral military agreement came up for renewal at the end of the decade, it would be essential to seek to amend its provisions to guarantee a supply of United States manufactured U-235 on a continuing basis for submarine use.

Anglo-American Disputes over Civil Nuclear Activities

The period from 1965 to 1970 was a very confusing and

contradictory one in Anglo-American nuclear relations as activities impinging upon the renewal of the 1958–9 military agreements were taking place in a number of disparate areas. Opposition from the Wilson government to the MLF concept had led to this idea being abandoned, and eventually replaced by the NATO Nuclear Planning Group arrangements, under which the British strategic bomber force, and later the Polaris missile submarines, were assigned to the NATO deterrent role envisaged in the Nassau Agreement, supplemented by an equivalent United States force.[5] The Non-Proliferation Treaty was signed in 1968, but care was taken to ensure that it contained no legal limitation upon continued Anglo-American transfers of strategic nuclear technology and materials, and, as it was solely concerned with dissemination and acquisition of nuclear weapons, it included no provisions related to nuclear submarine reactors.[6] The possibility that future arms control agreements might place limits on Anglo-American military transfers in the nuclear field became of real concern, however, once the US–USSR negotiations on strategic arms limitations commenced.[7]

Mr Wilson's Labour government persisted with the efforts initiated by its Conservative predecessor to join the EEC, and in so doing continued to reinforce the fears of those in the United States who believed that Britain was ultimately prepared to transfer nuclear weapons and submarine reactor data to France in order to secure entry. The Wilson policy was to emphasise Britain's ability to contribute its advanced technology to the EEC by entering into collaborative arrangements with other European countries in areas such as supersonic and subsonic airliners and advanced military aircraft, as well as a number of aspects of civil nuclear power.[8] The latter led to a series of acute conflicts with the United States which, while they had little direct connection to the military relationship, affected the general atmosphere in which the nuclear exchange agreements were to be amended at the end of the 1960s.

The starting point for these disagreements was the UKAEA's decision to develop the advanced gas-cooled reactor (AGR), in the belief that the higher steam temperatures possible with this plant, in comparison with both American light water designs and the indigenous magnox reactors, would lead to reduced electricity generating costs. This reactor used slightly enriched uranium as fuel. In May 1965 the CEGB asked the Ministry of Power to allow it to start construction of its first AGR station at Dungeness.[9] This proposal was accepted, but it was realised that the output from the low enrichment part of the Capenhurst military plant could not be expanded at a sufficiently rapid rate to allow the initial inventory of fuel for this and the five other stations in the programme to be manufactured in time for their planned completion in 1975.[10] The United Kingdom therefore attempted to negotiate an additional agreement with the United States for a supply of enriched material to manufacture into part of this initial inventory, the existing one merely covering the supply of material for experimental purposes.

This request occurred at a time when the United States policy towards civil nuclear power was undergoing a number of changes. The JCAE believed that it had a duty to assist the commercial development of civil power by United States companies, and to this end arrangements had been negotiated whereby both domestic and overseas sales of American-manufactured reactors were to be assisted by the inclusion of an assured 30-year supply of enriched fuel in the contract documents. This guarantee was underwritten by the AEC, and was regarded as essential for the expansion of nuclear power applications in other states. There existed no enrichment plants for civil fuel outside the United States at this time other than Capenhurst, and thus no overseas customer was likely to sign a contract for a reactor unless he was given fuel supply assurances. This situation was regarded as advantageous by the JCAE in another respect, as it meant that the United States, as sole fuel supplier, could insist that IAEA safeguards should be applied to all the reactor fuel exported, thus palliating concerns that the global expansion of nuclear power facilities would assist non-nuclear states to acquire nuclear weapons. A further development was that Congress had passed a bill in 1964 amending the 1954 Atomic Energy Act in a manner which enabled private companies and individuals to own special nuclear materials,[11] thus creating a legal framework within which fuel fabrication, uranium enrichment and fuel reprocessing could be carried out within the United States by private companies. The idea was that as the demands of the military programme declined from 1964 onwards, the AEC would convert some of its plants to civil use and sell them to commercial concerns, who would also have the legal power to build new ones. The AEC would then change to performing a regulatory role in relation to such plants, rather than owning them or promoting them. It was intended that this process would start with the AEC's enrichment plants, and as a first step it was to cease to sell or lease enriched uranium for domestic and foreign use after the end of 1968, and instead operate on the basis of 'toll' enrichment, an arrangement whereby the customer would pay directly for the energy input which had produced the enriched uranium he required.[12] This meant that after 1968 a private owner could buy uranium, and pay the AEC or a private concern to enrich it, thus obviating the need for private owners of enrichment plants to tie up capital in a uranium stockpile.

At this time there were only two reactor types competing with the United States light water reactors in world markets: the Canadian CANDU natural uranium fuelled design and the British AGR, with its requirement for uranium enriched to 1.5–2 per cent in U-235. Unfortunately, the AEA was not in a position to underwrite a 30-year supply contract for enriched AGR fuel with a foreign purchaser, and thus the British reactor construction industry was dependent upon its clients acquiring such a guarantee direct from the AEC under a bilateral agreement for cooperation. This automatically placed the British in a disadvantageous commercial position, despite American policy being based upon the idea that safeguards would only be acceptable if a stable and non-discriminatory supply of fuel was assured. Whatever may have been the AEC's policy in the matter, members of the JCAE were clear that they had no duty to assist United States commercial competitors, and thus the 1965 fuel supply request from the United Kingdom was subject to probing on the twin grounds that it would offer undue commercial advantages to United Kingdom reactor manufacturers, and that IAEA safeguards had to be mandatory upon the material supplied.[13]

The JCAE's attitude was coloured by the perceived reluctance of the United Kingdom government to place the CEGB reactors under IAEA safeguards, Bradwell only being opened up to this type of inspection in 1966, whereas the United States had agreed to place four of its power reactors under safeguards in August 1964.[14] The American reactors were not being used to supply plutonium to the nation's weapon programme, however, whereas plutonium from Bradwell had been exchanged for U-235 under the Anglo-American military agreement, and it was anticipated that output of this material from the other CEGB and SSEB reactors would be traded across the Atlantic through to the end of 1969. Thus any British acceptance of safeguards over all its civil reactors would have drastically affected the working of the existing military agreement. This situation appears to have been ignored by the JCAE, who also harboured suspicions that the United Kingdom might be prepared to sell AGRs and enriched fuel from Capenhurst to foreign customers without insisting that IAEA safeguards should be applied to them, thus allowing commercial gain to undermine the United States non-proliferation policy.[15] Attempts to alter the allied embargo on strategic material exports to enable power reactor sales to be made to Eastern Europe were seen to be part of this 'irresponsible' policy.[16] Thus the JCAE appears to have believed that it was necessary to use the British request for civil fuel as a lever both to ensure that the United Kingdom remained in step with American non-proliferation policy and to limit the commercial attractiveness of AGRs, which were seen by some members as the recipient of unfair assistance from the socialist British government.

The result was that after a year's hard negotiating, a new 'Agreement on the Civil Power Applications of Atomic Energy' was signed in August 1966, under which the United States was to supply up to 8000 kilograms of U-235 to the United Kingdom over the next ten years for Britain's domestic AGR programme.[17] Any transfer under this agreement was conditional upon the material being subject to IAEA safeguards, and thus Britain was forced to accept them over the six domestic AGR stations that were then believed to be in the programme. It was also made clear that Britain would be dependent upon American goodwill for the supply of fuel for any reactor exports, and that the United States would insist that such fuel and the recipient reactors would be subject to IAEA safeguards. In the event, no AGRs were sold to foreign concerns during the 1960s, while the delays in constructing and commissioning the British AGRs makes it unlikely that all of the material allocated under this agreement was actually transferred, as more British-produced material was available before completion of the reactors than originally calculated.

The British government is reported to have found the United States' actions over this agreement deeply offensive, not least because forcing safeguards upon United Kingdom civil facilities was seen as nonsensical, given the fact that Britain was a nuclear weapon state.[18] It was also felt that the small IAEA inspectorate should occupy itself checking on non-nuclear state facilities, rather than carrying out politically symbolic inspections of civil plants in nuclear weapon states. Any future export sales of British reactors were now seen to be dependent upon the United Kingdom having civil enrichment plants of its own with adequate capacity to cater for both domestic and foreign demand. Unfortunately Capenhurst's high energy input costs were a grave disadvantage, despite the capital costs of the plant having been subsidised by the Ministry of Defence. In late 1965, however, the Minister of Technology announced that the low enrichment part of the Capenhurst military plant was to be retained and refurbished to supply uranium fuel for the AGR programme.[19] This decision was undoubtedly made easier by the opportunity it offered to reemploy workers who had been made redundant as a consequence of the termination of military production.

The only effective long-term response to the United States stranglehold over fuel supplies was to develop a technology which allowed uranium to be enriched much more cheaply than the existing gaseous diffusion techniques. Britain had been working on such a technology, the gas centrifuge, since the mid-1950s. Data on this were classified as they could also serve as the basis for a military plant, but they had been the subject of information exchanges with the United States under the terms of the civil agreement for cooperation.[20] Designs for an effective gas centrifuge system were available by the mid-1950s but the lack of suitable materials for key components made further progress dependent on a technological breakthrough in the development of these substances. At this stage one of the leading researchers in the United States returned to his native Germany and published some of his findings, thus creating a complex situation as his research remained officially classified in America and Britain, but not in West Germany, as its non-nuclear status precluded it having any military nuclear secrets.[21]

In the second half of the 1960s it proved possible to develop appropriate materials in Britain to make the system work, and as a consequence negotiations started between Britain, West Germany and Holland at the end of the decade to form a consortium to exploit the new technology commercially. A memorandum on principles for cooperation was agreed in November 1968 and the Treaty of Almelo was signed in 1970 and ratified in 1971. This created two parallel commercial enterprises, URENCO Ltd and CENTEC GmbH, which built pilot plants at Capenhurst and in Holland.[22] This development was very unwelcome to both the AEC and the JCAE, for it was asserted that centrifuge plants could be more easily diverted to military use than gaseous diffusion ones, while allegations of British irresponsibility in this area were reinforced by a United Kingdom submission to the Eighteen Nation Disarmament Conference (ENDC) in 1962 which argued that if this technology was utilised in production plants, it would be impossible to guarantee that they would not be used for military purposes. Moreover, American plans to privatise the AEC's enrichment plants were disrupted by this development, as no commercial concern was likely to invest heavily in existing or new diffusion capacity if a cheaper method of enrichment would soon be available.[23]

These commercial differences soured Anglo-American relations in the civil field, and other British initiatives with Europe in this area served to reinforce the trend. These included participation in negotiations to join the French-led EURODIF enrichment consortia and Britain's British Nuclear Fuels Limited (BNFL) joining with the French CEA and the German KEWA to form a joint marketing company for reprocessing services, United Reprocessors GmbH, in November 1971.[24] Thus in civil nuclear power, Britain had turned its face against cooperation with its competitor, the United States, and had made common cause with the other European states who felt commercially disadvantaged by the United States domination of the market in enriched uranium.

Britain had been faced in 1964 with similar organisational problems to the United States over the future structure of its nuclear industries. Whereas the American policy was to try to transfer as many federal plants as possible into private hands, with the AEC retaining a regulatory role and control of the military programme, the British strategy, announced in July 1968, was to merge the reactor development division of the state agency, the UKAEA, with the three privately-owned reactor building consortia to form two new reactor design and construction companies. The fuel production and reprocessing activities of the UKAEA, including the military plants, were transferred to a state-owned company, BNFL, in April 1971, while in 1973 responsibility for the Aldermaston weapon design laboratories was transferred to the Ministry of Defence.[25]

Details of the transfers of fissile materials by type and quantity under the military exchange agreements between 1959 and 1969 remain secret, though the broad outlines of what was involved can be discerned from public sources. Between 1959 and 1964, British weapon-grade plutonium was bartered for either U-235 or tritium, or these latter materials were purchased direct. Between 1964 and 1971, the plutonium used in the exchanges came predominantly from CEGB and SSEB reactors. After 1971 the material exchanged by Britain came exclusively from the Calder Hall or Chapel Cross reactors. Certain other details of the transactions exist. The plutonium from CEGB and SSEB reactors was produced in fuel supplied by the AEA and reprocessed at Windscale between 1964 and 1 April 1969.[26] Thus the only reactors not potentially involved in the transactions were those at Wylfa and possibly Oldbury.[27] After April 1969 the material in used fuel rods remained the property of the CEGB and SSEB after reprocessing had taken place at Windscale, but it was not until the end of 1970 that the last of the plutonium produced under the original arrangements was transferred to the United States.[28] The plutonium reprocessed prior to April 1969 originated in fuel rods removed from reactors prior to mid-1968, and this, and the decision to open Bradwell to IAEA safeguards inspections in 1966, suggests that the bulk of it was a product of no more than 30 months' irradiation in the ten large reactors at Hunterston, Hinkley Point, Trawsfyndd, Dungeness and Sizewell, and that it contained high percentages of Pu-239. The massive increase in civil plutonium output from 1967 onwards coincided with the period when demand for highly enriched uranium to manufacture Polaris warheads was at its maximum. The start of reprocessing of civil fuel in 1964 was dependent on the opening of the B205 plant at Windscale, and the gradual switching of the military reactors to a civil fuel cycle. This reduced the amount of fuel arising from them passing through Windscale, and balanced off the increased demand for reprocessing services arising from the civil reactors. Estimates of the quantity of materials from civil sources traded under the military agreement are contained in Appendix 6.

The precise reasons for the decision to alter the fuel supply agreements between the electricity boards and the AEA remain difficult to discern. By then American military plutonium production had peaked, in line with reductions in the services' demand for plutonium. The British need for U-235 for Polaris warheads had also been fulfilled, and the continuing requirement was for relatively small quantities of this material for submarine reactors and tritium for warheads. Internationally, the United Kingdom had agreed in December 1968 to accept IAEA safeguards over all its civil nuclear installations once the Non-Proliferation Treaty became operative. This treaty was signed in July 1968, ratified by the United Kingdom in November 1968 and by the United States in March 1969. It would have been incompatible with these ratifications to continue a military trade in fissile materials produced in civil facilities beyond the end of March 1969, though in fact transfers under existing contracts continued to an unspecified date in 1970, which may itself have been determined by the entry into force of the NPT in March of that year. Thus the available evidence suggests that transatlantic military transfers of large quantities of fissile material, and therefore the use of civil plutonium in this trade, were terminated because of a combination of a reduction in military demand and the necessity to honour promises made during the NPT negotiations.[29]

The necessity to act in a manner consistent with the conditions the nuclear weapon states wished to impose upon the non-nuclear ones resulted in considerable difficulties in attempting to classify the barter of U-235 and tritium for civil plutonium. The fact that the transfers took place under the military agreement and the original American wish was to be free to use it for unrestricted purposes, such as building up the NATO stockpile, led to suspicions that British civil plutonium had been used to make United States nuclear weapons. However, in 1982, the United States Department of Energy was stated to have assured the British government that all the civil plutonium transferred prior to 1971 was still being used for non-weapon purposes, such as fast breeder experiments and the production of isotopes for medical activities.[30]

These civil and military nuclear events and activities during the 1960s formed the backdrop against which negotiations started in late 1967 to review the nuclear weapons information exchange arrangements and decide whether they were to terminate on 31 December 1969 as a result of the United States giving notice of this intention by the end of 1968.[31] In addition, the United Kingdom wished to negotiate a completely new amendment to the military agreement to cover the supply of fuel for all its submarine reactors, rather than just the *Dreadnought* one, and to extend the 1959 amendments under which weapon materials could be exchanged.

The Negotiations to Continue Anglo-American Nuclear Cooperation into the 1970s

The main hindrance to the renewal of the nuclear weapon data exchanges was the public commitment made by the British government in June 1967 not to develop a new generation of nuclear weapons.[32] If this was a serious statement of intent by the Labour government, rather than something purely for domestic political consumption, there seemed no point in any continued Anglo-American nuclear relationship in the military field other than the provision of tritium for stockpiled weapons and highly enriched uranium to be fabricated into submarine fuel. The attempt by Britain to continue the weapon information exchanges and extend those covering weapon materials suggested either that the public commitment to terminate nuclear weapon development was a pragmatic act of short-term political expediency which would soon be reversed, or that the requests for extensions were part of a strategy designed to acquire additional data and materials to trade with France in return for Britain's entry into the EEC. As a consequence of this air of uncertainty about the motives and intentions of the United Kingdom government, the negotiations with the Johnson administration on extensions to the Anglo-American agreements which commenced in late 1967 proved extraordinarily long and difficult. Considerable distrust was voiced over the apparently duplicitous nature of British activities and the Labour government's policies. Differences over American actions and policy in Vietnam did little to assist this process, though they had little direct impact on the detailed negotiations.

After much argument and hard bargaining, it had been agreed by September 1968 that the United States would not unilaterally give notice of its intention to terminate the weapon information exchange agreement at the end of the year, and thus the arrangements would remain operative until the end of 1974, as specified in the original 1958 agreement. It was not necessary to place this extension formally before the JCAE to permit objections to be raised to it, though there had been extensive informal discussions between the JCAE and the AEC on this topic in October 1967.

In parallel, negotiations and consultations had been taking place on submarine fuel supply arrangements, which would take the form of a further amendment to the 1958 agreement.[33] These were complicated by Admiral Rickover's desire to restructure the arrangements over the supply of materials and information relevant to nuclear submarine technology so that all requests for such transfers would be channelled exclusively through him. His aim was to prevent Britain having several parallel relationships in this area with American governmental agencies and commercial companies, which offered the opportunity for a policy of 'divide and rule' by negotiating separately with several of these ill-coordinated American organisations. In addition, some members of the JCAE were concerned about Britain transferring nuclear reactor information to other states without American permission: the worry once again appears to have been that this would be part of the price France would demand for British entry into the EEC.[34]

Concurrence on this new amendment was reached by mid-1968, and a draft agreement was signed on 27 September, but it was too late to lay the amendments before the JCAE for the statutory 60-day period, as representatives and senators had recessed to engage in the 1968 presidential and congressional elections. As a consequence the amendments were not laid before the new JCAE until January 1969, and formal executive hearings were held on this and the other arrangements on 10 March of that year.[35] All three AEC and Department of Defense witnesses supported the amendments to the military agreement which enabled America to supply Britain with submarine fuel, but it was made clear in the course of testimony 'that no transfer of naval nuclear propulsion technology or equipment or of materials' was to occur.[36] The amended agreement enabled the United Kingdom to supply uranium hexafluoride produced in

British facilities to the United States for toll enrichment in American plants. The JCAE was also assured that before the amendment would be implemented, the United Kingdom government would have to agree that all the existing provisions of the *Dreadnought* reactor transfer agreement would continue in force.[37]

The amended agreement meant that the United Kingdom was committed to use the enriched uranium for the fabrication of nuclear submarine fuel alone, and not to transfer an anglicised submarine reactor, its fuel or details of this technology to a third state, such as France, without first consulting the United States. The 'need to use' concept was to remain the basis for acquiescence to requests for toll enrichment. The British government apparently provided the guarantees demanded of them by the JCAE, and the new amended agreement, with its added submarine fuel clauses, was to run until 31 December 1979. It was ratified by Congress and the amendment came into force on 28 March 1969.[38]

The submarine fuel supply amendments had been relatively easy to agree as it could be argued without difficulty that an expanded British force of these boats was of positive assistance in furthering American security interests. The amendments to extend the weapon materials arrangements were subject to the same uncertainties that had surrounded the review of the weapon information exchanges and were thus more difficult to negotiate. The JCAE and the AEC insisted that Britain should offer assurances that no enriched uranium supplied for nuclear submarine fuel fabrication would be used in nuclear weapon manufacture without consultation, but the United Kingdom government was reluctant to accept such a restriction on its freedom of action. It eventually acquiesced to these limitations, and once the submarine agreement had been ratified, discussions started with President Nixon's new Republican administration on extending the material transfer provisions relating to its use in weapons. They were heavily influenced by two distinct issues: the lack of firm British development and production plans for new weapon designs and the timing of British requirements for fresh supplies of tritium from the United States. A low quantitative ceiling on transfers of tritium at a time when its shelf-life in weapons was uncertain could have created considerable operational difficulties for Britain, as it might not have allowed the United Kingdom sufficient time to construct and operate national production facilities for the material before the yields of its existing stockpile of weapons became uncertain. The precise details of the negotiations, and the detailed protocols that emerged from them, remain secret, but an amendment extending the weapon material supply clauses of the previous agreement to the end of 1974, in line with the duration of the weapon information exchange provisions, was signed on 16 October 1969 and sent to Congress when it reconvened in January 1970. No opposition was encountered, and it entered into force at the end of the statutory 60-day congressional review period on 8 April.[39]

The Anglo-American military nuclear relationship was gradually revitalised from 1972 onwards by Britain's entry into the EEC, the decision to start development of a new Polaris warhead, and the related commitment to recommence explosive testing. As a consequence, American doubts over the future of the British nuclear weapon development programme were reduced. The next review of the weapon information and materials agreements occurred at the end of 1973, at the same time as the Heath government was debating whether to sanction full-scale development and deployment of a new Polaris warhead. There was little dispute that they should continue, once the British government's commitment to the new warhead became known. A new amendment was therefore signed on 22 July 1974, extending the weapon material provisions to the end of 1979.[40] This occurred despite the return to power of a Labour government in the general elections of February and October 1974. Although this government remained publicly committed neither to acquire a successor to the Polaris force, nor to move towards the production of a new generation of nuclear weapons,[41] it sanctioned expenditure on the Polaris improvement scheme drawn up by its Conservative predecessor, and allow its associated programme of underground nuclear tests in Nevada to proceed.[42] Any disquiet felt in the United States by this contradictory policy was offset by Britain's entry into the EEC, which reduced fears that the United Kingdom would disseminate information to France in order to convince that government of its European credentials. In addition, the JCAE ceased to exist in 1975 when the AEC was abolished. The latter's responsibilities were split between the Energy Research and Development Agency (ERDA), soon to become the Department of Energy, and the Nuclear Regulatory Commission (NRC). Yet congressional pressures were growing for new United States policies to prevent nuclear proliferation, and the British decision of April 1976 to build a national tritium plant at Chapel Cross coincided with changes in American policy towards nuclear energy. The tritium decision symbolised an uneasy realisation that evolving United States' non-proliferation policies would inevitably create difficulties for the future of the materials supply agreements.

The Impact of Carter's Non-proliferation Policy

After the inauguration of President Carter in January 1977, the third American President to hold office in the space of thirty months, his administration moved swiftly to implement vigorstrategic arms control and non-proliferation policies. The latter had a number of domestic and international components, including discouragement of the reprocessing of civil light-water reactor fuel, rejection of the idea of using plutonium to enrich thermal reactor fuel and withdrawing support from the federally funded United States fast-breeder reactor project[43]. These actions directly impinged upon British activities in two areas. BNFL was committed to plans for large scale reprocessing of light-water reactor and AGR fuel at Sellafield. In addition, the down-grading of the United States fast-breeder project removed the major potential short-term civil use for British plutonium transferred under the military agreements.

Soviet proposals had been tabled in the SALT II negotiations to limit the diffusion of strategic technologies beyond the superpowers, and the new President's vigorous advocacy of a rapid movement towards a Comprehensive Test Ban Treaty (CTBT) was also seen as disturbing by some officials in the Ministry of Defence as well as personnel in the American weapon laboratories. It was believed that such a treaty could adversely affect British and American nuclear weapon development plans to a greater extent than those of the USSR, both because of the difficulty of defining a nuclear explosion and the ability of closed societies to carry out sizeable research explosions without arousing suspicions in the absence of effective provisions for on-site inspection and instrumentation. The possibility that a CTBT would be signed by the end of the 1970s provided an incentive for the Ministry of Defence to purchase new large laser equipment for Aldermaston in order to discover the degree to which some aspects of military nuclear research could be carried out in the laboratory. It was hoped that this equipment would enable simulation of the physics and mechanics of nuclear explosions to occur and reduce the need for full-scale explosive testing, as well as enabling a much better understanding of the small quota of tests that might result from the treaty negotiations. In addition, it had possible civil applications.[44]

A further effect of President Carter's policies and the passing by Congress in 1978 of the Nuclear Non-Proliferation Act was new contractual arrangements for the supply of civil reactor fuel which spilt over into the military field. It appears to have been decided that a continuation of the Anglo-American plutonium barter arrangements was incompatible with the administration's non-proliferation stance of not reprocessing used reactor fuel and separating out the plutonium within it, and that no further long-term barter agreements would be signed after the existing ones ran out at the end of 1979. This inability to make further long-term contracts with the United States for the supply of material to fabricate submarine fuel led to studies of methods of securing an indigenous source of supply independent of any future changes in United States government policies. These studies resulted in a decision to build a military centrifuge plant at Capenhurst to produce highly enriched uranium, though this was not announced until January 1980, eight months after Mr Callaghan's Labour government had been replaced by Mrs Thatcher's Conservative one.[45] It was stimulated by a belief that the centrifuge technology offered comparable economics for enriched uranium production to those anticipated from a continued reliance upon short-term toll enrichment contracts with the United States Department of Energy. Thus although Mr Wilson had been very scornful in 1965 of Conservative arguments that Britain's strategic nuclear weapons should constitute an independent capability, between 1976 and 1980 the Labour government were prepared to invest resources in new plants and equipment which would free the country from the very dependencies which he had earlier highlighted.

Trident and the Future

It was announced in July 1980 that the British government had reached agreement in principle with President Carter's administration on the purchase of the Trident C4 MIRVed missile system, less warheads, and was intending to fit it in a new class of British nuclear missile submarine. Over the next two years the details of how this decision was to be implemented were worked out, and in March 1982 it was announced that the Trident D5 missile, still in the development stage, would be purchased instead of the C4, with some slippage of the original in-service date for the new system. In addition, the new British submarine reactor, PWR-2, was to be fitted to the Trident boats.[46] The move from C4 to D5 had little effect upon the warhead programme, as both American missiles use the same MIRV reentry system and the intention was to limit the number of warheads carried by each British submarine to 128.[47] As with Polaris, Britain will have to produce an anglicised version of the American Trident warhead, using consultation techniques which conform to United States legislation, but it has been claimed that this task will be made easier by an ability to use the design concepts utilised in the development of Chevaline.[48]

The Trident decision stimulated a rebuilding and recruitment programme at Aldermaston to assist in the completion of the design tasks on the British Trident warhead, and to enable the necessary number of Chevaline warheads to be produced prior to 1986, which was scheduled as the date for initial production of the new warhead under the pre-D5 plans. An annual output of 30–50 missile warheads appears likely to be sustained for the next 15 years, while work is expected to start in 1986 on designing and developing a replacement for the existing tactical weapons. These 'boosted' bombs will, by the early 1990s, be reaching the point where they will need to be either totally refurbished or replaced by a new design.[49] As production of the tactical bomb in both naval and airforce versions appears to have been completed in the late 1970s and as its estimated shelf-life is between 20 and 25 years, a replacement would need to enter service in the period 1990–2000.[50] Newspaper reports indicate that the megaton weapons carried internally by the Vulcan aircraft were retired with them in 1982. Thus this was a year when substantial unilateral British nuclear disarmament occurred.

The manufacture of nuclear warheads incorporating thermonuclear materials has thus continued at a steady rate since the early 1960s, as Appendix Table A.4c illustrates, interrupted only by the gap between tactical weapon and Chevaline warhead production in the late 1970s and the effect of certain plutonium handling problems encountered at Aldermaston.[51] From the industrial and managerial perspective, the need to provide a steady flow of design, production and refurbishing work has been achieved by reworking strategic weapon stocks on roughly a ten-year cycle, with tactical weapon work smoothing out production troughs. By contrast, positive physics package development work came to a virtual standstill after 1965, and was not resumed until some five years later. All of these activities have been dominated by decisions taken at the highest political levels, the most significant of which were probably the Labour government's acquiescence to the continuation of the Chevaline warhead development and tactical weapon production programmes in 1974 and its decision, in April 1976, to insure against dependence upon American tritium supplies and the uncertainties of the United States political system by the construction of a new British production plant for this material. A fairly clear programme of work thus exists through to the 1990s unless existing political decisions and commitments are reversed.

This small but steady production programme and the resumption of active research and development work after the five-year break enabled Aldermaston personnel to maintain a constant dialogue with their United States counterparts, for while Britain was seriously engaged in ongoing military development activities, the 'need to know' basis of the exchange of nuclear weapon information remained operative. There exists therefore a total symbiosis between the continuity of positive British nuclear warhead development work, and the continuation of the Anglo-American information exchange arrangements within the limits agreed in 1958. To terminate that work would seriously limit the information exchanges, though the obligations to protect United States data would still remain. Moreover, the argument that any withdrawal of United States assistance to British military nuclear activities would produce a degradation in NATO security, because the United Kingdom could no longer sustain the current levels of its contributions to Western Europe's conventional defences, appeared to have the same persuasive power with American political leaders in 1980 as in 1959. Essentially the same arguments about cost savings and division of labour put forward by Dulles to the JCAE in support of the 1958 arrangements were again repeated at the news conference in Washington in July 1980, when the Trident decision was announced.[52] Thus despite changes in government and personnel, the underlying logic of the Anglo-American linkages in the nuclear warhead field has remained constant for a quarter of a century. However, any change in the constraints on the exchange of nuclear submarine design information, following the retirement of Admiral Rickover in 1982, is unlikely because of the strong links between this area of activity and civil LWR designs.[53]

The date for possible unilateral withdrawal from the information exchanges passed without any obvious problems at the end of 1978, and amendments extending the existing arrangements for the transfer of warhead data, materials and submarine fuel to the end of 1984 were negotiated in the course of 1979, without any desire being expressed by either party for a mutual agreement to terminate them. The formal agreement to extend the two material exchanges was signed in Washington on 5 December 1979, 12 days before the new Conservative Prime Minister, Mrs Thatcher, travelled there to discuss the transfer to the United Kingdom of Trident missiles and their associated technology.[54] It took the usual 60-day period to obtain congressional acquiescence to the new extensions, which entered into force on 25 March 1980, and were due to expire on 31 December 1984, a point eight months beyond the maximum possible period in office of the Thatcher government.[55] More significantly the review date for unilateral withdrawal from the information exchanges is the end of 1983, and the opportunity for this will not then arise again until the end of 1988.

The exchange of nuclear materials was still presenting problems at the end of 1979, however, because the policy of the Carter administration, influenced by non-proliferation considerations, was to limit nuclear material supply contracts to periods of months rather than years, thus sustaining the possibility that supplies would cease before alternative national sources of production could be commissioned. However, the new administration of President Reagan was prepared to offer the type of long-term supply arrangements that President Carter had opposed, and in April 1981 a contract was signed between the United States Department of Energy and the United Kingdom government, under which 100 000 SWU/year of toll enrichment capacity would be available for use by the United Kingdom for military purposes over the following five years.[56] This capacity has been calculated as producing an annual output of 338.5 kilograms of weapon-grade uranium for use in reactor cores.[57]

Assurance of supply had been the major motivation behind the studies undertaken by both the Labour and Conservative governments into the military centrifuge project, and once the Reagan administration offered a five-year enrichment contract, the urgent need to complete this insurance project no longer existed. As a result, construction of the military plant at Capenhurst, originally intended to be completed in 1985, was reported in August 1981 to have been slowed down, and its main function changed to manufacturing low enriched uranium to feed into American high enrichment plants.[58] This meant that the Labour Party, the originators in 1946 of self-sufficiency in military nuclear material production, having been forced by American policies increasingly to move back to this position between 1974 and 1979, now found that their Conservative successors were reverting to a policy of interdependence with the United States in this field. Thus the party whose leader had decried the existence of an independent deterrent was the one which felt it was necessary to take practical steps to achieve it in the nuclear materials area, while the party which had stoutly defended it in public had in practice shown itself more interested in creating a more interdependent relationship with the United States.

The 1981 five-year enrichment contract involved cash payments, rather than a barter of plutonium. Whether the latter will ever be reinstated may depend on a number of developments associated with the civil and military nuclear energy policies of both Britain and the United States. The first was the commissioning in 1980 of the tritium plant at Chapel Cross. In the United States, the Savannah River tritium production reactors have been operated so as to produce tritium and weapon-grade plutonium at the same time, and it is possible that the Chapel Cross process also involves the reactor being used in this way. The result could be an ability to produce in Britain about 173 grams of tritium and 38 kilograms of weapon-grade plutonium per year.[59] This would ensure that additional supplies of weapon-grade plutonium were available from the mid-1980s onwards for use in the production programme for Trident warheads and it might offer material for barter with the United States if required. It would also raise questions about the use of the civil B205 reprocessing plant at BNFL Sellafield for direct military purposes.[60]

A second change is that the United States has increased its production of weapon-grade plutonium to provide materials for the Reagan administration's plan to build 14 000 new nuclear warheads between 1981 and 1991. Moreover, the United States demand for additional plutonium has been such that it withdrew a significant number of plutonium-based weapons from its stockpiles in Europe and elsewhere in 1978–80 in order to recycle the material in their fissile cores. This increased demand has been a product not only of the acquisition of additional warheads but also the replacement of enriched uranium by plutonium in fissile core designs. To meet it, the new administration increased the power levels of its three operational Savannah River reactors, reactivated a fourth and changed the Hanford 'N' reactor from a civil to a military fuel cycle. Calculations suggest that the effect of these moves may be to increase American production of tritium and plutonium from the equivalent of about 1600 kilograms of plutonium in 1980 to over 4000 kilograms in 1984.[61] The Department of Energy has also started to mix 97 per cent Pu-239 with fuel-grade material containing 81 per cent in order to obtain weapon-grade material of 93 per cent composition.[62] The 81 per cent material was produced in the Hanford 'N' reactor when operated on a civil cycle, but British plutonium supplied from Calder Hall or Chapel Cross after 1971 would also have been suitable for this purpose. Indeed, the idea that British and American material can be kept separate while in United States ownership may be intrinsically misleading, as often material will become so intermingled that its origins become obscure: atoms cannot be labelled. This possibility was certainly envisaged in the military agreements.[63]

A further change was that the Reagan administration reversed a number of aspects of the Carter non-proliferation stance, in particular the policy of restricting funding for the development of a prototype commercial fast breeder reactor.

Carter's policy on fast breeder development, coupled with opposition to the idea of recycling plutonium through thermal reactors, had produced a situation where there was little short-term civil demand for the material. President Reagan's reversal of this policy meant that in the late 1980s the United States would need several tonnes of plutonium for its civil reactor development programmes. Officially 1300 kilograms of plutonium have been exported from the United Kingdom 'for civil purposes', but most of this material went to France as a result of an Anglo-American agreement, and was used in the 'Phoenix' and 'Super Phoenix' fast breeder development programmes.[64] Some consideration appears to have been given during 1981 to purchasing or leasing British civil plutonium for use in the American Clinch River prototype fast reactor, under the terms of the civil rather than military agreements.[65] It could have had the indirect effect of releasing limited quantities of American fuel-grade plutonium for weapon purposes, though its more likely impact would have been to allow the United States to maintain existing levels of plutonium stocks for emergency military use. It would thus have been convenient, but not essential, for the United States to have access to the British civil stockpile of plutonium, as U-235 could always be substituted for it in the early stages of fast reactor work. Had this purchase proposal been proceeded with, however, it could have been interpreted as a reestablishment of the military barter in a new guise, with cash acting as the intermediary in an indirect, rather than direct, transaction. It might also have been viewed as a means of offsetting British Trident costs incurred in the United States.

One additional activity occurring in America could have very unpredictable consequences for Anglo-American nuclear relations. Research is being funded to investigate methods of separating Pu-239 from other plutonium isotopes by the use of lasers. The effect of this would be to give all spent reactor fuel a potential for use in advanced nuclear weapons, and thus enable the United States to use its large store of irradiated LWR fuel for this purpose and the United Kingdom to do the same with its magnox fuel.[66]

Overall, therefore, the possibilities still exist for a continuing mutually advantageous trade in nuclear materials between the United States and Britain during the 1980s, though neither state seems to have an absolute need for the other in this area. Yet the precise details of the trade in these materials since 1958, and the use made of all the British plutonium exports to the United States, have not been divulged. This information remains classified and a full understanding of the trade would only be possible were the national security and non-proliferation implications of this information judged to be insignificant. Appendix 6 gives some guide to how much material may have been traded. Five possible, if speculative, end-uses for the totality of British plutonium transferred to the United States exist. One is in a reserve stockpile for emergency weapons use, or as a buffer stock in weapon manufacture; a second is in weapons; a third is in storage for later use in commercial fast breeder reactors; a fourth is in experiments to produce 'mixed-oxide' fuel for thermal reactors and fuel for FBRs; and a fifth for re-transfer to other OECD countries under civil agreements for cooperation.

The evidence that British plutonium has been used in the manufacture of United States weapons is somewhat contradictory. On the one hand, the aims of the original 1958 and 1959 exchange proposals included the provision that this material was to be supplied for unrestricted use by the United States, and specifically for inclusion in American tactical nuclear weapons. There exists no evidence to suggest that plutonium originating in the British military reactors was not used in this way. The situation with regard to material from the civil reactors is complicated by probable discrepancies between the initial aims of the Anglo-American agreements and the policies actually pursued. In 1958 it was envisaged that either some of the civil reactors would be requisitioned by the Ministry of Defence and used as military production ones, or that the initial discharges of fuel from them would be sent to the United States and used for military purposes. However, by the time the first civil reactors started to commission in 1962, the ideas of positioning unlimited numbers of nuclear weapons in Europe had been modified, and by 1964 the United States demand for military plutonium had passed its peak. Although Britain required additional fissile material from America for its military purposes, the United States demand could be met from national sources. As a consequence, Sir Alec Douglas-Home could state that although material from British civil, rather than military, reactors was to be sent to the United States under the military agreements, it was not to be used for weapon purposes.

Britain and the United States thus appear to be moving towards a more stable and harmonious military nuclear relationship in the 1980s than in the two decades that have preceded it. The political complications of British attempts to enter the Common Market no longer exist; an ongoing British nuclear warhead development programme is scheduled to continue throughout the decade and mutual resource savings still appear possible from a trade in nuclear materials. Yet this surprise-free future may not persist either because attempts to achieve the avowed objective of 40 years of military effort, that is the maintenance of a nuclear balance with the USSR, will fail with catastrophic results, or because domestic political forces within the United States and United Kingdom will lead to the termination of the existing arrangements. The most obvious of these is the opposition of some of the political parties in the United Kingdom to the Trident purchase, and the formal commitment of one of them, the Labour Party, to a policy of unilateral nuclear disarmament. For this reason, political decisions will continue to determine the nature of the Anglo-American nuclear relationships to the end of the century, rather than military or technical ones.

10 Old Age? The Implications of the Anglo-American Military Exchange Agreements for the Nuclear Disarmament of Britain

Introduction

Although Britain has been a nuclear weapon state for some 30 years, there has always existed a strong undercurrent of domestic opposition to this status, both outside of the party system in such pressure groups as the Campaign for Nuclear Disarmament (CND), and within it in sizeable sections of both the Labour and Liberal parties. The Labour Party in particular has adopted policies whilst in opposition pledging that, if it is returned to power during the 1980s, it will initiate a series of unilateral acts to alter Britain's political and military linkages with both Europe and the United States. The possibility thus exists that changes of government during the 1980s will lead to radically different policies towards nuclear weapons, including the cancellation of Trident and the initiation of a number of other measures of nuclear disarmament. Yet both the practical implications of these policies, and their likely consequences, remain largely unexplored. Four levels of nuclear disarmament can be visualised, involving increasing degrees of change in the 'surprise-free' situation described in the previous chapter. These are the relinquishment of a dedicated strategic nuclear weapon capability; a change to non-nuclear weapon status within NATO; the declaration of a nuclear weapon free zone in and around the United Kingdom; and the total destruction of all nuclear energy facilities in Britain.

A Nuclear State without Dedicated Strategic Weapons

This option implies that the Polaris missile submarines would be

prematurely retired in the later 1980s, and the Trident programme cancelled, leaving the United Kingdom with an indigenous tactical nuclear capability based upon dual-role aircraft or
cruise missiles, and totally reliant on the United States for both
strategic protection and battlefield weapons. An argument can
be advanced that such a tactical capability would still include a
residual element of strategic deterrence, in so far as the Tornado
aircraft could, on certain assumptions, be capable of bombing
Moscow.[1] Yet such a threat would have low technical credibility
compared with that posed by the Polaris and Trident systems.
Many would argue that in the event of hostilities it would invite a
preemptive strike, and that it is more dangerous to possess a
technically incredible strategic deterrent than no nuclear
weapons at all.

The effect of such a policy upon British nuclear development
and production capabilities would depend upon whether a
decision was taken to switch resources currently allocated to
strategic weapons to the development of new tactical, and
perhaps battlefield, weapons. If this transfer occurred it seems
likely that the workload of the 7000 employees at Aldermaston,
Burghfield Common and Cardiff[2] might have to be increased
while the strategic stockpile was being dismantled. Technical
exchanges with the United States could continue, but they
would be limited to obsolete and specific designs, as the main
area of American nuclear weapon development involves missile
warheads rather than gravity bombs. In the absence of such a
switch of resources, the workforce at Burghfield Common and
Cardiff would still need to be retained for several years to
dispose of the Polaris warheads, but there would be a considerable reduction of effort at Aldermaston. In addition, a cut-off of
further American information on nuclear weapon design would
probably occur, as was threatened in the late 1960s, but the
United Kingdom would still be obliged to protect in perpetuity
all the nuclear weapon information of United States origin in its
possession.

British tactical and battlefield nuclear weapons may be argued to have some final utility in a '1940' situation, where the
Soviet Union's forces had reached the Channel ports, were
threatening to invade the island, and could possibly be deterred
from this act by the threat of using nuclear weapons against an
invasion fleet. This scenario seems far fetched, however, for if
the United States had not succeeded in terminating the war by

threatening the use of nuclear weapons at this point, or actually used them, a British government would have few rational options other than negotiating a surrender on the best available terms. Thus consciously to relinquish strategic weapons but retain tactical or battlefield ones appears a most unsatisfactory policy offering low military utility and uncertain political value. A more logical alternative would be to opt for a policy of relinquishing all nationally-owned nuclear weapons.

A Non-nuclear Weapon State within NATO

One of the major arguments for Britain retaining a nuclear weapon capability, and the central justification for American assistance in sustaining it, is that it is the Western European states' contribution to the NATO nuclear deterrent force. Only Britain appears able to demonstrate to the United States that the Western European states are prepared to contribute fully to their own security in this area, as West Germany is debarred by treaty from possessing nuclear weapons,[3] while France rejects the idea that nuclear weapons can be used in defence of anything other than national territory. Any decision by Britain to abandon its nuclear weapon capability would lead to American perceptions of a lessening of the United Kingdom's commitment to national and Western European defence, and to the concept of mutuality in Anglo-American security relations. Both the political and military consequences of this are difficult to calculate, but both will be crucially dependent upon the degree of consultation with other NATO states before a decision on nuclear weapon destruction is taken and the use made of the resources previously devoted to the nuclear forces. Indeed the major political impact of such an action seems likely to be felt more in the attitudes of the United States, rather than the USSR, to Western Europe. There appear few reasons why the Russian leadership should alter its political view of Britain or its military contingency and targeting plans so long as American nuclear forces remain on British bases and the United Kingdom has access to United States nuclear weapons under 'key of the cupboard' rules.

The arguments for unilateral nuclear disarmament appear to encompass both the proposition that British nuclear forces are pretentious and would have an insignificant effect upon Soviet intentions, and the contrary assertion that they make a nuclear attack upon Britain more likely. While the official British justification for the force in 1980 was the value of two centres of strategic nuclear decision-making within the alliance, there does seem little doubt that a residual argument is the belief that in the absence of a national nuclear capability, the Soviet leadership might believe that they could mount nuclear attacks upon American bases in the United Kingdom without necessarily incurring an American nuclear response upon their own territory. Thus a national nuclear weapon capability is seen as an indispensable adjunct to the existence of United States nuclear weapon bases in Britain.

None of these hypotheses can be proven or disproven: they remain within the realms of political debate and judgement. What is rather more certain, however, are the practical difficulties which will be encountered if an act of national nuclear disarmament were to occur while Britain remained within NATO. Under these circumstances, there appears little possibility of such a move taking place under conditions of international inspection and verification, given the treaty commitments made by the United Kingdom to safeguard United States nuclear weapon data. The process would thus involve the dismantling of the existing stockpile of weapons over a number of years in the Burghfield Common and Cardiff factories, together with an immediate acceptance of full scope IAEA and EURATOM safeguards on all plants and materials in the United Kingdom nuclear fuel cycle. Nuclear weapon data exchanges with the United States would cease immediately, except possibly in the intelligence area, while any continuing supply of American weapon-grade uranium for submarine fuel would be based on purchase, rather than barter, to simplify the safeguards regime.

Abandoning nationally-owned nuclear weapons will thus produce rather complex and uncertain consequences for Britain's security position. Whilst it may be viewed as a significant anti-proliferation gesture by some Third World states, the lack of international verification of the process will detract from its impact, and it appears unlikely appreciably to alter the threat from Soviet military capabilities or the propensity of non-nuclear states under military threat to seek their own nuclear weapons. A reciprocal gesture of partial nuclear disarmament by the USSR appears unlikely. At one extreme, a judgement may be made that nuclear disarmament would at worst make little difference to Britain's security, and at best would enhance it considerably: at the other, it would seem likely to disrupt the NATO security system without similar consequences for the Warsaw Pact states. Only in a radically changed international political environment would it appear to offer the possibility of adding significantly to British and Western European security.

A Nuclear Weapon-free State outside of NATO

Discussion of this option is often accompanied by assumptions of a revolutionary change in British policy towards European security, which since the early 1950s has been based on the need to merge British defence concerns with Western European ones, and forge the closest links between European security policies and those of the United States. It is inconceivable that a decision by a British government to withdraw to 'fortress United Kingdom' in both the security and economic areas would not have profound consequences upon the attitudes both of other Western European countries and of the United States towards European security. A total United States withdrawal from Europe, an increased American military presence in West Germany and active hostility towards the United Kingdom are all possible consequences that could flow from it.

Any declaration by Britain of non-nuclear weapon status and withdrawal from NATO involves three main activities: the nuclear disarmament of British forces; the removal of all United States bases from the United Kingdom; and the removal of United Kingdom military forces from West Germany. This latter act would involve the abrogation of WEU treaty commitments, and would, in the short term, have very disruptive effects upon NATO plans for West European defence. It presents few practical difficulties, however, though many political ones. The other two activities involve very complex problems of implementation given probable United States disquiet at these moves.

The first set of difficulties relates to the process of national nuclear disarmament, and methods of convincing the Soviet Union and other states that this objective has actually been achieved. Two separable issues are involved: the verification of nuclear warhead destruction and accounting for all the fissile material produced for military use. Both would be the subject of American active concern, as all modern British nuclear warheads contain comingled United States information and materials, and the United Kingdom has treaty obligations in perpetuity, originating in the Quebec Agreement of 1944, to prevent their dissemination to third parties without mutual agreement. In addition, the United Kingdom would have to give due notice of withdrawal from its existing technical interchange arrangements with the United States. If this has not occurred by the last day of 1983, the arrangements could not be formally terminated before the end of 1989, unless a mutually agreed arrangement could be concluded prior to that date.[4] A hostile United States government would be unlikely to favour such termination unless the British government of the day was prepared to provide solid guarantees that its interests could be safeguarded.

Superficially, verification of nuclear weapon destruction appears to be a simple process. One obvious technique would be to use the type of input–output analysis discussed at length for destruction of strategic delivery systems within the Eighteen Nations Disarmament Conference (ENDC) in the early 1960s.[5] Under these arrangements, the systems were to be weighed by international observers; dismantled in secret by national technicians; reduced to scrap and then reweighed by the international team to verify that all of the system had been destroyed. With nuclear warheads weighing between 450 and perhaps 120 kilograms,[6] such a technique appears impractical. Unlike large bomber aircraft or missiles, it would be impossible for any international observer team to be certain that numbers of these British warheads had not been held back from destruction, for their dimensions and weight would make such retention very difficult to detect. In a further 1962 ENDC technical study,[7] Britain argued that given the then existing production facilities, it was impossible to ascertain with accuracy the past output of fissile material from production reactors, or the stocks of fissile material likely to be held by states which had conducted explosive testing programmes. It concluded that these uncertainties would enable up to 20 per cent of past output to be covertly stored for possible future military use. Although complete

weapons held back from destruction might gradually deteriorate because of corrosion and maintenance problems with their
non-nuclear components, and their potential yields would degrade rather more rapidly due to ageing of the tritium used in
them, it is difficult to see how an international inspection team
could be totally convinced that this act of 'cheating' had not
occurred. To compound the problem, it is unlikely that a British
government would permit inspection or weighing of the
warheads to be destroyed or provide details of the fissile material and thermonuclear fuel in them. Some weapon components
pose both radiation and toxic dangers to health and their
destruction might well have to take place by remote means
under tightly controlled conditions.[8] The United States would
almost certainly veto any international inspection of the
warheads and the dismantling process or the release of data on
critical masses as this could be argued to lead to dissemination of
American nuclear weapon data. In addition, non-nuclear state
members of any international inspection team would inevitably
acquire classified information on the construction of nuclear
weapons and the quantities of fissile material employed by their
observation of the act of nuclear disarmament, and thus this
process would become one of disseminating nuclear weapon
knowledge to non-nuclear states, contrary to the British commitments under Article I of the Non-Proliferation Treaty.[9] Thus
the very limited international technical verification of the destruction of the British nuclear weapons stockpile that seems
legally feasible is unlikely to be totally convincing to the USSR
or the non-nuclear states, and the credibility of the United
Kingdom's policy will rest almost entirely on the political intent
underlying it, together with the external policy alignment
adopted by the British government. This is not to argue that
such political acts would be insufficient to produce a belief
among responsible opinion that disarmament had occurred: the
problem would be that many outside Britain and some inside the
country would use those technical considerations to throw
doubt on the completeness and irreversibility of the act. For if
the USSR or France were to announce tomorrow that it had
chosen to destroy its nuclear weapons without detailed verification, how many people in Britain or the United States would
believe it?

The avowed destruction of the British nuclear weapon stock-

pile would not in itself constitute nuclear disarmament, however, as several technical issues would continue to undermine a
nuclear weapon-free posture. One concerns the disposal of the
fissile materials recovered from the scrapped weapons. While
the enriched uranium could be used as nuclear submarine fuel,
or diluted to act as fuel for civil reactors, the disposal of the
weapon-grade plutonium presents a more difficult problem. It
could be placed under IAEA safeguards and added to the
inventory of civil material currently stored at Sellafield awaiting
development of the commercial fast breeder reactor (CFBR)
but this would mean that the weapon material would remain on
national soil, possibly in metallic form, and would be easily
accessible for use in recreating a stockpile of first or second
generation atomic weapons in a national emergency. Britain
would also continue to possess an indigenous capability to revert
rapidly to nuclear weapon status as bomb-design information
and expertise would remain in existence for many years. A
politically symbolic 'burning of the books' or computer tapes
and closure of Aldermaston might well take place, yet the
knowledge possessed by bomb designers would remain in existence for two or three generations, and the supporting technologies are now so diffused and widespread that most outside
observers would simply not believe a British government which
argued that it had exorcised the relevant design expertise, and
could no longer revert to nuclear weapon status. Whether there
would be anything to gain from such a change of policy in an
emergency, however, can be debated, especially if the threat
was from a nuclear superpower. Yet the danger would be that in
such a situation, the mere existence of a British potential for
reversion to infant nuclear weapon status could stimulate a
preemptive nuclear attack upon its territory and facilities.

Two final problems which would still remain after an act of
national nuclear weapon disarmament concern the maintenance
of the British nuclear fleet submarine flotilla and the civil
nuclear fuel cycle. Currently no non-nuclear state possesses a
nuclear submarine reactor, and thus no experience exists of the
practical problems of applying IAEA and EURATOM
safeguards to a nation which has a legitimate military demand
for about 350 kilograms of weapon-grade uranium per year.[10]
Yet so long as the United Kingdom has this submarine capability, its associated fuel fabrication technologies and the means to

obtain a supply of weapon-grade uranium for it, the technical credibility of any move to non-nuclear weapon status will be open to question. Inspection of these military plants and facilities by the IAEA is unlikely to be easily conceded because of the clauses preventing the diffusion of technical information on nuclear submarine reactor technology and fuel fabrication contained in the 1958 agreement with the United States. Thus, so long as Britain retains these submarines in its fleet, the practical problems of convincing other states that Britain either is not, or could no longer be a nuclear weapon state would probably be compounded.

In 1982, Britain had in store some $14\frac{1}{2}$ tonnes of separated plutonium oxide originating from the CEGB magnox reactors; about $5\frac{1}{2}$ tonnes were tied up in fast reactor development work; some $14\frac{1}{2}$ tonnes were in reactors or awaiting reprocessing; and an unknown quantity produced by the BNFL military reactors remained stockpiled in metallic form.[11] This stock is increasing at the rate of about $2-2\frac{1}{2}$ tonnes per year (see Appendices 5a and 5b). All of this material is capable of being used in an emergency to make first or second generation nuclear weapons, though the resultant warheads would be of uncertain yield and have a limited shelf-life. Even if this stockpile, the BNFL reprocessing plant at Sellafield and the centrifuge enrichment plant at Capenhurst were placed under IAEA and EURATOM safeguards, the plutonium would still remain in the physical possession of the United Kingdom authorities. Moreover, the 1962 ENDC study concluded that an international inspection agency, using 1000 people to examine British activities alone, would only be able to detect, but not prevent, diversion of more than 2 per cent of fissile material from the fuel cycle.[12]

One possible conclusion from the preceding discussion is that to attempt merely to destroy Britain's nuclear weapon stockpile is at best a half-way house, and an unsatisfactory one at that. Technical doubts about the implementation of this policy may dominate other states' perceptions of it, irrespective of the stated political intentions of the British government. This raises the question of whether the real choice for Britain lies between maintaining a militarily credible strategic deterrent until politically acceptable multilateral arms control agreements can be negotiated and abandoning all forms of nuclear energy in the hope of reinforcing the technical credibility and political impact of a policy of nuclear disarmament.

Britain as a Nuclear-free Zone

The complete denuclearisation of Britain would involve the dismantling of those nuclear warheads in the national weapon inventory, removal of American bases, dismantling or scuttling of the nuclear submarine fleet, closing down all facets of Britain's nuclear industry and transferring all stocks of fissile materials out of the country. None of the three latter objectives would be easy to implement. The destruction of the national flotilla of nuclear fleet submarines, the only one of its kind within NATO other than that operated by the United States, would involve a major loss of conventional defence capabilities, given the emphasis that has been placed increasingly upon the use of this type of vessel in naval activities in the North Atlantic. Moreover, the effectiveness of any British maritime warfare capability divorced from the existing NATO infrastructure is debatable.[13] Thus, however desirable destruction of this force might seem to be from the perspective of increasing the technical credibility of nuclear disarmament, it is one which a neutralist British government would be very loath to take unless it was committed to both the unilateral nuclear and conventional disarmament of the country.

The existence of the civil nuclear fuel cycle and the plutonium stockpile are linked together, in so far as the current nuclear reactor systems only liberate between 0.25 and 1.5 per cent of the energy potentially available from their nuclear fuel.[14] To increase this percentage, it is necessary to use both the separated plutonium stocks and the depleted natural uranium from irradiated fuel rods and uranium enrichment operations to fuel fast breeder reactors. Thus any decision to abandon nuclear power in the interests of making an act of nuclear disarmament more convincing has to be related to the debates on national energy supply policy, and the role of nuclear power within it. This debate is complicated by the short-term impact of North Sea oil and gas supplies, the availability of reserves of coal capable of sustaining current national energy consumption levels for about 200 years, and the existence of an easily accessible energy potential equal to that of the coal reserves locked up within these stockpiled nuclear materials. The experiences of the early 1980s, with depressed demand for energy and falling oil prices, makes it difficult to focus upon the longer-term perspective which suggests that pressure upon finite supplies of fossil fuels will inevitably increase. In such circumstances, a government which released its available stocks of nuclear energy materials and made no investment in commercial fast breeder reactors (CFBRs), in the interests of pursuing a convincing policy of nuclear disarmament, would be described as either brave or foolhardy.

Future development of CFBRs necessitates the operation of thermal reactors and reprocessing plants for a significant number of years, together with the creation of a very large stockpile of plutonium.[15] If a British government were to seek to retain as many future options as possible in the energy supply field, it is difficult to see how this could be done without it having some effect upon the technical credibility of an act of unilateral nuclear disarmament, given the large quantities of plutonium, capable of at least emergency use in crude atomic weapons, that would have to be stockpiled in the United Kingdom and pass through its nuclear fuel cycle each year. Moreover, a decision to abandon nuclear energy development and close down all nuclear power stations and their associated plants would still leave the government with the problem of how to deal with the stocks of separated plutonium, which are the largest in the world. Are they to be retained in Britain or disposed of by sale, barter or gift to other countries, despite their military potential? The irony is that the only known method of effective final disposal is to transmute them into fission products in a fast burner, rather than breeder, reactor.[16] The drawback to such a process is that it would take decades to complete, would involve developing much the same technology as is applicable to a CFBR, and would be likely to be vociferously opposed by those who resist the further development of nuclear power on environmental safety grounds. Yet unless a policy of denuclearisation can include the implementation of a satisfactory method of disposing of the large British plutonium stockpile within the space of a few years, the technical possibility of reversion to nuclear status would remain.

History and Future Policy

The output of separated plutonium and enriched uranium from the British civil and military nuclear industries, together with 30 years' experience as a nuclear weapon state, is likely to detract from other states being totally convinced that a British government intent on nuclear disarmament has actually achieved that status. The act of scrapping the existing nuclear weapon inventory may itself take several years of difficult work by specialists, but of perhaps greater importance is the impossibility of verifying the results of past activities, and the economic and military penalties of dismantling both the civil nuclear energy system and the nuclear submarine fleet together with their supporting industrial infrastructure, despite their inherent potential to restore a stock of first or second generation atomic weapons to the country's armed forces at short notice. Those who assert that political intentions and commitments transcend residual technical capabilities can justifiably claim that these issues are minor matters of detail. Yet so long as plutonium stocks, weapon design knowledge and fissile material fabrication facilities remain in being in Britain, any public policy of denuclearisation is unlikely to be totally convincing to, or accepted by, the sceptical leaders of other states. At worst, some of them may dismiss declaratory policy as a fraud, and Britain would find it impossible to offer convincing technical proof to the contrary.

The unpalatable conclusion that emerges from this discussion is that Britain is likely to be viewed by potentially hostile states as a near-nuclear or first generation nuclear power even if it attempts to lose this status. Thus the relationship between the civil and military components of nuclear energy has created a situation where there appears no easy and clean escape from the complex pressures of nuclear weapon possession, while the historic and ongoing nuclear defence relationship with the United States gives a policy of nuclear disarmament an added dimension, and makes verification of it very difficult to implement. Yet this is an area where belief, rather than fact, and emotion, rather than reason, remain the dominant vocabulary of political debate. It is a difficult matter of judgement in such circumstances whether the preferred policy should be to accede to the moral urgings of those who wish to be untainted by the stigma of nuclear weapon possession and acceptance of doctrines of nuclear deterrence (even if the consequences that may result are totally unintended and unanticipated, and would themselves be judged inherently immoral), or stoically to accept that an existing nuclear weapon state will always be regarded as such, whatever its political claims to the contrary, and that its population has little choice but to attempt to sustain a technically credible strategic nuclear force at least cost, while still striving to achieve a multilateral nuclear disarmament agreement. Yet to be effective, such an agreement would have to overcome the same verification problems that confront a policy of unilateral disarmament. This only leaves the option of politically outflanking these problems by converting adversary relationships into cooperative ones. Thus the only realistic solution to the threat of nuclear war appears to be in the field of politics, rather than technology.

11 The United States, Britain and the Military Atom: Retrospect and Evaluation

Introduction

The preceding account of the evolution of American and British policies towards the development of nuclear technology for military purposes in the United Kingdom offers grounds for arguing that it can best be understood in the context of a chronological movement from one type of relationship to another. Concepts of dependency, interdependency and self-sufficiency play a central role in describing this progression, but the civil/military divide, the nature of state decision-making systems and weapon development processes are less visibly linked to these chronological stages, and, in some cases, impinge upon what was occurring in a random fashion. As a consequence the types of dependency, interdependency and self-sufficiency found within the Anglo-American nuclear relationship will be examined first (together with a breakdown of the period into chronological stages), followed by the interrelationship between these stages and the other ideas.

Chronological Stages and the Dependency/Interdependency Relationship

In retrospect, Britain's development of nuclear energy for military purposes has passed through six successive stages:
   (i) 1943–5: wartime integration;
  (ii) 1946–57: total insulation from the United States;
 (iii) 1958–64: reciprocal Anglo-American interaction, including the rapid creation of a British stockpile of nuclear

weapons; the plans for a mutually advantageous trade in fissile materials, and the switch to the use of American-manufactured strategic nuclear delivery systems;

(iv) 1965–70: the decline of the reciprocal relationship, due to the lack of an ongoing British nuclear weapon development programme and the complications created by attempts to enter the EEC;

(v) 1971–81: the partial regeneration of an active relationship as a consequence of the Chevaline project, offset by the parallel moves to make the United Kingdom visibly self-sufficient in the supply of nuclear materials for military purposes as a consequence of American arms control policies;

(vi) 1981 onwards: reinforcement of the active relationship coupled with reduced political pressures to attain overt independence in nuclear material supplies.

The relationship commenced with wartime integration, yet with a strong British intent to create a capacity for a national research programme into nuclear energy in the post-war period, including the ability to construct and detonate test devices. The dangers of being the junior partner in an integrated project were well demonstrated by the lack of bargaining power possessed by the British government in 1946, when the American President decided to stop any further interchange of information and materials between the two countries, in order both to pursue a policy of international control over atomic energy and to retain an American monopoly over nuclear weapons. This action was reinforced by the 1946 United States atomic energy legislation, which effectively transferred to Congress the power to decide whether interchanges with the United Kingdom should be restarted.

The chief characteristics of the subsequent period of insulation between the two nuclear projects were the inherently political nature of the British project which, in complete contrast to American activities, was aimed more at demonstrating an ability to make nuclear weapons than creating a stockpile of them, and the consistent efforts by United Kingdom negotiators to create a new cooperative, rather than integrative, relationship with the United States. These efforts were infused with a determination to avoid any conflict with the common interests of both states in building up the military strength of the Atlantic

Alliance against the USSR, resulting in no attempt being made to use Britain's potential bargaining power within their uranium supply relationship to obtain American concessions over information and nuclear material exchanges: indeed a third Windscale production reactor was foregone in recognition of this common interest in increasing the United States' inventory of nuclear weapons. Throughout this period various schemes for closer cooperation between Britain and the United States in the military applications of nuclear energy were discussed between officials and political leaders, though not with Congress, but at no time was Britain prepared to forego the capacity to produce the fissile material for nuclear weapons and conduct both military and civil experimental programmes with it. By contrast, there was a readiness to limit its independent bomb production facilities if access to weapons in the American nuclear stockpile or American manufacture of British owned nuclear bombs could be arranged. The low priority attached to the growth of a weapon stockpile was a reflection of the political motivations behind the United Kingdom programme, the lack of modern means of delivery, and the rather arbitrary nature of the stockpile target of 200 bombs. The tendency to subordinate production of British weapons to wider alliance considerations was continued by Churchill's government, where it was associated with the relatively low priority given until 1954 to weapon development beyond the Blue Danube design. Both of these policies were affected by the failure of the Windscale reactors to produce the quantities of plutonium expected of them in 1946. Yet the loan of 15 kilograms of this material for civil fast breeder experiments between 1954 and 1956 illustrates the general lack of political urgency attached to the accumulation of a substantial stockpile of weapons during this period.

Decisions had been taken in early 1953 to build two additional plutonium/power reactors at Calder Hall and freeze the design of the high enrichment plant for uranium at Capenhurst, but no significant change in the nature of the British nuclear programme was apparent until late in 1954. A number of linked actions were then initiated to try to give Britain a militarily significant stockpile of the most modern designs of nuclear weapons by the early 1960s. These included: the allocation of resources for an extensive explosive testing programme in Australia to develop atomic weapons of both greater yield and decreased weapon weight to yield ratios than the existing design; the expansion of military plutonium and high enriched uranium production capacity by building six additional production reactors and extending Capenhurst; the initiation of thermonuclear weapon development; the building of testing facilities in the Pacific; and the setting up of manufacturing facilities which would enable tens of weapons to be assembled each year. These decisions were a product of a juxtaposition of circumstances, including the realisation that the 1954 United States Atomic Energy Act was not going to make detailed Anglo-American collaboration any easier; the imminent arrival in squadron service of the first aircraft specifically designed to carry the Blue Danube bomb; the related adoption of nuclear deterrence as the conceptual basis of national defence policy; a belief that nuclear arms limitation agreements were inevitable towards the end of the 1950s; and the linked determination that Britain should possess similar technical capabilities to the other two nuclear states by the time they occurred.

These decisions had little immediate effect upon the absence of an Anglo-American dialogue in the weapon area, and paradoxically the first significant move towards technical collaboration between the two states occurred in the area of submarine reactor technology. The peculiarity about this event was that there was no possibility of any reciprocity by Britain in this technology. The American motivation appeared to be a belief that the close working relationship which then existed between the two navies would result in the nuclear submarines being constructed by the Royal Navy providing a positive contribution to the 'common defense'. The manner in which the executive branch in the United States attempted to by-pass the JCAE on this issue soured relations between the two, but the increase in international tension, the perceived need both to pursue arms limitation measures with the USSR and to strengthen Western European defences through the deployment of nuclear weapons, the close personal ties between the leaders of both countries and an expanding dialogue on nuclear matters after 1956, resulted in the National Security Council decision of October 1957 to seek amendments to the 1954 United States Atomic Energy Act in order to permit exchanges of weapons data and materials with the United Kingdom.

The period from 1958 to 1964 can be regarded as the time of

maximum interchange between the two countries. All British weapon design information was passed to the United States, while that country reciprocated with information which could assist with production designs for the new bombs and missile warheads that the United Kingdom was developing. Plans were laid to engage in a mutually beneficial trade in nuclear materials, based on the ability of the United States to produce weapon-grade uranium and tritium more cheaply than the United Kingdom and the attractive economics of producing weapon-grade plutonium in British military and civil reactors and bartering it for these American materials. Britain's use of American supplied nuclear materials and non-nuclear weapon components was dictated by two considerations: cost and time. With this United States assistance, the United Kingdom was in a position to place weapons in production and achieve its limited stockpile targets much earlier than otherwise might have been the case: by 1960–2 instead of 1967–8. It was calculated that national production plants for U-235 and tritium could be reactivated before any refusal by the United States to continue to supply them would have an effect upon the operations of the British nuclear submarine fleet or the reliability of its nuclear weapon stockpile. One paradox concerning the 1958 bilateral agreement was that it effectively terminated the submarine reactor data exchanges, the one existing technical exchange arrangement in the military nuclear area. Thus the net effect of these arrangements was to retain British independence in the supply of nuclear materials; to enable the United Kingdom to contribute a limited stockpile of nuclear weapons rapidly, and at reduced cost to the 'common defense'; to free some of its resources for other alliance defence tasks; to force it to develop an independent design and production capability for nuclear submarine reactors; and to persuade Her Majesty's Government to accept that all battlefield weapons available to British troops should be in United States' custody, in order to facilitate the American President's political control over the initial phases of any hostilities in Europe. In addition, a very close working relationship was forged between the two sets of national weapon design teams.

The honeymoon period of this new relationship, designed to maximise both states' defence resources, did not last long, and its ending was symbolised by the election of a new United States

President, the British government's attempts to negotiate entry into the Common Market and the greater willingness of Macmillan to make concessions to the USSR in return for arms limitation agreements. Difficulties over the American policy to be adopted towards French nuclear aspirations led to a National Security Council decision to try eventually to eliminate both Britain and France as nuclear states. However, these aspirations were soon overtaken by the need to use Britain's Christmas Island base for atmospheric testing, which in turn led to an involuntary expansion, rather than contraction, of areas for nuclear weapon data exchanges. At the higher political levels, suspicion persisted of British willingness to trade weapon and submarine reactor data with France in return for its acquiescence to EEC entry.

The British general election in late 1964, which returned the Labour Party to power under Wilson's leadership, generated considerable political rhetoric on the topic of the independence, or lack of it, of Britain 's nuclear forces. Wilson's view of the matter appeared to be that while the Conservative Party had publicly championed the idea of nuclear independence, in practice they had exchanged that status for one of dependency upon the United States in the years after 1958. This argument was primarily based on the closure of the British tritium production plants, the suspension of enriched uranium production at Capenhurst, and the commitment of British nuclear forces to a NATO role. The Labour Party in office continued the policy of acquiring U-235 for military use from the United States in exchange for plutonium from British civil reactors and produced and stockpiled nuclear weapons using this material, but halted physics package development work and explosive testing and redirected some of Aldermaston's efforts to civil projects. These decisions, plus Anglo-American friction in the civil nuclear field and the well-publicised policy of seeking entry into the EEC, created major difficulties when the information exchange arrangements were reviewed in 1968. The signing of the NPT in that year was linked with this, but the main problem was a belief that the United Kingdom's prime aim was no longer to contribute to the 'common defense'. The known commitment of Heath to closer British ties with Europe, and his public utterances about possible Anglo-French nuclear collaboration, resulted in little initial change in this situation after the Conservative Party's election victory in 1970, although the arrangements for obtaining nuclear submarine fuel had been placed on a more formal footing in 1969.

This situation started to change when the Conservative government initiated studies on a Polaris improvement or successor project, and eventually decided in principle to fund it and restart both warhead project work and explosive testing. The Conservative government's decision to move to full-scale development of the Chevaline warhead, taken after the ABM treaty had been signed by the USSR, was sustained by its Labour successor, which was then forced by American policies to take steps to limit the country's dependency upon the United States for tritium, and study methods of restarting national production of weapon-grade uranium. The reasons for its reversal of the policies of 1964–70 remain somewhat obscure, though there does appear to have been a fear that the advocates of more rigorous anti-nuclear proliferation legislation in Congress would create a situation where extensions to the military material exchanges might prove impossible to negotiate.[1] Thus, despite the political rhetoric, it is hard to escape the conclusion that, by 1979, the Labour Party leadership had been forced by circumstances to revert to a policy of moving British military nuclear capabilities to the position of self-sufficiency that was first achieved by Attlee's government in 1945–51.

The policy of the Conservative government after 1980 was characterised by a renewed emphasis upon a division of labour in the NATO defence structure, and a willingness to contribute to the 'common defense' at the highest level, that of nuclear deterrence. The Trident purchase was seen as necessary, both because of a belief that the only effective deterrent is a technically credible one, and because it, together with the nuclear submarine fleet, could be presented to the United States as a positive example of European willingness to contribute not only to their own defence but also to that of the United States. It was symbolised by a renewed willingness to accept dependence upon American facilities if substantial resource savings could be obtained.

These six historical phases of the Anglo-American nuclear relationship demonstrate that from the initial position of integration it moved to almost pure self-sufficiency. After 1958, the position of self-sufficiency remained in the submarine technology and material supply field, with any acquisitions from the United States being motivated by cost savings and insured against by the existence of reserve plant, stockpiling and the ability to produce new nuclear materials before the replacement of the old ones became essential. The situation with regard to warheads was rather more complex, as access to United States information almost certainly led to better weapon weight to yield ratios and more advanced weapons being placed into production earlier than would have been the case had purely national designs been used. The quantity and quality of the weapon design knowledge acquired by the United Kingdom prior to 1959, however, suggests that there was no reason why warheads of this kind could not have been designed by national efforts alone, though at considerably greater political and economic cost and over a longer period than actually occurred. Thus the effect of the weapon data interchange was to provide technically credible warheads using less resources than would otherwise have been the case. This arrangement rested on reciprocity and, in particular, on an active research effort in specific areas by Aldermaston. Although this reciprocity clearly declined between 1964 and 1970, it appears to have been sustained since that time. Overall, therefore, the judgement must be that these apparent dependencies cannot be classified as falling into the vulnerability category, but are rather sensitivities, which can be easily overcome, given appropriate inputs of resources.

The key to understanding the Anglo-American military relationship in nuclear energy is the acceptance by both states that it is in their mutual interest for Britain to have a technically effective strategic deterrent at minimum cost. So long as this mutual belief persists, the relationship seems destined to continue. Without American assistance, Britain would still possess an ability to design and manufacture nuclear warheads, though their technical effectiveness might be the subject of greater uncertainties than at present. Yet one of the major objectives of the relationship has been the political one of making American and European security indivisible. Since 1958 successive British governments have used it to sustain an effective position of self-sufficiency in nuclear warhead design and production, and to limit costs compared to a purely national project. Yet the successful implementation of this policy has rested above all on an ability to situate Britain's nuclear forces within the context of an alliance policy of maximising the 'common defense'.

The Civil/Military Dichotomy and Anglo-American Agreements for Cooperation

The use of nuclear energy for civil power generation, rather than military purposes, remained a future aspiration rather than an immediate possibility until 1954, while Anglo-American-Canadian control over the non-communist world's supplies of uranium gave them the power to limit other states' nuclear development programmes. In 1954 the uranium supply position eased, while the United States amended its atomic energy legislation to allow domestic commercial development of nuclear power. The next year, the United Kingdom government announced its intention to build a series of nuclear power stations aimed primarily at electricity generation, and the United States responded with the Shippingport project. The civil nuclear age had started.

In retrospect there appears to have been no clear vision until the early 1960s of the need to make a sharp distinction for non-proliferation purposes between the military and civil aspects of nuclear power. Indeed the history of Anglo-American activities from 1956 to 1964 is replete with examples of this distinction being ignored in order to build up military capabilities. The first occasion when this happened concerned the status of submarine reactors in the context of United States domestic legislation. By classifying them as civil reactors it proved possible to initiate transfers of information on their technology to Britain, the element of reciprocity being incorporated in demands for data on United Kingdom magnox power stations. This exercise was a blatant attempt to outflank the restrictions on military transfers to Britain, and was recognised as such when, in 1958, the sale of one of these reactors to Britain was brought within the terms of the military bilateral agreement between the two states.

Between 1957 and 1959 the USAEC became engaged in a series of activities which, had they reached fruition, would have made a mockery of the whole idea of the 'Atoms for Peace' programme. The idea was to use plutonium recovered from reactors supplied to foreign countries under this programme for military purposes. Opposition from both Japan and the State Department served to undermine these efforts, and the option was then examined of obtaining plutonium from British civil (that is, CEGB and SSEB) reactors instead. These and other considerations led the British government to contemplate operating some of them on a military fuel cycle, and one was modified to facilitate this. In parallel, it appears to have been originally envisaged that stocks of uranium enriched to a level below that of weapon grade would be transferred to the United Kingdom for further enrichment at Capenhurst and eventual use in weapons. Although there is no evidence to indicate that any of the CEGB stations have operated on a military fuel cycle, and transfers of low enriched uranium as feed to enable the Capenhurst plant to produce significant quantities of weapon-grade material do not appear to have taken place, what is not in doubt is the British Labour government's actions after 1964 in transferring plutonium obtained from CEGB and SSEB civil nuclear reactors to the United States under the terms of the military agreement between the two states. The further twist to this complex saga was that the United States government notified Britain that it had no immediate intention of using any British civil plutonium transferred under these arrangements for military purposes, and maintained, almost 20 years later, that it had not done so.

The reduction and, in Britain's case, virtual termination of fissile material production for military purposes after 1964, and the conversion of many of the military plants to perform civil roles, created the possibility of American and British civil nuclear activities being subjected to voluntary international safeguards. The belief was that this would assist in the construction of a regime for civil nuclear power and would both allow for the latter's worldwide development and prevent diversion of materials produced by it to military uses. For the United States, this presented few problems, as none of the military production reactors, other than Hanford 'N', were power/plutonium ones, though the uranium enrichment situation was somewhat more complex. The British position was the reverse, for while the low enrichment stages of Capenhurst could be classed as a civil plant so long as the high enrichment stages were inoperative, the Windscale facilities were required to reprocess both the output from the eight military reactors operating on a civil fuel cycle and the CEGB and SSEB used fuel, some of which was transferred to the United States prior to 1971 under the military agreement. It was largely because the British government wished to make as clear a distinction as practicable between military and civil activities, and thus have the option of placing the latter under voluntary safeguards, that the eight Chapel Cross and Calder Hall reactors were classed as military plants, while the CEGB and SSEB ones were deemed civil, even though all these reactors were operated in a manner which optimised electricity production. In line with this policy, it was decided to cease transferring plutonium from the civil reactors to the United States under the military agreement in 1970 and substitute material from the military ones. Other actions in conformity with it included sending only natural uranium hexafluoride gas from Springfields to America to undergo toll enrichment to weapon grade in American plants, rather than slightly enriched material from the civil Capenhurst plant, and constructing a separate military centrifuge plant at Capenhurst to provide slightly enriched feed materials for military U-235 production.

The second half of the 1960s produced considerable Anglo-American friction over both the commercial benefits of nuclear power development and nuclear exports, and their links with the system of IAEA safeguards designed to give timely warning of diversion of materials and plants to military purposes. This latter conflict was precipitated by the need for Britain to import part of its initial inventory of slightly enriched AGR fuel from the United States, and the resulting American attempts to use this to force the British government publicly to accept voluntary IAEA safeguards over its own civil reactors and any which its reactor-building companies might export. The American move generated considerable hostility in Britain, as it was suspected that the action had been primarily inspired by commercial motives. The consequence was to push the United Kingdom towards collaboration with Europe, rather than the United States, in the further development of civil nuclear technology. Thus while the two states remained close collaborators in the military area, they became competitors in the civil one.

Although the NATO 'key of the cupboard' nuclear weapon arrangements and the bilateral military nuclear information flows between Britain and the United States did not breach any legal obligations entered into upon signature of the NPT, they did open both countries to the charge that they were violating the 'spirit' of the treaty, whatever that might be. Furthermore, some of the Anglo-American nuclear interactions between 1956 and 1964 were historically embarrassing, for they appeared to breach the guidelines which later formed the basis of the international non-proliferation regime, and opened the two states to charges that they were engaging in the activity of 'do as I say, not as I do'.[2] There remains the suspicion that the lack of explicit public statements about the military material agreements by successive British governments is partly motivated by anxiety that what occurred would support this charge. The same argument also applies to the confidential safeguards agreements with EURATOM and the IAEA, as the dual use of fuel fabrication and reprocessing facilities appears to necessitate both plants and materials being moved in and out of the safeguards regime at the request of the British government. Yet in practice there was and is nothing in the Nuclear Proliferation Treaty (NPT) to prevent continued British and American nuclear collaboration for military purposes, with the exception of the direct transfer of complete weapons, while the military material agreements contain information on quantities, types and purities that was, and is, classified for both military security and anti-proliferation reasons. In addition, Britain is placed under no obligation by the NPT to submit any of its plants to IAEA safeguards: its action in doing so from 1966 onwards was a voluntary gesture to encourage others. The dual use of certain plants is largely a product of historical circumstances; the Ministry of Defence paid the majority of their construction costs and ministers were not prepared to provide additional money for further military plants, merely to simplify the voluntary operation of IAEA and EURATOM safeguards.

One consequence of these past activities is that at least three criteria for distinguishing between civil and military production activities have arisen in the Anglo-American context over the last 30 years. They are:

  (i) The isotopic composition of plutonium and uranium, and the related processes and plants used to manufacture it. Weapon-grade fissile material was produced in a military production reactor, or a power reactor operating on a military fuel cycle, or a specialist high enrichment plant. In the early years, this enabled military plants to be clearly identified, as well as military-grade material. After 1960, however, the ability to use the increasing numbers of power reactors to produce weapon-grade plutonium, the use of weapon-grade uranium as fuel for civil research reactors, and advances in physics package design which enabled fissile material with lesser percentages of the isotopes favoured for warhead construction to be used in nuclear weapons, all reduced the perceived importance of these technical distinctions.

(ii) The organisation performing the production activities and the legal owners of plants and materials. Thus the reactors owned and operated by the CEGB and SSEB have always been classed as civil ones, and those built by the UKAEA and now owned by BNFL as military ones, even if both were operated in a similar manner. However, prior to April 1969, all plutonium in civil fuel reprocessed by the UKAEA at Windscale was legally the property of that organisation, and it was thus legitimate to employ it for military purposes, even if the plant which produced it was a civil one.

(iii) The nature of the agreement under which material is transferred. Thus, so long as plutonium produced in civil reactors and used by the recipient for non-weapon purposes was transferred under a military agreement, or the material acquired in return was used in weapon production, the exchange was deemed to be a military one.

These criteria illustrate the contemporary difficulties of distinguishing between the civil and military atom, and the problems these are likely to produce if a British government were to attempt to implement a policy of nuclear disarmament. In particular, the continued operation of magnox reactors and stockpiling of separated plutonium from them, together with the existence of a nuclear submarine fleet and its support facilities, detract from the technical credibility of such a move.

The civil/military dichotomy has thus been, and will remain, a central issue in the Anglo-American nuclear weapon and submarine relationship, together with the degree to which their military activities are compatible with policies towards the international non-proliferation regime. It will also pose very difficult problems for any future attempt to create a non-nuclear armed Britain.

Decisions and Policy-making

Development programmes for British nuclear weapons have always been initiated by the high policy decisions of political leaders. These have set very broad technical objectives that development teams should strive to achieve, and also allocated resources to them. Government establishments, commercial organisations and civil servants have then been left to formulate instrumental strategies to achieve these broad objectives, such as the explosion of a megaton yield weapon. There is no overt evidence to suggest that nuclear decisions have ever escaped from political control by the Prime Minister of the day and selected members of his Cabinet, though it appears that the full Cabinet has been consulted only infrequently, and, even then, given little detailed information on projects. Any argument that these activities represent a case of sectoral policy or low politics is undermined by these initial, higher-level political decisions and choices.

The main high policy acts related to the British nuclear project can be readily identified. The first group was the move to send the Maud Report to the United States, the subsequent decision not to participate in a joint Anglo-American project, and its reversal in order that British scientists and engineers could assist with the Manhattan Project. This latter decision was taken in the spirit of the wartime idea of the 'common defense'. A second group comprised the decision by the Attlee administration to implement a policy of developing an independent British nuclear project , and included plans to explode a nuclear device similar to the Nagasaki bomb, and to produce weaponised versions of it in very small numbers. A third group of decisions included the action of the Churchill government in 1954 in attempting to demonstrate Britain's ability to make a thermonuclear weapon and greatly to expand and accelerate fissile material production in order to support an extensive nuclear weapon manufacturing programme. The fourth group involved the reduction of the experimental thermonuclear programme, the reorientation of the material and weapon production programme after the agreements with the United States, the stockpiling of relatively low numbers of strategic and tactical bombs, the decision to rely on United States 'key of the cupboard' weapons in other roles, and the development of a relatively large nuclear submarine fleet. Two further significant political decisions were those to reduce the nuclear warhead development programme after 1965, and then to revive it in 1969–70 in order to study and develop the Chevaline warhead and reentry vehicle. All these decisions were made by the political leadership on the basis of the deterrent, rather than war-fighting, role of nuclear weapons. The use of this criterion is particularly marked in the period up to 1954, where it was politically visible attainments which were being aimed at rather than extensive military capabilities: 'the art not the article'. Again, in 1954, the political target of exploding a megaton bomb was chosen because of the demonstration effect inherent in achieving a similar level of nuclear technology to the two superpowers. Finally, neither the V bombers nor the Polaris force were intended to be anything other than a minimum deterrent force: indeed in so far as Britain has made decisions on force size by reference to strategic doctrines, it has been ideas of limited assured destruction or minimum deterrence that have predominated. The function of the independent strategic nuclear force has never been to fight a war but to produce a political effect via the technically credible capability to threaten Moscow and other major Soviet cities with destruction. The parallel political message conveyed by the force to the United States has been that the United Kingdom is a reliable European ally willing to contribute appropriate resources to the common defence pool, and willing to take equal risks to those shouldered by America in defence of NATO countries and the territory of the United States itself. It is this posture which has made the United States willing to assist the United Kingdom in its military nuclear programme.

There is little doubt, however, that political leaders have felt constrained when they have moved beyond high policy decisions to more instrumental questions of the best technical method of achieving political objectives. So long as the high policy issues were of the type 'Do we attempt to explode a megaton device at the earliest possible moment?' little detailed understanding of nuclear technology was required. When their nature changed radically to become questions such as 'what ABM defences will exist in the USSR in ten years time, how might they be overcome, does Britain need a new warhead to do it, and how much will it cost?' political leaders found themselves limited in their understanding of the options open to them by their lack of detailed knowledge, and thus were unable fully to comprehend the complex scientific and technical issues involved, leaving them increasingly dependent upon advice from officials. This was compounded by the perceived overriding need to protect the credibility of Britain's small nuclear deterrent by a blanket of state security, which ruled out the use of advisers from outside the governmental service. Yet at the same time this increased dependence on officials offered political decision-makers a method of excusing their ineffective or incompetent activities while in office. The problem posed for the British political system by the necessity to have considerable background knowledge in order to master complex areas of activity still remains unresolved, as the Chevaline experience has highlighted. Moreover, although the House of Commons Defence Committee has raised many issues in connection with the Trident purchase, it, and leading politicians both in and out of office, appear to find it impossible to convey effectively to the British public the complex interlinkages of alliance politics and technology, and of European, as against British, security policies.

Until the early 1960s, British nuclear warhead programmes were initiated by political directives and the nuclear specialists attempted to implement them as best they could. After 1965, when the development of nuclear weapon technology became focused upon detailed and problematic issues of reentry vehicle design, missile warhead configurations, defence systems and nuclear hardening, the changed nature of these choices made politicians increasingly dependent upon their advisers when making decisions, though they always retained the option, exercised after 1965, to wind down all development and adopt a policy of nuclear disarmament. Whether a more open discussion of these issues and a wider dissemination of knowledge would have led to altered policies is difficult to evaluate, given the contemporary political and administrative structures of Britain.

In the United States, however, the situation was, and is, very different. The Manhattan Project and its British counterpart had both been initiated by secret decisions of the political leadership, but by late 1945 the American Congress had full knowledge of the expenditure on the nuclear project and was preparing to legislate to ensure civilian control over any further nuclear development. The creation of the AEC and the JCAE led to American nuclear weapon, submarine reactor and power reactor development policy becoming the subject of a three-cornered tug-of-war between these two bodies and the Executive. Moreover, the JCAE, unlike a House of Commons Committee, was cleared to receive and discuss all of America's nuclear secrets, including those acquired from Britain, and through its control over AEC budget allocations, it was able to acquire policy-making powers. These were reinforced by the nature of the United States system of public administration, in which federal agencies both acquire their executive powers and are constrained in their activities by congressional legislation. Thus it was the JCAE which ultimately stood in the way of expanded atomic energy cooperation between Britain and the United States in the early 1950s; which drafted the 1954 Atomic Energy Act; which campaigned for an expansion of military plutonium production; which insisted on pushing ahead with a demonstration nuclear power program; and which provided the political power base for Admiral Rickover's single-minded development of naval propulsion reactors. The conflicts between the JCAE and other groups with responsibilities for atomic energy were exacerbated in the mid-1950s by Eisenhower's appointment of Strauss, the AEC chairman, as his personal adviser on nuclear matters, as well as the successful strategy adopted by the Defense Department and the AEC of evading JCAE opposition to the transfer of nuclear submarine design information to Britain by use of a legal technicality. During this period additional complications in the relationship between the AEC and the Department of Defense arose from the question of which organisation had the power to determine whether the transfer to other states of military information on nuclear weapons was in the national interest. In addition, the AEC and the State Department were in conflict over proposals to use plutonium arising from foreign reactor operations under the 'Atoms for Peace' programme for military purposes.

These are just some of many examples of the way in which no one group or agency made American policy over nuclear energy. Further examples can be found in the 1960s and 1970s especially over Britain's non-proliferation policy and relations with France. Policy was, as Allison hypothesises, the product of tugging and hauling between several groups, and it certainly could not be seen as a product of purposeful activity by a unified decision-making organisation, as appeared to be the case in the United Kingdom. It was this contrast between the governmental structures of the two countries which led to Admiral Rickover's concern that Britain, in its relations with the United States agencies, might succeed in pursuing a policy of divide and rule.

In their dealings with the United Kingdom, however, many American officials did discover that they had escaped from congressional scrutiny and had almost become free agents. This appears to have been especially true of dealings in the weapon design area, where the secrecy surrounding transfers tended to place them outside of detailed congressional scrutiny, and it can be argued that a transnational Anglo-American professional guild of weapon design had arisen. It also applied to the dominant role played by Admiral Rickover in the nuclear submarine reactor technology area. These secretive transatlantic dealings, tinged with elements of court politics, appear to have escaped any but the most superficial public scrutiny by the full Congress and the House of Commons and can be classified as multi-bureaucratic in their nature. It is unclear to what extent the semi-permanent status and professional authority of several of the non-elective actors in the nuclear energy field enabled them to persuade more transient political leaders to acquiesce to legal obligations which may considerably limit the freedom of future British governments to undertake acts of nuclear disarmament.

Weapon Development Processes

Even though a concerted attempt has been made in this study to describe the outputs from the British weapon and submarine reactor development process, it has not proved possible to provide detailed insights into the nuclear weapon development process itself. There exists no simple relationship between the explosion of experimental devices and production weapons of the type that exists between, for example, prototype aircraft and production models. Indeed it remains unclear whether any of the British test explosions have been of production warheads, except possibly for the test in 1974, which may have been staged to investigate the tritium ageing effect.

What does emerge, however, is that the United States and the

United Kingdom proceeded, independently, along very similar lines of nuclear warhead development, starting with atomic devices and moving on to more complex thermonuclear ones. In addition, it appears that the main technique for accelerating the development of nuclear warheads was similar to that found useful in other technologies: experimenting with several concepts at once in order to insure against failure of one or several of them. After 1958, the process of British warhead development becomes somewhat obscure, as the evidence that exists gives no clear indication of whether the designs for strategic and advanced tactical warheads were refined by explosive testing alone, or by the incorporation of data from American test results. More recently, the use of advanced computation techniques and very large lasers, able to simulate the processes encountered in nuclear explosions, has reduced the need for large numbers of test explosions and served to camouflage further the activity of nuclear weapon development from public view.[3]

The British experience also demonstrated that factors external to the project were of crucial importance in these development programmes. It was the political demand for more rapid development after 1954 which accelerated the project, and it was political, and not technological considerations which led to suspension of explosive testing in 1958, and again after 1965. Yet the relationship between nuclear weapon development and production activities was similar to that found in other defence projects in respect of timescales and costs. Thus it was not until the 1955 decision to embark upon series production of atomic weapons that very substantial investment had to be made in production facilities, while weapons did not become available in numbers until the end of the decade, despite the first test explosion having occurred in 1952. Similarly, although the first test of a thermonuclear device occurred in 1957, it was the early 1960s before a production weapon entered the stockpile (see Appendix 4c).

Retrospect and Prospect

The development of nuclear energy in the United Kingdom for both military and civil purposes is one of the few examples of a state enterprise which has grown from nothing in 1940 to a large, thriving and expanding industry in the 1980s. It is an historic irony that the British Labour Party, which under Attlee was largely responsible for the initial development of its military sector, should now be the main proponent of its closure. Its future will be decided at the British ballot box, with debate centring on emotive arguments about the inherent immorality of weapons of mass destruction, the absolute and opportunity costs of the delivery systems for nuclear weapons, the risks that their existence and possession generate, and the horrific consequences of their use. Yet there is no necessary correlation between non-possession of nuclear weapons by a state and their non-use upon its territory, or between the hoped for consequences of an act and its actual results.

The nuclear disarmers of the 1980s, in common with those of the 1950s, argue for a changed security system in Europe and the two objectives are intimately interrelated. Yet at least four issue areas may well be ignored or misunderstood in this debate over British possession of nuclear weapons, both because there is a lack of knowledge in the public domain concerning them and because they involve mastery of complex questions which rest in the no-man's-land between the realm of technology and that of politics. One is the subtle and intangible nature of many of the linkages in the NATO security system. There is a great temptation to view deterrence and defence as solely national activities, rather than corporate, interstate ones, and this has been exacerbated by the manner in which British nuclear weapons have been viewed as the ultimate guarantee of the sovereign integrity of the United Kingdom. This residual justification, although important in public debate, offers little insight into why United Kingdom governments should have consistently sought closer nuclear collaboration with the United States, and why the United States was, after 1957, prepared to offer it. Understanding of this phenomenon can only be found in corporate concepts of security, in intangible phrases such as the 'common defense' and in the way that ideas of reciprocity and mutual advantage have underlain actions. United Kingdom governments since the late 1940s have consistently acted on the basis of these latter principles, and through them have forged a unique linkage with the United States. Ideas of reciprocity and assisting in the 'common defense' of both Europe and the

United States also offer insights into American willingness to assist the United Kingdom first to expand its strategic nuclear weapon capabilities and nuclear submarine fleet, and then to sustain them. They differentiate the United Kingdom sharply from France, the only other West European nuclear power, which has always conceived of its nuclear forces in national rather than alliance terms. The diplomatic functions fulfilled by the British force are thus much more subtle than those underlying the French one, and are based on the belief that no defence of Western Europe is possible on a state-centric basis, and that the national nuclear forces of lower-rank states can only be justified by reference to their contribution to a larger alliance system. Thus the dominant external rationale for a British strategic deterrent was, and is, the *contribution* it makes to NATO's nuclear forces and to the security of the United States, rather than any ability to offer a last-ditch defence of a militarily isolated and threatened United Kingdom. It is not so much its technical ability to destroy Moscow, but its unique ability to cause the USSR to believe that the security of the United States and the rest of Western Europe is indivisible, that can be argued to create the maximum deterrent effect against Soviet military adventures. Although the official 'two centres of decision' rationale for Trident may appear to contradict this argument, in fact it is merely a gloss upon it, for the link with United States deterrent forces maximises deterrence arising out of the threat of 'independent' action by the United Kingdom.

The origins of these often intangible ideas can be found in the wartime Atlantic alliance, and its substance was reinforced by the threat of a direct nuclear attack upon the United States from the mid-1950s onwards. They have been embraced by the leaderships of all British political parties while in office, though not always by their followers, for there have always existed political undercurrents in both political parties moving in the direction of a more 'Gaullist' position of national nuclear independence. Advocacy of an altered relationship with NATO, through British nuclear disarmament, is related to profound idealogical concerns over the direction of American external policies and whether they still promote British and European interests, as well as the basic dichotomy between ideologies of left-wing socialism and right-wing free enterprise. In particular, it is feared that the nuclear relationship with the United States could lead the United Kingdom into a nuclear war originating in a localised conflict or issue remote from Britain's interests and contrary to its ideological sympathies. This possibility has concerned British leaders since the Quebec Agreement in 1944. It led to Attlee's dash to Washington during the Korean War, and was one of the issues Macmillan was concerned to clarify when he became Prime Minister in 1957. Thus the reciprocal consequences of the Anglo-American nuclear relationship have always been appreciated by British political leaders, though not necessarily its detailed nature.

Yet there exists a second level or issue area of more tangible Anglo-American nuclear activity which may be regarded as contradictory to this first one. This is the nature of the technical relationship in the military aspects of nuclear energy between the two states. It involves contradictions in so far as British policy at this level has been to accept non-recurrent assistance from the United States if it saved time and money, or improved the quality of a weapon design, but never to acquiesce to a situation where United States actions could immobilise either the Royal Navy's submarine fleet or British nuclear warheads. These principles have been followed consistently since 1958, but their full implications have remained obscure, enabling the resultant operational forces to be variously characterised as either dependent upon the United States for their continued technical credibility, or independent and self-sufficient. Thus where there may appear to be short-term dependency this has been offset by stockpiling and, in the longer term, by the ability to reactivate plants or, in the last resort, to switch civil plants to military production. Thus although the political objectives of the British military exploitation of nuclear energy may have involved generating a symbiosis with United States security forces, the technical objectives appeared to be geared to the contrary aim of sustaining a position of independence.

The political systems of the United States and the United Kingdom, and particularly the role of committees of their legislatures, constitute a third issue area in need of greater clarification. Information is essential to democratic decision-making, but when that information is such that it is judged to have the potential to produce adverse consequences for the state, and possibly even mankind, compromises to restrict its availability have to be made. In the United States, the problem of protecting such information, while yet enabling Congress to sustain its legislative and policy-making roles, was solved by creating the bipartisan JCAE and its successors, whose members and staff had access to all technical, design and intelligence information in the nuclear field. Members remained on the committee for lengthy periods and gained considerable expertise in the area, though this did not always enable them to understand the technical information they were given. By their control over budgetary allocations and legislation, they were able to make policy, as well as block activities they objected to. They remained a group apart from their colleagues, due to their security clearances, but given the reliance of Congress upon recommendations from specialist committees in conducting its business, this position was not unduly anomalous. Although members of the JCAE had access to nuclear secrets, the rest of Congress did not, and they and their committee staff were liable to prosecution under the Atomic Energy Acts for unauthorised disclosure. Congress operates its own system for giving security clearances to members sitting on such committees, and these individuals must not allow other congressmen or non-security-cleared members of their own staff access to US classified or restricted data, or to British nuclear weapon information in the possession of the American government. Thus, by virtue of the nature of the American political system, Congress's role within it and the use it makes of its committees, the legislature in the United States appears to have played a substantial role in policy-making and monitoring in the military nuclear area. How effectively it performed this role is difficult to judge.

The British system of government differs significantly from that of the United States, for in practice Parliament does not make state policy, and such separate agencies of government as exist are held responsible to departments and their ministers. There is no system of security clearance for MPs or ministers, other than the taking of the Privy Councillor's oath, and this has led to decisions involving access to nuclear secrets being taken in small Cabinet committees restricted to such oath-takers. Parliament has consistently refused to have MPs cleared for access to highly classified information, and thus its committees, including those charged with scrutiny of departmental activities such as the Defence Committee, do not have any right of access to information above confidential level, although this may be relaxed by ministerial decision to allow the disclosure of material classified as secret. All important nuclear operational design and intelligence data is classified above this level. If greater scrutiny of detailed nuclear issues by Parliament is deemed desirable, three alternatives exist. One is to set up a committee comprised entirely of Privy Councillors similar to the one set up to conduct the Falklands inquiry. A second is for a small number of MPs of all parties to be cleared to see highly classified papers, with the attendant possibility that some might be denied clearance. Such MPs would then be exposed to the full consequences of the Official Secrets Act in the event of unauthorised disclosure. A third would be for nuclear data to be declassified to enable a public debate to occur, even if this meant releasing information that few non-specialists would fully understand, and which could be of assistance to those in non-nuclear weapon states attempting to develop and produce their own physics packages. Thus in the absence of a positive desire by MPs to accept restrictions on their freedom of speech and action, and to take a permanently bipartisan approach to nuclear matters, a British decision-making process on nuclear weapon issues that appears unduly covert in comparison with American practice is almost inevitable.

Nuclear disarmament, and how it might be implemented, is the fourth issue area that merits greater attention. Politics has often been characterised as the art of the possible, but it is also an area in which aspirations and reality meet. Forty years of Anglo-American nuclear relations have left a legacy of arrangements and legal commitments that, in theory at least, cannot be ignored. If a British government attempted unilaterally to terminate them in an illegal manner, this could lead to a hostile United States reaction. Britain is now in possession of much important nuclear defence information: the United States is unlikely to stand idly by if the security of this material appears to be in jeopardy. Legally, the existing arrangements are not open to unilateral termination until the end of 1989 at the earliest, in the absence of a general election during 1983. Practically, it will take several years for the British nuclear weapon inventory to be dismantled, and several decades before weapon design knowledge capable of producing first generation nuclear weapons accompanies its possessors to the grave. Moreover, the American agreements and the NPT will prevent effective international technical verification of any unilateral British nuclear disarmament process. Even if an act of nuclear weapon disarmament occurs in the future, the plutonium stockpile, and possibly both an FBR programme and the nuclear submarine facilities, will offer the ability to revert to nuclear status at very short notice. Thus four decades of military development of nuclear energy no longer offer Britain a practical choice of either remaining a nuclear state or being reborn as a virginal, non-nuclear one: the best that could be hoped for is that political actions and rhetoric will lead other states to accept Britain's claim to non-nuclear status, though their cynical and realist leaders and professional advisers are likely to continue to be influenced by capabilities rather than intent. In short, the choice for Britain may be restricted now to what level of nuclear capability offers the greatest security: the possibility of recapturing non-nuclear innocence disappeared during the decade between 1955 and 1965, without the majority of the British population or their legislators being fully aware of it.

Appendix 1

TABLE A.1 *British experimental nuclear explosions, 1952–82*

Date	Place	Yield	Placement	Comments
3.10.52	Monte Bello	15–20 kt	Ship	Experimental device similar to US Mk III warhead.
14.10.53	Woomera	15–20 kt	Tower	Experimental tests of Blue Danube production designs.
26.10.53	Woomera	15–20 kt	Tower	Experimental tests of Blue Danube production designs.
16.5.56	Monte Bello	> 20 kt	Tower	Experimental tests of modified Blue Danube designs.
19.5.56	Monte Bello	> 20 kt	Tower	Experimental tests of modified Blue Danube designs.
27.9.56	Maralinga	> 20 kt	Tower	Experimental tests of modified Blue Danube designs in association with weapon effects tests.
4.10.56	Maralinga	< 20 kt	Surface	Experimental tests of modified Blue Danube designs in association with weapon effects tests.
11.10.56	Maralinga	< 20 kt	Air	Experimental tests of modified Blue Danube designs in association with weapon effects tests.
22.10.56	Maralinga	> 20 kt	Tower	Experimental tests of modified Blue Danube designs in association with weapon effects tests.
15.5.57	Christmas Island	< 1 megaton ?	15 000 ft	Experimental megaton thermonuclear device.
31.5.57	Christmas Island	< 1 megaton ?	15 000 ft	Experimental megaton thermonuclear device.
19.6.57	Christmas Island	< 1 megaton ?	15 000 ft	Experimental megaton thermonuclear device.
14.9.57	Maralinga	< 20 kt	Tower	Experimental tests linked to Red Beard development programme.
25.9.57	Maralinga	> 20 kt	Tower	Experimental tests linked to Red Beard development programme.
9.10.57	Maralinga	> 20 kt	Balloon	Experimental tests linked to Red Beard development programme.

Date	Location	Yield	Type	Description
8.11.57	Christmas Island	> 1 megaton	15 000 ft	Experimental thermonuclear device: first fully effective megaton test.
28.4.58	Christmas Island	c. 10 megatons	15 000 ft	Experimental thermonuclear device
22.8.58	Christmas Island	< 1 megaton	Balloon	Experimental primary/boosted tactical design?
2.9.58	Christmas Island	c. 10 megatons	15 000 ft	Experimental thermonuclear device.
11.9.58	Christmas Island	c. 10 megatons	15 000 ft	Experimental thermonuclear device.
23.9.58	Christmas Island	< 1 megaton	Balloon	Experimental primary/boosted tactical device?
25.4.62–11.7.62	Christmas Island			British participation in 25 US atmospheric tests including Polaris warhead test.
1.3.62	Nevada	< 20 kt	Underground	Experimental thermonuclear device linked to Skybolt warhead programme.
7.12.62	Nevada	< 20 kt	Underground	Experimental thermonuclear device linked to Skybolt warhead programme.
17.7.64	Nevada	< 20 kt	Underground	Experimental device to obtain improved fissile weight/yield ratios – failure.
10.9.65	Nevada	20–200 kt	Underground	Repeat of above – success – one source gives yield as 15 kt.
23.5.74	Nevada	20–200 kt	Underground	Ageing test of megaton bomb primary at expiry of calculated shelf-life?
26.8.76	Nevada	20–150 kt	Underground	Experimental devices to obtain special shapes, improved weight/yield and hardening characteristics, linked to Chevaline advanced warhead development programme.
11.4.78	Nevada	20–150 kt	Underground	Experimental devices to obtain special shapes, improved weight/yield and hardening characteristics, linked to Chevaline advanced warhead development programme.
18.11.78	Nevada	20–150 kt	Underground	Experimental devices to obtain special shapes, improved weight/yield and hardening characteristics, linked to Chevaline advanced warhead development programme.

Date	Place	Yield	Placement	Comments
29.8.79	Nevada	20–150 kt	Underground	Experimental devices to obtain special shapes, improved weight/yield and hardening characteristics, linked to Chevaline advanced warhead development programme.
26.4.80	Nevada	20–150 kt	Underground	Experimental devices to obtain special shapes, improved weight/yield and hardening characteristics, linked to Chevaline advanced warhead development programme.
24.10.80	Nevada	<20 kt	Underground	Experimental devices to obtain special shapes, improved weight/yield and hardening characteristics, linked to Chevaline advanced warhead development programme.
17.12.80	Nevada	<20 kt	Underground	Experimental devices to obtain special shapes, improved weight/yield and hardening characteristics, linked to Chevaline advanced warhead development programme.
12.11.81	Nevada	20–150 kt	Underground	Experimental device.
25.4.82	Nevada	20–150 kt	Underground	Experimental device.

SOURCES
Carter and Moghissi, *op. cit.*
International Defence Review, vol. XIV no. 1 (1981). Research Institute of National Defence, *Nuclear Explosions 1945–1972: Basic Data*, FOA4 Report A 4505 – A1 (Stockholm, April 1973).
O. Dahlman and H. Israelson, *Monitoring Underground Nuclear Explosions* (Elsevier, 1977) p. 389. *SIPRI Yearbook 1982* (Taylor & Francis, 1982).

Appendix 2

TABLE A.2   *Numbers of British strategic nuclear delivery vehicles, 1955–70*

Year ending	Type and number in operational service	Total
1955	8 Valiant	8
1956	48 Valiant	48
1957	56 Valiant, 17 Vulcan	73
1958	48 Valiant, 24 Vulcan, 16 Victor	88
1959	48 Valiant, 24 Vulcan, 24 Victor	96
1960	40 Valiant, 40 Vulcan, 32 Victor (8 NATO Valiant)	112 (120)
1961	24 Valiant, 48 Vulcan, 32 Victor (16 NATO Valiant)	104 (120)
1962	72 Vulcan, 48 Victor (24 NATO Valiant)	120 (144)
1963	48 Vulcan, 24 Blue Steel Vulcan, 40 Victor, 8 Blue Steel Victor (24 NATO Valiant)	120 (144)
1964	48 Vulcan, 24 Blue Steel Vulcan, 16 Victor, 16 Blue Steel Victor (24 NATO Valiant)	104 (128)
1965	48 Vulcan, 24 Blue Steel Vulcan, 16 Blue Steel Victor	88
1966	48 Vulcan, 24 Blue Steel Vulcan, 16 Blue Steel Victor	88
1967	48 Vulcan, 24 Blue Steel Vulcan, 16 Blue Steel Victor	88
1968	40 Vulcan, 24 Blue Steel Vulcan, 16 × 3 Polaris	64 + (16 × 3) 48
1969	48 Vulcan, 16 Blue Steel Vulcan, 48 × 3 Polaris	64 + (48 × 3) 144
1970	56 Vulcan (16 in Cyprus) 48 × 3 Polaris	56 + (48 × 3) 144

On the assumption that in the period 1964–8 some of the Vulcans were assigned two thermonuclear weapons each, the number of deliverable warheads carried by British long-range offensive systems has remained static in the 200 range since 1960. If the Chevaline system involves 6 warheads this number may increase to 288 from 1983–4 onwards, while a Trident D5 reequipment in the 1990s would lead to an increase in the maximum number of warheads to a figure of $(8 \times 16 \times 3)$ 384. These figures assume one missile submarine will always be out of commission on refit.

SOURCE Jackson, *V-Bombers* (Ian Allen, 1981).

Appendix 3

The calculation of plutonium production in natural uranium reactors

The starting point for any consideration of plutonium production is the fissioning, as a consequence of neutron bombardment, of one atom of the 0.711 per cent of the isotope U-235 present in natural uranium. This produces heat, fission products and on average 2.5 neutrons. Three possible consequences result from this production of neutrons in a purpose-built reactor; they may generate more fissions in U-235; they may be captured by U-238 the predominant isotope in uranium to form Pu-239, and later Pu-239 may itself capture a further neutron to form Pu-240, and so on, or they may be absorbed by reactor fuel canning material, graphite or other moderating material, concrete and the reactor control rods. A plutonium production reactor has therefore to be designed to minimise loss of neutrons to reactor materials, and to achieve the best possible compromise between the use of neutrons to produce U-235 fissions, and thus generate more neutrons, and their use to transmute U-238 into Pu-239. A reactor being operated to maximise plutonium 239 production will tend to operate at lower thermal power and with reduced electricity generating capability than a power producer, and its fuel will be completely changed approximately once every 4–6 months, rather than the more normal period of once every 4–6 years for a power producer.

The discussion of plutonium production is normally conducted by comparing the number of U-235 atoms destroyed to the number of Pu-239 atoms created: the so-called 'conversion ratio'. This is limited to about 0.8 in magnox reactors, but in the absence of detailed figures on the amount of uranium in them, this information cannot be used to arrive at approximations of the amount of plutonium individual reactors produce. A second method is to relate the thermal power or heat output of the reactor, or alternatively its electricity output, to plutonium production. This can be done if information is available on the amount produced for given periods of operation at specified power levels (e.g. one (1) day at 1000 Mw(th) or 1000 Mw(th)/days). Although these figures are usually given as Mw(th) days/tonne, a simplifying assumption can be made to ignore the quantity of uranium fuel and thus relate plutonium output directly to thermal output. Thermal output and electricity output are linked to give the thermal efficiency of a reactor, in which the latter figure is expressed as a percentage of the former. Two magnitudes for electrical output are usually available: a figure of gross electricity generation by the turbo-alternators and a net electricity output figure, arrived at by subtracting the power absorbed by reactor machinery such as pumps, compressors, etc., from the gross figure. Thermal efficiency can be based on either figure, and this sometimes leads to difficulties as it may be unclear which is being referred to.

The type of plutonium produced in any reactor is related to the period of time the fuel rods remain under irradiation. Beyond figures of about 400 Mw(th) days/tonne, some of the Pu-239 previously produced by reactor operations may itself fission, thus reducing net plutonium production. In addition, such material has a reduced percentage of Pu-239, and almost pure quantities of this are preferable for weapon purposes. Calculations of plutonium production in British natural uranium reactors are thus most usefully based on two alternative assumptions:

(i) that the fuel is irradiated to about 300–400 Mw(th) days/tonne; or

(ii) that it is irradiated to levels of 2000–4000 Mw(th) days/tonne.

The difference involves keeping fuel rods in a reactor for 3–6 months or 4 years.

Figures for plutonium production at 300–400 Mw(th) days/tonne range from one kilogram per 1000 Mw(th) days to 760 grams. Both Wohlstetter *et al., Swords from Ploughshares* (Chicago University Press, 1979, p. 168) and L. Beaton, *Must the Bomb Spread?* (Penguin, 1966, p. 91) offer the first figure, though the balance of evidence suggests that it is too high. The most useful and authoritative source is probably H. Rose and J. J. Syrett, 'Long term reactivity changes', *Journal of the British*

Nuclear Energy Conference, vol. IV (1959) p. 180. They publish a graph relating plutonium production to irradiation levels, based upon data from the Windscale and Calder Hall reactors. This suggests that about 800 grams of Pu-239 were produced for every 1000 Mw(th) days of initial reactor operations (i.e. a 100 Mw(th) reactor operating for 10 days). Another source gives a slightly lower figure of 0.760 ± 0.008 grams/1000 Mw(th) days (D. S. Craig *et al.*, 'Long irradiation of natural uranium', Geneva Conference Paper P/205, in *Progress in Nuclear Energy*, series II, *Reactors*, vol. II (Pergamon, 1961) p. 125). Given that the two latter sources base their figures upon experimental observations, calculations of military plutonium output have been standardised on the higher of these two. Thus the average figure used to calculate military-grade plutonium production in gas-cooled, graphite-moderated reactors is 800 grams per 1000 Mw(th) days.

Plutonium production at 3000 Mw(th) days is given by two sources as 670 grams/1000 Mw(th) days (Rose and Syrett, op. cit. and A. B. McIntosh and L. Grainger 'Plutonium and nuclear power', *Journal of the British Nuclear Energy Society* (1962) p. 3) while W. Marshall offers a figure of 685 grams or 250 kg per 1000 Mw(th) year ('Nuclear power and the proliferation issue', *Atom*, 258 (April 1978) p. 79). These lower figures are a result of Pu-239 fissioning, and thus some of it is destroyed and reduces the net amount being created. In addition, some Pu-239 becomes transmuted into further isotopes – Pu-240, 241, 242, etc. This gives rise to two distinct figures for plutonium production, one giving the total weight of all isotopes, and a second, or equivalent figure, which is an artificial creation indicating the fissile worth of the resulting mixture. Thus although Marshall ('The use of plutonium', *Atom*, 282 (April 1980) p. 89) gives a figure of 617 equivalent kilograms as the output of a 1000 Mw(e) magnox reactor operating continuously for one year, this translates into a total weight of plutonium of 754 kilograms, similar to the figure of 750 kilograms quoted by Mr Lamont in a parliamentary answer on 3 March 1980 (*HC Report* 980, Col 10).

Since electricity production figures are readily accessible for all British magnox reactors, Marshall's figure of 754 kilograms has been used as the basis for calculations of plutonium production from reactors operating on a civil fuel cycle, rather than figures based on thermal output. However, the result is at best an approximation, both because reactors differ in their thermal efficiency and because plutonium output will be significantly affected by the degree of burn-up of their fuel. Since this appears to have been gradually extended over the years this average figure will tend to underestimate plutonium production in the early years and overestimate it in the later ones.

Appendix 4

TABLE A.4a *Estimates of weapon-grade plutonium created in British military reactors, 1951–64 (in kg)*

Year	Reactor Windscale 1	Windscale 2	Calder 1	Calder 2	Calder 3	Calder 4	Chapel Cross 1	Chapel Cross 2	Chapel Cross 3	Chapel Cross 4	Annual production	Cumulative production (gross)
1951	14	10	—	—	—	—	—	—	—	—	24	24
1952	19	26	—	—	—	—	—	—	—	—	45	69
1953	19	26	—	—	—	—	—	—	—	—	45	114
1954	28	35	—	—	—	—	—	—	—	—	63	177
1955	25	30	—	—	—	—	—	—	—	—	55	232
1956	25	30	—	—	—	—	—	—	—	—	55	287
1957	25	30	8	40	—	—	—	—	—	—	103	390
1958	21	25	50	50	30	—	—	—	—	—	176	566
1959	—	—	50	50	50	26	30	4	—	—	210	776
1960	—	—	50	50	50	50	50	50	37	26	363	1 139
1961	—	—	50	50	50	50	50	50	50	50	400	1 539
1962	—	—	50	50	50	50	50	50	50	50	400	1 939
1963	—	—	50	50	50	50	50	50	50	50	400	2 339
1964	—	—	50	50	50	50	50	50	50	50	400	2 739

NOTES
(a) The figures for the Windscale reactors are based on the following assumptions about their thermal capacities:
 (i) Before 1953 the first reactor was operated at 76 Mw(th) and the second at 104 Mw(th) compared to a design rating of 115 Mw(th) (see M. Gowing with L. Arnold, *Independence and Deterrence*, vol. II (Macmillan, 1974), p. 347).
 (ii) In 1954, increased power outputs were obtained by using slightly enriched uranium fuel (*ibid.*, p. 401). The revised thermal ratings for the two reactors have been estimated at 110 and 140 Mw.
 (iii) From 1955 onwards production of tritium reduced their plutonium production capacity. In the absence of information, it has been assumed that it had an effect equivalent to reducing the thermal ratings to 100 and 120 Mw(th).
(b) All Calder Hall and Chapel Cross reactors are assumed to have been operated at 200 Mw(th) (R. F. Pocock, *Nuclear Power* (Unwin Brothers, 1977) p. 34, and H. G. Davey, 'Commissioning and operation of "A" station, Calder Hall', *Journal of the British Nuclear Energy Conference*, vol. III (1958) p. 108).

(c) The standard figure of 800 grams of plutonium produced per 1000 Mw(th)/days has been used as the basis for all output calculations (see Appendix 3).

(d) It has been assumed throughout that all reactors operated for the equivalent of 314 days per year at full power, i.e. 86 per cent of the available time.

(e) All figures have been rounded to the nearest kilogram.

(f) Total British military fuel cycle plutonium output seems likely to have been equivalent to that produced by about eight months full power operations of the five US Savannah River military reactors.

TABLE A.4b   *Estimates of plutonium available for weapon production (kg), 1951–82*

Year ending	Annual production [a] (material held in cooling ponds or reactors [b])	Material entering reprocessing plant	Reprocessing losses, and material in plant liquors [c]	Net annual plutonium output	Material destroyed in tests or diverted to civil use [d]	Annual increase in material available for weapon production	Cumulative total of material available for weapon production
1951	24	0	0	0	0	0	0
1952	45	24	12	12	6	6	6
1953	45	45	16	29	12	17	23
1954	63	45	10	35	15	20	43
1955	55	63	1	62	0	62	105
1956	55	55	1	54	30	24	129
1957	103	55	1	54	13	41	170
1958	176	103	2	101	20	81	251
1959	210	176	4	172	—	172	423
1960	363	210	4	206	—	206	629
1961	400	363	7	356	—	356	985
1962	400	400	8	392	8	384	1 369
1963	400	400	8	392	—	392	1 761
1964	400	400	8	392	4	388	2 149
1965(e)	—	400	8	392	4	388	2 537

NOTES

(a) Annual production rates in reactors are based on Appendix 4a.

(b) It is assumed that this plutonium was either in reactors or in cooling ponds at the end of the year.

(c) Reprocessing losses and plutonium in the plant is assumed to have been an arbitrarily large proportion of production until 1955, and reprocessing losses are then estimated at 2 per cent of throughput thereafter.

(d) Material destroyed in tests is calculated on the basis that the three tests in 1952 and 1953 consumed 6 kg each, the 1956 tests 5 kg and thereafter tests consumed 4 kg each. In 1954, 15 kg were transferred to the FBR research programme, and this is assumed to have been returned for military use in 1957, hence the low figure of 13 kg consumed in that year despite the 7 test explosions. No allowance is made for material destroyed in safety tests, at least one of which took place in Australia.

(e) It is assumed that military cycle plutonium production ceased at the end of 1964, and that since that date, plutonium in new weapons has been obtained by recycling the material produced by dismantling old ones.

TABLE A.4c   Estimates of British nuclear weapon inventory, 1950–82

Year ending	Cumulative total of plutonium available for weapon production	Pu in weapons	Pu in stockpile, being recycled, in course of manufacture or transferred to USA	Blue Danube (6 kg)	Red Beard (RAF) (4 kg)	Red Beard (RNF) (4 kg)	Megaton Blue Steel (3 kg)	Megaton gravity bomb (3 kg)	Tactical bomb (RAF & RN) (3 kg)	Polaris single warhead (3 kg)	Chevaline single warhead (2 kg)	Annual production of warheads	Total number of warheads in inventory
1953	23	6	17	1	—	—	—	—	—	—	—	1	1
1954	43	24	19	4	—	—	—	—	—	—	—	3	4
1955	105	60	45	10	—	—	—	—	—	—	—	6	10
1956	129	84	45	14	—	—	—	—	—	—	—	4	14
1957	170	132	38	22	—	—	—	—	—	—	—	8	22
1958	251	204	47	22	18	—	—	—	—	—	—	18	40
1959	423	344	79	22	48	5	—	—	—	—	—	35	75
1960	629	524	105	22	83	15	—	—	—	—	—	45	120
1961	985	822	163	22	141	30	—	2	—	—	—	75	195
1962	1 369	1 075	294	10	150	40	20	65	—	—	—	102	285
1963	1 761	1 190	571	—	147	38	60	90	—	—	—	65	335
1964	2 149	1 275	874	—	144	36	60	120	5	—	—	35	365
1965	2 537	1 324	1 213	—	141	34	58	140	10	—	—	25	383
1966	2 537	1 301	1 236	—	138	32	56	136	15	—	—	5	377
1967	2 537	1 311	1 226	—	135	30	54	133	20	10	—	15	382
1968	2 537	1 351	1 186	—	132	28	52	130	25	30	—	25	397
1969	2 537	1 341	1 196	—	110	25	40	127	30	70	—	45	402
1970	2 537	1 335	1 202	—	80	22	20	124	35	130	—	65	411
1971	2 537	1 293	1 244	—	50	10	—	121	40	190	—	65	411

1972	2 537	1 226	1 311	—	20	—	118	45	219	—	34	402
1973	2 537	1 218	1 319	—	—	—	115	75	216	—	30	406
1974	2 537	1 305	1 232	—	—	—	112	110	213	—	35	435
1975	2 537	1 392	1 145	—	—	—	109	145	210	—	35	464
1976	2 537	1 479	1 058	—	—	—	106	180	207	—	35	493
1977	2 537	1 566	971	—	—	—	103	215	204	—	35	522
1978	2 537	1 653	884	—	—	—	100	250	201	—	35	551
1979	2 537	1 636	901	—	—	—	97	247	198	5	5	547
1980	2 537	1 639	898	—	—	—	94	244	195	20	15	553
1981	2 537	1 692	845	—	—	—	91	241	192	60	40	584
1982	2 537	1 631	906	—	—	—	50	238	189	100	40	577

NOTES

This table is merely intended to convey a general picture of how the production and dismantling programmes have been scheduled. The arbitrary assumption has been made that the amounts of plutonium in each weapon are as indicated in parentheses. For later weapons they are considerably below the critical mass of 4 kg with beryllium reflector (see G. Hildenbrand, 'Nuclear energy, nuclear exports and non-proliferation of nuclear weapons' reproduced in *Nuclear Proliferation Factbook* (US Library of Congress, 23 September 1977) p. 382), but this appears justified as it is assumed that both plutonium and U-235 have been used in them. The slow decrease in inventory figures for each type is a product of the assumed practice of carrying out reliability checks by totally dismantling a small sample of weapons each year for laboratory examination. It should be noted that in the 1950–70 period a number of the weapon types, especially Blue Danube and Red Beard, were probably procured in such a way that up to twice as many non-nuclear assemblies were in existence as there were nuclear cores. The estimates in this table relate solely to the nuclear components and *not* to these sets of non-nuclear assemblies.

TABLE A.4d   *Estimates of fuel-grade plutonium production in British military reactors, 1965–81*

Year	Electrical output (gross): Calder Hall reactors (000 Mwh(e))[a]	Electrical output (gross): Chapel Cross reactors (000 Mwh(e))[a]	Total electrical output (gross) of military reactors (000 Mwh(e))	Gross Pu production (kg)[b]
1965[c]	1 500	1 500	3 000	258
1966	1 537	1 815	3 352	289
1967	1 685	1 584	3 269	281
1968	1 862	1 401	3 263	281
1969	1 828	1 617	3 445	297
1970	1 956	1 719	3 675	316
1971	1 906	1 865	3 771	325
1972	1 910	1 930	3 840	331
1973	1 871	1 921	3 792	326
1974	1 865	1 916	3 781	325
1975	1 427	1 852	3 279	282
1976	1 250	1 849	3 099	267
1977	1 020	1 702	2 722	234
1978	1 268	1 757	3 025	260
1979	1 289	1 626	2 915	251
1980	1 196	1 601	2 797	241
1981[d]	1 629	1 629	3 258	280
Cumulative totals	26 999	29 284	56 283	4 844

NOTES

(a) The electricity production figures are taken from *Operation of Nuclear Power Stations, 1974* (Office for Official Publications of the European Communities, Luxembourg, 1975) p. 45–6, and *Operation of Nuclear Power Stations, 1980* (Office for Official Publications of the European Communities, Luxembourg, 1979) pp. 60–1. They are electrical gross production figures, and thus include electricity consumed by the power station's own pumps, etc.

(b) The basis for the plutonium production calculation is the figure for all isotopes of 754 kg per 1000 Mw(e) year of magnox reactor operation given by W. Marshall, 'The use of plutonium', *Atom*, 282 (1980) p. 89. This method of calculation using an average figure contains considerable inaccuracies, as it tends to understate production in the early years and may exaggerate it in the later ones, when the reactor fuel was subject to greater irradiation and hence more of the plutonium in it fissioned. The estimates are for gross plutonium production in reactors, and take no account of reprocessing losses. They are *not* for the amount of separated plutonium metal in the stockpile in 1981, as some of the cumulative plutonium production remained in the reactors and some was in cooling ponds. Both together probably amounted to 3–4 years' production. Thus the *generation* figure for the end of 1979 is probably equivalent to a *separation* figure for 1982–3.

(c) This is an estimated figure as no actual figures are available.

(d) This figure is derived from the monthly *Operation of Nuclear Power Stations* (Office for Official Publications of the European Community, Luxembourg, December 1982) p. 5. In the late 1970s, figures for thermal energy produced by the military reactors began to be published but for consistency electricity generation figures have been used throughout these calculations.

Appendix 5

TABLE A.5a   *Estimate of plutonium produced in CEGB and SSEB magnox reactors, 1962–9*

	pre 1966	1966	1967	1968	Cumulative totals
Thermal energy generated by reactors[a] (000 Mwh)	79 864	64 923	76 112	76 681	297 580
Plutonium production[b] (kg)	2 662	2 056	2 283	2 173	9 174
Plutonium reprocessed prior to April 1969[c] (kg)	665	1 179	1 750	1 147	4 741

NOTES
(a) Figures for thermal output calculated from *Operation of Nuclear Power Stations, 1974*. Gross electricity output has been converted to thermal output using the ratio of the 1974 figures as a constant.
(b) It is assumed that the rate of plutonium production gradually declined after 1965 as the amount of plutonium in the reactors increased and some of it fissioned. To simulate this effect pre-1966 production has been based on the military cycle figure of 800 grams per thousand megawatt days, 1966 on 760 grams, 1967 on 720 grams and 1968 on 680 grams, the latter approximating to Marshall's average civil cycle production figure of 250 kilograms per thousand megawatt years.
(c) To simulate the effect of withdrawing 25 per cent of the fuel from the reactor each year, which over the 4-year period would contain steadily increasing amounts of plutonium, each year's production has been divided by four, and then aggregated from 1966 onwards in cumulative fashion (i.e. pre-1966 = pre 1966 ÷ 4; 1966 = (pre-1966 ÷ 4) + (1966 ÷ 4); 1967 = (pre-1966 ÷ 4) + (1966 ÷ 4) + (1967 ÷ 4) etc.). For 1968 only half the estimated output is used in the calculation, as it is assumed that June 1968 was the latest date for discharging fuel if it was to be reprocessed by April 1969. The cumulative figure produced is more likely to be an overestimate of the material available, rather than the opposite.

TABLE A.5b   *Estimate of cumulative plutonium production from CEGB/SSEB magnox reactors, 1962–81*

Year	Gross electrical output of all reactors[a] (000 Mwh(e))	Gross plutonium production[b](kg)
pre-1966	22 373	1 926 kg
1966	18 599	1 601
1967	21 906	1 886
1968	24 524	2 111
1969	24 028	2 068
1970	21 634	1 862
1971	23 707	2 041
1972	25 227	2 171
1973	23 657	2 036
1974	29 392	2 530
1975	26 508	2 282
1976	30 456	2 621
1977	30 496	2 625
1978	27 173	2 339
1979	26 864	2 312
1980	22 734	1 957
1981	22 730	1 956
Cumulative total	42 200 800	36 324 kg

NOTES

(a) Source: *Operation of Nuclear Power Stations.*
(b) Calculated on basis of Marshall's figure of 754 kg per 1000 Mw years(e).

Appendix 6

TABLE A.6   *British nuclear submarines*

Type	Name	Date of commissioning
SSK-Fleet/submarines	*Dreadnought*	4.1963
	Valiant	7.1966
	Warspite	4.1967
	Churchill	7.1970
	Conqueror	11.1971
	Courageous	10.1972
	Swiftsure	4.1973
	Sovereign	7.1974
	Superb	11.1976
	Sceptre	2.1978
	Spartan	9.1979
	Splendid	late 1980
	Trafalgar	laid down 1978
	Turbulent	laid down 1979
	Tireless	laid down 1981
SSBN-Polaris missile submarine	*Resolution*	10.1967
	Repulse	9.1968
	Renown	11.1968
	Revenge	12.1969

SOURCE J. E. Moore, *Warships of the Royal Navy* (Jane's, 1981) pp. 16–20.

NOTES
(1) The intention appears to be to acquire a 'steady state' flotilla of about 18 SSK.
(2) HMS *Dreadnought* was decommissioned in 1982.
(3) In addition to the reactors in submarines, there is also a shore-based installation at HMS *Vulcan* at Dounreay, which will be replaced in 1985–6 by a new design, PWR-2.
(4) 37 cores have been built for British submarine reactors to mid-1981 (Fishlock, 'New design for submarine reactors', *Financial Times*, 12 June 1981, p. 29).

Appendix 7

Quantities of materials traded across the Atlantic under the military agreements

There is no easy way of ascertaining how much fissile material has been traded between the United Kingdom and the United States under the terms of their military agreements. A number of indicators do exist, however, and permit some speculative estimates.

(a) The manufacture of 37 nuclear submarine reactor cores by the United Kingdom through to 1981 would require a minimum of (37×40) 1480 kg of weapon-grade uranium (figure of 40 kg derived from *Dreadnought* core). There also seems likely to be a requirement for one replacement core per reactor every four to seven years. This suggests that between 1980 and 1984 some 15 to 20 cores may have to be manufactured, requiring 600 to 800 kilograms of weapon-grade uranium, or an average 120 to 160 kilograms per year. If all supplies of uranium used in submarine reactor fuel have come from America then at least 1500 kilograms of British plutonium were transferred there prior to 1980 if the trade was conducted on a gram-for-gram basis.

(b) The other use of U-235 has been in weapons. This trade appears to have occurred principally during the 1960s, and involved plutonium from CEGB and SSEB magnox reactors. As indicated in Appendix 5a, about $4\frac{1}{2}$ tonnes had probably been reprocessed by April 1969 when this mode of exchange was terminated. In addition, the figure of about $36\frac{1}{4}$ tonnes of plutonium these reactors were capable of producing through to the end of 1981 can be compared with the 33 tonnes which were officially accounted for by a minister in the Department of Energy on 1 April 1982 (*Hansard*, Issue No. 1238, Vol. 20/21, Written Answer Col 169) the unquantified balance consisting of transfers to the United States prior to 1971. This suggests that between three and four tonnes of plutonium have been sent across the Atlantic in exchange for an equivalent amount of U-235.

(c) It appears possible that prior to 1964 some weapon-grade plutonium was traded for U-235 on the basis of 1:1.76 units. If the figures in Appendix 4c are reasonable estimates of British weapon requirements, it is possible that up to 600 kilograms of British plutonium of this grade could have been traded for about a tonne of U-235, during these initial exchanges.

(d) Almost the only estimate of weapon-grade uranium production from Capenhurst before the closure of the high enrichment plant in 1963 is that contained in N. Brown's *Nuclear War: the Impending Strategic Deadlock* (Pall Mall, 1964). He gives a figure of 10 000 lb (4536 kg), though it is unclear on what basis he has made this assessment. It is possible to arrive at an estimate of the separative work capacity of the British high enrichment plant (400 000 SWUs), and hence its annual capacity for production of weapon-grade uranium (about 1 400 kilograms). Without knowledge of the electricity inputs into Capenhurst between 1956 and 1963, however, no informed estimate of production appears possible, though a figure of about four tonnes would appear to be a reasonable guess.

(e) The best estimate that can be made is that up to eight tonnes of weapon-grade uranium was probably manufactured or acquired up to 1971. How much of this is in weapons will depend on their design: at 16 kg per warhead, this quantity would allow 500 to be manufactured. Since that date a further 1500 kg may have been acquired, in exchange for the equivalent quantity of fuel-grade plutonium from Calder Hall and Chapel Cross, to fuel nuclear submarine reactors.

(f) It remains unclear whether tritium has been acquired by purchase or barter or how much tritium is incorporated into weapons. Given US production during the Carter administration of 9 kg per year, it seems likely that an annual demand in gram quantities is involved: possibly half a kilogram every five years is sufficient for Britain's needs. On a barter basis, this would involve an exchange of 36 kilograms of weapon-grade plutonium, or 63 kilograms of fuel-grade material (figures derived from Cochran in National Resources Defense Council, *No More Atoms for Peace* (Washington, 1981). At the most, this suggests that an additional 75–250 kilograms of plutonium have been transferred to the United States in exchange for tritium.

Notes and References

1   Prologue: Themes for Analysis

1. Considerable technical controversy exists over what constitutes weapon-grade fissile material. In the 1950s this was taken to be uranium containing 90 per cent of the U-235 isotope and plutonium containing 97 per cent of the Pu-239 isotope. The former material was manufactured in enrichment plants, the latter in nuclear reactor fuel, which was then passed through a reprocessing plant to separate the plutonium from other materials. Recent studies have argued that in theory uranium and plutonium with much lower concentrations of these isotopes could be used to make weapons. A. de Volpi, *Proliferation, Plutonium and Policy* (Pergamon Press, 1979), pp. 59–118, 285–7 and 297–327; and SIPRI, *Nuclear Energy and Nuclear Weapon Proliferation* (Taylor & Francis, 1979) pp. 398–401.

2. The conversion of a large low enrichment plant to high enrichment, while not easy, is possible. It involves rearranging the process in order to ensure sufficient enriched material is flowing through the high enrichment part of the plant to allow it to operate effectively. It may also be feasible to process the same material a number of times in the same plant. The use of low enriched uranium (3–5 per cent U-235) enables a reactor to operate under conditions where appreciable absorption of neutrons is taking place, such as a water-cooled and moderated environment. Natural uranium would not produce a significant yield of plutonium under such circumstances, and a very large reactor would be involved, whereas enriched uranium enables a very compact unit to be built. For a discussion of these issues and the links between civil and military nuclear programmes see A. Wohlstetter *et al.*, *Swords from Ploughshares* (Chicago University Press, 1979) pp. 33–46 and 151–217; and T. Greenwood, G. W. Rathjens and J. Ruina, *Nuclear power and weapons proliferation*, *Adelphi Paper No. 130* (IISS, 1976).

3. For a succinct account of this early US policy see US House of Representatives: Committee on International Relations, *Science, Technology and American Diplomacy*, vol. 1 (Washington, GPO, 1977) pp. 57–122. The contemporary unease stems largely from fears that an Iraqi research reactor, destroyed by an Israeli air raid in the summer of 1981, was intended for use in a military programme, despite Iraq being a non-nuclear state party to the NPT and the reactor being subject to IAEA safeguards inspections.

4. This argument applies especially to plutonium, where 97 per cent +

263

Pu-239 was originally classified as weapon grade. More recently it has been stated that plutonium with a Pu-239 content of more than 93 per cent is classed as weapon grade. Hearings on H.R. 2969 [H.R. 3413] *Department of Energy Authorisation Legislation (National Security Programs) for Fiscal Year 1982:* before the Procurement and Military Nuclear Systems Subcommittee of the Committee on Armed Services, 97th Congress, 1st session. Statement by F. C. Gilbert, Assistant Secretary for Nuclear Materials, DoE, p. 170.

5. Enrichment plants would be operating uneconomically if they produced weapon grade U-235 because the commercial demand for reactor fuel is for 3–5 per cent enrichment only. Reactors would operate uneconomically because weapon-grade plutonium is produced by irradiating the fuel for only a short time, and then discharging it. This not only reduces the amount of time the reactor is available to make electricity, but it would also increase uranium consumption (assuming no reenrichment and recycling) at least eightfold.

6. These include the high-temperature reactors and experimental prototypes of fast breeder reactors. However, none of these types is currently in use for commercial electricity production.

7. For an account of the issues and arguments surrounding the negotiation of this treaty see SIPRI, *Postures for Non-Proliferation* (Taylor & Francis, 1979) pp. 74–129.

8. The pledges of the parties on these points are contained in Articles I, II and IV of the treaty.

9. A non-nuclear state which signs the NPT automatically pledges itself to accept IAEA safeguards and inspections over all its nuclear plants. This safeguard system is not intended to prevent diversion, but only to give timely warning of it having occurred. For a discussion on this point see M. Imber, 'NPT safeguards: the limits of credibility', *Arms Control*, vol. 1, no. 2 (Sept 1980) 186–7.

10. Currently, the majority of British voluntary safeguards inspections are made by EURATOM, not the IAEA. The EURATOM/UK/IAEA relationship over safeguards is rather complex. After the 1957 EURATOM treaty had been signed between the six EEC states, an Agreement for Cooperation was negotiated with the United States under which EURATOM would act as the safeguarding agency for materials and equipment supplied to them by that country. When the NPT had been negotiated, an agreement was sought to prevent duplication between the IAEA and EURATOM safeguarding activities. This was eventually signed on 21 February 1977, by which time there were seven non-nuclear EURATOM states. When the United Kingdom joined the EEC and EURATOM it was necessary to alter the existing arrangements resulting from a pledge at the end of 1967 that it would submit its civil nuclear facilities to IAEA safeguards. These negotiations were concluded with the signing of a UK/EURATOM/IAEA agreement which entered into force in August 1978.

11. In the United Kingdom, the basic distinction is between the civil programme administered by the Central Electricity Generating Board (CEGB) and the South of Scotland Electricity Board (SSEB) and the military programme administered by British Nuclear Fuels Limited

(BNFL) and the United Kingdom Atomic Energy Authority (UKAEA). However, since BNFL reprocesses the SSEB and CEGB fuel, the distinction is less than perfect. In the United States, the civil programme is mainly in the hands of non-federal bodies such as commercial electricity undertakings and the military one is administered by the Department of Energy.

12. This justification was the one offered by India in 1974 when it conducted an underground nuclear test.

13. The possibility that a non-nuclear state might decide to build a submarine power reactor is incorporated into para. 14 of INFCIRC 153 (corrected), the standard agreement that a non-nuclear state signs with the IAEA when it accepts mandatory full scope safeguards under Article III of the NPT. Under this provision, material can be withdrawn from safeguards for military applications.

14. Cf. L. Freedman, 'Logic, politics and foreign policy processes', *International Affairs*, vol. 52 (1976) 434–49.

15. W. Wallace, *The Foreign Policy Process in Britain* (RIIA, 1975) p. 11.

16. Ibid.

17. Ibid., p. 12.

18. Ibid.

19. Ibid., pp. 13 and 15.

20. C. P. Snow, *Science and Government* (Oxford University Press, 1961) p. 56.

21. Ibid.

22. Ibid., p. 57.

23. Ibid., p. 60.

24. Ibid., p. 63.

25. Even when information is made publicly available through House of Commons committee reports and investigations it is often in the form of carefully tailored statements which do not give a full picture of what actually happened. For some examples of this from the early 1950s see J. Simpson, 'Understanding weapon acquisition processes: a study of naval anti-submarine aircraft procurement in Britain, 1945–1955', unpublished PhD thesis (University of Southampton, 1976) especially pp. 488–527.

26. Cf. R. G. Head, 'Decision-making on the A-7 attack aircraft program', unpublished PhD thesis (Syracuse University, 1971) p. 568.

27. R. J. Coulam, *Illusions of Choice* (Princeton University Press, 1977) pp. 12–13; J. D. Steinbruner, *The Cybernetic Theory of Decision: New Dimensions of Political Analysis* (Princeton University Press, 1974) pp. 26–7; and G. T. Allison, *Essence of Decision* (Little, Brown, 1971) p. 67.

28. Coulam, ibid., pp. 14 and 15.

29. Ibid., pp. 24–34.

30. Allison, op. cit., p. 67.

31. Ibid.

32. Coulam, op. cit., pp. 17–26, and Steinbruner, op. cit., Chapters 3 and 4.

33. W. I. Jenkins, *Policy Analysis* (Martin Robertson, 1978) p. 70.

34. H. Sapolsky, *The Polaris System Development* (Harvard University Press, 1972) esp. p. 232.

35. Allison, op. cit., p. 144.
36. Ibid.
37. K. Kaiser, 'Transnational relations as a threat to the democratic process' in R. O. Keohane and J. S. Nye Jr. (eds), *Transnational Relations and World Politics* (Harvard University Press, 1971) p. 358.
38. Ibid.
39. M. J. Peck and F. M. Scherer, *The Weapon Acquisition Process: an Economic Analysis* (Harvard, 1962) p. 24.
40. Ibid.
41. Ibid.
42. Ibid., p. 362.
43. T. A. Marschak (ed.), *The Role of Project Histories in the Study of R & D*, Rand Paper P-2850 (Santa Monica, 1965) p. 3.
44. This was the procedure adopted with considerable success in the US Polaris A1 programme. Sapolski, op. cit., pp. 140–1.
45. Marschak, op. cit., p. 16.
46. Peck and Scherer, op. cit., p. 310.
47. I have derived this listing from the review of the literature on the subject contained in Simpson, op. cit., pp. 23–9, 38–41 and 589–92.
48. Three examples of British aircraft projects illustrate this point. The Gannet anti-submarine aircraft took from October 1945 to September 1949 to achieve the first flight of a prototype, but it was January 1955 before it reached Fleet Air Arm squadrons (Simpson, ibid.). Work on the Avro Vulcan bomber started in early 1947, the prototype first flew in August 1952, and it entered squadron service in July 1957, while work on the Handley Page Victor started in early 1947, the prototype first flew in December 1952, and it entered squadron service in April 1958. (R. Jackson, *V-Bombers* (Ian Allen, 1981) pp. 10, 42, 51, 70 and 79.)
49. There now exists an extensive literature on the role of non-state actors in international relations. For a representative study see R. W. Mansbach, Y. H. Ferguson and D. E. Lampert, *The Web of World Politics* (Prentice-Hall, 1976) pp. 20–45 and 273–99.
50. Machiavelli was one of the earliest political thinkers to make use of this dichotomy. *The Prince*, trans. J. B. Atkinson (Bobbs-Merrill, 1976) pp. 68–9, 149, 163, 171, 203 and 349.
51. A rather wider distinction exists in some of the academic literature between self-sufficiency and dependency. This concentrates on the linkages between the economic development of Third World states and their trade dependency upon developed countries, as well as the polarisation of their social structures into a small, wealthy, ruling elite and the rest of the population. Some writers have argued that this has led to significant links between these elites and those in Western states. For a discussion of this social, rather than power, meaning of the term, see R. D. Duvall, 'Dependence and dependence theory: notes towards precision of concept and argument', *International Organisation*, vol. 32 (Winter 1978) 62–3.
52. This distinction first appears to have been used by Kenneth Waltz in his chapter 'The myth of interdependence' in C. Kindleberger (ed.), *The International Corporation* (MIT Press, 1970) p. 210.
53. The question of whether international interdependence is growing has

been the subject of considerable debate. For a study based on this view see R. N. Cooper, *The Economics of Interdependence* (McGraw-Hill, 1968). For an opposing view see Waltz, ibid.

54. For a comprehensive discussion of these issues see, for example, A. O. Hirschman, *National Power and the Structure of Foreign Trade* (University of California Press, 1945).

55. The concept of 'need' is one which is open to several interpretations. For an interesting discussion of the distinction between needs and values see J. Burton, *Deviance, Terrorism and War* (Martin Robertson, 1979) pp. 58–84.

56. Cf. M. W. Hoag, 'What interdependence for NATO?', *World Politics*, vol. XII, no. 3 (April 1960) 369–72 and T. A. Callaghan, *US/European Economic Cooperation in Military and Civil Technology* (Washington, Center for Strategic and International Studies, Georgetown University, 1975) pp. 40–64.

57. Cf. J. G. Ruggie, 'Collective goods and future international collaboration', *American Political Science Review*, vol. 66 (Sept 1972) 874–93.

58. For a good discussion of these issues see B. M. Russett (ed.), *Economic Theories of International Politics* (Markham Publishing Co., 1968) pp. 17–49.

2 Conception: 1940–6

1. This was first accomplished experimentally by Hahn and Strassman in Berlin late in 1938. See R. G. Hewlett and O. E. Anderson Jr., *The New World, 1939–1946* (Pennsylvania State University Press, 1962) pp. 10 and 11.

2. For the full text see M. Gowing, *Britain and Atomic Energy, 1939–1945* (Macmillan, 1964) Appendix I, pp. 389–93.

3. For a discussion of the impact of German activities upon the British project see R. W. Clark, *The Birth of the Bomb* (Horizon Press, 1961) p. 41.

4. Gowing, op. cit., Appendix II, p. 394.

5. Ibid., p. 395.

6. Ibid., p. 98 and p. 108.

7. A summary of the committee's conclusions is given in ibid., p. 105.

8. Hewlett and Anderson, op. cit., p. 32.

9. Ibid., p. 43.

10. A. J. Pierre, *Nuclear Politics* (Macmillan, 1972) p. 26.

11. Gowing, op. cit., pp. 122–6.

12. Natural uranium has two main isotopes, in the proportion of 1 part of U-235 to 140 parts of U-238. These isotopes cannot be separated by chemical means and use has to be made of the slight difference in their weights. This can be done in the gaseous diffusion method by manufacturing the gas uranium hexafluoride and pumping it through a fine membrane. As the molecules of the lighter U-235 tend to pass through the membrane more easily than those of U-238, the gas on the far side is slightly enriched in U-235. By arranging for this enriched material to be

passed through a large number of such membranes, uranium hexafluoride containing an increasing proportion of U-235 can be produced. The degree of enrichment possible is slight at each stage, and this, plus the difficulty of finding materials that are not attacked by the gas, made the building of such a plant very difficult. For a discussion of British ideas on such an enrichment plant in 1941, see Appendix IV to the Maud Report in Gowing, op. cit., pp. 416–25, and on United States ideas towards the end of 1942, see Hewlett and Anderson, op. cit., pp. 97–101.

13. The ability of natural uranium to sustain a chain reaction in a nuclear reactor is critically dependent upon the ability of neutrons to hit and split the nuclei of the U-235 atoms it contains. They have a better chance of doing this if they are moving relatively slowly at 'thermal' speeds, rather than the speed at which they are ejected from a fissioning nucleus. The latter type of 'fast' neutrons have a tendency to be captured and absorbed by U-238 to form Pu-239. It is thus necessary to enclose the uranium in a moderator, which will slow the neutrons down, but not absorb them. Such moderators have low atomic weights, and the best ones are heavy water and graphite. Heavy water is present in ordinary water to the extent of one part in 5000.

14. The French had been working actively on the possibility of a chain reaction using slow neutrons, and their government had purchased the entire stock (180 kg) of heavy water from the Norwegian Hydroelectric Company for this purpose. When it was clear that France was about to surrender, this heavy water was transported to Britain by Drs Halban and Kowarski, two of the three leading scientists working on the project. Britain then purchased the heavy water and employed the French scientists in its nuclear project. They also made arrangements for dealing with the issue of the patents which the French scientists had taken out on the processes they had been developing. This involvement led to considerable complications towards the end of the war over the degree to which the French government had a right to use the results of the British work in which the French had participated, and indirectly have access to American information. To complicate matters further, the nuclear reactor that was being built on the basis of this work was situated at Chalk River in Canada. See Gowing, op. cit., pp. 49–52, 187–99, 209–15 and 289–96.

15. For a detailed discussion of the technology involved in the American project see Hewlett and Anderson, op. cit., pp. 62–5, 141–67 and 168–73.

16. When uranium 238 captures a neutron it produces uranium 239 which then decays rapidly into neptunian 239, which in turn decays in a matter of days into plutonium 239, which is fissionable. Although Britain had acquired the heavy water reactor project from France, it was felt in 1941 that the most realistic way to obtain fissionable material was to separate out uranium 235. In the United States, however, work on plutonium was given equal priority to that on U-235. Ibid., pp. 53–6 and 105–13.

17. Gowing, op. cit., p. 132.

18. For a summary of the reasons impelling the British towards this decision see the minute of Sir John Anderson to the Prime Minister, 30.7.42, reproduced in ibid., pp. 437–8.

19. The recommendation to build a full-scale diffusion plant was contained in the Lewis Report of December 1942, and approved by the President at the end of the year. Hewlett and Anderson, op. cit., pp. 112–15.

20. Ibid., pp. 78–83.

21. L. R. Groves, *Now It Can Be Told: The Story of the Manhattan Project* (Harper, 1962) p. 11.

22. Gowing, op. cit., p. 154.

23. This presidential decision appears to have been influenced by the discovery that an Anglo-Russian agreement for the exchange of scientific information had been signed in September. See ibid., p. 155 and Hewlett and Anderson, op. cit., pp. 267–8.

24. Gowing, ibid., pp. 157–60.

25. Accidents played a part in this. Roosevelt instructed Bush, who was in London, to *renew* information exchanges at the end of July, but the message was garbled in transmission and he received a message to *review* them. Pierre, op. cit., pp. 43–4; Gowing, ibid., pp. 160–4.

26. Gowing, ibid., pp. 166–71.

27. Ibid., pp. 439–40 for the full text of the Quebec Agreement.

28. Ibid., pp. 172–3.

29. For a full discussion of these activities see ibid., pp. 297–319.

30. Ibid., pp. 269–96.

31. Ibid., pp. 256–60.

32. The original British work on the bomb had been based on the idea of firing two subcritical masses of U-235 towards each other in the manner of a projectile in a gun. This method was used for the Hiroshima U-235 bomb, but it appears that there was no direct British contribution to this work. A plutonium bomb could not use this technique because of the danger of a premature fission, and it thus had to be detonated by surrounding a grapefruit-size subcritical mass of plutonium with explosives, and by a controlled implosion subjecting the mass to such pressures that it became critical. Ibid., pp. 263–4.

33. Ibid., pp. 260–6.

34. Ibid., pp. 250–6. There is an interesting parallel between the use made of the British as consultants to the American project when it ran into difficulties and the role of German scientists in the USSR's gaseous diffusion project. See P. Pringle and J. Spigelman, *The Nuclear Barons* (Holt, Rhinehart & Winston, 1981) p. 477, ref. 60.

35. It has been suggested that the incoherence of United States' policy-making over atomic energy was in part a natural consequence of Roosevelt's decision-making style. In order to retain control of situations, and ensure that he alone was in a position to make a final decision on key issues, the creation of complex, overlapping networks of communication and jurisdiction was encouraged between agencies of government, none of which was strong enough to act independently. See R. Neustadt, *Presidential Power* (Wiley, 1960) p. 157 and A. M. Schlesinger Jr., *The Age of Roosevelt*, vol. 2 (Houghton Mifflin, 1959) p. 528.

36. Hewlett and Anderson, op. cit., pp. 322–4.

37. Ibid., pp. 324–5.

38. Ibid., p. 326.

39. Gowing, op. cit., pp. 245–50.
40. Ibid., pp. 346–63 and Hewlett and Anderson, op. cit., pp. 326–7.
41. Gowing, ibid., Appendix 8, p. 447.
42. Hewlett and Anderson, op. cit., p. 328.
43. Ibid., pp. 331–6.
44. Ibid., pp. 339–40.
45. Ibid., pp. 408–11.
46. Ibid., pp. 417–18.
47. Ibid., p. 420.
48. Ibid., pp. 422–3.
49. Ibid., pp. 431–48.
50. Ibid., pp. 452–5.
51. Ibid., pp. 456–61 and M. Gowing with L. Arnold, *Independence and Deterrence*, vol. 1 (Macmillan, 1974) pp. 64–73 and 78–81.
52. Hewlett and Anderson, ibid., p. 462 and Gowing, ibid., pp. 74–7 and 82–6.
53. Hewlett and Anderson, ibid., pp. 469–77.
54. Ibid., pp. 477–81 and Gowing, *Independence and Deterrence*, vol. 1, pp. 92–100.
55. Alan Nunn May was a British subject who had been employed at the University of Bristol in 1940, and was one of the first physicists to undertake experimental work for the Maud Committee. He was later sent to Canada to form part of the Anglo-French-Canadian team developing the Chalk River heavy water reactors. In February 1946, following the defection of a member of the Russian Embassy staff in Canada, it became known that a spy ring had been operating there which was responsible for passing atomic information and materials to the USSR. Among those arrested and convicted for these acts was Nunn May. Hewlett and Anderson, ibid., p. 501 and Gowing, *Independence and Deterrence*, p. 105.
56. Hewlett and Anderson, ibid., pp. 482–530.
57. Gowing, *Independence and Deterrence*, vol. 1, p. 111.
58. The idea of United States policy-making being a product of bureaucratic politics among individuals and agencies with little purposeful policy emerging, rather than rational ends/means activity by a monolithic actor, first acquired a substantial academic following after the publication of G. T. Allison's article 'Conceptual models and the Cuban missile crisis', *American Political Science Review*, vol. 63, no. 3 (Sept 1969) 689–718.
59. William Penney (now Baron Penney) had been a mathematics professor at Imperial College London before the war, working on the borders of applied mathematics, theoretical physics and theoretical chemistry. In the early part of the war he worked for the Home Office and the Admiralty on high explosive effects. In 1944 he went to Los Alamos, where he became especially expert on the blast and shock effects of the bombs, and observed the Nagasaki explosion. It has been stated that 'Few Americans know more [than him] about the operational aspects of the bomb'. Gowing, *Independence and Deterrence*, vol. 2, pp. 6–7.
60. Ibid., vol. 1, pp. 112–13.
61. It is probably these exchanges which are being referred to by Pringle and Spigelman, op. cit., p. 481, ref 83, when they state that 'it is now accepted

that despite Groves and the McMahon Act, there was an exchange of atomic information during 1947–49 and it was due to Portal'.

62. Hewlett and Anderson, op. cit., pp. 626–7 and 631.
63. Professor Sir James Chadwick had been the discoverer of the neutron in 1932, and in 1939 was a highly respected Professor of Nuclear Physics at Liverpool University, a member of the Maud Committee and the director of the group undertaking fast neutron research. In September 1943 he went to the United States as head of the British Tube Alloys mission and technical adviser to the British members of the CPC. Gowing, *Britain and Atomic Energy*, pp. 18–20, 38–9 and 173.
64. Ibid., p. 324.
65. Ibid., p. 325.
66. Ibid., p. 329.
67. In 1932 Professor John Cockcroft and E. T. S. Walton had been the first scientists to split an atom by artificial means. In 1939 Cockcroft was about to take up a Chair at Cambridge. He was a member of the Maud Committee, and at the end of 1943 had been appointed director of the Anglo-Canadian team at Montreal and Chalk River. Gowing, *Independence and Deterrence*, vol. 2, pp. 4–6.
68. Gowing, *Britain and Atomic Energy*, p. 334.
69. Ibid.
70. It has been argued that this was largely a product of the manipulative abilities of Sir Edward Bridges, the secretary of the Cabinet, who believed that the atomic bomb project should be insulated from the effects of party politics. He was also alleged to have ensured that control of atomic energy policy effectively remained with the Prime Minister, and to have recommended that a start be made on building the bomb. Pringle and Spigelman, op. cit., pp. 78–85.
71. For a discussion on the institutional arrangements for atomic energy in the post-war period see Gowing, *Independence and Deterrence*, vol. 1, pp. 19–59.
72. Ibid., pp. 166–7.
73. Ibid., pp. 167 and 172.
74. Hewlett and Anderson, op. cit., p. 216. Although the Hanford reactors were designed to produce 250 megawatts of heat, they proved to be susceptible to a greater neutron loss than had been calculated due to the production of the fission product xenon 135. This necessitated a larger than anticipated fuel charge to achieve the design power levels. The likely output from these reactors can be calculated using the method outlined in Appendix 3. The later 'N' reactor at Hanford, a similar water-cooled and moderated design, produces 4000 megawatts of heat. Its output as a military plutonium producer appears to be approximately 866 kilograms a year. (Figures derived from *No More Atoms For Peace*, Natural Resources Defense Council Inc. (Washington, July 1981) pp. 2 and 3 and *Hearings on H.R. 2969*, p. 171.) On the basis of operating at full power for 86 per cent of the time, it will produce 0.69 grams of plutonium per 1000 megawatt days of operation. This indicates that the plutonium production rate of an early Hanford-type water-cooled production reactor can optimistically be estimated at 0.7 grams per 1000 megawatt days. This would

give an annual plutonium production for such a reactor, assuming operations on full power for 86 per cent of the year, of 55 kilograms. Aggregate calculations of this type are only approximations, but they do give an indication of the rough quantities of material involved.

75. Gowing, *Independence and Deterrence*, vol. 1, pp. 169–70. No thought appears to have been given in these deliberations to the need to produce isotopes with short half-lives to initiate the chain reaction in atomic weapons, and the vulnerabilities in their supply that would be created by having only one production reactor. However, the option would always exist of producing them in research reactors.

76. Lord Portal was appointed Controller of Production, Atomic Energy, in the Ministry of Supply in early 1946. This appointment was made by the Prime Minister and Portal was given power to report direct to him. His relationship with the Minister of Supply was thus somewhat unclear. For a discussion of these issues see ibid., pp. 29–30, and Pringle and Sigelman, op. cit., pp. 78–85.

77. Gowing, *Independence and Deterrence*, vol. 1, pp. 370–8.

78. Ibid., pp. 382–5 and K. B. Jay, *Britain's Atomic Factories* (HMSO, 1954) pp. 21–3.

79. Gowing. *Independence and Deterrence*, vol. 1, p. 176.

80. Ibid., pp. 176–9.

81. Ibid., p. 174.

82. Considerable confusion surrounds the question of whether or not the original V bomber specification B35/46 issued in early 1947 included provision for the carriage of an atomic bomb. Gowing, ibid., reports that this was not in the RAF operational requirement for the aircraft, but another source indicates that the specification did include a statement that the aircraft had to be capable of carrying a 'special bomb' measuring $60'' \times 290'' \times 80''$ and weighing 10 000 lb (R. Jackson, op. cit., p. 10). The bomb dropped on Nagasaki also weighed 10 000 lb, and was $60''$ in diameter and $128''$ long (Hewlett and Anderson, op. cit., photo opposite p. 401). In addition, 'special bomb' was the pseudonym used by the United States Army Air Force in the operational orders for the nuclear bomb attacks on Hiroshima and Nagasaki (ibid., p. 394). In fact the bomb mentioned in the B35/46 specification was a lighter, developed version of the 'Tallboy' 12 000-lb high explosive bomb used by the RAF in the later stages of the Second World War for precision attacks on hardened targets. It was anticipated that this would have considerable penetrative powers against targets such as submarine shelters when dropped from the V bomber operational height of about 50 000 feet, and would need a casing of advanced aerodynamic design if the intended accuracies were to be achieved. The development work undertaken on these casings by the Royal Aircraft Establishment at Farnborough was later utilised in the design of the initial nuclear weapons, which were $24'$ long and weighed 10 000 lb. An extensive series of drop tests on their casings was conducted in Britain from late 1952 onwards using early examples of the V bombers (Jackson, op. cit., p. 20).

83. Gowing, *Independence and Deterrence*, pp. 179–83.

3 The American Nuclear Weapon Programme: from Scarcity to Abundance

1. The term 'laboratory weapon' was used to describe the type of bomb dropped on Nagasaki, and indicated its unsuitability for long-term storage or rapid military use. D. A. Rosenberg, 'American atomic strategy and the hydrogen bomb decision'. *Journal of American History*, vol. 66 (1979–80) p. 66.

2. For a full analysis of the problems of restructuring the wartime project see *Investigation into the United States Atomic Energy Project*. Hearings before the Joint Committee on Atomic Energy, 81st Congress, 1st Session (USGPO, Washington, 1949). This includes Oppenheimer's comment that 'I do not believe that you could have expected a very flourishing performance between the summer of 1945 and the fall of 1947' (Part 7, 13 June 1949, p. 311). while W. J. Williams explained that the Manhattan Project 'was not set up as a long range job, because from the beginning it was not known which processes would prove efficient, practicable, or if any of them would definitely prove so. So for that reason much of the construction ... was temporary ... The Commission knew ... they would be operating under peacetime conditions. They had to set up programs that would extend over a long period' (Part 7, 22 June 1949, p. 462).

3. D. E. Lilienthal, *The Journals of David E Lilienthal*, Vol. II. *The Atomic Energy Years, 1945–1950* (Harper & Row, 1964) pp. 165–6; R. G. Hewlett and F. Duncan, *A History of the United States Atomic Energy Commission*, Vol. II. *Atomic Shield 1947–1952* (Pennsylvania State University Press, 1969) p. 47 and D. A. Rosenberg, 'US nuclear stockpile, 1945–50', *Bulletin of the Atomic Scientists* (May 1982), p. 26 (hereafter cited as 'US nuclear stockpile')

4. For a discussion of the British programme see pp. 62–89 below. The Soviet programme is examined in detail in D. Holloway, 'Entering the nuclear arms race: the Soviet decision to build the atomic bomb, 1939–45', *Social Studies in Science*, vol. 2 (Sage, 1981) pp. 159–97.

5. Rosenberg, op. cit., p. 66 states categorically that 'all weapons produced from 1946 until late 1948 were Mark III "Fat Man" plutonium implosion bombs'.

6. Hewett and Duncan, op. cit., pp. 39–40. For an explanation of the basis for the estimate of Hanford output see Chapter 2, ref. 74. I have assumed that the core of each bomb contained up to six kilograms of plutonium.

7. Ibid., p. 40.

8. Hewlett and Anderson, op. cit, p. 646.

9. Ibid., p. 631.

10. In the summer of 1944 it had been estimated that one bomb would be available in August 1945 and a further three by the end of the year. Ibid., p. 253. Figures for the US stockpile through to June 1948 have been declassified: D. A. Rosenberg, 'US nuclear stockpile', p. 28. One source states that eight were in store at the end of 1946. C. Pincher, *Inside Story* (Sidgwick & Jackson, 1978) p. 154.

11. Hewlett and Duncan, op. cit., pp. 62–3 and 141–7.

12. Rosenberg. op. cit., pp. 65–6.
13. I have used the term 'warhead' throughout this study to refer to the nuclear explosive part of any nuclear weapon. An alternative description is the physics package. It appeared to be standard practice with first and second generation weapons to stockpile twice as many non-nuclear assemblies as warheads.
14. S. F. Wells, Jr., 'The origins of massive retaliation', *Political Science Quarterly* (Spring 1981) p. 48.
15. Rosenberg, op. cit., pp. 66 and 71; Wells, ibid., p. 48 and Hewlett and Duncan, op. cit., pp. 175–6.
16. *Investigation into the United States Atomic Energy Project*, Part 7, 13 June 1949, pp. 347–8.
17. Rosenberg, op. cit., pp. 64–6.
18. Ibid., p. 66.
19. Ibid., p. 68.
20. Ibid., p. 65; Rosenberg, 'US nuclear stockpile', p. 28; and S. M. Millett, 'The capabilities of the American nuclear deterrent, 1945–1950', *Aerospace Historian* (March 1980) p. 28.
21. Rosenberg, ibid., pp. 67–8.
22. The public face of this debate is seen in the B36 *v.* supercarrier controversy which was analysed by P. Y. Hammond, 'Super carriers and B36 bombers: appropriations, strategy and politics' in H. Stein (ed.), *American Civil-Military Decisions* (University of Alabama Press, 1963), pp. 465–554. The debate within the military establishment appears to have been a more principled one, however, and centred around the relationship between the use of nuclear weapons against the USSR and its impact upon the actions of that country. Ibid., pp. 70–9.
23. RG 218, Records of the US Joint Chiefs of Staff, CCS 471.6 (8–15–45) Sec 9, SU JIC Policy Memo no. 2, 29 March 1948. *Agreed Statement on Estimated Russian Atom Bomb Production.* In this, the Joint Intelligence Committee of the JCS estimated that the earliest date for the first Soviet test explosion would be mid-1950, and that the USSR could possess a stockpile of 50 bombs by 1955. The probable date was specified as mid-1953, with a stockpile of 20 weapons being achieved by mid-1955.
24. RG 218. Records of the US Joint Chiefs of Staff, CCS 471.6 USSR (11–8–49) SI JIC 502(1), 31 January 1950. *Implications of Soviet Possession of Atomic Weapons*, Appendix A, p. 4 and p. 5 and Appendix B, pp. 19 and 21. A detailed study was later undertaken by the Joint Intelligence Committee to estimate the scale and nature of a Soviet attack upon the United Kingdom up to mid-1952. See RG 218, Records of the US Joint Chiefs of Staff, CCS 092 USSR (3–27–45) Sec 55, JIC 435/52. 7 February 1951. *Estimate of the Scale and Nature of a Soviet Attack on the United Kingdom between Now and mid-1952.*
25. See, for example, *Memorandum by Chief of Staff, USAF to JCS on Military Requirements for Atomic Weapons.* RG 218, Records of the US Joint Chiefs of Staff, CCS. 471.6 (11–3–51) Section 1, 12 November 1951. This indicated on p. 4 that the USAF 'ideal' requirement was 5000 weapons by 1955–6 excluding tactical weapons, but this was being ignored and stockpile targets were being tailored to fit the estimated output of materials from existing facilities.

26. An interesting reflection of this conflict is found in the Chief of Naval Operations' response to JCS 2215–1: Joint Chiefs of Staff view on *Department of Defense Interest in the Use of Nuclear Weapons*. RG 218, Records of the US Joint Chiefs of Staff, CCS 471.6 (11–3–51) Sec 1. This insisted that the sentence 'developments now underway in the Tactical Air Command (TAC) and in Naval and Marine aviation are pointed towards full exploitation of their capabilities in this field' should be inserted after 'The Strategic Air Command (SAC) as now constituted and equipped, has to a large extent developed around the atomic weapon'. It also contained the bald statement that 'the acquisition by the United States of its foreign bases has been dictated largely by atomic weapon considerations' (p. 1). The need to plan for the development and production by January 1955 of weapons which could be used as a 'direct contribution to the defense of the signatory nations of the North Atlantic Pact' had been accepted in May 1949, and a requirement specified in terms of numbers and kilotonnage *Military Considerations on Delivery of More Powerful Atomic Weapons*. RG 218, Records of US Joint Chiefs of Staff, CCS 471.6 (8–15–45) Sec 15. JCS 1823/14, 13 January 1948.
27. This question is fully discussed in Gowing, *Independence and Deterrence*, vol. 1, pp. 358–73.
28. For a table listing annual US procurement figures for uranium concentrates and their source, see Hewlett and Duncan, op. cit., Appendix 5, p. 674.
29. Ibid., p. 179.
30. For the basis of this calculation see supra Chapter 2, ref. 74 and ibid., pp. 271–2.
31. A. Cave-Brown (ed.), *Operation: World War III* (Arms and Armour Press, 1978) p. 18.
32. A rather sketchy study had been conducted in January 1948 of the need for such weapons. It was based on the proposition that the same amount of fissionable material could be incorporated in ten 20-kiloton bombs as in seven 100-kiloton ones and the latter would collectively devastate 70 square miles compared with the 34 square miles threatened by the former. However, it was emphasized that requirements would be dependent on the existence of large urban targets, and relatively few of these existed in the USSR. *Military Considerations on Delivery of More Powerful Atomic Weapons*, Sec 3, 1948. This requirement was incorporated in a memorandum on *Production Objectives for the Stockpile of Atomic Weapons* sent by the Chief of Staff, US Air Force to the JCS on 27 May 1949, RG 218, Records of the US Joint Chiefs of Staff, CCS 471.6 (8–15–45) Sec 15, JCS 1823/14. This contained the conclusions of the *ad hoc* committee set up by the JCS in October 1948 to specify the military requirements for atomic weapons through to 1956, and was the detailed basis for the JCS request to the AEC for the expansion of fissile material production.
33. Hewlett and Duncan, op. cit., pp. 175–6. Eniwetok is an atoll in the Marshall Islands in the Central Pacific. It was chosen as a testing ground because of its remoteness, its excellent harbour and its convenient location 300 miles away from a US naval base.
34. *Production Objectives for the Stockpile of Atomic Weapons*, pp. 86, 91–2 and 94 of Annex B specifies four types of atomic weapon intended to

make up the 1956 stockpile. Three were specified in terms of kilotonnage, but these figures have yet to be declassified. (Other contemporary documentation would suggest they were 100, 20 and possibly a figure in the range of 1–10 kilotons.) The fourth was the earth penetrator weapon. This had to use a gun mechanism, presumably because an implosion device was regarded as less able to withstand the forces created by impact and penetration before exploding. For a more detailed discussion of the requirements of this type of weapon, which also has a bearing on the development of missiles and artillery warheads, see *Memorandum by Chief of Staff, USAF to JCS on Military Requirements for Atomic Weapons*, 11 December 1951, pp. 1 and 2.

35. H. P. Green and A. Rosenthal, *Government of the Atom* (Atherton 1963) pp. 6–10 and 236–7.
36. Hewlett and Duncan, op. cit., p. 182.
37. Ibid., Appendix 2, p. 669.
38. Ibid., p. 371.
39. These were now based on more detailed information than was available in March 1948, when it was estimated that the Soviet stockpile would comprise 20 to 50 bombs by mid-1955. By February 1950 it had been concluded that the USSR had at least one production reactor in operation and was building a uranium enrichment plant. This led to estimates of 120 to 200 weapons by mid-1954, with 50 bombs being available in mid-1952. *Implications of Soviet Possession of Atomic Weapons*, Appendix A, p.6. This document also indicates that after January 1955 it was assumed that the USSR would have the capability 'decisively' to disable the United States by employing its stockpile of 300 bombs in a surprise attack if effective means of delivery were available (pp. 6a–8). Consideration was also given to the employment of nuclear weapons against UK and Canadian targets in the period after January 1951. The document is remarkable for the worst-case assumptions that underpin its assessments and 'guesstimates' of Soviet capabilities: its guideline appeared to be 'if it is remotely conceivable, the USSR will do it'.
40. The General Advisory Committee (GAC) was created by the 1946 Atomic Energy Act 'to advise the Commission' (which comprised five Commissioners) 'on scientific and technical matters ... It was to be composed of nine members, who shall be appointed from civilian life by the President' (Section 2b) The AEC's other advisory committee was the Military Liaison Committee. In the immediate post-war years the GAC had a very significant role in policy-making, due to the lack of experience of the commissioners and the leading part played by many of its members in the Manhattan Project.
41. Hewlett and Duncan, op. cit., pp. 383–95 and H. York, *The Advisors: Oppenheimer, Teller and the Superbomb*, (W. H. Freeman 1976) pp. 41–65 and Appendix, pp. 150–9.
42. Wells, op. cit., p. 49.
43. This point is alluded to in York. op. cit., p. 100. For a more detailed discussion see Pringle and Spigelman, op. cit., p. 516, note 253. It was also the view of the GAC and Penney that yields of close to one megaton could be obtained by developing fission bomb technology. Gowing, *Independence and Deterrence*, vol. 2, p. 474.

44. See York, ibid., pp. 62–5 for the arguments of Teller and the other scientists. Rosenberg, op. cit., p. 87 makes the point that the AEC's Military Liaison Committee 'placed emphasis on the problem of technological competition and the psychological importance of the H bomb, rather than its military mission'.
45. Rosenberg, ibid., pp. 81–3 emphasises the key role played by this Committee in shaping the JCS positive attitude to the proposal, despite opposition from its military planning and targeting organisations.
46. Ibid., p. 84 and Hewlett and Duncan, op. cit., pp. 406–9.
47. York, op. cit., p. 69 concludes that although Fuchs's interrogation was known to the United States government prior to the H bomb decision, it did not affect the result in any way. Rosenberg, ibid, pp.84–6 indicates that the key shift in attitude towards the H bomb by the military occurred as a consequence of a memorandum sent to the Military Liaison Committee by its army member General Loper, on 16 February, in which he hypothesised that if (thanks to Fuchs) the USSR had commenced a determined nuclear weapon development programme in 1943, it was conceivable that the USSR might have a stockpile equivalent to that of the United States and be already well advanced in production of the H bomb. This possibility led the JCS and the National Security Council to urge that the H bomb programme should proceed 'as a matter of the highest urgency'. Contributory factors that led to the possibility of a Soviet H bomb programme being taken seriously were that Fuchs has worked on theoretical aspects of H bombs while at Los Alamos and that intelligence reports indicated that the USSR had initiated 'a very large, heavy water production program' (*Implications of Soviet Possession of Atomic Weapons*, Appendix B, p. 23). The construction of heavy water reactors, in addition to their existing graphite-moderated ones, was taken to be a sign of their interest in producing tritium for H bombs, radiological warfare material or U-233 from thorium (cf. GAC report, York, op. cit., p. 153). It appears that the worst-case assumption was made that its purpose was tritium production, for an H bomb production programme. While this may have been part of the purpose of the Soviet programme, there are also indications that U-233 production was another aim, as unlike the US programme, the USSR used U-233 in test weapons (David Holloway, 'Research note: Soviet thermonuclear development', *International Security* vol. 4 no. 3 (Winter 1979–80) p. 195). In *Implications of Soviet Possession of Atomic Weapons*, Appendix A, p. 6 dated 9 February 1950, it states that 'Prior to the disclosure of the Fuchs' leaks the estimate of the Soviet bomb stockpile was as follows: this estimate will probably be materially revised upwards:

    mid-1949 1 exploded
    mid-1950 10–20
    mid-1951 25–45
    mid-1952 45–90
    mid-1953 70–135,

A year later in its *Estimate of the Scale and Nature of a Soviet Attack on the United Kingdom Between Now and mid-1952*, p. 5, these figures had become 50 bombs by mid-1951 and 120 by mid-1952, indicating that the previous estimates made *after* the Soviet explosion had been moved forward by about one year following Fuchs's arrest.

48. Figures for the plutonium foregone as a consequence of tritium production are contained in *Hearings on H.R. 2969*, p. 172. This states that one kilogram of tritium can be equated with 72 kilograms of plutonium in terms of the production capability of a reactor. Only part of the reactor capacity can be used to make tritium, and during the late 1970s each reactor at Savannah River was producing annually one kilogram of tritium and about 470 kilograms of plutonium, thus reducing potential plutonium output by about 13 per cent. *No More Atoms for Peace* op. cit., p. 2.
49. Hewlett and Duncan, op. cit., p. 415. York, op. cit., pp. 122–213, discusses the construction of a large linear accelerator to produce tritium by bombarding lithium 6 with neutrons, but this method proved uneconomic. In addition he points out (p. 27) that several types of thermonuclear fuel could be used in a hydrogen bomb, including pure deuterium, deuterium plus tritium and lithium deuteride.
50. Hewlett and Duncan, ibid., p. 430 and *No More Atoms for Peace*, p. 2.
51. Hewlett and Duncan, ibid., pp. 493–531.
52. Ibid., p. 496.
53. For a full description of NSC 68 and the crosscutting issues of nuclear *v.* conventional capabilities and strategic nuclear *v.* tactical nuclear ones, see S. F. Wells, 'Sounding the tocsin: NSC 68 and the Soviet threat', *International Security,* vol. 4, no. 2 (Fall 1979) pp. 116–58.
54. Hewlett and Duncan, op. cit., p. 524.
55. Ibid., p. 532 and pp. 553–4.
56. Ibid., p. 534.
57. Ibid., p. 550.
58. The 1950 figure is based on the data in Chapter 2, footnote 74, pp. 271–2, where the output of each Hanford reactor is estimated as 55 kilograms per year: four operated throughout that year. The 1956 figure is based on the five Savannah River reactors having a capacity for producing about 4040 kilograms of plutonium (*No More Atoms for Peace*, pp. 2, 3) and the six smaller Hanford reactors producing about 330 kilograms.
59. Hewlett and Duncan, op. cit., pp. 557–9.
60. Ibid., pp. 576–8 and 580–1.
61. Ibid., p. 586.
62. Green and Rosenthal, op. cit., pp. 238–9.
63. I have assumed that the two larger Hanford reactors had a plutonium output capacity midway between the later 'N' reactors' 866 kilograms and the earlier reactors' 55 kilograms.
64. H. Morland, 'The H-bomb secret', *The Progressive*; vol. 43, no. 11 (Nov 1979) 14–23 and more especially 'Errata', *The Progressive*, vol. 43, no. 12 (Dec 1979).
65. York, op. cit., pp. 78–81 and Hewlett and Duncan, op. cit., pp. 590–2.
66. Hewlett and Duncan, ibid., p. 535 and M. W. Carter and A. A. Moghissi, 'Three decades of nuclear testing', *Health Physics*, vol. 33 (July 1977) p. 60.
67. York, op. cit., pp. 84–5.

68. Ibid., p. 26. See also Carter and Moghissi, op. cit., p. 60.
69. Morland, op. cit., p. 19.
70. Hewlett and Duncan, op. cit., p. 548.
71. York, op. cit., pp. 212–16.
72. Hewlett and Duncan, op. cit., pp. 75–6.
73. Ibid., pp. 185–221.
74. A useful indicator for the 1952 figure is the increase in the number of United States aircraft capable of delivering an atomic bomb. The figures were 397 for the end of the 1950 fiscal year, 518 for the same date in 1951 and 639 in 1952. RG 218, Records of the United States Joint Chiefs of Staff, CCS 471.6 (6–15–45) Sec 19, MLC 34 – *Memorandum from Military Liaison Committee to the Atomic Energy Commission* on *Basis of Procurement for certain Items for Stockpile*, 7 July 1950.

4 Gestation: the Programme to Explode a British Atomic Device, 1947–52

1. Gowing, *Independence and Deterrence*, vol. 1, p. 180.
2. In the absence of detailed information on the first bomb design, it must be assumed that only part of the aerodynamic casing was used to carry the warhead, the rest containing fusing and other systems, or being empty. Pictures of the 24-foot weapon suggest that it was somewhat similar to a German V2 rocket in shape. Given the height at which it was intended to be released, its speed as it approached the ground must have been substantial. See A. Brookes *V-Force* (Jane's 1982).
3. Gowing, *Independence and Deterrence*, vol. 1, p. 171.
4. Ibid.
5. Ibid., p. 189.
6. It is unclear from the official history what were the origins of the erroneous information on the Hanford reactors. Although the figures for thermal power were probably based on the original design rating for these plants, the output calculations appear to have contained errors which were not discovered until after the arrest of Klaus Fuchs in 1950. See Chapter 2, footnote 74 and ibid., vol. 2, p. 401.
7. Ibid., vol. 1, pp. 190–1. The site had been a Royal Ordnance Factory and was known as Sellafield. To avoid confusion with another nuclear site at Springfields, the name was changed to Windscale. In 1981 its name officially reverted to Sellafield.
8. Ibid., pp. 192–3.
9. Ibid., vol. 2, pp. 391–3. In 1957, the inadequate control system resulted in some graphite channels in a Windscale reactor catching fire and distorting, producing an inability to discharge some of the fuel and the latter then burning.
10. Ibid., pp. 394–5.
11. Ibid., p. 399.
12. Ibid., p. 400.
13. Ibid., pp. 347 and 401.

14. Ibid., p. 389. In practice, enrichment back to normal levels did not result in material identical to natural uranium, as some non-fissile U-236 was created during reactor operations, and thus the percentage of this material present in the resultant uranium was far greater than before.
15. The basis for these figures is that originally the reactors had a combined output of 180 Mw(th) which was later increased to 240 Mw(th). The figures assume that they operated for 314 days per year and produced 800 grams of plutonium per 1000 megawatt days. For a discussion on the source of the 800 gram figure see Appendix 3. There is also a suggestion in ibid., vol. 1, pp. 445–6 that in 1952 the output potential of the second, more efficient, Windscale reactor was 40 kilograms of plutonium per year, giving a combined output of less than 80 kilograms.
16. The figure for the amount of plutonium required for the Hurricane assembly and the Blue Danube weapon is derived from Gowing, ibid., vol. 2, pp. 347–8. The original 1946–8 calculations (ibid., vol. 1, pp. 167–8 and 217) were based on 100 kilograms of plutonium producing 15 bombs, i.e. 6.67 kilograms per weapon. For the Hurricane test, 15 per cent less than this is reported to have been requested, i.e. 5.67 kilograms, though the actual core may not have contained as much fissile material as this.
17. Hewlett and Anderson, op. cit., p. 630.
18. Gowing, *Independence and Deterrence*, vol. 2, pp. 405–22.
19. Ibid, vol. 1, pp. 186–7 and 214 and S. Menaul, *Countdown* (Hale, 1980) p. 33.
20. This work formed part of the background to a report on 'future developments in weapons and methods of war' submitted to the Chiefs of Staff Committee in July 1946. See *The Times*, 15 June 1981, p. 2.
21. Gowing, *Independence and Deterrence*, vol. 1, p. 216.
22. D. A. Rosenberg, op. cit., pp. 67–8.
23. In 1949 a committee of the US Joint Chiefs of Staff conducted a planning exercise into the possible course of a world war breaking out in 1957, code named Dropshot. This assumed that 7 British bomber groups comprising 210 aircraft would be available to the NATO allies, as against 19 from the United States. The implication of the figures for atomic bomb and conventional bombing aircraft is that the UK force would carry some atomic weapons. Cave-Brown, op. cit., pp. 201 and 289–90. This planning figure of 210 aircraft may not be unconnected with the target figure of 200 weapons by 1957.
24. Gowing, *Independence and Deterrence*, vol. 1, pp. 215–17.
25. This table is based on the magnitudes suggested in ibid., p. 217 and figures given in ibid., pp. 167–8 for the output of the Hanford reactor. They suggest that it was anticipated that approximately 6.67 kilograms of plutonium would be required for each UK bomb. In practice, both output figures for the reactors and the amount needed for each weapon were overstated – see supra, refs 15 and 16.
26. Ibid., pp. 217–19 and 223.
27. Ibid., vol. 2, pp. 426–41.
28. Ibid., p. 427.
29. Ibid., vol. 1, pp. 440–3, but more especially Brookes op. cit. pp. 36–9.
30. Gowing, ibid., vol. 2, p. 295.
31. A fast breeder is a reactor which utilises neutrons moving at both high and

lower 'thermal' speeds. By building the core of the reactor from enriched uranium or plutonium, the neutrons from a fission reaction are used more effectively, a much smaller reactor is possible, and the moderator can be dispensed with. In addition, the core can be surrounded with a blanket of U-238, a waste product of the U-235 enrichment process, and neutrons generated by the chain reaction in the reactor core will convert some of this material into plutonium. In theory this could lead to more plutonium being created in the blanket than is consumed in the reactor core, hence the name fast breeder reactor. If the reactor is not surrounded by uranium it becomes in effect a method of burning up plutonium or U-235 only, and is then termed a fast reactor or fast burner. Existing power reactors use neutrons travelling at thermal speeds, and have moderators to slow down the speed of neutrons and increase their chances of producing fission in a U-235 atom. It is because of this that such reactors are often called thermal ones.

32. Gowing, *Independence and Deterrence*, vol. 2, pp. 274–6.
33. Ibid., pp. 265–90.
34. Ibid., p. 290 and vol. 1, pp. 445–6.
35. Ibid., vol. 2, p. 295.
36. Ibid., vol. 1, pp. 445–7.
37. For a detailed recent discussion of this problem, see A. De Volpi, op. cit., Appendix L, pp. 297–327. This suggests that the presence of Pu-240 complicates weapon design because it: (i) leads to the need to increase the mass and radius of the fissile core of the weapon; (ii) introduces extraneous and unpredictable sources of radiation and heat into the weapon assembly. This can lead to reductions in the yield of the weapon, the possibility of it being physically disabled and problems in storing the completed assembly. The possibility of physical disablement arises from the fact that plutonium metal changes its characteristics if it is heated. It is in its most dense state, and hence has a minimum critical mass, below 115°C (the alpha phase). If its temperature rises above this figure it expands, creating not only a need for more material to form the critical mass but also changes in physical configuration. Above 115°C, plutonium is stable in the delta phase (310–450°C): above and below these figures it shrinks. This creates two options for weapon designers: (i) minimise the amount of plutonium used by maintaining its temperature prior to detonation below 115°C and thus use only plutonium containing a minimum of Pu-240; (ii) stabilise the plutonium in the delta phase by adding gallium, and accept the penalties of a greater requirement for plutonium and the impact of having very hot metal in the core of the weapon, with subsequent effects on its design. Such a weapon could, however, use cores containing significant quantities of isotopes of plutonium other than Pu-239 (p. 62). Gowing indicates that the British weapons were stabilised in the delta phase (ibid., vol. 2, footnote p. 467), and thus the problems they faced were physical shrinkage if the temperature boundaries were crossed, and the impact of the heat generated by the core upon the rest of the weapon.
38. Gowing, ibid., vol. 1, p. 448 and R. F. Pocock, *Nuclear Power* (Unwin, 1977) pp. 30–3.
39. Gowing, ibid., pp. 448–9 and vol. 2, p. 291.

40. These figures are based upon the calculations in supra, ref 16, which indicate that 25 Hurricane size cores could be manufactured from 140 kilograms of plutonium, and the data in Table 3.1 which indicates that the output of the high enrichment plant would add 20 to 21 cores to the annual output figure.

41. Gowing, *Independence and Deterrence*, vol. 2, pp. 462–70.

42. For an account of this test see ibid., pp. 476–95.

43. Gowing, ibid., vol. 2, pp. 472–4 fails to make it clear that the Hurricane device was similar to the US Mark III 'laboratory weapon' of 1945. It possessed all its operational limitations, although it benefited from advances in electronic and explosive research over the intervening seven years, and its nuclear efficiency might have been better. The Blue Danube production weapon, however, was similar to the US Mark IV assembly of 1948 and possessed many of its operational advantages over the Mark III.

44. Ibid., pp. 461–73.

45. Ibid., p. 473 and Hewlett and Duncan, op. cit., p. 673.

46. Jackson, op. cit., p. 20.

47. Gowing, *Independence and Deterrence*, vol. 2, pp. 448–52.

48. Ibid., p. 452 and vol. 1, p. 437. All non-nuclear component production was undertaken in Royal Ordnance factories, rather than being subcontracted to commercial firms.

49. Ibid., vol. 2, pp. 436–7, 448 and 474.

50. For a discussion on this point see Hewlett and Duncan, op. cit., p. 415.

51. Gowing, *Independence and Deterrence*, vol. 2, pp. 474–5.

52. Ibid., vol. 1, pp. 184–5.

53. Ibid., p. 94.

54. Hewlett and Duncan, op. cit., pp. 264–71 and *Science, Technology and American Diplomacy*, op. cit., pp. 57–122.

55. Hewlett and Duncan, ibid., p. 272.

56. Ibid., pp. 274–5.

57. Ibid., pp. 277–9.

58. Ibid., pp. 279–84 and Gowing, *Independence and Deterrence*, vol. 1, pp. 249–52. The document is reproduced in Gowing, pp. 266–72.

59. Gowing, ibid., pp. 254–6.

60. Hewlett and Duncan, op. cit., pp. 286–93.

61. Ibid., pp. 293–5 and Gowing, *Independence and Deterrence*, vol. 1, pp. 258–62.

62. Gowing, ibid., p. 263.

63. Contemporary US war plans envisaged the Soviet Army reaching the Channel ports in 60–90 days, and then launching an invasion of Britain with 45 000 airborne troops and 100 000 seaborne ones, backed up by 350 000 reserves. Soviet attempts to obtain air superiority over the United Kingdom were assumed from the outbreak of hostilities in order to prevent US strategic bombers using British bases. *Estimate of the Scale and Nature of a Soviet Attack on the United Kingdom between Now and mid-1952*, pp. 7 and 9.

64. Hewlett and Duncan, op. cit., pp. 299–304, and Gowing, *Independence and Deterrence*, vol. 1, pp. 275–9.

65. Gowing, ibid., pp. 283–4 and Hewlett and Duncan, ibid., p. 306.

66. Gowing, ibid., p. 289.
67. Ibid., p. 293.
68. Ibid., pp. 294–5 and Hewlett and Duncan, op. cit., pp. 308–10.
69. Gowing, ibid., pp. 296–7.
70. Ibid., vol. 2, p. 449.
71. Ibid., vol. 1, p. 298 and Hewlett and Duncan, op. cit., pp. 310–14.
72. Gowing, ibid., pp. 299–303.
73. Ibid., pp. 303–4 and pp. 325–7.
74. Hewlett and Duncan, op. cit., pp. 480–3.
75. Gowing, *Independence and Deterrence*, vol. 1, p. 304.
76. Ibid., pp. 304–5. Positive vetting involves attempting to discover adverse information about an individual's loyalty and behaviour. The contemporary British system merely involved checking that no such information existed in police records, etc. and the Conservative government was opposed to extending this procedure, partly because officers swore allegiance to the Crown and ministers were Privy Councillors, and partly because in the United States many people were only second generation citizens whereas most of the British population could trace their citizenship back for centuries. After 1955 positive vetting started to be introduced for all new AEA and Ministry of Defence employees, mainly because it was seen as a necessary prelude to closer cooperation with the United States in nuclear matters.
77. Ibid., pp. 307–8.
78. Ibid., pp. 311–18.
79. *494 HC Debs* Col 280, Written Answers, 6 December 1951 and ibid., p. 318.
80. Gowing, *Independence and Deterrence*, vol. 1, pp. 410–11 and pp. 415–16, and Hewlett and Duncan, op. cit., pp. 574–5.
81. Gowing, ibid., pp. 411–14, 416 and 441–2.
82. Ibid., pp. 413–14.
83. Ibid., p. 442 and 448–9.
84. Strauss, who had been the AEC commissioner largely responsible for the furore which led to the limiting of interchange under the 1948 *modus vivendi*, became both AEC chairman and atomic energy adviser to the President on 1 July 1953. Green and Rosenthal, op. cit., pp. 12–13. Nichols is stated to have been 'a hostile critic of the British programme' in Gowing, ibid., p. 294.

5 Translating the Art into the Article: Initial British Nuclear Weapon Testing and Production

1. Gowing, *Independence and Deterrence*, vol. 1, pp. 406–7. Memo from Churchill to Lord Cherwell, November 1951: 'I have never wished since our decision during the war that England should start the manufacture of atomic bombs ... We should have the art rather than the article ... There is however no point in our going into bulk production even if we were able to.'

2. Ibid., p. 445.
3. Carter and Moghissi, op. cit., p. 69, Jackson, op. cit., p. 20 and Pincher, op. cit., p. 176.
4. Jackson, ibid., p. 19.
5. Ibid., pp. 20–2.
6. Gowing, *Independence and Deterrence*, vol. 2, p. 475.
7. R. N. Rosencrance, *Defense of the Realm* (Columbia University Press, 1968) pp. 224–5.
8. The reasons for this relate to the fact that the critical mass of a bare sphere of pure metallic Pu-239 is approximately 11 kilograms, and that of U-235 about 48 kilograms. A kilogram of fully fissioned fissionable material has an explosive power equivalent to about 17 kilotons. Assuming the necessity to limit the fissionable material in the core of an explosive device to less than that of its critical mass, and further assuming a 30 per cent conversion ratio of fissile material into energy, the maximum yields possible from a Pu-239 weapon appear to be about 56 kilotons and for a U-235 weapon about 245 kilotons. Thus any attempt to develop a fission bomb with yields up to 200 kilotons necessitates the use of either U-235 alone or a high proportion of this material in the fissile core. The figures are taken from De Volpi, op. cit., p. 85 and pp. 208–9.
9. For an extended discussion of this activity see Chapter 6, pp. 112–13 below.
10. Jackson, op. cit., p. 18.
11. For a discussion of the consequences of this realisation see Sir R. Powell, 'The evolution of British defence policy, 1954–1959', in F. E. C. Gregory, M. Imber and J. Simpson (eds), *Perspectives upon British Defence Policy, 1945–70* (Adult Education Department, University of Southampton, 1978) pp. 40–2.
12. For a discussion on the justification for attributing this date to the decision see ref. 42 below.
13. R. A. Devine, *Blowing in the Wind* (Oxford University Press, 1978) pp. 3–35 and 58–74.
14. Ibid., p. 21, pp. 58–9 and 124–5.
15. For a concise discussion on the links between this policy and 'Atoms for Peace' see *The Prohibition of the Production of Fissionable Material for Weapon Purposes* (Committee on Disarmament (CD)/90, 17 April 1980) pp. 2–3.
16. Gowing, *Independence and Deterrence*, vol. 1, pp. 424–36 summarises the background to this reorganisation and Cherwell's role in it.
17. Cmd 8986.
18. For a brief discussion of the Waverley Report and its effects see R. Williams, *The Nuclear Power Decisions* (Croom Helm, 1980) pp. 21–5.
19. This judgement is confirmed by statements in Pierre, op. cit., p. 143 that in 1958 'American officials were ... amazed to learn the full extent of Britain's knowledge and expertise', and by Rosencrance, op. cit., p. 252, that 'American scientists were apparently amazed at British progress in weapon designs and later made use of certain British concepts.'
20. See *Minutes of Thirty-seventh Meeting of the General Advisory Committee to the US Atomic Energy Commission* (Washington, 4, 5 and 6 November,

1953) p. 9 (partially declassified December 1979). This states that the contemporary system to obtain and analyse data on all foreign explosions was not 'geared to detection in the Southern Hemisphere; and it would probably miss for example, a Russian shot on a whaler in the South Seas'. In a letter attached to the minute dated 30 December, from Dr Bethe to Strauss, chairman of the AEC, a proposal was made (p. 2) to ask the UK to pass on their deductions from analysis of US test debris while the US would do the same for the UK. This suggests that some analysis of the UK programme had taken place, but the detection system was not optimised to obtain detailed information on these tests.

21. Menaul, op. cit., p. 62.
22. Ibid., pp. 63–7.
23. Ibid., p. 76.
24. Ibid., pp. 67–8.
25. This episode involved a most bizarre interaction between politics, nature and advanced technology. Christmas Island was first 'discovered' by Captain Cook in 1777, but no attempt was made to impose a British administration on the island until it was annexed in 1888. In the early part of the nineteenth century the area was visited by American whaling ships, and by the 1850s the commercial exploitation of guano (bird-droppings) as fertiliser had started on a number of Pacific Islands. In addition an Englishman had landed on Fanning Island, one of the northern Line Islands, and started a coconut plantation. In 1856 American commercial interests obtained government protection for their guano operations through the passage of the Guano Act by Congress. This Act empowered the President to claim jurisdiction over any unoccupied island which no other state had laid claim to, for the purpose of allowing guano to be removed from it. S. F. Beamis in his authoritative *A Diplomatic History of the United States*, first published in 1936, 4th ed (Henry Holt & Co., New York, 1955) claimed that Christmas Island was one of about 80 guano islands occupied by the United States under the powers contained in this Act (p. 402: footnote 1). However, it appears that little guano actually existed on Christmas Island, and after 1865 what was there was exploited by the Anglo-Australian Guano Company. In addition, British-owned and run coconut plantations had been established and operated both there and on Fanning and Washington Islands after the annexation in 1888.

The Guano Act resulted in a major diplomatic incident between Britain and the United States in 1937 when Britain attempted to incorporate the Phoenix Islands to the west of the Line group into its colony of the Gilbert and Ellis Islands. The United States claimed the provisions of the Guano Act gave them sovereignty over the group, and the US Navy was instructed to occupy Canton and Enderbury Islands. The dispute was resolved in 1939 by the declaration of a joint condominium over them. In 1941, the United States was allowed to build an air base on Christmas Island, but it remained under British administration. To prevent a repetition of the 1937 episode, it was necessary to undertake research to establish whether Beamis's claim was correct. As it appeared no American had actually dug for guano on the island, it was then accepted that the British claim to sovereignty was uncontested. See also A. Coates, *Western*

Pacific Islands (HMSO, 1970) p. 48 and W. D. Morell, *Britain and the Pacific Islands* (Oxford University Press, 1960) p. 264.

26. Menaul, op. cit., pp. 69–70, 80–7.
27. Gowing, *Independence and Deterrence*, vol. 1, pp. 372–92.
28. Ibid., pp. 400–1.
29. Ibid., pp. 364–5.
30. Ibid., pp. 382 and 386.
31. Ibid., p. 386.
32. For an overview of the build-up of the force see Appendix 4. The target figure for the number of Blue Danube and Red Beard bombs available for immediate RAF use appears to have been 140. This would be consistent with a total inventory of about 200 weapons, given the need for maintenance and inspection on a regular basis. D. Campbell, 'Digging up the past', *New Statesman*, 8 May 1981, states that until 1965 these bombs were stored at two sites, Faldingworth near Lincoln and Barnham in Norfolk. Each site held 70 bombs, with provision for the fissile cores to be stored separately from the non-nuclear components.
33. UKAEA Historian's office, AERE Harwell, *The Development of Atomic Energy: Chronology of Events, 1939–1978*, p. 15.
34. The nuclear efficiency of the Calder Hall type of reactor proved to be greater than calculated, as they operated at a power rating of 200 Mw (th) when optimised for military plutonium production, rather than the design rating of 150 Mw (th). Assuming a production rate of 0.8 grams of plutonium per 1000 megawatt days, and the reactors running for 314 days per year, this meant each was capable of producing about 50 kilograms of military plutonium per year, rather than the 40 kilograms originally calculated. Eight reactors plus the two Windscale plants would thus have given a annual output of about 460 kilograms, rather than the 380 kilograms initially believed possible. For a discussion of the basis for these estimates see Appendix 4a.
35. The basis for this figure is 6 kilograms of plutonium per warhead.
36. UKAEA, *Sixth Annual Report* (1959–60) p. 8, para. 53 and R. F. Pocock, *Nuclear Power* (Unwin, 1977) pp. 122–3.
37. UKAEA, *Fourth Annual Report* (1957–8) p. 8, paras 60–2.
38. D. Campbell, 'The wings of the green parrot', *New Statesman*, 17 April 1981, p. 10. 'Green parrot' was not the code name for a nuclear bomb: the weapon he refers to was Red Beard.
39. I base this figure on the following assumptions:
    (i) Each Calder Hall type reactor was, in 1955, assumed to be rated at 150 Mw(th) and capable of producing 40 kg of plutonium a year, and the Windscale ones had a combined output of 55 kg.
    (ii) The output from the Capenhurst plant was intended to be increased by an arbitrary 50 per cent over the original target figure of 300 kg per year.
    (iii) Each bomb used 6 kg of plutonium or 15 kg of uranium 235 or a mixture of both in these proportions. On this basis, some 375 kg of plutonium and 450 kg of enriched uranium would be available for bomb manufacture, giving a theoretical maximum capability of producing 92 bombs of this type per year.

40. Powell, op. cit., pp. 40–2.
41. *Statement on Defence*, Cmd 9391 (1955) p. 3.
42. Considerable differences of opinion exist in public sources over the date for the start of the British thermonuclear weapon programme. Anthony Eden in *Full Circle* (Cassell, 1965) p. 368 gives 1952 as the date of the decision, as does N. Moss, *Men who Play God* (Gollancz, 1968) p. 135. R. N. Rosencrance, op. cit., p. 165 also names 1952 but quotes a 'highly placed observer' as saying that 'in our work after 1952, we followed several ideas that turned out to be quite wrong. It was not until 1954 that we were well on our way to the H-bomb.' However, Macmillan, in a speech to the House of Commons on 1 April 1957, indicated clearly that the decision had been discussed by the Cabinet in (late?) 1954. *HC Debs 568* Col 44, 1 April 1957. The discrepancy seems to result both from working back from the assumption that the 1957 tests were of weapons, rather than experimental devices; from the limited amount of theoretical work that was done between 1952 and 1954, the preliminary discussions that occurred on possible alternative ways of obtaining a thermonuclear explosion and from the experimental work to produce more efficient atomic physics packages which was a necessary precondition for the construction of a thermonuclear device. However, it was not until the 1955 *political* announcement that resources were mobilised fully to support this line of development.
43. Gowing, *Independence and Deterrence*, vol. 1, pp. 443–5.
44. Ibid., pp. 437–9.
45. Ibid., p. 438.
46. Ibid., p. 439.
47. Pringle and Spigelman, op. cit., p. 516, footnote 253.
48. For yields see Carter and Moghissi, op. cit., p. 70. For an indication of the weapon effects element in the tests see *International Defence Review*, vol. 12, no. 7 (July 1979) 1107–10 and Menaul, op. cit., pp. 76–8.
49. Menaul, ibid., Jackson, op. cit., p. 24 and Brookes. op. cit., p. 74.
50. Carter and Moghissi, op. cit., p. 70.
51. Considerable controversy surrounds the exact rate of progress made by both the US and the USSR thermonuclear programmes. Neither state had a weaponised H-bomb by 1954, though the US Castle tests during March–May 1954 were of devices 'readily adaptable for delivery by aircraft' (York, op. cit., p. 85). The exact nature of the USSR Joe 4 test in August 1953 also remains in some dispute mainly because it only yielded 170–400 kilotons. This raises the possibility that it was not a full H-bomb design, but either a 'boosted' bomb or a possible third type in which fusion reactions were used to increase the fission yield. See York, op. cit., pp. 89–93 and I. Bellany, 'The origins of the Soviet hydrogen bomb: the York hypothesis', *RUSI Journal*, vol. 122, no. 1 (March 1977) 57. The basic data for the table is taken from ibid., pp. 60–1, 68 and 70.
52. It is unclear how far the United Kingdom had advanced by 1957 towards the type of fusion primary device employing a hollow sphere of Pu-239 within a slightly larger one of U-235, described in Morland, op. cit. To have designed and constructed a test device using a segmented and hollow spherical core rather than two solid hemispheres would imply that Alder-

maston had access to very advanced computational facilities. There is also no positive evidence that tritium boosting or U-235 were used in the primary, and it is possible that early devices used triggers constructed from solid hemispheres of plutonium.

53. R. W. Clark, *The Greatest Power on Earth* (Sidgwick & Jackson, 1980) pp. 293–4.

54. There were two official reports on this accident, Cmnd 302 and Cmnd 471 (HMSO, 1958). See also Pocock, op. cit., p. 30 and pp. 61–73.

55. UKAEA, *Second Annual Report* (1955–6) p. 8, para. 34 and *Fourth Annual Report* (1957–8) p. 10, para. 66.

56. Menaul, op. cit., pp. 78–80 and 83–6 and Jackson, op. cit., pp. 29–33. Jackson states that the yield of the first device was approximately one megaton, and that 'codenames for British thermonuclear devices were subsequently applied to the warheads rather than to the complete weapons' (p. 33).

57. For a description of the Castle series see York, op. cit., pp. 85–6.

58. Pincher, op. cit., p. 178 and Brookes, op. cit. (caption to picture of Grapple explosion).

59. See H. Macmillan, *Riding the Storm* (Macmillan, 1971) p. 564 and *Minutes of Thirty-seventh Meeting of the General Advisory Committee to the Atomic Energy Commission*, pp. 14–15. Although the substance of these latter documents remains classified it seems clear that there were two Soviet explosions in 1953 in addition to those listed in public sources, Joe 6 and 7. They were small-yield tests at altitude, and their precise aim baffled the committee, although there was an assumption that they were for anti-aircraft purposes.

60. Jonathan Alford, the Deputy Director of the IISS made reference to this yield figure in a review of Menaul's book in *SURVIVAL* (July/August 1981) p. 188. He indicated that all three tests in the 1958 series were of this magnitude, and also provided the figures for the personnel involved.

61. Macmillan, *Riding the Storm*, p. 459.

62. Ibid., p. 561.

63. For a detailed account of the evolution of these negotiations see US Dept of State, *Geneva Conference on the Discontinuance of Nuclear Weapon Tests* (Department of State Publication 7258, Disarmament Series 4) released October 1961, pp. 1–20.

64. Blue Steel was an air-launched, rocket-propelled stand-off bomb, designed for carriage by the V bombers. Work had started on the weapon in 1954, and a development contract had been let to Avro's in 1956. By late 1958, trials had begun with full-size test vehicles. Jackson, op. cit., pp. 90–3 and Brookes, op. cit., pp. 124–8.

65. Devine, op. cit., p. 153.

66. Macmillan, *Riding the Storm*, op. cit., pp. 306–7.

67. CD/90, op. cit., p. 6.

68. Devine, op. cit., p. 6.

69. CD/86, *Report on a Comprehensive Nuclear Test Ban* (24 March 1980) pp. 9–12.

70. Dates taken from *Operation of Nuclear Power Stations, 1979* (Office for Official Publications of the European Communities, Luxembourg, 1980) pp. 60–1.

71. Williams, op. cit., p. 41 and *A Programme of Nuclear Power*, Cmd 9389 (HMSO, 1955).
72. *HC Debs 590* Cols 228/9-Written Answers 1.8.58.
73. *Economist*, 21 June 58, p. 1107.
74. This figure is obtained by the methods described in Appendix 4. It is confirmed by a statement by Dr Walter Marshall, then the Deputy Chairman of the UKAEA, in 'Nuclear power and the proliferation issue', *Atom*, vol. 258 (April 1978) 79 that 'roughly speaking each 1000 Mw of thermal nuclear reactor produces 250 kilograms of plutonium each and every year of operation'. If this statement assumes that the reactor is worked for 365 days, a more normal 80 per cent operating schedule would produce roughly 200 kilograms. The three stations mentioned by Maudling appear to have been Hinkley Point, Dungeness and Sizewell.
75. Assuming 6 kilograms of plutonium per warhead. On this basis, the scheme offered Britain a potential to produce up to 300 weapons per year using plutonium alone.
76. Pocock, op. cit., p. 125.
77. By 1951, the United States had an inventory of 400 bombs–supra p. 60. The exaggerated public perceptions of the size of the British stockpile are well illustrated by an article written by the *Manchester Guardian*'s scientific correspondent in 1956 when he stated that Britain had 'at least a thousand' atomic bombs. A. J. R. Groom, *British Thinking about Nuclear Weapons* (Frances Pinter, 1974) p. 131.

6 The Making of an Atomic Alliance

1. Gowing, *Independence and Deterrence*, op. cit., vol. 1, pp. 406–7.
2. Pincher, op. cit., p. 148.
3. For a full account of the controversy surrounding the Dixon–Yates contract see A. Wildavsky, *Dixon–Yates: A Study in Power Politics* (Yale University Press, 1962).
4. The motives and context for this speech are discussed in Pringle and Spigelman, op. cit., pp. 121–4.
5. Pierre, op. cit., p. 138 and Green and Rosenthal, op. cit., p. 124.
6. 526 *HC Debs* Col 56, 5 April 1954.
7. Green and Rosenthal, op. cit., pp. 125–6.
8. Ibid., pp. 156–67.
9. *US Code Congressional and Administrative News*, vol. 1, 83rd Congress, 1954, Public Law 703, Section 3e and 144b.
10. Ibid., Section 123b and 123c.
11. Pierre, op. cit., p. 129.
12. *Agreement . . . for Cooperation on the Civil Uses of Atomic Energy*, Treaty Series no. 55 (1955) Cmd 9560 (HMSO, 1955).
13. Ibid., Article IC (ii) and Article IB.
14. Ibid., Article IC (i).
15. Ibid., Article II D2 (b) and Article IIIA.

16. Ibid., Article IA.
17. *Agreement ... for Cooperation regarding Atomic Information for Mutual Defence Purposes*, Treaty Series no. 52 (1955) Cmd 9555 (HMSO, 1955).
18. Ibid., Article II.
19. H. Macmillan, *Tides of Fortune* (Macmillan, 1969) p. 566, notes that in November 1954 'no arrangements had yet been made to specify which enemy targets, especially those most important to the United Kingdom, would be dealt with immediately by American bombers'.
20. Hearing before the Sub-committee on Agreements for Cooperation, Joint Committee on Atomic Energy, *Amending the Atomic Energy Act of 1954 – Exchange of Military Information and Material with Allies,* 85th Congress, 2nd Session (1958), p. 378 – statement by Senator Clinton Anderson. Anderson stated the date was June/July 1954, but the context of his remarks suggests that he actually meant 1955.
21. Ibid.
22. Ibid.
23. This dispute arose out of the confused nature of the legislative process which produced the 1954 Act. Section 144b started by stating that information could be passed to allies for planning and training purposes, but then limited this to those exchanges which 'in the joint judgement of the Commission and the Department of Defense ... will not reveal important information concerning the design or fabrication of the nuclear components of an atomic weapon'. The AEC argued that this latter section had to be interpreted in the light of a previous clause which prevented transfer of all 'Restricted data relating ... to external characteristics ... including size, weight, shape, yields and effects'. This disagreement effectively negated most of the provisions of the US–UK bilateral agreement for cooperation, but also affected the continental air defence agreement with Canada. It was later claimed that 'certain areas of cooperation with Canada, as well as with other nations, became rather difficult and impossible ... We found that in connection with safety devices, the training of personnel in the actual handling of weapons, that this made their adequate training and operational readiness for the utilisation of these weapons very difficult and essentially impossible.' Hearings before the Subcommittee on Agreements for Cooperation, Joint Committee on Atomic Energy, *Exchange of Military Information and Materials with the United Kingdom, France, Canada, The Netherlands, Turkey, Greece and the Federal Republic of Germany,* 86th Congress, 1st Session (1959) p. 14. Statement by General Loper, Chairman, Military Liaison Committee, AEC.
24. *Amending the Atomic Energy Act of 1954,* p. 97. Statement by Hon. D. A. Quarles, Deputy Secretary of Defense.
25. Executive Order 10841 – *Executive Order Concerning International Cooperation,* 30.9.1959, and ibid., p. 175. Answer by Mr Strauss, chairman of the AEC to questions by Senator Pastore, chairman of JCAE Subcommittee.
26. The history of the development of submarine reactors in the United States, the role of Admiral Rickover and his relationships with the USN, the AEC and the JCAE is examined in detail in R. G. Hewlett and F.

Duncan, *Nuclear Navy, 1946–1962* (University of Chicago Press, 1974) pp. 153–224.

27. *Amending the Atomic Energy Act of 1954*, p. 576.
28. Cmd 9560, op. cit., Article IC(iii).
29. *Amending the Atomic Energy Act of 1954*, pp. 576–7.
30. Ibid.
31. Vice-Admiral Ian McGeoch, 'The British Polaris project', in Gregory, Imber and Simpson, op.cit., p. 123.
32. N. Polmar, *Atomic Submarines* (Van Nostrand, 1963) p. 60, states that in 1953 there existed an unofficial division of labour between the USN and the RN with the former concentrating its submarine development work upon nuclear power and the latter upon hydrogen-peroxide propulsion in order to eliminate costly duplication of effort. The implication was that the results of each programme would be freely available to the other partner.
33. *Amending the Atomic Energy Act of 1954*, pp. 576–7.
34. This point was emphasised by Admiral Rickover in testimony before the JCAE in 1958, when he stated 'we have not gotten anything' from the British on submarine reactors, ibid., p. 165.
35. The origins of this link were that in 1952 Rickover's team and Westinghouse were engaged in designing a large pressurised water reactor for use in aircraft carriers. It was also viewed by a coalition of political forces as a means of developing nuclear power as a government enterprise in contrast to the incoming Republican administration's policy of leaving this task to private industry. In early 1953 the carrier reactor was deleted from the defence programme, thus terminating the AEC's only experimental power reactor. The JCAE and the AEC then became engaged in complex political manoeuvres to have funding for a power reactor, based on the carrier design, included in the 1954 AEC Budget, despite opposition from the Executive. In parallel there was a conflict within the Commission over whether the new reactor should compete with Calder Hall and be a rapidly built adaptation of the original design, with Rickover's navy team managing its construction or should be produced by a more leisurely process intended to lead to a reactor with superior economics. The first approach was adopted in June 1953, and the United States thus became committed to the development of light water civil power reactors, initially under the management of the USN. Hewlett and Duncan, *Nuclear Navy*, pp. 225–34.
36. Ibid., p. 362.
37. Green and Rosenthal, op. cit., p. 16.
38. The Shippingport reactor went critical on 2 December 1957, and was operating at full power by the end of the year. It was essentially a technology demonstration project, though only in the nature of its fuel charge, consisting of a mixture of weapon-grade and natural uranium, did it differ radically from later designs. By contrast the first Calder Hall reactor, of equivalent capacity to Shippingport, had started generating electricity in August 1956. Hewlett and Duncan, *Nuclear Navy*, pp. 225–34.
39. Green and Rosenthal, op. cit., pp. 262–5.

40. *Amendment to Agreement ... for Cooperation on the Civil Uses of Atomic Energy of June 15, 1955*, Treaty Series no. 35 (1956) Cmd 9847 (HMSO, 1956).
41. *Amending the Atomic Energy Act of 1954*, p. 456.
42. Ibid., pp. 518–19.
43. Green and Rosenthal, op. cit., pp. 92–3 and 95–6.
44. The strength of feeling among JCAE members on the subject of Executive 'trickery' can be gauged by their prolonged exchanges with the Secretary of State, Mr Dulles, on the subject in public hearings in May 1958. *Amending the Atomic Energy Act of 1954*, pp. 458–61.
45. B. Goldschmidt, *Les Rivalités atomiques, 1939–1966* (Fayard, Paris, 1967) pp. 225–7.
46. *Amending the Atomic Energy Act of 1954*, p. 171.
47. Ibid., p. 162.
48. 'The British Polaris project' in Gregory, Imber and Simpson, op cit., p. 129.
49. *Amending the Atomic Energy Act of 1954*, p. 171.
50. Ibid.
51. Ibid., p. 164.
52. *Exchange of Military Information and Materials with the United Kingdom, France, etc.*, p. 54.
53. *Amending the Atomic Energy Act of 1954*, p. 166.
54. 'The British Polaris project' in Gregory, Imber and Simpson, op. cit., p. 131.
55. The decision to use an American reactor in *Dreadnought*, the first British nuclear submarine, resulted in it going to sea at least three years before a comparable boat with a British designed and built reactor could have been commissioned. It also enabled the first of the *Valiant* class of fleet submarines to be ordered in August 1960, using the American reactor design built under licence in Britain. This in turn made it possible by December 1962 to regard building Polaris missile submarines as an activity in which most of the development risks were known and understood. Ibid., pp. 131–2. Rickover himself estimated the time saving as a minimum of three years and the cost saving as $50–75 million. *Amending the Atomic Energy Act of 1954*, p. 499.
56. Ibid., p. 169.
57. Rolls-Royce had developed the motors through a technical assistance agreement with Rocketdyne, and the missile used a Sperry inertial guidance system developed in the United States. Janes, *All the World's Aircraft, 1959–60* (Sampson, Low, Marston, London, 1959) p. 408.
58. M. H. Armacost, *The Politics of Weapons Innovation: The Thor–Jupiter Controversy* (Columbia University Press, 1969) pp. 54–179 gives a full account of this competitive development exercise and the factors behind it.
59. Ibid., p. 191.
60. The formal agreement was not signed until February 1958. *Exchange of Notes ... Concerning the Supply to the United Kingdom of Intermediate Range Ballistic Missiles*, Treaty Series no. 14, Cmnd 406 (HMSO, 1958).
61. Armacost, op. cit., pp. 196–7.

62. H. Macmillan, *Riding the Storm*, p. 261.
63. Ibid., p. 566.
64. Armacost, op. cit., p. 194, footnote 35.
65. *Amending the Atomic Energy Act of 1954*, pp. 175 and 189.
66. J. Baylis, 'The Anglo-American relationship in defence' in J. Baylis (ed.), *British Defence Policy in a Changing World* (Croom Helm, 1977) p. 78, but more especially, Menaul, op. cit., p. 91.
67. *Amending the Atomic Energy Act of 1954*, p. 181.
68. Ibid., p. 520.
69. *Nuclear Engineering*, vol. 1, no. 2 (May 1956) p. 86 and vol. 1, no. 3 (June 1956) p. 128.
70. Ibid., vol. 3, no. 24 (March 1958) pp. 127–8.
71. Ibid., vol. 2, no. 16 (July 1957) p. 296.
72. Ibid., vol. 2, no. 13 (April 1957) p. 133.
73. Ibid., vol. 3, no. 28 (July 1958) p. 75. The desire of the JCAE to ensure that detailed information on Calder Hall and other British gas-cooled reactor technology had been obtained in return for the submarine reactor is reflected in insistent questioning on whether information on this topic had been obtained from Britain. *Amending the Atomic Energy Act of 1954*, pp. 172 and 173. The JCAE held Executive Session hearings on foreign reactor programmes, especially the British one, in May 1956: ibid., p. 517. Admiral Rickover was also questioned on this topic in public hearings on the amendment proposals on 28 May 1958, and stated that some information had been given to the AEC on Calder Hall but that a formal proposal to exchange American information on submarine reactors for British data on gas-cooled ones had been rejected by Britain. Ibid., pp. 501–3.
74. Devine, op. cit., p. 60.
75. Macmillan, *Riding the Storm*, p. 301.
76. Ibid., p. 306.
77. Ibid., p. 315.
78. Ibid., p. 323 and *The Times*, 26 October 1957.
79. Macmillan, Ibid., p. 327 and Carter and Moghissi, op. cit., p. 70.
80. *Amending the Atomic Energy Act of 1954*, p. 448.
81. *US Code Congressional and Administrative News*, 85th Congress, 2nd Session (1958) vol. 11, Atomic Energy act of 1954 – Amendment, House Report, p. 2818.
82. Ibid., Appendix A, p. 2837.
83. 'Special nuclear material' was defined in the 1954 Act (Section 20E) as 'plutonium, uranium enriched in the isotope 233 or the isotope 235 and any other material that the Commission pursuant to the provisions of Section 51, determines to be special nuclear material'.
84. *Exchange of Military Information and Material with the United Kingdom*, p. 59. Letter to Dr F. Libby, acting chairman, USAEC from Senator Anderson, chairman JCAE, 13 March 1959.
85. Supra, Chapter 5, pp. 109–10. Military-grade plutonium, containing very high percentages of Pu-239, is obtained by irradiating fuel in a reactor for a relatively limited period of time (typically some four to six months), and then reprocessing it to separate out the plutonium. Calder Hall type

reactors had to be shut down to discharge this fuel, but the civil magnox reactors were designed to be fuelled and defuelled while still operating, in order to produce electricity for extended periods of time in their role as base-load stations for the British electricity grid. Thus whether the intention was to operate these stations in a similar manner to the Calder Hall ones, discharging a full fuel load every four to six months, or merely to make much more frequent 'on-load' fuel changes than normal, remains unclear. This ability to remove fuel from the reactor while it was still operating meant that quantities of military-grade plutonium could also be produced in part of the reactor while it was being operated in a near optimal manner for electricity production. Such reactors thus blurred the boundaries between civil and military fuel cycles by being able to operate on both types simultaneously. However, there is no hard evidence to suggest that they were ever used in either of these specifically military ways. Plutonium with high percentages of Pu-239 was a natural product of these civil reactors, even when they were operated in a manner which optimised their electricity production. Fuel ideally remained in them for about four years, but to maintain economical power output it was necessary to manage the fuel inventory in a manner which allowed batches of fuel to become exhausted and be replaced in rotation. Until this continuous cycle had been established, a process which took about three to four years, some fuel would be withdrawn after only limited levels of irradiation, and the plutonium in it would undoubtedly be of weapon grade. See letters to the editor, *Guardian*, 19 August 1982, p. 12.

86. Figures calculated from Pocock, op. cit., p. 156.

87. Additional drawbacks to the American non-military fuel as a source of plutonium were that it was more difficult to reprocess than magnox fuel, and uneconomic given the relatively small quantities available. In addition, it usually contained much lower percentages of Pu-239 than magnox fuel, due to its higher level of burn-up and irradiation.

88. *Amending the Atomic Energy Act of 1954*, p. 5. Letter from Mr Strauss to the chairman of the subcommittee on agreements for Cooperation.

89. The scheme in its initial form involved the United States acquiring a maximum of 6667 kilograms of plutonium from Britain at $30 gram, and selling tritium and U-235 to her, the latter at a price of $16 gram. This would have provided sufficient revenue to purchase up to 12 500 kilograms of U-235. Ibid., pp. 59–60, 74, 112, 205 and 242.

90. Ibid., p. 219. *Exchange of Military Information and Material with the United Kingdom*, p. 58 and M. F. Imber, 'Mitrany's functionalism, the International Atomic Energy Agency and the development of safeguards against the proliferation of nuclear weapons' (unpublished PhD thesis, University of Southampton, 1981) pp. 124–6.

91. *Amending the Atomic Energy Act of 1954*. Evidence by Mr Dulles, Secretary of State, pp. 452–3 and 462; statement of US proposals to UN Disarmament Subcommittee, 29 August 1957, p. 407, and statement on need for UK rapidly to attain stockpile, p. 282. The amounts of U-235 the United States and the USSR were prepared to contribute to the 'Atoms for Peace' programme reinforces this point. The initial US offer was for 5000 kg of U-235, with 50 kg being offered by the USSR and

20 kg by the UK. US House of Representatives, *Science, Technology and American Diplomacy*, vol. 1. p. 185.

92. *Amending the Atomic Energy Act of 1954*, pp. 110, 223–7 and 239–40.
93. Ibid., pp. 103 and 140.
94. *Exchange of Military Information and Material with the United Kingdom*, pp. 63 and 64.
95. Ibid., p. 61.
96. *Atomic Energy Act of 1954 – Amendment*, p. 2826 and *Amending the Atomic Energy Act of 1954*, pp. 102–3.
97. *Agreement ... for Cooperation on the Uses of Atomic Energy for Mutual Defence Purposes*, Treaty Series no. 41 (1958) Cmnd 537 (HMSO, 1958). Article II A4 and *Amending the Atomic Energy Act of 1954*, p. 189.
98. *Amending the Atomic Energy Act of 1954*, p. 243.
99. Ibid., pp. 229–30.
100. Ibid., pp. 202–4.
101. Ibid., p. 235.
102. Ibid., p. 141.
103. Ibid., pp. 217–18.
104. The saga of the conflict between the AEC and the JCAE over the revolving fund had started in early 1957, when the AEC discussed with the JCAE methods of assisting overseas sales of reactors and fuel. At that time the fund was seen as being applicable to civil sales only. When the question of purchases for military purposes arose in late October, the AEC's principal justification was that the Department of Defense was refusing to forecast its requirements more than three years ahead, and it was therefore prudent to buy all the militarily useful plutonium that was available. Several JCAE members had been advocating following the British lead and building plutonium/power reactors at Hanford as part of a civil reactor development programme, and purchases from Britain undermined this argument. The AEC tried to compromise with its opponents by reducing the term for contracts from 15 to 7 years and the initial funding from $200 million to $50 million, but the JCAE remained implacably opposed to the idea of the AEC acquiring an independent source of funds, and thus reducing its sensitivity to congressional pressures. Eventually the proposal was withdrawn by the AEC on 7 March. Ibid., pp. 42–3, 54, 74–6, 202–3, 207, 218, 229–30 and 233. See also Green and Rosenthal, op. cit., pp. 138–40.
105. Green and Rosenthal, ibid., pp. 262–5.
106. *Amending the Atomic Energy Act of 1954*, pp. 104, 196 and 298.
107. *Atomic Energy Act of 1954–Amendment*, p. 2835.
108. *Amending the Atomic Energy Act of 1954*, p. 187.
109. Ibid., pp. 166–7.
110. Ibid., pp. 501–2.
111. Ibid., pp. 146, 170, 178 and 183. Canada was also to be treated differently from the other allies as the United States wished to transfer package power reactors to power early warning radar sites in the joint continental defence system, ibid., p. 97.
112. Ibid., p. 105.

113. *Atomic Energy Act of 1954–Amendment*, p. 2825.
114. Devine, op. cit., p. 210.
115. Macmillan, *Riding the storm*, p. 474.
116. Macmillan's exact comment was that 'with American working arrangements made, our autumn tests are not a "must". Without these, they are vital to the safety and strength of Britain and we must go on.' Ibid., p. 491.
117. Ibid., p. 492.
118. Ibid., p. 294.
119. *Atomic Energy Act of 1954–Amendment*, p. 2827.
120. Ibid., p. 2826.
121. Cmnd 537, op. cit.
122. Macmillan, *Riding the Storm*, p. 496.

7 The Nuclear Alliance in Operation, 1959–63

1. For a discussion of the procedures for the exchanges and their nature see *Amending the Atomic Energy Act of 1954,* pp. 171 and 179, and *Exchanges of Military Information and Material with the United Kingdom,* pp. 63–4.
2. Macmillan, *Riding the Storm,* p. 560.
3. Ibid., pp. 561–2.
4. American weapon designers had been aware of this possibility since at least 1953, when the Russian nuclear tests Joe 5–7, which were not publicly recorded, revealed the probability that the USSR's chemical explosive technology for implosion devices was in advance of that used by the US. At the time Rabi, chairman of the General advisory Committee stated that 'the gains to be obtained from success in this direction are enormous both in the reduction in size of large fission weapons and even more importantly in the possibility of making smaller fission weapons of simple design and great economy of fissionable material. It is well known that both the Russians and the British are very expert in the field of chemical explosives. It is conceivable to us that they may have made significant advances in this field.' *Minutes of the Thirty-Seventh Meeting of the General Advisory Committee.* Letter to Strauss dated 7 November 1953.
5. Macmillan, *Riding the Storm*, p. 500. He also noted (p. 564) that 'in some respects we are as far, and even further, advanced in the art than our American friends ... They are keen that we should complete our series [of tests] especially the last megaton, the character of which is novel and of deep interest to them.'
6. *Exchanges of Military Information and Material with the United Kingdom,* pp. 49–51. The UK agreement was stated to be the model for the one with France which is discussed in detail. Each submarine core contained 40 kilograms of U-235, and 300 kilograms allowed for seven years of full power operation (i.e. for 14 cores), with a burn-up of 112 kilograms of

U-235, reprocessing losses on 6 cores of 18 kilograms and 4 cores in stock at the end of the 10-year period.

7. For details of the performance of this aircraft see Janes, *All the World's Aircraft, 1963–64* (Sampson, Low, Marston, London, 1964) pp. 119–20. It had a range without bomb-load and with maximum fuel of 3630 miles compared with the Valiant's operational range of 3430 miles if it carried a Blue Danube bomb over half this distance, and 4500 miles without this bomb-load.

8. For a description of this process see Campbell, 'Wings of the green parrot' op. cit., p. 12.

9. Between 80 and 100 Scimitars were built, and a limited number were adapted for the nuclear strike role with additional external fuel tanks and bomb-aiming equipment. Jane's, *All the World's Aircraft, 1963–64*, p. 156.

10. *Exchange of Military Information and Material with the United Kingdom*, p. 64.

11. Ibid.

12. Ibid., p. 66.

13. *Report of the Joint Committee on Atomic Energy*, 86th Congress, 2nd Session HR672 – *Proposed Amendments to the Agreement for Cooperation with the United Kingdom, and Proposed Agreements for Cooperation with the Republic of France, Canada and the Netherlands, the Federal Republic of Germany and Greece, on the Uses of Nuclear Energy for Mutual Defense Purposes*, 15 July 1959, p. 12.

14. In 1959, the AEC's posted price for plutonium from civil reactors for weapon use was $30 a gram and this formed the basis for the barter. *Exchange of Military Information and Material with the United Kingdom*, p. 58. It appears that this applied to material for a civil fuel cycle, as until July 1962 the AEC's schedule of prices was.

Percent of Pu-240	$ Price/gm
0	45.00
2	41.50
4	38.00
6	34.50
8	31.00
8.6 +	30.00

15. *HC Debs* 607 – Oral Answer 22.6.59 Col 849. This episode led to objections from Labour MPs over the moral and practical consequences of using these civil facilities for military purposes. In addition, there was considerable adverse comment in the technical press as it was believed to undermine the commercial prospects for magnox power stations by implying that they were only economically viable if the plutonium they produced was sold for military purposes. See, for example *Nuclear Engineering*, August 1958, p. 318 and September 1958, pp. 362 and 400.

16. *HC Debs* 630, 21 November 1960, Col 774–778. Debate on Electricity Amendment Bill. This bill amended section 2(7) of the 1957 Electricity Act.

17. Letter from chairman of JCAE to acting chairman of AEC, 13 March

1959. *Exchange of Military Information and Materials with the United Kingdom*, pp. 58–9. The contents of this letter are difficult to unscramble, but they suggest that negotiations had taken place in 1958 to allow the AEC both to purchase plutonium from British civil reactors for unrestricted use and to exchange 20 per cent enriched uranium for plutonium on a gram-for-gram basis. In the second part of the letter it is stated that the uranium was to be used 'in production reactors for reactor materials for military use'. This appears to be a garbled interpretation of a proposal that it would be fed into the Capenhurst enrichment plant to produce U-235 for use in submarine fuel and weapons.

18. This assessment is based on a table of separative work and input figures for various levels of U-235 enrichment contained in *Uranium Enrichment Services Criteria and Related Matters*, Hearings before the Joint Committee on Atomic Energy, 88th Congress, 2nd Session, August 1966 (USGPO, 1966) p. 352. The key figures are that 'to produce 1 kg of 20% enriched uranium from natural requires 41.35 Separative Work Units (SWUs), while to produce 1 kg of 90% from natural requires 206.992 SWUs'. Using slightly different figures (those found in V. V. Abagian and A. M. Fishman, 'Supplying enriched uranium', *Physics Today* (August 1973) p. 23), A. Wohlstetter *et al.*, op. cit., p. 39 estimate the output of the Capenhurst plant, using a natural uranium feed, as 1586 kilograms of highly enriched uranium per year. On this basis, 18 years of operations would have yielded 28 500 kilograms, but such an estimate may be discounted as Wohlstetter's figures appear to be based on data for the later civil plant.

19. For an explanation of the technical reasons for this see SIPRI – *Nuclear Energy and Nuclear Weapon Proliferation*, p. 400.

20. *Exchange of Military Information and Materials with the United Kingdom*, p. 145. Letter from AEC to President, 2 May 1959.

21. Ibid., pp. 60–1, and *Atomic Energy Act – Amendment*, p. 2826.

22. Ibid., p. 66.

23. *Amendment to the Agreement . . . for Cooperation on the Uses of Atomic Energy for Mutual Defence Purposes of July 3, 1958*, Treaty Series no. 72 (1959) Cmnd 859 (HMSO, 1959).

24. Pringle and Spigelman, op. cit., pp. 202–4 and 506–7.

25. Imber, op. cit., pp. 126–31.

26. COCOM, the Coordinating Committee for Export Controls to Communist Countries, included the NATO states and Japan, and harmonised the export restrictions of the Western allies towards the Communist Bloc. Pringle and Spigelman, op. cit., p. 507.

27. Ibid., p. 546.

28. Ibid., p. 526. This states that there was a meeting of the club in February 1963 in South Africa and another in February 1967 at the United States Embassy in London.

29. E.g. Campbell, 'Wings of the green parrot', p. 12.

30. For example the 1958 *Report on Defence*, Cmnd 363, stated that 'British megaton bombs are now in production and deliveries to the RAF have begun' (para. 6) but in the February 1959, *Progress on the Five Year Defence Plan*, Cmnd 662, it was merely reported that 'the production of

British megaton weapons is proceeding steadily' (para. 3).

31. G. Wilmer, 'TSR-2: Yesterday's answer to tomorrow's problem', *Air Enthusiast*, no. 14, 1981, pp. 24–6, states that the concept of carrying two Blue Water missiles, each with a 1000 lb (450 kg) one megaton warhead, on TSR-2 aircraft was studied in depth up to the missile's cancellation in August 1962.

32. These weapons were revealed publically in the 1963 *Statement on Defence*, Cmnd 1936, p. 67, para. 5, which recorded 'the further development of a tactical nuclear weapon which was intended in the first place for tactical operations by the Buccanneer and TSR-2 ... In addition, it has now been found that the weapon can be adapted speedily and cheaply to give a strategic nuclear punch. This weapon will make it possible to continue to operate the V bombers in a variety of ways, and can be used tactically as the complement to Blue Steel.'

33. Wilmer, op. cit., pp. 24 and 25, discusses nuclear bombing techniques in detail, and states that there was a development programme during the 1960s to meet the RAF requirement OR 1177 for a modification kit which would enable both the low- and high-yield nuclear weapons to be dropped at low level. Once this was completed, the V bombers and Canberras adopted low-level flight as the preferred method of penetrating hostile airspace.

34. H. Macmillan, *Pointing the Way* (Macmillan, 1972) pp. 251–5.

35. The precise nature of the link between the Skybolt purchase, the setting up of the US submarine base in Holy Loch, and the acquisition of Polaris at a later date has always been rather obscure. For a perceptive discussion of this linkage, see J. Baylis, *Anglo-American Defence Relations, 1939–1980* (Macmillan, 1981) pp. 67 and 68, also Brookes op. cit., p. 115. On the numbers of Skybolts see C. Gardener, *British Aircraft Corporation* (Bookclub Associates, 1981) p. 34. Skybolt was to be purchased instead of a developed version of the Blue Steel cruise missile, and was to be carried by about 50 Vulcan Mark II aircraft. This decision resulted in a reduction in the numbers of Mark II V bombers on order. Thus by the end of the decade it was envisaged that the dedicated strategic nuclear force would be reduced to less than 100 operational warheads.

36. On weights and dimensions see Campbell, 'Wings of the green parrot', p. 12. On the relationship between the two types of bomb see *Statement on Defence*, Cmnd 1936, p. 67, para. 5.

37. Pierre, op. cit., p. 156.

38. Jane's, *Weapon Systems, 1971–72* (Sampson, Low, Marston, London, 1971) p. 103, Brookes, op. cit., pp. 124–8, and Jackson, op. cit., pp. 90–4; both give succinct histories of the development of Blue Steel.

39. Cambell, 'Digging up the Nuclear past', states that Barnham, one of the two Blue Danube and Red Beard storage bases, was closed in 1965, but the other base, Faldingworth was extended 'in the 1960s' and an additional base was built at Machrihanish in South-west Scotland. Brookes, ibid., p. 107, states that Faldingworth continued to be the main storage base until the 'early seventies'.

40. *Statement on Defence*, Cmnd 1936, p. 67, para. 5, and Morland, op. cit., pp. 18–19.

41. Jackson, op. cit., p. 35.
42. Macmillan, *Tides of Fortune*, p. 576.
43. For a short official description of the contemporary British delivery systems which rely on US nuclear ordnance and those using British bombs, see 'Memorandum submitted by the Minister of Defence' in *The Future of the United Kingdom's Nuclear Weapons Policy*, Sixth Report from the Expenditure Committee Session 1978–79, HC Paper 348 (HMSO, 1979) p. 293.
44. The most frequently cited set of figures for the size of the United Kingdom stockpile are those given by Leonard Beaton in *Would Labour Give Up the Bomb?* published by the *Sunday Telegraph*, August 1964, pp. 12–14. In this, he speculated that Britain possessed 300 thermonuclear and 1200 atomic bombs. No account was taken of American weapons available to British forces in these figures. They appear to have been a gross overestimate, as simple arithmetic demonstrates that had they been correct, each bomb would on average have contained less than 2 kilograms of plutonium. However, what was correct was that by 1964, the British had a very substantial stockpile of weapons in comparison with the situation four years earlier.
45. One particularly Machiavellian acquaintance has suggested that had CND not arisen spontaneously the Ministry of Defence might well have been forced to create it in order to convince the Russian leadership that Britain possessed a large arsenal of nuclear weapons at a time when, in fact, there were very few in its stockpile.
46. *Strategic Nuclear Weapons Policy*, Fourth Report from the Defence Comittee, Sessions 1980/81, HC paper no. 36, 1981. Appendix to Minutes of Evidence, p. 179.
47. The announcement of the decision to terminate production at Capenhurst in 1963 led to a debate in the House of Commons during which some details were given of the Anglo-American arrangements. *HC Debs* 667, 1962–63, Cols 965–975, 19 November 1962. It is also referred to in the Report of the Select Committee on Science and Technology, 1966–7, *United Kingdom Reactor Programme*, HC 381, XVII (HMSO, 1967) pp. 264–5, para. 1270.
48. *Statement on Defence 1964*, Cmnd 2270 (HMSO, 1964) para. 28.
49. Glen T. Seaborg, *Kennedy, Khrushchev and the Test Ban* (University of California Press, 1981) p. 104.
50. H. Macmillan, *At the End of the Day*, 1961–1963 (Macmillan, 1973), p. 121.
51. Ibid., p. 476.
52. Ibid., pp. 123 and 334–5.
53. Ibid., p. 335.
54. Ibid., pp. 180–220.
55. H. Kissinger, *The White House Years* (Weidenfeld and Nicolson/Michael Joseph, 1979) p. 90.
56. Seaborg, op. cit., pp. 108–9.
57. Ibid., pp. 111–15.
58. Ibid., pp. 117–19.

59. Ibid., p. 127.
60. Macmillan, *At the End of the Day*, p. 146.
61. Seaborg, op. cit., p. 126.
62. Ibid., pp. 134–5, and Macmillan, *At the End of the Day*, p. 154.
63. Macmillan, ibid., p. 168.
64. Seaborg, op. cit., p. 192.
65. Carter and Moghissi, op. cit., pp. 63–4.
66. Seaborg, op. cit., p. 157.
67. Ibid., p. 223 and Macmillan, *At the End of the Day*, p. 173.
68. Macmillan, ibid., p. 341.
69. Seaborg, op. cit., p. 110.
70. Macmillan, *At the End of the Day*, p. 343.
71. Ibid., pp. 534–5.

8 The Mature Technology: from Polaris to Chevaline

1. *Further Documents Relating to the Conference of The Eighteen-Nation Committee on Disarmament*, Misc 20(1964) Cmnd 2486 (HMSO, 1964) Document No. 4 (ENDC/131); Document No. 5 (ENDC/132) and Document No. 6 (Statement by Sir Alec Douglas-Home to the House of Commons, 21 April 1964).
2. Ibid., Document No. 6 and *HC Debs* 693, Col 1098.
3. *Statement on Defence 1964*, Cmnd 2270 (HMSO, 1964) para. 26.
4. All Sellafield buildings have a number, hence B205.
5. UKAEA, *Tenth Annual Report*, 1963–4, p. 3, para. 16. The money does not appear to have been paid in equal instalments presumably because of the effect of a reducing interest component. In the 1969–70 UKAEA *Sixteenth Annual Report*, £23.35 million was reported to have been transferred and in the 1970–1 one £20.6 million. The most detailed account of the situation is contained in the 1969–70 Report which states (p. 109, paras 10–12): 'The plutonium production facilities at Windscale were provided initially for military purposes, but the plant was later expanded to provide capacity also for civil production. In particular, a new and expanded main chemical processing plant (known as the B205 plant) was completed in 1963–64 at a cost of some £16 m ... the capital costs incurred by the authority in providing facilities for the production of fissile materials for military purposes are being reimbursed by a series of eight annual payments (including interest on outstanding balances) from the Defence Budget, which started in 1964–65. The amount included in respect of the Windscale site covered virtually the whole of the B205 plant based on the proportion of its capacity assumed to have been provided to meet normal military requirements. The remaining capacity of the B205 plant was attributed to other continuing production for the Defence Department and to civil production. The share of the capital costs attributed to these continuing activities has been recovered through

depreciation charges over a six year period (although the Authority normally use a ten year period for the depreciation of chemical process plants). Thus by the end of 1969–70 the capital costs of the fixed assets at the Windscale site had been almost wholly written off in the Authorities books either in the amounts covered by the payments from the Defence Budget or through the depreciation charges included in the costs of the continuing production for the Defence Budget and others.' By March 1970 the plant was valued at £6.36 million , 40 per cent of its capital cost of £15.9 million. This whole situation was always rather artificial, given the Ministry of Defence's standard practice of paying for capital expenditure as it was incurred. Thus had the UKAEA never been created in 1954 and had military production remained the responsibility of the Ministry of Supply, the Ministry of Defence would have paid for the capital charges of these plants as they were incurred and written them off. The formation of the UKAEA meant that the charges became its responsibility, and also that the direct financial costs to the Ministry of Defence of the expanded production programme after 1955 were deferred for about three years. All the plants built in this period were eventually converted to civil use except the high separation plant at Capenhurst which was mothballed, and thus what appeared to be £300 million of wasted defence expenditure was utilised for civil purposes.

6. The plants involved were principally the Springfields fuel facilities and the Windscale separation plant. A further specialist military plant had also been constructed at Windscale to purify plutonium scrap from old weapons and manufacturing processes and remove any build-up of the element Americium from it. This is produced if spontaneous fissions cause PU-240 to gain a neutron.

7. H. Wilson, *The Labour Government, 1964–1970* (Weidenfeld and Nicholson/Michael Joseph, 1971) p. 54.

8. The tests occurred on 17 July 1964 and 10 September 1965. Mr Wilson's comments on them were that the 'test which took place last September . . . was a repeat of a test that failed a year earlier under the previous Government . . . [It] was a test for economy purposes which had failed a year earlier at great cost. We repeated it and succeeded with it . . . if it became necessary, for similar reasons, to have a further test we should have one, but we succeeded in that test, so it is not necessary to repeat it a second time.' *HC Debs 728*, Oral Answers, 12 May 1966, Cols 591–2. These comments imply that the two tests were not proof tests of the Polaris warheads, but were part of a broader-based research and development programme.

9. Black Knight was designed and produced as a cheap launcher to conduct tests on Blue Streak reentry vehicles at the least possible cost. A significant number of units were ordered but the testing programme was still in its early stages when Blue Streak was cancelled. It was then continued as a general Anglo-American/Australian research programme, with some 22 firings taking place through to November 1965. Jane's, *All the World's Aircraft*, 1967–8 (Sampson Low, Marston, London, 1967) p. 486.

10. *Ministry of Defence: Chevaline Improvement to the Polaris Missile System*, Ninth Report from the Committee of Public Accounts, Session 1981–82,

HC 269 (HMSO, 1982) pp. 9 and 10.

11. Carter and Moghissi, op. cit., p. 63.

12. Information on the maintenance needs of the Polaris warheads and British nuclear bombs is sparse and somewhat contradictory. It appears that half the warheads carried by a Polaris submarine are removed at the armament depot at Coulport after each patrol, but it has been stated that 'aside from replenishing essential components at particular times, which is fairly rare anyway measured in years ... we do not envisage regular returns to base for regular servicing'. However, 'nuclear weapons themselves have a finite weapon life. Initially, when weapons were first designed that was a relatively short period. With improvements in technology it is being extended, but it is still measured in 10, 20, 25 year periods and when weapons get to that sort of age they have to be replaced.' Oral evidence by Mr D. C. Fakley, Assistant Chief Scientific Adviser (Nuclear) Ministry of Defence reported in *Strategic Nuclear Weapons Policy*, p. 175 and p. 178. At the same hearing, Mr C. C. Fielding, the Director of Aldermaston, stated that they were 'required to take back inservice weapons for any kind of checking and refurbishment' (p. 170). Campbell, 'Wings of the green parrot', p. 11 and Pincher, op. cit., pp. 305–6, however, suggest that a regular movement of Polaris warheads occurs between Coulport and Aldermaston, while Campbell also states that the fully assembled thermonuclear bomb has an effective 'life' of only about 30 days. The implication appears to be that one of the major advances in nuclear weapons technology between the late 1950s and early 1960s was that techniques were developed which enabled fissile cores to remain in nuclear warheads for prolonged periods of time.

13. J. Simpson, 'The Polaris executive: a case study of a unified hierarchy', *Public Administration*, vol. 48 (Winter 1970) pp. 386 and 388.

14. This programme was 'to study phenomenon associated with the re-entry of bodies into the earth's atmosphere and some aspects of anti-missile defence'. T. B. Millar, *Australia's Defence* (Melbourne University Press, 1965) p. 135.

15. Carter and Moghissi, op. cit., pp. 64 and 69. In particular a 1.4 megaton device was exploded at 40 000 ft in July 1962, and four smaller devices at 100 000 ft in October of that year. In the same month there were three similar Soviet high-altitude explosions and in one of them missiles were believed to have been fired through the area of the explosion.

16. Campbell, 'Wings of the green parrot', p. 12.

17. *Strategic Nuclear Weapon Policy*, p. 178.

18. L. Freedman, *Britain and Nuclear Weapons* (Macmillan, 1980) p. 39.

19. UKAEA, *Eleventh Annual Report* (1964–5) p. 16.

20. *HC Debs* 747, Col 223–4, Written Answers, 7 June 1967.

21. *HC Debs* 748, Col 299, Oral Answers, 13 June 1967.

22. H. Wilson, op cit., p. 408.

23. Freedman, *Britain and Nuclear Weapons*, Appendix 3 provides a convenient table of these expenditures derived from Defence White Papers. It illustrates how expenditures on special nuclear materials drifted downwards from a peak of £55 million in 1966–7 to £20 million in 1971–2 while R & D on nuclear forces moved from £33 million in 1966–7 to £17

million in 1970–1. It is unclear whether the special nuclear material figures included the compensation payment to the UKAEA for the premature termination of programmes in 1964.

24. D. Fishlock, 'Britain's £2 billion new warhead', *Defense Week*, 7 April 1980, p. 12.
25. Carter and Moghissi, op. cit., p. 71. China exploded its first nuclear device on 16 October 1964 and its first device involving tritium on 9 May 1966.
26. *Ministry of Defence*, p. 12.
27. Freedman, *Britain and Nuclear Weapons*, p. 37.
28. F. Hussain, 'The future of arms control: Part IV: The impact of weapon test restrictions', *Adelphi Paper*, no. 165 (IISS, 1981) p. 14.
29. Freedman, *Britain and Nuclear Weapons*, pp. 47–8 and D. Fishlock, 'Revealed: Chevaline's £1 bn secrets', *Financial Times*, 14 July 1981, p. 17.
30. *Ministry of Defence*, p. 1.
31. D. Owen, *The Politics of Defence* (Jonathan Cape, 1972) p. 207.
32. Baylis, op. cit., pp. 107–9 notes that during this period observers in Washington detected a lack of interest by the Heath government in exploring further nuclear collaboration with the United States, perhaps for fear of disturbing the prospects of a smooth entry into the EEC by actions reminiscent of the Nassau episode in 1962–3.
33. *Ministry of Defence*, pp. vi and 1.
34. Freedman, *Britain and Nuclear Weapons*, p. 44.
35. Ibid.
36. See *Ministry of Defence*, pp. 9 and 11.
37. Ibid., p. 1.
38. This was the period of the 'three-day week', the miners' strike and the restrictions on oil supplies following the Middle East war. One indirect consequence of the latter was that Lord Carrington, the Defence Minister, was made Minister for Energy on 8 January, thus disrupting the normal flow of political decision-making in the Ministry of Defence.
39. *Ministry of Defence*, p. 20.
40. On this point and the question of who in the Labour Cabinet was fully informed about what was taking place, see especially Fishlock, 'Britain's $2 billion new warhead', p. 13.
41. *Ministry of Defence*, p. 24.
42. Ibid., p. 2.
43. Ibid., p. 13.
44. Ibid., p. 25.
45. Ibid., p. 20.
46. Ibid., p. 2.
47. Ibid., pp. 17 and 18.
48. Freedman, *Britain and Nuclear Weapons*, p. 48 suggests that the name was based on the mistaken belief that it meant a fleet-footed mountain goat. Although this story appears to have gained considerable credence in defence circles, the truth is rather more mundane: it just happened that this was the next on the list of code-names that were acceptable to the Ministry of Defence. It was realised rapidly that its meaning of a horse or pertaining to horses might have unfortunate connotations, but by then it

had already been used in US–UK correspondence.

49. *Ministry of Defence*, p. 2.

50. See Appendix 1 for full listing.

51. Freedman, *Britain and Nuclear Weapons*, p. 52 states that this test was part of the Chevaline programme and that it enabled Aldermaston to ascertain whether or not it was a feasible project. However, it normally takes at least a year to plan a test, suggesting that this one had been decided upon in early 1973 before the Chevaline development decision had been taken. In addition, if it was part of the Chevaline programme it would mean that no tritium ageing experiments were conducted on the early 1960s weapon designs when they reached the end of the shelf-life of their initial inventories of tritium. F. Hussain, *Adelphi Paper*, p. 14 states that the only way to evaluate the impact of this phenomenon upon individual weapon designs was to detonate them at the end of this planned shelf-life. Such a test could have been justified more easily than the Chevaline programme, as it was clearly necessary to ensure the continued technical credibility of British nuclear weapons. It would only have been unnecessary if American data on this phenomenon were directly applicable to the British weapon designs.

52. There still remains considerable uncertainty over the number of nuclear warheads in the Chevaline system. The consensus appears to be six of about 40 kilotons yield each (e.g. *International Defence Review*, vol. XIV, no. 1, 1981). However, Freedman, *Britain and Nuclear Weapons*, p. 49 notes that only three warheads plus dummies may be involved, and that the idea of six of 40 kilotons yield originated in a memorandum by the IISS to the Defence and External Affairs Subcommittee of the House of Commons Expenditure Committee in 1973 (*Nuclear Weapon Programme*, Twelfth Report, Session 1972–73 HC 399 (HMSO, 1973) p. 3). Although Mr Brezhnev also publically stated that six warheads are involved (interview with *Der Spiegel*, 2 November 1981 reprinted in *Survival*, vol. XXIV, no. 1 (Jan/Feb 1982) p. 34), my personal judgement is that three is the more likely number!

53. *Strategic Nuclear Weapons Policy*. Oral Evidence by Mr Fakley, pp. 172 and 4.

54. Wilson, op. cit., p. 55, stated that Britain 'would still be dependent after the completion of the Polaris programme in 1968, on the Americans for certain specialised materials essential to the maintenance of our missile force'. He then went on to quote from his House of Commons speech: 'The question is whether after 1968 we shall be in a position to supply all the fissile materials required to maintain the effectiveness of our warheads, having regard to the half-life of those materials and so on.' The significance of 1968 was that at the end of that year the US could have given notice of its unilateral intention to cease to supply Britain with tritium under the terms of the amended 1958 Military Agreement for Cooperation.

55. For a full discussion of the tritium ageing problem see Hussain, op. cit., pp. 13 and 14.

56. Ibid., p. 8 suggests that it is less than ten years.

57. Ibid., p. 14.

58. One of the more significant unilateral arms control acts of the Carter administration between 1977 and 1981 was to limit the output of military plutonium and tritium to that manufactured by three production reactors at Savannah River, operating at two-thirds capacity. This meant that they collectively produced about 3 kilograms of tritium and 1400 kilograms of weapon-grade plutonium per year. It has been estimated that constructing 1000 neutron weapons would double the amount of tritium in the United States weapon stockpile, and that producing this material would be the main technical constraint upon the deployment of the weapon. *No More Atoms for Peace*, pp. 1–2.

59. A key element in this decision appears to have been the coincidence in the timing of Britain's need for significantly increased quantities of tritium for its nuclear weapon programme, the tritium ageing problem and the presidential elections in late 1980. The realisation that the presidency might change hands before the tritium transfers were completed, and thus expose Britain to a damaging embargo, made a national plant to maintain the viability of at least part of the British nuclear force in such circumstances appear essential. Until this point, the assumption had been that if a President was to refuse to supply Britain, there would always be a 3–4 year period in which the British force would still remain technically viable and within which a national tritium production plant could be constructed. The assumption in Whitehall that a new President is always likely to be less amenable than his predecessor is discussed in Freedman, *Britain and Nuclear Weapons*, p. 44.

9 Reactors, the Trade in Military Nuclear Materials and Trident

1. *The Future of the United Kingdom's Nuclear Weapon Policy*, 'Options for the UK's future nuclear weapons policy', memorandum by F. Hussain, Appendix 1, pp. 188 and 190 and D. Fishlock, 'New design for submarine reactors', *Financial Times*, 12 June 1981, p. 29.

2. UKAEA, *Ninth Annual Report* (1962–3) para. 18. In August 1959, Rolls-Royce announced that they were to construct a plant to manufacture reactor cores for nuclear submarines, using fuel supplied by the UKAEA. Pocock, op. cit., pp. 128–9.

3. D. Fishlock, 'New design for submarine reactors'.

4. Captain J. E. Moore, *Warships of the Royal Navy* (Janes, 1981) pp. 16–20 lists four attack submarines and four 'R' class missile submarines as in commission at the end of 1971, in addition to HMS *Dreadnought* and *Vulcan*.

5. Wilson, op. cit., pp. 48–51. For a full account of the MLF saga see J. D. Steinbruner, op. cit.

6. The NPT prohibits transfers of complete weapons between all states but movements of weapons data and materials are only restricted between a nuclear and a non-nuclear one and between two non-nuclear ones. Nuclear weapon states are thus free to make such transfers. The possibility

that a non-nuclear state might wish to operate a submarine reactor was recognised by the IAEA, and it is covered by the provisions of para. 14 of INFCIRC 153 (corrected), the standard agreement under which a non-nuclear state accepts IAEA full-scope safeguards. Under this provision, a non-nuclear state can withdraw materials from safeguards for military applications, but this provision has never been utilised, and the procedures for this, and the attitudes of the members of the IAEA's Board of Governors, who would probably have to approve the arrangements, remain unclear.

7. Freedman, *Britain and Nuclear Weapons*, p. 44. This concern was reinforced in 1972 when Article IX of the ABM Treaty contained a restrictive non-transfer clause, though the United States consistently refused to discuss such clauses in its bilateral negotiations with the USSR over offensive strategic weapons.

8. In the period 1964–70 Britain continued with development of Concorde; participated in the airbus consortium; was a party to both the European Launcher Development Organisation and the European Space Research Organisation; joined with France in the Jaguar, AFVG, Martel and three helicopter projects; and discussed with France, Germany and Holland the creation of a number of Western European consortia in the civil nuclear energy field.

9. For a full discussion of the AGR programme see R. Williams, op. cit., pp. 114–46.

10. *International Agreements for Cooperation – 1966*, Hearings before the Subcommittee on Agreements for Cooperation of the Joint Committee on Atomic Energy, 89th Congress, 2nd Session (USGPO, 1966) p. 74 and pp. 101–3. For an account of the conversion of Capenhurst to a civil plant see D. Fishlock, 'A fuel that Britain can export successfully', *Financial Times*, 25 April 1968.

11. This was the *Private Ownership of Special Nuclear Materials Act*, Public Law 88–489. It added a new section 161v to the US 1954 Atomic Energy Act (as amended).

12. *Uranium Enrichment Services Criteria and Related Matters*, especially Appendix 5, pp. 317–23, Appendix 6, pp. 324–32 and Appendix 7, pp. 334–46.

13. The conflict between the idea of the AEC as a 'neutral' global supplier of enriched uranium and the commercial advantages of this role to the US nuclear reactor industry is well illustrated in the statement recorded in *International Agreements for Cooperation – 1966*, pp. 95–7. For the assertion that the United States would not make 30-year supply commitments to fuel AGRs sold to other countries, see p. 90.

14. Ibid., p. 25 and pp. 73–4.

15. Ibid., pp. 93–4.

16. Ibid., Appendix 8, pp. 183–6 contains correspondence on the COCOM decision.

17. Ibid., pp. 145–51.

18. Report of speech by B. Goldschmidt (ex-Director of International Relations for French CEA), *Nuclear News* (Journal of American Nuclear Society) (January 1981) p. 38.

19. Williams, op. cit. p. 133.

20. UKAEA, *Tenth Annual Report* (1963–4) p. 7, para. 31.
21. G. Zippe, J. W. Beams and A. R. Kuhltan, 'The development of short bowl ultracentrifuges', Progress Report No. 1: ORO-210; UVA/ORL-2400-58-PR-1.
22. For an account of these developments see *Science, Technology and American Diplomacy*, vol. 1, pp. 261–4. This suggests that a mixture of concern over nuclear proliferation and the commercial impact of the new technology were at the heart of American unease over this development. For the details of the organisation see C. Allday, 'Some experiences in formation and operation of multinational uranium-enrichment and fuel-reprocessing organisations' in A. Chayes and W. Bennett Lewis (eds), *International Arrangements for Nuclear Fuel Reprocessing* (Ballinger, 1977) pp. 177–81. The Treaty of Almelo is found in Cmnd 4315 (HMSO, 1970).
23. ENDC/60 submitted 31 August 1962 and speech by Representative Holifield, chairman of JCAE, *Congressional Record: House*, Vol. 115, 91st Congress, 1st Session, 14 April 1969, pp. 8902–7.
24. Chayes and Bennett Lewis, op. cit., pp. 182–5.
25. Pocock, op. cit., pp. 201–4 and Brochure on AWRE. Prepared by Ministry of Defence Public Relations and the Central Office of Information, undated p. 44.
26. Letter from F. E. Bonner, Dep. Chairman CEGB to R. V. Hesketh, 26 May 1982.
27. The dates of first criticality of CEGB and SSEB magnox reactors were:
    Berkeley: 8.1961 and 3.1962
    Bradwell: 8.1961 and 4.1962
    Hunterston: 9.1963 and 3.1964
    Hinkley Point: 5.1964 and 10.1964
    Trawsfynydd: 9.1964 and 12.1964
    Dungeness: 6.1965 and 9.1965
    Sizewell: 6.1965 and 12.1965
    Oldbury: 8.1967 and 12.1967
    Wylfa: 11.1969 and 9.1970
    Operations of Nuclear Power Stations 1974, pp. 49–59. Assuming six months to work up to a full power, a further year before 25 per cent of the fuel is discharged, and at least six months in cooling ponds, fuel from these reactors could have started to be reprocessed at Windscale two years after first criticality. This ties in with shipments in 1964 of plutonium produced at Berkeley and Bradwell and makes it unlikely that material from either Oldbury or Wylfa went to the United States if official statements are correct.
28. See *Hansard* No. 1253, Part I, Cols 4389: Written Answer by Mr John Moore, 27 July 1982.
29. For an extended discussion on the difficulties of classifying these activities as civil or military see J. Simpson, 'Power, plutonium and politics', *ADIU Report*, vol. 4, no. 3 (May/June 1982) 7–13.
30. *Hansard* No. 1253, Part I, Cols 4389. Moore's exact words were that 'the bulk of the material is in the form of "coupons" for the zero energy fast reactor critical assembly and in the core of the fast flux test facility. Both of

these are part of the United States fast reactor programme. The remaining small quantity is in use for experimental purposes elsewhere on the civil programme for example at Argonne and Battelle. It is therefore clear that the assurance given to the United Kingdom government in 1964 has been fulfilled.'

31. The initial 1958 agreement had specified in Article XII that the termination date was to be ten years after its entry into force, but Article 5 of the 1959 amendments to this agreement extended this date to 31 December 1969. The conditions for unilateral termination specified in the 1958 agreement remained in effect, allowing such termination to occur only if at least one year's notice of the intention to do so was given prior to the end of each period covered by the agreement (i.e. by 31 December 1968, 1973, 1978, 1983, 1988, etc.). If no notification of termination had been given by these dates, the information exchanges were to be automatically extended. In practice, however, their substantive content has always depended on the detailed nature of the arrangements for these transfers.

32. *HC Debs*, 748, Oral Answers, 13 June 1967, Col 299.

33. *Congressional Record: House*, vol. 115, 91st Congress, 1st Session, 11 March 1969, *Amendment to United States–United Kingdom Defense Agreement on uses of Atomic Energy*, p. 5967.

34. Ibid., Extension of Remarks, Hon. William Bates, 12 March 1969, p. 6280.

35. Ibid., p. 5976.

36. Ibid.

37. Ibid.

38. Ibid., p. 6279 and *Amendment to the Agreement . . . for Cooperation on the uses of Atomic Energy for Mutual Defence Purposes of July 3, 1958*, Treaty Series no. 85 (1969) Cmnd 4119 (HMSO, 1969).

39. *Congressional Record*: Senate, vol. 116, Part 1, 91st Congress, 2nd Session, 26 January 1980, p. 1122 and *Amendment to the Agreement . . . for Cooperation on the uses of Atomic Energy for Mutual Defence Purposes of July 3, 1958*, Treaty Series no. 46, (1970) Cmnd 4383 (HMSO, 1970).

40. *Amendment to the Agreement . . . for Cooperation on the uses of Atomic Energy for Mutual Defence Purposes*, Treaty Series no. 65 (1975) Cmnd 6017 (HMSO, 1975).

41. *The Labour Party Manifesto* (1979) pp. 37–8.

42. Freedman, *Britain and Nuclear Weapons*, pp. 52–3.

43. For an account of these policies see J. S. Nye, 'Non-proliferation: A long term strategy', *Foreign Affairs*, LVA(3) (April 1978) 601–23.

44. D. Fishlock, 'Vulcan and Helen: Lasers of unusual power', *Financial Times*, 5 March 1981.

45. D. Fishlock, 'Navy freezes nuclear fuel plant project', *Financial Times*, 27 August 1981.

46. The way in which the issues of number of missiles, type of submarine reactor, tactical weapon fit, type of missile, nature of missile storage facilities, programme phasing and timing and numbers of warheads evolved can be best appreciated by reference to *Strategic Nuclear Weapons Policy*.

47. These points are summarised in Defence Open Government Document

82/1, *The United Kingdom Trident Programme*, especially paras 29 and 30. It is unclear from this whether the intention is to carry 16 missiles with 8 warheads or 9 missiles with 14 warheads or some combination.

48. *Strategic Nuclear Weapons Policy*, pp. 172 and 174.

49. Ibid., pp. 171, 175 and 178.

50. Ibid., and p. 163. In his evidence to the committee, Mr Fielding, the Director of Aldermaston, emphasised that the establishment was only capable of undertaking one major project at a time. He indicated that work on new tactical designs would begin in 1986 once the Trident production programme had started, and that the latter would last to 1994–6 when tactical weapon production would recommence. At that point, some of the existing free-fall bombs would be at the end of their 25-year shelf-life.

51. In 1978, ten buildings involved in manufacturing plutonium were closed following the discovery of unacceptable levels of the material elsewhere on the site. By late 1980, four had been returned to production, but the impact of this closure upon the Chevaline programme has yet to be disclosed. Ibid., p. 172.

52. Official Text of Background Briefing released by the White House, 15 July 1980. *US Sale of Trident One Missiles to UK*, p. 5.

53. *The Times*, 16 November 1981.

54. P. Hennessy, 'Planning for a future nuclear deterrent', *The Times*, 5 December 1979.

55. *Amendment to the Agreement ... for Cooperation on the Uses of Atomic Energy for Mutual Defence Purposes of July 3, 1958*, Treaty Series no. 61, Cmnd 7976 (HMSO, 1980).

56. *Nuclear Fuel*, 13 April 1981, p. 9.

57. Using the tables in *Uranium Enrichment Services Criteria and Related Matters*, p. 352, in which a kilogram of 90 per cent enriched uranium is produced by 206.992 SWUs, the figure for 90 per cent U-235 would be 483.11 kilograms. This suggests that the quoted figure is somewhat conservative for 97 per cent enriched.

58. Fishlock, 'Navy freezes nuclear fuel plant project'.

59. This calculation is based on figures for tritium production at Hanford given in *Hearings on H. R. 2969*, p. 171, and an assumed weapon-grade production rate of 0.8 grams per megawat day for Chapel Cross. This reactor, assuming it operates for 314 days per year and has had its power rating reduced to the 1963 military level of 200 Mw(th) would, in theory, produce 50 kilograms of plutonium annually. The 'N' reactor at Hanford can produce about 3 kilograms of tritium and 650 kilograms of plutonium, the tritium being produced at an opportunity cost of 72 kilograms of plutonium. Applying similar ratios to plutonium and tritium production at Chapel Cross, speculative estimates of 173 grams of tritium and 37.5 kilograms of weapon-grade plutonium per year can be obtained.

60. The safeguards agreements between Britain, Euratom and the IAEA are confidential documents, but they are based on the principle of safeguarding both facilities and material passing through them. Other than a small plant at Dounreay for fast reactor fuel and the military plutonium 'cleaning' plant at Sellafield, the only reprocessing plant known to be

operating in Britain is the B205 magnox one.

61. *No More Atoms for Peace*, pp. 2–3.
62. *Hearings on H.R. 2969*, p. 170.
63. This covered by Article 1, Section C-1 of the 1958 Agreement as amended in 1959.
64. *HC Debs*, 21 December 1981 – *Debate on Plutonium (Exchange Agreement)* Col 736 and Seaborg, op. cit., p. 110.
65. *Debate on Plutonium (Exchange Agreement)*, ibid., Col 738; see also D. Fishlock, 'The plutonium hot potato', *Financial Times*, 27 October 1981.
66. This plan has generated considerable controversy in the United States. *New York Times*, 11 September 1981, p. A20 and 22 September 1981, p. C1 and *The Energy Daily*, 28 September 1981, p. 4.

10 Old Age? The Implications of the Anglo-American Military Exchange Agreements for the Nuclear Disarmament of Britain

1. An argued case for this option is provided in my Memorandum to the House of Commons Defence Committee, *Strategic Nuclear Weapons Policy*, pp. 299–306.
2. P. Hennessy, 'Disarming Britain', *The Times*, 15 May 1981, states that 5000 people are employed at Aldermaston and 2000 at Burghfield Common and Cardiff.
3. Under Protocol III, Article 1 and Annexes I–IV of the Paris Agreements of 23 October 1954 which led to Germany and Italy joining the Western European Union, a treaty organisation established by the UK/ France/Benelux through the Brussels Treaty of 1948, Germany agreed not to manufacture nuclear weapons.
4. This arises from the terms of the 1958 agreement as amended in 1959. Unilateral termination is only possible at the end of each five-year period commencing on the last day of December 1959 *but* notice must be given of this decision at least one year in advance. Thus notice must be given by the last day of December 1983 to terminate at the end of 1984. However such termination would absolve neither party from the duty not to disseminate any nuclear information and material exchanged under the agreements other than by mutual agreement.
5. ENDC/54, Presented 1 August 1962.
6. I have obtained these figures from the weight of the 1 megaton bomb given by Campbell in 'Wings of the green parrot', and by dividing the payload of the Polaris missile by the six nuclear warheads some sources attribute to the Chevaline reentry system.
7. ENDC/60 submitted 31 August 1962.
8. The radiation dangers from the limited quantities of the isotope Pu-240 in nuclear warheads were one of the main justifications given by the American government in 1981 for developing laser enrichment to obtain pure

Pu-239 for weapons. *New York Times*, 22 September 1981.

9. Article I states that: 'Each nuclear-weapon state Party to the Treaty undertakes not to transfer to any recipient whatsoever nuclear weapons ... directly or indirectly; and not in any way to assist, encourage, or induce any non-nuclear state to manufacture ... nuclear weapons.'

10. I have used the 1981 supply agreement with the United States for access to 100 000 SWU per year as the basis for this figure.

11. *Weekly Hansard No. 1238*, 1 April 1982, Written Answers, Col 169.

12. ENDC/60, op. cit.

13. Current maritime warfare techniques appear to be based upon the use of several different NATO sensor systems to provide information on the position of potentially hostile ships and submarines. In the absence of this information, the effectiveness of a national fleet of nuclear submarines would be considerably degraded.

14. In a natural uranium reactor only the 0.7 per cent of U-235 is subject to fission initially, and this is the basis for my, admittedly conservative, lower figure. The same argument applies to AGR fuel rods enriched to 2 per cent U-235. In neither case have I made any allowance for fissions in the Pu-239 produced as the reactor is operating.

15. For an overview of the stockpile likely to be accumulated through to the year 2000, see *The Windscale Inquiry*, Report by Hon. Mr Justice Parker, vol. I (HMSO, 1978) p. 27. This suggests that eventually some 55 tonnes of separated plutonium might be in existence if none were absorbed in CFBR programmes.

16. For a discussion of the differences between a fast breeder and a fast burner or incinerator reactor see W. Marshall, 'The UK fast breeder programme' in C. Sweet (ed.), *The Fast Breeder Reactor* (Macmillan, 1980) pp. 93–101, especially p. 97.

11 The United States, Britain and the Military Atom: Retrospect and Evaluation

1. For the substance of this debate see K. Kaiser, 'The great nuclear debate: German/American disagreement', *Foreign Policy*, vol. 30 (Spring 1978) p. 93; M. Brenner, 'Carter's non-proliferation policy', *ORBIS*, vol. 22, no. 2 (Summer 1978); F. Williams, 'The United States Congress and non-proliferation', *International Security*, vo. 3, no. 2 (Fall 1978) pp. 45–60; and A. G. McGrew, 'Nuclear revisionism: the United States and the nuclear non-proliferation act of 1978', *Millenium*, vol. 73, no. 3 (Winter 1978–9) pp. 237–50.

2. Cf. Lord Chalfont, the Minister for Disarmament in the Wilson government, speaking to the ENDC during the negotiations leading up to the NPT. '"Do as I say, not as I do" is a logically indefensible precept, but in an imperfect world it may be a necessary one for a particular short period of history' quoted in SIPRI, *Postures for Non-Proliferation*, p. 129.

3. See *Aviation Week and Space Technology*, 23 August 1982, pp. 72–5. This states that the use of large computers at the Los Alamos weapon laboratory during the late 1970s reduced the number of explosive tests needed for successive generations of American weapons from 23 to 6.

Bibliography

1 Government Publications (all London: HMSO)

(i) British Command Papers

Cmd 8986   *The Future Organisation of the United Kingdom Atomic Energy Project* (Waverley Report) 1953

Cmd 9389   *A Programme of Nuclear Power*, 1955

Cmd 9391   *Statement on Defence: 1955*

Cmd 9555   *Agreement ... for Cooperation regarding Atomic Information for Mutual Defence Purposes*, Treaty Series no. 52, 1955

Cmd 9560   *Agreement ... for Cooperation on the Civil Uses of Atomic Energy*, Treaty Series no. 55, 1955

Cmd 9691   *Statement on Defence: 1956*

Cmd 9847   *Amendment to the Agreement ... for Cooperation on the Civil Uses of Atomic Energy of June 15, 1955*. Treaty Series no. 35, 1956

Cmd 9860   *Amendment to the Agreement ... for Cooperation in the Civil Uses of Atomic Energy*, Treaty Series no. 35, 1956

Cmnd 124   *Defence: Outline of Future Policy: 1957*

Cmnd 126   *Final Communiqué from the Bermuda Conference*, Misc no. 10, 1957

Cmnd 302   *Accident at Windscale no. 2 Pile on 10 October 1957*, 1957

Cmnd 338   *Report of the Committee appointed by the Prime Minister to Examine the Organisation of Certain Parts of the United Kingdom Atomic Energy Authority* (Fleck Committee) 1957

Cmnd 363   *Report on Defence: 1958*

Cmnd 471   *Final Report (of the Committee on the Windscale Accident)*, 1958

Cmnd 406   *Exchange of Notes ... Concerning the Supply to the United Kingdom of Intermediate Range Ballistic Missiles*, Treaty Series no. 14, 1958

Cmnd 537   *Agreement ... for Cooperation on the Uses of Atomic Energy for Mutual Defence Purposes*, Treaty Series no. 41, 1958

Cmnd 662   *Progress on the Five Year Defence Plan*, 1959

Cmnd 859   *Amendment to Agreement ... for Cooperation on the Uses of Atomic Energy for Mutual Defence Purposes*, Treaty Series no. 72, 1959

Cmnd 952   *Report on Defence: 1960*

Cmnd 1083   *The Nuclear Power Programme*, 1960

Cmnd 1288   *Report on Defence: 1961*

Cmnd 1639   *Statement on Defence 1962: The Next Five Years*

Cmnd 1857   *Documents on Disarmament*, Misc no. 32, 1962

313

Cmnd 1915 *Bahamas Meetings, December 1962. Texts of Joint Communiqués*, 1962
Cmnd 1936 *Statement on Defence: 1963*
Cmnd 2108 *Polaris Sales Agreement*, Treaty Series no. 59, 1963
Cmnd 2166 *Amendment to Article IV of the Agreement . . . for Cooperation in the Civil Use of Atomic Energy*, Treaty Series no. 82, 1963
Cmnd 2270 *Statement on Defence: 1964*
Cmnd 2335 *The Second Nuclear Power Programme*, 1964
Cmnd 2353 *Documents on Disarmament*, Misc no. 12, 1964
Cmnd 2486 *Further Documents Relating to the Conference of The Eighteen-Nation Committee on Disarmament*, Misc no. 20, 1964
Cmnd 2592 *Statement on the Defence Estimates: 1965*
Cmnd 2901 *Statement on Defence Estimates: 1966. Part I: The Defence Review*
Cmnd 3203 *Statement on the Defence Estimates: 1967*
Cmnd 3357 *Supplementary Statement on Defence Policy: 1967*
Cmnd 3540 *Statement on the Defence Estimates: 1968*
Cmnd 3927 *Statement on Defence Estimates: 1969*
Cmnd 4119 *Amendment to the Agreement . . . for Cooperation on the Uses of Atomic Energy for Mutual Defence Purposes of 3 July 1958*, Treaty Series no. 85, 1969
Cmnd 4290 *Statement on the Defence Estimates: 1970*
Cmnd 4315 *Treaty of Almelo*, 1970
Cmnd 4383 *Amendment to the Agreement . . . for Cooperation on the Uses of Atomic Energy for Mutual Defence Purposes of July 3, 1958*, Treaty Series no. 46, 1970
Cmnd 4592 *Statement on the Defence Estimates: 1971*
Cmnd 4694 *Agreement for Cooperation on the Civil Uses of Atomic Energy . . . Signed at Washington on 15 June 1955 as Amended*, Treaty Series no. 31, 1971
Cmnd 4891 *Statement on the Defence Estimates: 1972*
Cmnd 5231 *Statement on the Defence Estimates: 1973*
Cmnd 5976 *Statement on the Defence Estimates: 1975*
Cmnd 6017 *Amendment to the Agreement . . . for Cooperation on the Uses of Atomic Energy for Mutual Defence Purposes*, Treaty Series no. 65, 1975
Cmnd 6432 *Statement on the Defence Estimates: 1976*
Cmnd 6735 *Statement on the Defence Estimates: 1977*
Cmnd 7099 *Statement on the Defence Estimates: 1978*
Cmnd 7474 *Statement on the Defence Estimates: 1979*
Cmnd 7976 *Amendment to Agreement . . . for Cooperation on the Uses of Atomic Energy for Mutual Defence Purposes*, Treaty Series no. 61, 1980

(ii) Other British Official Publications

Fifth Report of Select Committee on Estimates, *United Kingdon Atomic Energy Authority*, HC 316–7, 1958–9
ENDC/54   1 August 1962
ENDC/60   31 August 1962

Nuclear Energy in Britain, COI Reference Pamphlet no. 208, 1962

Report of the Select Committee on Science and Technology, *United Kingdom Reactor Programme*, HC 381, XVIII, 1966–7

Fourth Report of the Select Committee on Science and Technology. *United Kingdom Nuclear Power Industry*, HC 401, 1968–9

Twelfth Report from the Defence and External Affairs Subcommittee of the House of Commons Expenditure Committee, *Nuclear Weapon Programme*, HC 399, 1972–3

Second Report of the Select Committee on Science and Technology, *Nuclear Power Policy*, HC 350, 1972–3; HC 444, 1971–2 and HC 223, 1972–3

Special Report 4, Select Committee on Science and Technology, *Fast Breeder Reactor*, HC 625, 1975–6

The Windscale Inquiry, Report by the Hon. Mr Justice Parker, 1978

Sixth Report from the Expenditure Committee, Session 1978–9, *The Future of the United Kingdom's Nuclear Weapons Policy*, HC Paper 348, 1979

Defence Open Government Document, *The Future United Kingdom Strategic Nuclear Deterrent Force*, 80/23

Fourth Report from the Defence Committee, *Strategic Nuclear Weapons Policy*, Session 1980–1, HC 36, 1981

Defence Open Government Document, *The United Kingdom Trident Programme*, 82/1

First Special Report from the Defence Committee, Session 1981–2, *Strategic Nuclear Weapons Policy*, HC 266, 1982

Ninth Report from the Committee of Public Accounts, Session 1981–2, *Ministry of Defence: Chevaline Improvement to the Polaris Missile System*, HC 269, 1982

Annual Reports of AEA, CEGB and SSEB

(iii) United States Official Publications

Hearings before the JCAE. *Investigation into the United States Atomic Energy Project*, 81st Congress, 1st Session, 1949

Hearings before the JCAE. *Amending the Atomic Energy Act*, 82nd Congress, 2nd Session, 1952

Hearings before the JCAE. *Legislation Concerning Long-Term Utility Contracts*, 83rd Congress, 1st Session, 1953

US Code Congressional and Administrative News, vol. 1, 83rd Congress, 1954, *Public Law 703*

Hearings before the Subcommittee on Agreements for Cooperation of the JCAE. *Amending the Atomic Energy Act of 1954 – Exchange of Military Information and Material with Allies*, 85th Congress, 2nd Session, 1958

Hearings before the JCAE. *Proposed EURATOM Agreements*, 85th Congress, 2nd Session, 1958

Hearings before the JCAE. *Proposals Under Power Demonstration Program*, 85th Congress, 2nd Session, 1958

Reports of the Joint Committee on Atomic Energy, 86th Congress, 2nd Session, HR 672, HR 1849, HR 2299, S 1654

US Code Congressional and Administrative News, 85th Congress, 2nd Session, 1958, vol. 11, *Atomic Energy Act of 1954 – Amendment – House Report*

Hearings before the Subcommittee on Agreements for Cooperation of the

JCAE. *Exchange of Military Information and Materials with the United Kingdom, France, Canada, the Netherlands, Turkey, Greece and the Federal Republic of Germany*, 86th Congress, 1st Session, 1959

US Department of State, *Geneva Conference on the Discontinuance of Nuclear Weapon Tests*, Department of State Publication 7258, Disarmament Series 4, October 1961

Hearings before the Subcommittee on Agreements for Cooperation of the JCAE. *International Agreement for Cooperation, 1966*, 89th Congress, 2nd Session, 1966

Hearings before the JCAE. *Uranium Enrichment Services Criteria and Related Matters*, 89th Congress, 2nd Session, 1966

Congressional Record: House. *Amendment to United States: United Kingdom Defense Agreement on Uses of Atomic Energy*, vol. 115, 91st Congress, 1st Session, 1969

US Library of Congress, *Nuclear Proliferation Factbook*, 1977

US House of Representatives: Committee on International Relations, *Science, Technology and American Diplomacy*, 3 vols, 1977

Hearing before the House of Representatives Subcommittee on Procurement and Military Nuclear Systems, *Proposed Department of Energy Authorisation Legislation (National Security Programs) for Fiscal Year 1982*, 97th Congress, 1st Session

(iv) US Archival Material

(a) **Records of the United States Joint Chiefs of Staff**

Military Considerations on Delivery of more Powerful Atomic Weapons, RG218/CCS 471.6 (8-15-45) Secs 13 and 15, JCS 1823/1, 13 January 1948

Agreed Statement on Estimated Russian Atom Bomb Production RG218/CCS 471.6 (8-15-45) Sec 9, SUJIC Policy Memo no. 2, 29 March 1948

Production Objectives for the Stockpile of Atomic Weapons RG218/CCS 471.6 (8-15-45) Sec 15, JCS 1823/14, 27 May 1949

Implications of Soviet Possession of Atomic Weapons RG218/CCS 471.6 USSR (11-8-49) SUJIC 502(i) 30 January 1950

Memorandum from Military Liaison Committee to the Atomic Energy Commission on the Basis of Procurement for Certain Items for Stockpile, RG218/CCS 471.6 (6-15-45) Sec 19, MLC 34, 7 July 1950

Estimate of the Scale and Nature of a Soviet Attack on the United Kingdom between Now and mid-1952. RG218/CCS 092 USSR (3-27-45) Sec 55, JIC 435/52, 7 February 1951

Memorandum by Chief of Staff, USAF to JCS on Military Requirements for Atomic Weapons, RG218/CCS 471.6 (11-3-51) Sec 1, 12 November 1951

Department of Defense Interest in the Use of Nuclear Weapons, RG218/CCS 471.6 (11-3-51) Sec 1

(b) **Minutes of the Thirty-seventh Meeting of the General Advisory Commission,** Washington, 4–6 November 1953

2 Books and Reports

Allison, G. T. *Essence of Decision* (Little, Brown, 1971)

Armacost, M. H. *The Politics of Weapons Innovation: The Thor–Jupiter Controversy* (Columbia University Press, 1969)

Barnaby, C. F. and Thomas, G. P. (eds) *The Nuclear Arms Race* (Frances Pinter, 1982)

Bartlett, C. J. *The Long Retreat: A Short History of British Defence Policy* (Macmillan, 1972)

Baylis, J. (ed.) *British Defence Policy in a Changing World* (Croom Helm, 1977)

——. *Anglo-American Defence Relations, 1939–1980* (Macmillan, 1981)

Bell, C. *The Debatable Alliance: An Essay in Anglo-American Relations* (Oxford University Press, 1964)

Beamis, S. F. *A Diplomatic History of the United States*, 4th edn (Henry Holt & Co., 1955)

Beaton, L. *Must the Bomb Spread?* (Penguin, 1966)

Blackett, P. M. S. *Atomic Weapons and East–West Relations* (Cambridge University Press, 1956)

Brookes, A. *V-Force: The History of Britain's Airborne Deterrent* (Jane's 1982)

Brown, N. *Nuclear War: The Impending Strategic Deadlock* (Pall Mall, 1964)

Burton, J. W. *Deviance, Terrorism and War* (Martin Robertson, 1979)

Callaghan, T. A. *US/European Economic Cooperation in Military and Civil Technology* (Center for Strategic and International Studies, Georgetown University, 1975)

Cave-Brown, A. (ed.) *Operation: World War III* (Arms and Armour Press, 1978)

Chayes, A. and Bennett Lewis, W. (eds) *International Arrangements for Nuclear Fuel Reprocessing* (Ballinger, 1977)

Clark, R. W. *The Birth of the Bomb* (Horizon Press, 1961)

——. *The Greatest Power on Earth* (Sidgwick & Jackson, 1980)

Conant, J. B. *Anglo-American Relations in the Atomic age* (Oxford University Press, 1952)

Coates, A. *Western Pacific Islands* (HMSO, 1970)

Cooper, R. N. *The Economics of Interdependence* (McGraw-Hill, 1968)

Committee on Disarmament. *Report on a Comprehensive Nuclear Test Ban* (CD/86, 1980)

——. *The Prohibition of the Production of Fissionable Material for Weapon Purposes* (CD/90, 1980)

Coulam, R. J. *Illusions of Choice* (Princeton University Press, 1977)

Craig, D. S., *et al.*, 'Long irradiation of natural uranium', Geneva Conference Paper, P/205 in *Progress in Nuclear Energy*, series II, vol. II (Pergamon, 1961)

Dahlman, O. and Israelson, H. *Monitoring Underground Nuclear Explosions* (Elsevier, 1977)

Devine, R. A. *Blowing in the Wind* (Oxford University Press, 1978)

Drivers, D. *The Disarmers: A Study in Protest* (Hodder & Stoughton, 1964)

Durie, L. and Edwards, R. *Fuelling the Nuclear Arms Race* (Pluto, 1982)

Eden, A. *Full Circle* (Cassell, 1965)

Eisenhower, D. D. *Mandate for Change 1953–56* (Doubleday, 1963)

——. *Waging Peace 1956–61* (Doubleday, 1965)

EUROSTAT. *Operation of Nuclear Power Stations* (Office for Official Publications of the European Communities. Annual Publication)

Freedman, L. *Britain and Nuclear Weapons* (Macmillan, 1980)

Gardner, C. *British Aircraft Corporation* (Book Club Associates, 1981)

Goldschmidt, B. *Les Rivalités atomiques, 1939–1966* (Fayard, Paris, 1967)

Gowing, M. *Britain and Atomic Energy 1939–1945* (Macmillan, 1964)

Gowing, M. (with Arnold, L.): *Independence and Deterrence,* 2 vols (Macmillan, 1974)

Green, H. P. and Rosenthal, A. *Government of the Atom* (Atherton, 1963)

Greenwood, T., Rathjens, G. W. and Ruina, J. *Adelphi Paper No. 130: Nuclear Power and Weapons Proliferation* (IISS, 1976)

Gregory, F. E. C., Imber, M. and Simpson, J. (eds). *Perspectives upon British Defence Policy, 1945–1970* (Adult Education Department, University of Southampton, 1978)

Groom, A. J. R. *British Thinking about Nuclear Weapons* (Frances Pinter, 1974)

Groves, L. R. *Now It Can Be Told: The Story of the Manhattan Project* (Harper, 1962)

Head, R. G. '*Decision-making on the A-7 attack aircraft program*' (unpublished PhD thesis, Syracuse University, 1971)

Hewlett, R. G. and Anderson, O. E. Jr. *A History of the United States Atomic Energy Commission,* vol. I, *The New World, 1939–1946* (Pennsylvania State University Press, 1962)

Hewlett, R. G. and Duncan, F. *A History of the United States Atomic Energy Commission,* vol. II, *Atomic Shield 1947–1952* (Pennsylvania State University Press, 1969)

——. *Nuclear Navy, 1946–1962* (University of Chicago Press, 1974)

Hirschman, A. O. *National Power and the Structure of Foreign Trade* (University of California Press, 1945)

Hussain, F. *Adelphi Paper No. 165: The Future of Arms Control: Part IV: The Impact of Weapon Test Restrictions* (IISS, 1981)

Imber, M. F. *Mitrany's Functionalism. The International Atomic Energy Agency and the Development of Safeguards against the Proliferation of Nuclear Weapons* (unpublished PhD thesis, University of Southampton, 1981)

Jackson, R. *V-Bombers* (Ian Allen, 1981)

Jay, K. B. *Britain's Atomic Factories* (HMSO, 1954)

——. *Calder Hall* (Methuen, 1956)

Jenkins, W. I. *Policy Analysis* (Martin Robertson, 1978)

Keohane, R. O. and Nye, J. S. Jr. (eds). *Transnational Relations and World Politics* (Harvard University Press, 1971)

Kindleberger, C. (ed.). *The International Corporation* (MIT Press, 1970)

Kissinger, H. *The White House Years* (Weidenfeld and Nicolson/Michael Joseph, 1979)

Lilienthal, D. E. *The Journals of David E. Lilienthal,* vol. II. *The Atomic Energy Years 1945–1950* (Harper & Row, 1964)

Machiavelli, N. *The Prince* (Bobbs-Merrill, 1976)

Macmillan, H. *Tides of Fortune, 1945–1955* (Macmillan, 1969)

——. *Riding the Storm, 1956–1959* (Macmillan, 1971)

——. *Pointing the Way, 1959–1961* (Macmillan, 1972)

——. *At the End of the Day, 1961–1963* (Macmillan, 1973)

Mansbach, R. W., Ferguson, Y. H. and Lampert, D. E. *The Web of World Politics* (Prentice-Hall, 1976)

Marschak, T. A. (ed.). *The Role of Project Histories in the Study of R & D* (Rand Paper P-2850, Santa Monica, 1965)

Menaul, S. *Countdown* (Hale, 1980)

Millar, T. B. *Australia's Defence* (Melbourne University Press, 1965)

Moore, J. E. *Warships of the Royal Navy* (Jane's, 1981)

Morell, W. D. *Britain and the Pacific Islands* (Oxford University Press, 1960)

Moss, N. *Men Who Play God* (Gollancz, 1968)

Natural Resources Defense Council Inc. *No More Atoms for Peace* (mimeo. Washington, 1981)

Neustadt, R. *Presidential Power* (Wiley, 1960)

——. *Alliance Politics* (Columbia University Press, 1970)

Owen, D. *The Politics of Defence* (Jonathan Cape, 1972)

Peck, M. J. and Scherer, F. M. *The Weapon Acquisition Process: an Economic Analysis* (Harvard University Press, 1962)

Pierre, A. J. *Nuclear Politics* (Macmillan, 1972)

Pincher, C. *Inside Story* (Sidgwick & Jackson, 1978)

Pocock, R. F. *Nuclear Power* (Unwin, 1977)

Polach, J. G. *EURATOM* (Oceana, 1964)

Polmar, N. *Atomic Submarines* (Van Nostrand, 1963)

Pringle, P. and Spigelman, J. *The Nuclear Barons* (Holt, Rinehart & Winston, 1981)

Research Institute of National Defence. *Nuclear Explosions 1945–1972: Basic Data*, FA04, Report A4505-A1 (Stockholm, 1973)

Rosencrance, R. N. *Defense of the Realm* (Columbia University Press, 1968)

Russett, B. M. (ed.). *Economic Theories of International Politics* (Markham Publishing Co., 1968)

Sapolsky, H. *The Polaris System Development* (Harvard University Press, 1972)

Schlesinger, A. M. Jr. *The Age of Roosevelt*, 2 vols (Houghton Mifflin, 1959)

Seaborg, G. T. *Kennedy, Khrushchev and the Test Ban* (University of California Press, 1981)

Simpson, J. *Understanding weapon acquisition processes: a study of naval anti-submarine aircraft procurement in Britain, 1945–1955* (Unpublished PhD thesis, University of Southampton, 1976)

SIPRI. *Nuclear Energy and Nuclear Weapon Proliferation* (Taylor & Francis, 1979)

——. *Postures for Non-Proliferation* (Taylor & Francis, 1979)

——. *SIPRI Yearbook 1982* (Taylor & Francis, 1982)

Snow, C. P. *Science and Government* (Oxford University Press, 1961)

Snyder, W. P. *The Politics of British Defence Policy, 1945–1962* (Ohio State University Press, 1964)

Stein, H. (ed.). *American Civil-Military Decisions* (University of Alabama Press, 1963)

Steinbruner, J. D. *The Cybernetic Theory of Decision: New Dimensions of Political Analysis* (Princeton University Press, 1974)

Strauss, L. *Men and Decisions* (Doubleday, 1962)

Sweet, C. (ed.). *The Fast Breeder Reactor* (Macmillan, 1980)

UKAEA Historian's Office. *The Development of Atomic Energy: Chronology of Events, 1939–1978* (AERE Harwell, 1979)

Volpi, A. de. *Proliferation, Plutonium and Policy* (Pergamon Press, 1979)

Wallace, W. *The Foreign Policy Process in Britain* (RIIA, 1975)

Waltz, K. N. *Foreign Policy and Democratic Politics: The American and British Experience* (Little, Brown, 1967)

Wildavsky, A. *Dixon-Yates: A Study in Power Politics* (Yale University Press, 1962)

Williams, R. *The Nuclear Power Decisions* (Croom Helm, 1980)

Wilson, H. *The Labour Government, 1964–1970* (Weidenfeld and Nicolson/Michael Joseph, 1971)

Wohlstetter, A. (*et. al.*). *Swords from Ploughshares* (Chicago University Press, 1979)

York, H. *The Advisors: Oppenheimer, Teller and the Superbomb* (W. H. Freeman, 1976)

3 Articles

Allison, G. T. 'Conceptual models and the Cuban missile crisis', *American Political Science Review*, vol. 63 no. 3 (Sept 1969)

Bellany, I. 'The origins of the Soviet hydrogen bomb: the York hypothesis', *RUSI Journal*, vol. 122, no. 1 (March 1977)

Brenner, M. 'Carter's non-proliferation policy', *ORBIS*, vol. 22, no. 2 (Summer 1978)

Buzzard, Rear Admiral Sir A. W. 'The H-bomb: massive retaliation or graduated deterrence', *International Affairs*, vol. XXXII, no. 2 (April 1956)

Campbell, D. 'The wings of the green parrot', *New Statesman*, 17 April 1981

——. 'Digging up the nuclear past', *New Statesman*, 8 May 1981

Carter, M. W. and Moghissi, A. A. 'Three decades of nuclear testing', *Health Physics*, vol. 33 (July 1977)

Dawson, R. and Rosencrance, R. N. 'Theory and reality in the Anglo-American alliance', *World Politics*, vol. XIX, no. 1 (Oct 1966)

Davey, H. G. 'Commissioning and operation of "A" station, Calder Hall', *Journal of the British Nuclear Energy Conference*, vol. 3 (1958)

Duvall, R. D. 'Dependence and dependence theory: notes towards precision of concept and argument', *International Organisation*, vol. 32 (Winter 1978)

Epstein, L. D. 'Britain and the H-bomb, 1955–1958', *Review of Politics*, vol. XXI (August 1959)

Freedman, L. 'Logic, politics and foreign policy processes', *International Affairs*, vol. 52 (1976)

Goldberg, A. 'The atomic origins of the British nuclear deterrent', *International Affairs*, vol. XL, no. 2 (July 1964)

——. 'The military origins of the British nuclear deterrent' *International Affairs*, vol. XL, no. 4 (Oct 1964)

Gott, R. 'The evolution of the independent British deterrent', *International Affairs*, vol. XXXIX, no. 2 (April 1963)

Groom, A. J. R. 'US–Allied relations and the atomic bomb in the second world war', *World Politics*, vol. XV, no. 1 (Oct 1962)

Hesketh, R. V. 'Plutonium exports', *Science and Public Policy* (April 1982)

Hoag, M. W. 'What interdependence for NATO?', *World Politics*, vol. XII, no. 3 (April 1960)

Holloway, D. 'Research note: Soviet thermonuclear development', *International Security*, vol. 4, no. 3 (Winter 1979–80)

——. 'Entering the nuclear arms race: the Soviet decision to build the atomic bomb, 1939–45', *Social Studies in Science*, vol. 2 (Sage 1981)

Imber, M. 'NPT safeguards: the limits of credibility', *Arms Control*, vol. 1, no. 2 (Sept 1980)

Kaiser, K. 'The great nuclear debate: German/American disagreements', *Foreign Policy*, vol. 30 (Spring 1978)

Marshall, W. 'Nuclear power and the proliferation issue', *Atom*, vol. 258 (April 1978)

——. 'The use of plutonium', *Atom*, vol. 282 (April 1980)

Martin, L. W. 'The market for strategic ideas in Britain: the "Sandys era"', *American Political Science Review*, vol. LVI, no. 1 (1962)

Millett, S. M. 'The capabilities of the American nuclear deterrent, 1945–1950', *Aerospace Historian* (March 1980)

Morland, H. 'The H-bomb secret', *The Progressive*, vol. 43, no. 11 (Nov 1979)

——. 'Errata', *The Progressive*, vol. 43, no. 12 (Dec 1979)

McIntosh, A. B. and Grainger, L. 'Plutonium and nuclear power', *Journal of the British Nuclear Energy Society* (1962)

McGrew, A. 'Nuclear revisionism: the United States and the nuclear non-proliferation act of 1978', *Millennium*, vol. 7, no. 3 (Winter 1978/79)

Owen, Sir Leonard. 'Nuclear engineering – the United Kingdom: the first ten years', *Journal of the British Nuclear Energy Society* (1963)

Pierre, A. J. 'Nuclear diplomacy: Britain, France and America', *Foreign Affairs*, vol. XLIX, no. 2 (Jan 1971)

Rose, H. and Syrett, J. J. 'Long-term reactivity changes', *Journal of the British Nuclear Energy Conference*, vol. 4 (1959)

Rosenberg, D. A. 'American atomic strategy and the hydrogen bomb decision', *Journal of American History*, vol. 66 (1979–80)

——. 'US nuclear stockpile, 1945–1950', *Bulletin of the Atomic Scientists* (May 1982)

Ruggie, J. G. 'Collective goods and future international collaboration', *American Political Science Review*, vol. 66 (Sept 1972)

Sokolski, H. 'Atoms for peace: a non-proliferation primer', *Arms Control*, vol. 1, no. 2 (Sept 1980)

Schilling, W. R. 'The H-bomb decision: how to decide without actually choosing', *Political Science Quarterly*, vol. LXXVI (March 1961)

Scherfield, Lord. 'Britain's nuclear story: 1945–52: Politics and technology', *Round Table*, no. 258 (April 1975)

Simpson, J. 'The Polaris executive: a case study of a unified hierarchy', *Public Administration*, vol. 48 (Winter 1970)

——. 'Power, plutonium and politics', *ADIU Report*, vol. 4, no. 3 (May/June 1982)

Thomson, Sir G. 'Britain's drive for atomic power', *Foreign Affairs*, vol. XXXV, no. 1 (Oct 1956)

Wells, S. F. Jr. 'Sounding the tocsin: NSC 68 and the Soviet threat', *Interna-*

tional Security, vol. 4, no. 2 (Fall 1979)

——. 'The origins of massive retaliation', *Political Science Quarterly* (Spring 1981)

Williams, F. 'The United States Congress and non-proliferation', *International Security*, vol. 3, no. 2 (Fall 1978)

Wilmer, G. 'TSR-2: yesterday's answer to tomorrow's problem', *Air Enthusiast*, no. 14

Index

SIMPSON: The Independent
Nuclear State